Their Sex

A book in the series

LATIN AMERICA OTHERWISE

Languages, Empires, Nations

Series editors: Walter D. Mignolo, Duke University,

Irene Silverblatt, Duke University, Sonia Saldívar-Hull,

University of California at Los Angeles

Gender, Labor, and Politics

in Urban Chile, 1900–1930

Labors

Appropriate to

Their Sex

Elizabeth Quay Hutchison

Duke University Press   Durham & London   2001

© 2001 Duke University Press

All rights reserved

Printed in the United States of

America on acid-free paper ∞

Designed by C. H. Westmoreland

Typeset in Adobe Garamond

with Franklin Gothic display

by Keystone Typesetting, Inc.

Library of Congress Cataloging-

in-Publication Data appear on the

last printed page of this book.

About the Series

Latin America Otherwise: Languages, Empires, Nations is a critical series. It aims to explore the emergence and consequences of concepts used to define "Latin America" while at the same time exploring the broad interplay of political, economic, and cultural practices that have shaped Latin American worlds. Latin America, at the crossroads of competing imperial designs and local responses, has been construed as a geocultural and geopolitical entity since the nineteenth century. This series provides a starting point to redefine Latin America as a configuration of political, linguistic, cultural, and economic intersections that demand a continuous reappraisal of the role of the Americas in history, and of the ongoing process of globalization and the relocation of people and cultures that have characterized Latin America's experience. *Latin America Otherwise: Languages, Empires, Nations* is a forum that confronts established geocultural constructions, that rethinks area studies and disciplinary boundaries, that assesses convictions of the academy and of public policy, and that, correspondingly, demands that the practices through which we produce knowledge and understanding about and from Latin America be subject to rigorous and critical scrutiny.

Women were key participants in Chile's transformation into an urban and industrial society during the first decades of the twentieth century. By 1912, they made up one third of Santiago's factory workers, and were the majority labor force in textile, clothing, and tobacco enterprises. Their growing presence in urban life earned them editorials in the press along with the apprehension of both radical and conservative organizations, troubled by their well being. Yet their significance has been, for the most part, ignored by scholars.

Elizabeth Quay Hutchison's study of these tumultuous times brings gender back into play. She investigates the way the gendered division of labor constrained women's possibilities in the labor market, and burdened them with double work; how the growing numbers of women in urban Chile provoked concern among male-dominated labor organizations while spawning the development of radical socialist feminist movements; how reformers working within the government and the Catholic Church, alarmed by the "woman question," promoted programs that constrained what Chile's women could become. *Labors Appropriate to Their Sex,* recognizing the singular importance of gender as an analytical category, returns women to the complex political and economic relations of early-twentieth-century urban Chile; it makes us, therefore, understand Latin America Otherwise.

In memory of

Pablo Andrés Candia Gajardo

1969–1996

For Regina

Contents

List of Tables   xi
List of Illustrations   xiii
Acknowledgments   xv
Introduction   1

I Working-Class Life and Politics

1. Gender, Industrialization, and Urban Change
in Santiago   19
2. Women at Work in Santiago   36
3. "To Work Like Men and Not Cry Like Women":
The Problem of Women in Male Workers' Politics   59
4. *Somos Todas Obreras!* Socialists and Working-Class
Feminism   97

II Women Workers and the Social Question

5. Women's Vocational Training: The Female Face of
Industrialization   143
6. *Señoras y Señoritas*: Catholic Women Defend the
Hijas de Familia   171
7. Women, Work, and Motherhood: Gender and
Legislative Consensus   198
Conclusion: Women, Work, and Historical Change   233

Appendices   245
Abbreviations   257
Notes   259
Bibliography   325
Index   339

List of Tables

1. Population of the Department of Santiago by Sex, 1895–1930   25
2. Number of Industrial Establishments and Workers in Santiago, 1895–1925   27
3. Average Family Expenses as Percent of Family Income, Santiago, 1911–1925   32
4. Women Active in the Chilean Workforce, 1895–1930   39
5. Sectoral Distribution of Economically Active Women, 1895–1930   43
6. Percentage of Economically Active Women Employed in Chilean Industry, Domestic Service, and Commerce, 1895–1930   44
7. Feminization of Chilean Industry, Domestic Service, and Commerce, 1895–1930   44
8. Men and Women in Selected Occupations in Chile, 1907   46
9. Women Workers Employed by Santiago Factories, 1910–1925   48
10. Distribution of Women Workers in Chilean Manufacturing by Type of Factory, 1912–1925   50
11. Sectoral Feminization of the Chilean Factory Workforce, 1912–1925   50
12. Women Homeworkers Interviewed by Elena Caffarena, 1924   53
13. Workers' Societies and Membership in Chile, 1870–1923   61
14. Literacy in the Department of Santiago, by Sex, 1885–1920   65
15. Women's and Mixed-Sex Workers' Associations, Santiago, 1906–1908   70
16. Enrollment and Attendance in the Santiago Girls' Vocational School, 1892, by Area of Specialization   152
17. Founding Dates of Provincial Girls' Vocational Schools   156
18. Weekly Hours of Instruction in Several Girls' Vocational Schools, 1909   157
19. Number of Diplomas Granted in the Vocational High School by Area of Specialization, 1915–1924   158
20. Enrollment in Private Girls' Vocational Schools, 1909   175
21. Compliance with Maternity and Day Care Law (DL 442), 1925   229

List of Illustrations

1. Map of Santiago, 1897   24
2. Santiago market scene, circa 1900   26
3. Santiago's *conventillos*, 1900–1923   31
4. Laundrywomen in a *conventillo*, circa 1900   33
5. Census list of professions, Province of Santiago, 1885   40
6. Seamstresses selling shirts, Santiago, circa 1910   47
7. Women at looms, Gratry Textile Factory, Viña del Mar, 1908   49
8. Packing department, Chilean Tobacco Company, Santiago, circa 1910   51
9. Juana Roldán de Alarcón of Santiago's Sociedad Protección de la Mujer   64
10. "Gallery of Presidents for Workers' Societies," *El Obrero Ilustrado*, 1906   71
11. Chilean Liberty, Confectioners' Union, 1926   90
12. Masthead of *La Alborada*, feminist workers' publication, 1906   104
13. Asociación de Costureras "Protección, Ahorro i Defensa," 1907   115
14. Audience for the first anniversary of the Asociación de Costureras, July 1907   116
15. Masthead of *La Palanca*, "A feminist publication of emancipatory propaganda," 1908   120
16. Girls' Vocational School exhibit, Women's Exhibit, 1927   145
17. Machine sewing class, Girls' Vocational School, Curicó, circa 1925   148
18. Commercial class, Girls' Vocational High School, Santiago, circa 1925   151
19. Primary school domestic economy class, Women's Exhibit, 1927   161
20. Sales clerks, Casa Francesa and Gath y Chaves department stores, 1913   185
21. Sindicato "Aguja, Costura y Moda," 1923   195
22. Cover of industrialists' publication, *Boletín de la Sociedad de Fomento Fabril*, 1911   203
23. Elena Caffarena de Morice, Labor Office inspector, circa 1927   228

Acknowledgments

It hardly seems possible to acknowledge all that so many teachers, friends, colleagues, and family have done for me these many years, as I counted Santiago's seamstresses and scoured the chilly archives for evidence of their lives. I can at least try to thank them all here, offer the book itself as testimony to their generous support, and hope some day to have the opportunity to return their many kindnesses.

The administrators and staff of the Chilean National Library and Archives have shown considerable forbearance and professionalism with my many research requests. I am particularly grateful to José Apoblazo Guerra, María Eugenia Barrientos Harbín, Fernando Castro, Manuel Cornejo, Elda Opazo, and Carmen Sepúlveda. I have relied at different times on the able research assistance of Teresa Gatica, Ivonne Urriola, and Fernanda Caloiro. Hugo Castillo produced some of the photographic reproductions that accompany the text, and Gonzalo Catalán and Roberto Aguirre of the Chilean National Library generously granted permission for their use. Without the very professional help of Valerie Millholland of Duke University Press, this book (among other things) would never have materialized. Several anonymous readers at Duke University Press inspired necessary revisions, and Miriam Angress and Jonathan Director have guided me patiently through the mysteries of manuscript production. Shaun Driscoll of Camera Graphics Imaging supplied excellent reproductions; and Tiffany Thomas offered indispensable aid in proofreading and indexing the book.

A project of this scope has depended, of course, on multiple forms of institutional support, which have ranged from grants to teaching and other employment opportunities. The University of California at Berkeley, the Fulbright Foundation, and the Mellon Foundation offered crucial support for my doctoral research, and the Ford Foundation repeatedly employed me in Santiago as a consultant, allowing me to extend my stay in Chile and granting me respite from my research activities. I also extend my thanks to Alicia Frohmann of the Facultad

Latino Americano de Ciencias Sociales (FLACSO) and to Nicolás Cruz and Anne Pérotin-Dumon of the Catholic University's Instituto Histórico for arranging for me to teach at those institutions. I am especially indebted to the students who attended those courses for their participation and enthusiasm, as I am to scholars at FLACSO, the Centro de Desarollo de la Mujer (CEDEM), SUR Profesionales, the Catholic University's Instituto Histórico, and the University of Santiago who have facilitated publication and presentation of new scholarship on Chilean women's history.

Of all the debts I have incurred, the intellectual ones will, I hope, be most evident in these pages. At the University of California, Berkeley, I had the good fortune to work with Tulio Halperín Donghi, who drew out this reluctant historian with his encyclopedic knowledge of Latin American history and rigorous, always incisive critiques. Linda Lewin and Francine Masiello also guided me through the rigors of doctoral study and offered helpful suggestions as my research took shape.

I also extend my gratitude to my Chileanist colleagues in the United States. For better or for worse, Iván Jaksic made me a Chileanist, nurturing my curiosity about the Chilean military regime and teaching me to appreciate historical approaches to understanding social conflict. I thank him here for his years of guidance and unflagging support for my work. Heidi Tinsman and Thomas Klubock have also—perhaps unknowingly—continually inspired me with their scholarship and solidarity, ever since they corralled me on Pio Nono one January eve. I also thank Karin Rosemblatt and Ericka Verba for their continued personal and professional support, as well as my other fine colleagues in the growing field of Chilean gender studies, including Lisa Baldez, Corinne Pernet, and Margaret Power.

María Soledad Zárate Campos has contributed in myriad ways to the long labor of this book, broadening my intellectual horizons and demonstrating over and again that *si, se puede*. A diverse array of scholars have at one point or another offered encouragement, commentary, or other crucial support for my efforts, including Robert Buffington, Sandra McGee Deutsch, Elizabeth Faue, Alicia Frohmann, Thelma Gálvez, Donna Guy, Asunción Lavrin, Elizabeth Lira, Brian Loveman, Jorge Olivares, Anne Pérotin-Dumon, Julio Pinto, Jorge Rojas, Anthony Rosenthal, Anindyo Roy, Gabriel Salazar, the late Cecilia Salinas, Cynthia Sanborn, Marc Stein, Barbara Weinstein, and Alex Wilde. I am enormously grateful to Peter Winn, who read the dissertation and suggested how I might make this a better book.

Most recently, my colleagues in the History Department and the Latin American and Iberian Institute at the University of New Mexico have provided a terrific new work environment, where they have shown me the great personal and intellectual benefits that come with real collegiality. In particular, I thank Melissa Bokovoy, Kimberly Gauderman, Jane Slaughter, Samuel Truett, and the late Robert Kern for their encouragement and friendship. Judy Bieber and Linda Hall, as well as other Latinamericanists and historians at UNM, have all helped to make UNM my professional home, where dedicated undergraduate and graduate students continually inspire me to be a better historian and teacher.

Many "families" have fed me, kept me healthy, made me sleep, and helped me keep all of this in perspective. The Hutchison family, of course, gave me a love of history and social justice; my adopted *familias—polaca, Platero,* and *Ford*—saw me through the hardest years of this project with love and humor, and the *familia maestravidiana* kept me dancing. My own family, which enjoyed the happy arrival of Dante Santiago Quay Manocchio between copyediting and proofs, has simply made life a joy. Linda Garber, Margy Hutchison, and Regina Manocchio encourage me to pursue my dreams and tell me when to rest from them. To all my families, friends, teachers, students, and colleagues, thank you.

Introduction

I told the head of investigations and the Criminal Judge that I have been dressing as a man for four years and that I did this, first, in order to better protect my honor as a woman, and second, to earn more so that I could live. Dressed as a man, I am more respected and no one propositions me. In this way I can work without anyone making me uncomfortable or bothering me. Dressed as a woman, I could not live among men nor work in whatever job [I wished]. Work for women is scarce and very badly paid. I preferred to look for another way to satisfy my physical necessities without upsetting my spiritual inclinations.
—Laura Rosa Zelada, November 26, 1903

In November 1903, the Santiago and Valparaíso newspaper-reading public were entertained by the revelations of an illiterate young woman named Laura Rosa Zelada, also known as Honorio Cortes. The nineteen-year-old bakery employee was discovered to be a woman in man's clothing, arrested for dressing in disguise, and thrown in jail. According to lawyer Agustín Bravo Cisternas—who dubbed her "Laura, Virgin of the Forest" in his account—Zelada had fled her rural home and an abusive brother-in-law four years earlier, shed her skirts for pants, and gone to work in and around Santiago as a servant, fruit seller, hotel employee, and baker. In the above petition for her release, Zelada argued that she was not guilty of the crime of wearing a disguise, because she had dressed as a man only to earn a decent living and to protect her honor. When charges were dropped and she was released, Zelada disappeared without a trace.[1]

During the six months of her imprisonment, Zelada's case became the talk of the town. As the details of the case emerged, she was lauded as a local heroine in urban newspapers, which also took advantage of the situation to produce titillating accounts of cross-dressing throughout history. One editorial defended Zelada's right to wear pants and mocked the charges that had been made against her, arguing that she had "cut her hair and become a better man than any Deputy or Senator."[2] The bulk of editorials, however, focused on the economic logic of Zelada's actions. Journalists from the working-class daily *El Chileno*, for example, followed the case closely, justifying Zelada's masquerade in light of women's limited occupational choices: "If she had not changed her clothes, she would have been a laundress, a seamstress, which is to say, a slave to someone who only pays her enough so that she doesn't die right away."[3] Publicity about Zelada's arrest provoked widespread sympathy for her plight, reflecting the common perception that working women were unduly exploited. Zelada's case was also used to illustrate complaints about women's low wages, poor working conditions, excessive sexual vulnerability, and desperate poverty. By dressing as a man to survive and to protect her honor, Zelada had apparently won more fans than critics.[4]

The most extensive and revealing treatise in Zelada's defense was penned by her lawyer, who included a chapter about her case in his legal polemic, *La mujer a través de los siglos* (Women Through the Centuries). Bravo Cisternas rendered a detailed account of Zelada's hardships and defended her cross-dressing as a rational economic choice: "She solved the economic problem regarding women's capacities in male occupations and found a way for a woman to get a better salary and more respect from men."[5] According to Bravo, "the Virgin of the Forest" had chosen the only virtuous option available to a woman who had to support herself, and she should not have been punished for it. On the contrary, he argued, Zelada's actions should be considered exemplary until legal reforms that would improve the lot of working women could be implemented.

The scandal generated by Zelada's arrest was only one manifestation of widespread public concern for the plight of working women in early-twentieth-century Chile. Labor organizers, elite Catholic women, industrialists, and legislators all debated the nature and propriety of women's paid work as they confronted a rapidly changing society. As urban and industrial growth engulfed Santiago and women literally went out to work, traditional gender and social arrangements came under intense scrutiny. What did it mean that poor women could not, or would not, tend exclusively to domestic responsibilities? How should the state or private organizations intervene to ensure healthy future generations of workers? These queries spurred private and public efforts for the aid, protection, and organization of women workers that characterized the era of the social question in Chile.

In part, this preoccupation was a result of the increasing evidence of women in the urban labor force around the turn of the century; according to the 1885 national census, women constituted 35 percent of the national workforce, and their work was concentrated in manufacturing, service, and commercial activities in urban centers. Women working for wages outside the home had become not only more numerous, but also more visible against the backdrop of the dramatic urban transformations of the late nineteenth century. Much of the public concern about the mushrooming urban population, therefore, focused on the unseemly presence of *women* in the city: as factory workers, street sellers, domestic servants, and prostitutes. In the still predominantly rural society of nineteenth-century Chile, women's work, though necessary for family survival, was not paid or public; in the burgeoning capital, by contrast, women and their work were everywhere in evidence. This study explores the origins, motives, and objectives of debates on women's urban work in Chile over the first three decades of the twentieth century to show how these debates influenced broader developments in labor politics, women's activism, and state formation. In this fashion, the Chilean case illuminates how gender affects and is affected by social transformations linked to urban and industrial growth in Latin America prior to the 1930s.

Public outcry over working women's condition was just one aspect of a society that anxiously confronted far-reaching social and economic changes. This period spans a critical juncture in Chilean development, from the aftermath of the Second War of the Pacific (ending in 1883) through the Ibañez era, a period in which a set of crucial socioeconomic and political changes transformed Chile's territory, demography, and administration. Many of these changes stemmed from Chile's acquisition of vast nitrate fields in its second great war with Peru; taxes from the export of nitrates to Europe funded the growth of the Chilean state and encouraged national integration through the development of transportation networks. The so-called Parliamentary Republic that followed, initiated with the fall of Balmaceda in 1891, described a thinly disguised version of oligarchic rule, one riven by increasing levels of class conflict in the new century.

Changes linked to the export of nitrates also dramatically transformed the living and employment options of working people. Rural wage laborers, already migrating in search of work, turned to the city in hopes of finding some opportunity for economic advancement and freedom from rural peonage. The promise of employment in nitrates and related industries sparked massive migration of male peons from rural to urban areas: urban centers expanded from 34 to 49 percent of the population between 1885 and 1930, and Santiago's growth peaked at almost 5 percent a year between 1885 and 1895. Male artisans and workers found in the city increased employment opportunities as production diversified to supply domestic markets for luxury and essential goods. The emergence of an urban proletariat and the enactment of literate male suffrage (1885) contributed to the foundation of the first workers' parties in the late 1880s. Subsequent labor organization and conflict in port, mining, and industrial centers presaged the conflictive, repressive relations between workers and their employers that would come to characterize labor relations under the Parliamentary Republic.[6]

Women also formed an integral part of these changes, as they too turned to the city in search of employment. Since the 1860s, women had begun to abandon the shrinking family economies of the countryside and take up residence in the *ranchos* (shacks) that circled Santiago.[7] To sustain what were often female-headed households, women mixed domestic agriculture with cottage industries and local commerce in the urban periphery. As Santiago increased in importance as the administrative and residential center for Chile's aristocracy in the late nineteenth century, demand for female domestic services increased and urban space was reorganized to accommodate elite plans for the city. Relocated to slums at the city's center, poor women and men were drawn into a cash economy, and consequently women became more dependent on either male family members or their own scarce wages for survival.

The growth of urban population and domestic consumption also provided some women with another option: factory work in clothing, textile, cigarette, and food production. By the last decade of the nineteenth century, Chile's early industrial production was well underway, supplying the growing domestic markets for clothing and food. The average size of factories grew from seventeen to thirty workers between 1895 and 1925; by 1918, 43 percent of all industrial workers in Chile were employed in factories of one hundred or more.[8] Citing their superior dexterity, docility, and sobriety, industrialists actively recruited women and children to manufacturing employment, thereby ensuring a sizable and inexpensive workforce for textile, food, and clothing production. By 1912, women made up a solid third of Santiago's factory workers, where they predominated in the clothing, textile, and tobacco industries by a ratio of 3 to 1. All told, approximately one tenth of the wage-earning women of Santiago worked in factory production, including those who retrieved factory piecework to complete in their homes.[9]

Because of women's visible role in these socioeconomic transformations, this was the period in which attention to the plight of working women was first ignited. The fact of women's manual employment—and its high visibility in the city—disturbed and offended a wide variety of social actors, from anarchists to senators, who seized on the figure of the woman worker as proof of social decay. At the turn of the century, labor organizers referred with increasing frequency to the plight of working women, diagnosing this pressing issue according to the various dictates of anarchist or socialist ideology. In parallel fashion, Chilean elites initiated a variety of private and legislative projects to protect, train, and mobilize working-class women, revealing their competing visions for the preservation of Chilean society and its values. The simultaneous growth of middle-class employment in clerical, sales, and professional jobs evidenced Chile's gradual shift to a more middle-class, urban society and spurred new concerns over the nature of female employment. The growing presence of women in these sectors not only buttressed the emancipatory designs of middle-class feminists, but also prefigured the feminization of state welfare activities in the 1930s.

Despite the abundant evidence of female participation in the urban workforce in the twentieth century, existing studies of the urban working classes in Chile have been generally inattentive to women's participation and to gender as an analytic category. Until very recently, labor historians have relegated women workers to the very margins of narratives on industrial development and class formation in Chile.[10] This failure to consider women as worthwhile subjects of working-class history has been misleading: it not only overlooks female agency, but also conflates the experience of male workers with the process of class formation itself, dictating the periodization, subjects, and sources for its study.[11] The fact that labor historians have viewed women as only a secondary workforce obviates the reality that, historically and currently, almost one of every four Chilean "workers" is female. This was, and is, not simply a "natural" division of labor: women's position in the labor market—in Chile as elsewhere—has been constrained by material conditions on the one hand (including the double duty performed by working mothers) and normative and institutional exclusions on the other (barring women's access to "skilled" and more permanent jobs).[12] The characteristics of women's participation in the labor force—in a variety of settings and conditions—have challenged scholars first to incorporate women into labor history and then to question prevailing wisdom about the construction of working-class identities, consciousness, and agency.

Fortunately, the development of Chilean social history in recent years has mandated that women and other "popular subjects" be included as historical subjects, and has begun to provide a more complete picture of working-class development.[13] When working-class women have been discussed, however, most authors have not sufficiently challenged the normative analytic dichotomy between the male as worker and the female as mother, which tends to obscure women's productive and sometimes public contributions, both as workers and as labor militants. As Joan Scott has observed, gender is a remarkably powerful mechanism in class formation because "sexual difference is invoked as a 'natural' phenomenon; as such it enjoys a privileged status, seemingly outside question or criticism."[14] Historians who, in like fashion, fail to question the apparent immutability of gender roles have overlooked an important analytical tool for understanding labor and workers' politics. For example, women have often been given short shrift in research on working-class political movements because many historians have tended to dispense with female participation in labor politics with the observation that women were more "passive" than men, without asking how or why this might have come about.[15] By presenting instances of female activism as exceptions that confirm the rule of female passivity, these accounts fail to consider the fact that male-led labor movements have historically offered conditional support for the mobilization of women workers, whose demands have consequently been structured around the twin goals of cross-gender solidarity and increasing male wages. The ways labor movements have drawn on and manipulated gender ideology to great political gain have been amply documented in a variety of historical cases and periods.[16] In the Chilean case, historians' continuing tendency to view working-class women first as housewives and only secondarily as workers has inhibited closer scrutiny of their participation in the labor force, as well as its implications for workers' political movements.[17]

Like the labor movement, debates on the social question have provided one of the central reference points for Chilean histories of the period, which have explored the ideological, political, and institutional parameters of public debate and legislative action under the Parliamentary Republic.[18] However, the substantial literature on Chilean industrial relations has described the evolution of the social question in Chile as an exclusively male phenomenon: male politicians and employers debating the fortunes and control of male miners and industrial workers. Because they have focused solely on conflicts between working men and their male employers, historians have tended to overlook the ample evidence of public concern for working women.[19] Even though contemporaries themselves addressed concerns about women's changing role in society in the context of debates on the social question, historians have divided research on "the worker question" and "the woman question" into separate projects concerned exclusively with their respective male and female subjects.[20]

Finally, the growing field of Chilean women's history has offered a partial response to this elision of working women from the historical record.[21] Although early studies of women's political participation tended to emphasize middle-class professional women's leadership in the gradual transformation of Chilean women's roles,[22] recent scholarship has begun to flesh out working-class women's agency and experience by examining their labor, community ties, and political participation. Guided by a variety of distinct theoretical orientations,[23] these studies have confirmed the need to revise the "master narratives" of both labor and political history in Chile.[24] Chilean women's labor history promises to illuminate how the persistent identification of men with wage work and women with reproduction reflects gender hierarchies that influence working-class men and women in the home as well as in labor politics. Given the incipient development of the field of working-class women's history in Chile, the methodological sweep of this study extends from the first step of compensatory history (in which women are reconstituted as subjects) to the task of posing new questions about previous interpretations of female agency and influence in historical processes. What happens when we place working-class women at the center of historical narratives about organized labor, the rise of feminism, and state formation? We see, first, that Chilean working-class women struggled to reconcile the need for wages with changing expectations about working-class domesticity and class solidarity; working women's concerns with gender "rights" and their capacity to achieve them were therefore quite different from those demonstrated by elite feminists of the period. Second, we see that the *problem* of women's work was often constructed quite differently by women's erstwhile protectors—union leaders, legislators, elite women, and state officials—than it was by women themselves. Nevertheless, it was outsiders' continuing attention to women at work that fundamentally shaped the emerging urban labor movement, early protective legislation, and private and state welfare activities in the early twentieth century, effectively limiting the range of choices for women who needed to work for wages in the urban economy. Therefore, this focus illustrates how changes in the panorama of women's paid, manual labor accompanied the growth of the city and sparked the attention of social actors who saw in working women the illustration of a society in crisis and the springboard for necessary reforms.

Much of the existing history of Latin American women in the modern period has focused, understandably, on the increasing access of middle-class women to education and professional employment and on the corresponding emergence of movements for gender equality, in which women and their male allies challenged the civil codes and suffrage restrictions of their respective countries.[25] The present study intentionally circumvents this narrative of liberal feminism not because it is unimportant, but rather because without further development of the social history of women's labor, deceptive generalizations about women's "progress" in the modern era remain seductive.[26] Recent scholarship has demonstrated that liberal feminism was not the only movement that emerged in defense of women's "interests" during the century of "the woman question" in Latin America. As Lavrin has shown, liberal feminists borrowed selectively from competing feminists' claims and built their projects for social reform on existing class and political networks.[27] Similarly, proponents of "other feminisms," often social Catholic in orientation, drew attention to the plight of working women to achieve conservative political and social goals.[28] Of all the varieties of feminism circulating in early-twentieth-century Chile, this study examines working-class feminism most closely, fleshing out its substance and significance within socialist unionism, precisely because this discourse clearly illustrates the constraints on and opportunities for working women's political action in this period. This approach not only privileges working-class actors—particularly women—but also allows us to examine the claims they made on behalf of working women, which were quite different from those of liberal or conservative feminist movements of the period. Each of these "mixed feminisms" provided an arena for women's struggle to change their social condition (or that of others), leaving a rich and complex record of their social agency.

This study has also been enriched by recent studies of Latin American working women that examine how gender is articulated in the process of class formation, particularly in terms of cultural representations of working-class women. A number of recent North American studies have examined the "cultural paradox of the woman worker," referring to the central discursive paradigm that makes women's workforce participation suspect, dangerous, or at the very least requiring an explanation. This tension has been amply documented in Ann Farnsworth-Alvear's study of the Antioqueña textile industry in the 1920s, where she argues that the "fictive category" of *la mujer obrera* (the woman worker) shaped both industrial discipline and the resistance of women textile workers.[29] Other studies have shown that the discourse that emerged in conjunction with women's factory work in much of Latin America has shaped their employment on a structural level—through the creation of industrial training programs, charitable work, and protective legislation—as well as at the level of experience, influencing how working women view themselves and their work. Oral histories have therefore frequently revealed how women employ a "language of necessity" or turn to available life scripts of working-class social motherhood to justify their employment.[30]

Chilean representations of la mujer obrera during the first three decades of the twentieth century confirm that the paradox of the woman worker was a powerful stimulus to social reform, but it was not the only available paradigm for workers' own actions. As union militants struggled to resolve the tension between working-class aspirations for viable patriarchy on the one hand and the challenges presented by female employment outside the home on the other, representations of working women became relatively *less* paradoxical, as competing representations of women as active agents in revolutionary struggle became available. Where we do glimpse women's own agency and voice, there is also evidence for what Deborah Levenson-Estrada has called "the gray area of women's experience of gender 'imperfection.'"[31] Women militants active in the labor associations of early-twentieth-century urban Chile justified their appropriation of a male role in a variety of ways, in some cases feminizing that role by evoking the feminine traits of virtue and self-sacrifice, and in others embracing the model of "virile" activism for the greater good of class revolution.[32] Militant women workers both manipulated prevalent assumptions about their vulnerability and asserted through their activism a claim to the "manly" characteristics of organized labor. By looking at the interplay between "fictions" and "realities" of working women's experience, we gain a greater appreciation of how constructions of la mujer obrera might have shaped women's economic opportunities and community solidarity in early-twentieth-century Chile.

Like most projects in social history, the task of reconstructing Chilean working-class women's experience in this period began with the search for relevant sources. Because many women were engaged, then as now, in informal employment that allowed them to fulfill domestic obligations, quantitative data are weak and incomplete indicators of their employment. Women's work was also characterized by a high degree of instability, as women moved between jobs in search of better working conditions and wages and more time for domestic duties. Given the diverse nature of female employment, this study draws on a variety of sources to reconstruct how, when, and where women worked in the city. Although contemporaries demonstrated ample concern for the effects of female employment, data on women's working conditions and wages were not collected in any systematic fashion. Data on women's work thus had to be gleaned from labor inspectors' reports, factory surveys, and the published census. Law theses concerned with the social question occasionally provided case studies of working-class women amidst legislative analysis and foreign bibliographies. Journalists, on the other hand, regularly focused their attention on abuses and developments in the most common forms of female employment: manufacturing, domestic service, commerce, and prostitution. Labor Office records, trade magazines, and factory rules provide some indication of how women's work was organized in certain highly feminized industries.

The search for sources also quickly revealed how the story of women's work is also a narrative about the emergence of organized labor, the consolidation of the state, and elite projects for social control of the working classes. The state's earliest attempts to protect women in the workplace were documented in congressional debates, legislative proposals, and ministerial records. The abundant labor press of the period reveals all sorts of information on working-class women, from doctrinal statements on "the woman question" to meeting announcements, denunciations of employers, and flowery poetry.[33] These observers gathered and disseminated information on working women in the service of their respective causes, offering various solutions to the perceived crisis. However divergent their ideological positions, their views tend to converge on the premise that if women were to continue working outside the home, their activities had to be monitored and protected in the interest of the public good.

As the present study shows, historical documents that describe women at work—in both quantitative and qualitative terms—are infused with the cultural norms, symbols, and ideologies that differentiate male and female qualities and behaviors, particularly in the sphere of employment. For example, all of these sources share a marked bias toward the definition of work as only waged, and usually industrial, employment, so much so that women's activity in other areas can be drawn only from anecdotal information. Moreover, methods of data collection and the use of results reveal the political and social aims of each group with respect to workers and their families, as well as their assumptions and expectations about women in the labor force. In the end, many of these sources reveal more about how women's work was valued, rationalized, and contested than about the reality of women's work in any objective sense.

Divided into two parts, this book sketches out the changes in women's paid employment and a series of developments that followed in two major arenas: the labor movement and the private and state projects of Chilean elites. The first chapter sets the stage for this discussion by describing the processes of industrialization and urbanization in Chile in terms of migration, housing, and the urban labor market. Chapter 2 charts the economic activities of urban women, challenging accepted interpretations of women's economic role in Chile's industrial growth. Previously, historians have taken at face value census figures that show a dramatic decline in women's industrial work after 1907. Closer examination reveals that women's participation shifted rather than evaporated: the use of female labor in domestic sweatshops and changing definitions of employment combined to informalize women's labor, making much of it disappear from census records by 1930.

Chapters 3 and 4 examine how workers' organizations responded to women's increased visibility in the urban workforce. Whereas some leaders relied on available discourses of female emancipation to unionize working women, labor organizers also utilized images of female victimization in the workplace, both to shame employers and to assert male workers' rights to control and protect working-class women's labor and sexuality. Although working-class feminist criticism sometimes emerged to protest gender inequalities in Chilean working-class politics, this challenge was limited by a tacit consensus between men and women about the gender roles they deemed appropriate for each sex and the gendered codes of respectability to which they aspired. The surge in socialist unionization among women workers between 1900 and 1908, often referred to as *feminismo obrero* (worker feminism), illustrates the inflexibility of gender roles even under the pressure of a rapidly changing workforce and a challenge from the more radical worker feminists. Although socialist organizers' attention to women workers attenuated in the subsequent two decades, women continued to participate in labor associations, occasionally raising the banner of worker feminism in later years for the benefit of cross-gender solidarity.

Part 2 explores how women's paid labor became the locus of anxiety for social elites—industrialists, educators, aristocratic women, social reformers, and legislators—who were alarmed by the changes induced by industrial and urban growth. Chapter 5 describes how industrialists and their state allies set out to modernize Chilean industry and rescue women from poverty by establishing industrial schools for girls. The innovative potential of this project was constrained, however, by the school administrators' acceptance of existing occupational segregation, which, compounded by consistently low female wages, made female training and certification in industrial skills superfluous to improving their position in the labor market. Instead, the schools evolved into a mechanism for improving poor women's morals and domestic skills in an effort to discipline potentially unruly working-class men. Chapter 6 examines how elite women addressed what they perceived as a gendered social crisis through attempts to educate, organize, and protect women workers. Aristocratic Catholic women, who had long supported religious and vocational programs for poor women, were compelled to take further action by the increasing participation of middle-class and even aristocratic women in economic activities. Alarmed by radical labor's organizing among women workers, they also turned to organizing women in the workplace in hopes of staving off what they perceived to be the impending social and moral impact of industrialization. In the 1910s and 1920s, Catholic women's societies countered leftist mobilization by establishing worker cooperatives and Catholic unions for women workers.

Finally, women workers became the explicit subject of congressional debate in these decades, as politicians considered implementing social legislation in response to the social question. Taking their cue from the private charitable organizations and international laws that preceded them, prominent legislators urged their colleagues to provide women and children with state protection, securing several largely uncontroversial measures passed (but not enforced) after 1910. Chapter 7 analyzes how and why legislators debated laws and regulations designed to limit what they considered to be the untoward effects of female employment on working-class families. The timing and content of labor legislation for women reveals how assumptions about masculinity and femininity—in relation to wage work, family survival, and reproduction—shaped the state's response to the social question as a whole. As recent scholarship on the welfare state elsewhere has shown, such policies were gendered not only because many of them were directed at women, but also because they derived from gendered assumptions about human capabilities, the nature of the state, and social organization.[34] However divided they might have been over the social question itself, opposing politicians agreed on the necessity of state intervention to protect working mothers. Private charities and gender-specific legislation thus paved the way for the comprehensive and paternalistic Labor Code of 1924. Although little in this Code was effectively enforced prior to the 1930s, these regulations consolidated men's role as breadwinner and further narrowed opportunities for women in the labor market.

One of the keys to understanding how gender operates historically in any society has been the sexual division of labor, by which economic activities come to be identified as appropriate for either men or women. In urban Chile at the turn of the century, such gendered divisions, including the low value attached to women's labor, had already become firmly entrenched in cultural understandings. The phrase commonly employed to describe women's occupations—"labors appropriate to their sex" (*labores propias de su sexo*)—relied on a supposedly natural and therefore immutable division of labor by sex. In fact, as forms and levels of female employment were transformed, women's "appropriate" work would become a contested category, as working women and other social actors tried to explain, challenge, or justify the kinds and conditions of female employment. Although the growing presence of women in formerly male arenas such as the industrial workshop was readily acknowledged around 1900, their presence there was considered—by all but their employers—detrimental and temporary. Women who earned money for their labor outside the home continued to be defined as exceptions to the rule of the working-class homemaker, which confirmed and justified women workers' confinement to female occupations and their correspondingly low wages. Nevertheless, as the case of Laura Zelada demonstrates, working women did not always accept such constraints on their choices, but regularly subverted them (by performing "male" work), challenged them (through strikes and labor actions), or adapted them to their own advantage (through recourse to protective legislation and vocational training). Through their own actions, women demonstrated their agency, if not by refashioning definitions of "appropriate work," then by working around such exclusions in order to survive.

This study of the "labors appropriate to their sex" demonstrates how this very concrete manifestation of sexual hierarchy shaped women's economic options, structured urban working-class communities, and affected debates about the well-being of Santiago's working poor. Although certain norms concerning gender and work came under public scrutiny in the social transformations of the period, prevailing constructions of gender roles and identity continued to shape labor movement strategies, the development of the industrial relations system, and elite administration of private and public welfare for the working classes. Gender norms and their changing content therefore crucially informed the process of class formation and urban change in this critical period of Chilean history.

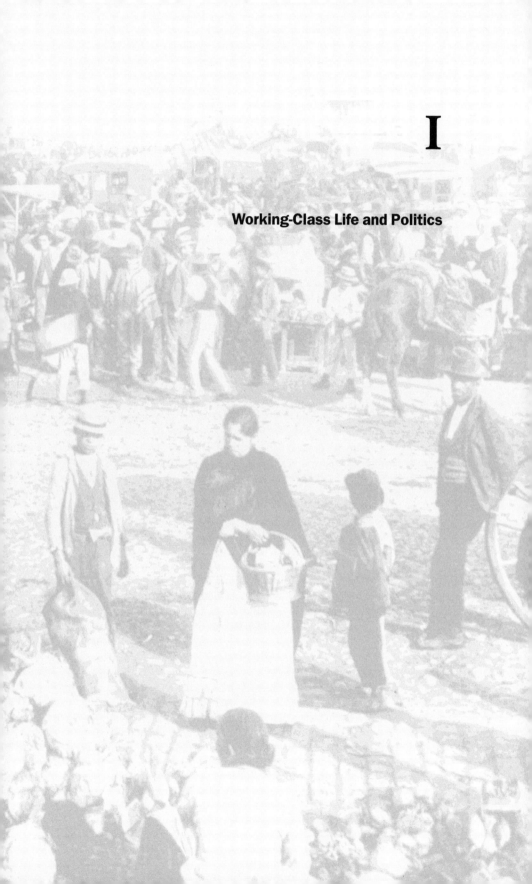

I

Working-Class Life and Politics

During the decades flanking the turn of the century, the city of Santiago made manifest the social distance between the growing wealth of a few and the grinding poverty of the many in increasingly dramatic terms. While profits from the nitrate industry funded the palatial homes of Santiago's aristocratic families, rural unemployment and poverty sent scores of women and men into the city in search of work in wealthy homes and industrial workshops. The history of "the city of the poor" and "the death of the people" is also a history of an emerging public awareness of working-class women's subjugation within that scheme.[1] The story of where these women lived and worked and of how they participated in working-class political movements forms a crucial part of the history of class formation and the politics of the left in Chile.

Part I begins with two chapters that describe the transformation of the urban areas and labor markets of urban Chile in the early twentieth century, focusing on how such changes shifted the contours of working-class urban life and impacted women and men in different ways. Not only did more women than men migrate to urban areas in search of work, but they also facilitated male migration and family survival in the increasingly cash-based economy of the city. As women and children became a crucial labor pool for factory expansion in textile and clothing production, as well as an important source of labor for making tobacco, chemical, and leather products, these new workers in fact "invaded" the streets and tram cars of Santiago and Valparaíso. However, these formal employment opportunities did not at once eliminate women's simultaneous responsibility for domestic reproduction, nor their participation in informal and illegal employment. Determining how, where, and for what women labored in this shifting economy is an important step in sketching the urban panorama of early-twentieth-century Chile.

These socioeconomic transformations also triggered increasing conflicts between workers and their employers, stimulating working-class organization and the circulation of radical labor ideologies in Chile. Chapters 3 and 4 explore how representations of women in relation to wage work shaped the discourse and platforms of labor militants, both male and female, at this crucial stage in the genesis of the Chilean labor movement. The discourse on women workers that emerged in the first decade of the twentieth century—made necessary in large part by the incessant focus on the social question at all levels of public debate— required that labor leaders acknowledge women's presence in the work-place and propose forms of female organization, if only to bring the erosion of male industrial wages through female employment to an end. Despite the prevailing consensus that women—and their families—were better off when women stayed at home, images of working women in this period were adapted to the exigencies of mobilization through labor propaganda that lauded, naturalized, and explained this "unfeminine" behavior. By the 1920s, the intensity of attention to "the woman ques-tion" had declined, reflecting the success of socialist cross-gender strat-egies, which both legitimated working women's demands and buttressed campaigns for the male family wage.

I

Gender, Industrialization, and

Urban Change in Santiago

Beneath the apparent calm of Chile's Parliamentary Republic (1891–1924), demographic and economic forces combined to produce important changes in the urban environment, transforming the structure of life and labor for working people in Santiago. Hard on the heels of the rapid population expansion of the city in the 1890s, nitrate export earnings funded urbanization and industrial growth and sponsored the consolidation of the national state and its infrastructure. Because the unequal distribution of wealth was also a primary characteristic of these developments, economic profit was concentrated in the hands of a tiny landholding elite and small middle sector, whereas the vast majority of the population labored outside the benefits of economic growth.[1]

However, many of these changes were rooted in the earlier economic expansion of the period following Chilean independence. National development accompanied the strengthening of an authoritarian government as the state established ports and railroads to facilitate primary exports. The effects of this integration into the world economy reached into the organization of agricultural and mining production. The three-pronged colonial organization of production—concentrated in the Central Valley's agriculture, northern mining fields, and the country's three main urban centers—was not fundamentally altered in the economic organization of independent Chile. The relative economic importance of these three sectors shifted, however, as world markets for Chilean exports rose and fell over time.[2]

First, an export boom in wheat to California and Australia in the 1840s, accompanied by increasing domestic consumption in mining and urban centers, generated easy wealth for the former colonial landowning class. Landowners increased production to meet this demand not by modernizing agricultural techniques, but through increasing labor demands and expanding their land holdings, effectively expelling rural workers and their families from traditional tenant-farming arrangements (*inquilinaje*).[3] The accelerated concentration of lands in the hands of the former colony's rural elite of the Central Valley was a fundamental factor in the mobility and subsequent proletarianization of rural labor; labor payments were monetarized, domestic production for exchange was practically eliminated, and pressure on lands forced *inquilinos*—especially young men—to migrate in search of other work.[4] Even when the export boom itself ended in 1856, these now land-rich Central Valley haciendas relied on a system of rural peonage (poorly paid or servile labor) to supply growing markets in northern Chile and in Peru. This development froze rural labor relations into a semifeudal system of economic and political control over rural workers that lasted well into the twentieth century.

Second, the development of nitrate mining and exports, which dated from the late 1860s in the Chilean north and increased dramatically with Chile's acquisition of Peruvian nitrate fields in 1883, established the fundamental basis for Chilean economic and political organization through the 1920s. Although a majority of the mines that passed into Chilean hands were foreign-owned, they generated huge tax revenues for the state, thereby providing the economic foundations of politics under the Parliamentary Republic. The Civil War of 1891 reestablished a strong legislature in Chile, which was subsequently dominated by a closed and largely ineffective debate over issues of national interest.[5]

Chile's nitrate economy also stimulated the expansion and reorganization of the industrial workforce. Although the Chilean nitrate sector conforms to some degree to the model of a foreign export enclave, the nitrate economy also crucially stimulated Chile's early industrialization. Early industrial development was tied to the fate of the nitrate economy; periodic depressions in that economy (1896–1898, 1907, 1909, 1914, 1919–1920, 1922, 1926–1927) brought emigration and unemployment to mining areas and inflation and recession to the industrial centers. In fact, the principal ingredients of industrial growth were closely linked to the development of the nitrate enclave, which facilitated national economic integration, the availability of capital for investment in industry, and demographic shifts that increased domestic markets for manufactured goods. Brian Loveman sums up these links: "Unlike a true economic enclave, the nitrate economy spurred national economic integration. . . . Operation of the industry created markets for Chilean agriculture and lumber, coal, and processing industries and induced development of service and support activities."[6] The development of a national port and railroad system after the second War of the Pacific subsidized agricultural production, integrated regional markets, and contributed to the mobility of labor.

The argument that Chilean industrialization began with the import-substitution policies of the 1930s has long since lost credence, but the lack of reliable data has made it difficult to calculate reliable growth rates for industry in the earlier period. Marcelo Carmagnani has argued that after the depression of 1895–1899, industrial growth averaged 7.5 percent per year through 1910.[7] Henry Kirsch's estimate hovers around the much lower figure of 3 percent real annual growth for the same period, perhaps because he includes such factors as protectionist policies and currency devaluation in that calculation.[8] The overall pattern of industrial production from 1895 to 1930 in Chile was, however, apart from the depression of 1914–1915, one of capitalist industrialization.

The historically weak manufacturing sector received extra support in the 1880s with the founding of the Society for Factory Development (Sociedad de Fomento Fabril or SOFOFA) and the Ministry of Industry and Public Works. Both agencies studied European economic policies and lobbied for increased protection for domestic manufactures, as well as technical training for Chilean workers and recruitment of foreign technicians. The industrialists' link with the state was strong: many SOFOFA members held government posts, and by 1925 the organization managed to establish permanent representation on several parliamentary councils.[9]

Mining and agricultural capitalists in Chile took advantage of opportunities to diversify their investments in the area of industry. To some extent, this choice was supported by the monetarization of the economy; the state frequently devalued currency, the overall effect of which was to increase import-export revenues for investment and the substitution of imported for domestically produced goods. Growth of national income and urban population thus generally favored the redirection of capital investment to the manufacturing sector. According to Oscar Muñoz, in addition to iron and copper foundries, these investments financed machine shops and factories for food, beer, furniture, and construction materials.[10] Though not necessarily the most profitable sector, production for domestic markets in food and clothing increased dramatically in this period, and by 1917 these sectors led industrial production in terms of employment and capital investment.[11] Significantly, these were the very industries that employed the highest proportion of women in the manufacturing sector.

Migration, Urban Growth, and Industrialization

Beneath its stable exterior, Chile at the turn of the century was characterized by the extreme contrast between national development that
brought economic prosperity to a handful of families and new forms of
urban poverty to more and more working people. That is, the migration
and urbanization linked to Chile's particular form of economic development, combined with continuing unequal distribution of wealth, increased levels of urban poverty and social dislocation that contrasted
dramatically with the new urban mansions of the nitrate-rich elites. The
urban influx of unskilled men and women alarmed these elites, who
undertook to isolate and remedy the increasing urban blight. This period of extreme political stability, then, was also characterized by public
outcry and working-class protest over "the social question." Despite the
significant differences between Chile and industrial Europe, where the
discourse on the social question first developed, Chilean elites were
almost unanimously convinced that their country faced—or would soon
be faced with—transformations of a similar nature.

Accompanying larger changes in the structure of the national economy was the steady growth of Chilean cities. Compared with the steady
growth rates in the national population, these figures reflect the accelerated pace of urbanization in the late nineteenth and early twentieth
century. Urban expansion was primarily the result of internal migration,
as rural migrants swelled urban centers (defined in the census as cities
with 20,000 or more inhabitants) from 34 to 49 percent of the total population between 1895 and 1930.[12] Santiago's 1885 population of 177,271
grew steadily at 4.09 percent per year until 1895, after which yearly
growth rates declined to about 2.5 percent.[13] Elites' alarmed response to
this influx of rural poor to the *ranchos* (shanties) that ringed the city
culminated in the municipal administration of Vicuña Mackenna, who
in 1872 fixed the city limits at the "beltway" (*camino de cintura*) and
oversaw the eviction of poor families from urban ranchos and their
relocation to horrid rental housing in the city's center. By 1875, Santiago
had virtually become two cities, the poorer half of which fed the night-
mares of the richer. Intendant Vicuña Mackenna reported in 1872 that
"Santiago is . . . a kind of double city that has, like Peking, a quiet and
laborious district and another that is brutal, demoralized and savage."[14]
In geographical terms alone, Santiago doubled in area between 1872 and
1915, with an average annual growth of fifty hectares after 1895.[15]

Foreign immigration also contributed to the growth of urban centers such as Santiago, Valparaíso, Antofagasta, and Iquique, but total foreign immigration never reached the proportions it did in neighboring Argentina. In fact, Chile's Central Valley lost more workers than it gained prior to 1895; Salazar estimates that about 200,000 Chileans left for Australia, California, Peru, northern and southern Chile, and Argentina in this period.[16] After peaking in 1890 with 11,001 in net immigration, Chile received a mere 8,462 immigrants in 1907 (compared to Argentina's 119,861).[17] In the same year, most immigrants to Chile were Peruvian (20.62%) and Bolivian (16.33%), followed by Spanish (13.94%) and Italian (9.68%) immigrants, many of whom became shopkeepers and businessmen in Chile's urban centers.[18] Immigrant artisans found good use for their talents: trades such as tailoring were established in Chile only through the arrival of foreign artisans.

The steady expansion of Santiago's population after 1885 has been attributed to several factors linked to the nitrate enclave: the growth of transportation networks, regional migration linked to seasonal agriculture, the sporadic nature of nitrate employment, and the development of the capital as the administrative and residential center for Chile's aristocracy. Each of these elements made the city more attractive to rural migrants, who hoped to find in the city some opportunity for economic advancement and freedom from rural peonage. Another crucial factor contributing to Santiago's urbanization was the migration of mining and landowning elites to the country's administrative and cultural center. The marked growth of the state and public administration after 1892 also attracted midlevel bureaucrats and their families to reside in the capital. The growth of these populations is evident in the construction boom of the city's wealthy neighborhoods, where city planners and architects constructed palatial homes, avenues, and parks in the garden city style of European capitals.[19] At the same time, rapid urban growth exacerbated previous forms of poverty; poor nutrition, epidemic disease (1872 and 1876), and the increasing instability of family life characterized the working-class environment of nineteenth-century Santiago.[20]

Forced out of rural areas by successive crises in agriculture and wars, women outnumbered male migrants to Santiago so that the growing "barbarous city" of the 1860s was also in large measure a city of women. As increasing numbers of unemployed *jornaleros* (day laborers) abandoned the shrinking family economies of the countryside after 1860, large numbers of women brought their families to settle in the ranchos that circled Santiago. These family units were often supported by women who mixed cottage industries, commerce, and some home

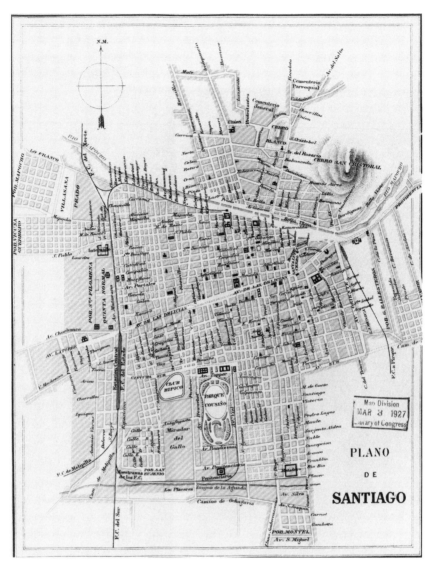

1. Map of Santiago.
Source: F. A. Fuentes L., 1897.
Courtesy of the U.S. Library of Congress,
Geography and Maps Division.

Table 1 Population of the Department of Santiago by Sex, 1895–1930

Year	Women	Men	Total	Women per 100 Men
1895	168,789	143,678	312,467	117
1907	219,270	184,505	403,775	118
1920	300,625	252,873	553,498	118
1930	447,532	392,033	839,565	114

Sources: República de Chile, Dirección General de Estadística, *Censo de la Población de Chile, 1895* (Santiago, 1895), 2: 186; *Censo 1907*, 467; *Censo 1920*, 45; *Censo 1930*, 1: 52.

manufacturing with service (laundry, cooking, cleaning) for wealthy families in the capital. The 1907 census showed that women outnumbered men in the national population by a ratio of 113 to 100; in the Department of Santiago this ratio reached the level of 118 women per 100 men (see table 1).[21] Because natural population growth did not become a factor in urban birth and death statistics until the 1920s, this ratio was largely the result of gendered patterns of rural-to-urban migration.[22] Whereas Santiago drew women from rural areas with the promise of safe, lucrative employment in well-to-do homes, male migratory destinations were more diverse and unstable. Men left rural areas largely in search of work in nitrate production, national railway construction, and the expanding port system. Compared to the seasonal and migratory nature of nineteenth-century male peonage, opportunities for female income were exclusively urban, tying women to wage work in populated areas.[23]

Once in the city, the experience of rural migrants also differed according to sex. Outside of the incipient manufacturing workforce and workshops survived the *rotos* (the "broken ones"), male migrant workers who survived by piecing together odd jobs in domestic service or commerce.[24] The distance between this marginal group and the more established lower class (*bajo pueblo*) was not great; male migrants could establish themselves in regular commerce or service work fairly easily or hope to find a better-paying job in industry at some point.[25] The women of this marginal class, however, had a harder time of it; contemporary sources lamented the eternal plight of laundresses and seamstresses who struggled with underpaid, intermittent work to support families against the rising cost of living.[26]

Most women arrived in Santiago during this period to work as domes-

2. Santiago market scene, circa 1900. *Source:* Marie Robinson Wright, *The Republic of Chile: The Growth, Resources and Industrial Conditions of a Great Nation* (Philadelphia: George Barrie and Sons, 1904), 358.

tic servants or set up their families in modest ranchos on rented unproductive lands that surrounded the southern and western periphery of the Department of Santiago. These women of nineteenth-century suburban Santiago subsisted on the animal and vegetable produce of their tiny plots as well as on income from weaving and other cottage industries. As markets for their handicrafts decreased with the establishment of clothing factories, most poor women survived by commercial and service activities (such as food production and peddling, washing, and sewing), and a relatively small number found employment in the manufacturing workshops and factories of the city. As chapter 2 shows, certain industrial tasks were reserved for the cheaper, ostensibly more nimble hands of women workers, but many women found these jobs incompatible with their domestic responsibilities. Because the labor movement and protective legislation failed to remove these limitations—or significantly improve women's wages—factory work in situ remained the purview of younger, childless women as the century wore on.

As for the manufacturing sector, Santiago's urban proletariat grew through the combination of migrant populations with the artisans and shop workers of the nineteenth-century city. Historian Luís Alberto Romero has extensively documented the existence of small industries and artisanal production in Santiago before 1850. Stimulated principally

Table 2 Number of Industrial Establishments and Workers in Santiago, 1895–1925

Year	Establishments	Workers	Workers per Establishment
1895	1,052	17,567	16.7
1905	954	16,505	17.3
1906	1,086	25,183	23.1
1910	1,172	26,046	22.2
1912	1,232	28,511	23.1
1925	1,147	34,486	30.0

Source: Adapted from DeShazo, *Urban Workers*, Table 1.6, p. 16.

by the consumption habits of the resident elite and the de facto protectionism of Chile's distance from Europe, tailoring, cobbling, beer, and carriage workshops became increasingly commonplace in nineteenth-century Santiago, employing the artisans who sustained the Sociedad de Igualdad (Society of Equality) and participated in the early expressions of worker politics in the 1850s.[27] In the last decades of the nineteenth century and the first decades of the twentieth, however, the industrial workforce underwent quantitative and qualitative shifts, with important implications for the female workforce. Although it is difficult to estimate the size of manufacturing workshops prior to the industrial census of 1909, by 1918 it was clear that "the vast majority of manufacturing workers in Chile . . . toiled not in artisan shops but in industrial establishments [of four or more workers]."[28] Small establishments continued to dominate the industrial sector numerically, but by 1918 more than 43 percent of all industrial workers in Chile were employed in factories of one hundred or more.[29] Although available statistics on the factory workforce are based on a limited sampling, they show that the average size of factories surveyed employing more than four workers grew from 17 to 30 workers between 1895 and 1925 (see table 2). The growth of factory size corresponded to the formation of large-scale monopolies; according to DeShazo, "By [1927], one or two major firms had established near or complete control in the production of cigarettes, cement, paper products, shoe-making machinery, beer, cookies, candy, glass products, refined sugar, chemicals, cloth, and matches."[30]

Both anecdotal and fragmentary statistical evidence reveal the expansion and concentration of manufacturing in the provinces of Santiago and Valparaíso, especially after 1880.[31] According to the Industrial Census, almost 80 percent of the factories in existence by 1895 were founded after 1880.[32] War demands further stimulated industrial production and investment in new machinery, most importantly in the leather, beer, and textile sectors. In Santiago, industry was concentrated in the southern and eastern sectors of the city, near railroad depots.[33] Although 41 percent of the Chilean active population was still employed in agriculture in 1895, the increasing concentration of poor and relatively unskilled workers in Santiago led to a transformation of the urban landscape.[34]

Life and Work of Santiago's Working Poor

This so-called brutish population of day laborers, artisans, domestics, and prostitutes inhabited Santiago's "other half." The rotos who made up the mushrooming population of Santiago of the late nineteenth century would become the better-known proletariat of labor histories of the twentieth. How did the men and women of these communities—in the crowded cités and conventillos (tenement houses) that still mark the urban landscape—eke out their existence in the era of "the social question"? What were their living conditions and employment opportunities? Most important, how did men and women experience these conditions in different ways?

The campaign to regulate and then eliminate the modest ranchos that surrounded Santiago began in 1857 with a municipal order authorizing elimination of the ranchos and indemnification of their owners.[35] Despite repeated attempts to implement this order (in 1857 and 1861), little urban renovation went into effect until the Vicuña Mackenna administration of the 1870s. The eruption of popular protest in response to economic crisis (1874) and the spread of epidemic disease in the late 1880s provoked elite efforts to divide the city and protect the decent people (gente decente) from the "hordes of hungry people, the new invasion of barbarians that punishes all improvident civilizations."[36] The expansion of the city into previously rural areas was aided by the creation of municipal districts, sanctioned by the 1891 Law of Autonomous Community, which allowed municipal authorities to parcel out and sell the ranchos that surrounded Santiago.[37] This campaign was rationalized in elite accounts of the unhygienic and unsightly "city of the poor" that ringed their fair capital. The newer plots were in turn purchased by middle-class employees fleeing the rising rental prices of the old city. Despite efforts to eliminate ranchos altogether, some 5,272 still surrounded Santiago by the 1895 census.[38]

Land speculation pushed urban workers toward the working-class neighborhoods at the heart of the genteel old city, located near factories and commercial centers. Once there, they had little choice but to crowd in with relatives or to rent a room in one of the numerous overpriced and overcrowded conventillos of the city center. These city slums formed the backdrop for the rising tide of misery among Santiago's poor, in which disease, overcrowding, and violence were the rule of daily life. Santiago intendant Vicuña Mackenna was horrified by living conditions in Santiago's conventillos, in part because of the generalized fear that these disease-ridden constructions would contribute to citywide epidemics (which they did): "In the conventillo the rooms are humid, dark, airless; rainwater comes in, there are holes a meter deep (as I have seen many times); they are, in a word, a certain, active and powerful cause of death."[39]

The conventillo, which quickly became the predominant form of working-class housing in the early twentieth century, was defined as a building in which individual rooms were rented out to a working-class family or group of workers. A central patio served as a common cooking and washing area for the building's residents, whose sewage washed into the street through a central, usually inadequate, open canal. Rooms with windows onto or access from the street could be 75 percent more expensive than interior apartments and often served as storefronts for selling prepared foods.[40] The slightly roomier and more expensive cités—out of reach for all but the most fortunate working-class families—represented little improvement over tenement housing. The uncleanliness of the conventillos and the misery of their inhabitants was a constant source of journalistic, literary, medical, charitable, and bureaucratic debate, and became the primary focus of many city reform arguments.

These conventillos allowed landlords to achieve maximum profit on valuable urban lands simply by subdividing apartments into smaller rooms with separate entrances, and they also confined working-class poverty to interior spaces in the city: "The conventillo was conceived of as the urban solution to the problem of the poor who had been driven from their ranchos, which at the same time preserved speculation in urban real estate."[41] Although DeShazo has argued that most conventillo owners in 1903 were simply trying to make a living from renting their single properties, Isabel Torres's study of government surveys in 1918 and 1922 reveals a clear pattern of elite slumlording.[42] In the 1918 survey by the *Revista de Habitación*, 57 out of 319 conventillos were owned by public figures (e.g., politicians and intellectuals), and approximately 40 conventillos were operated by people who owned four or more of them. By 1922, these numbers had increased to 103 conventillos owned by public figures, 61 of which belonged to "slumlords"; one owner, Luís Cornejo, controlled an impressive 20 conventillos and three others operated 8 conventillos each. According to Torres, conventillo owners included businessmen Carlos Ossandón and Alfredo Matte, politician Horacio Fabres, engineer Luis Harnecker, and historian Enrique Matte Vial. This pattern of conventillo ownership helps explain why government efforts to improve or demolish the buildings were largely ineffective. When the High Council on Housing ordered that 1,319 rooms be demolished in 1918, for example, only 23 percent of the 321 units actually destroyed belonged to public figures.[43]

Concentrated in the south and northwestern sectors of the city center, conventillos' principal characteristic was overcrowding, a problem that worsened over the first three decades of the twentieth century. The surveys conducted by the Offices of Labor and Statistics yielded a mean of 2.48 to 3.32 persons per room from 1906 to 1912,[44] and the government housing council calculated population density at 3.4 persons per room in 1916 and 3.36 in 1920.[45] The average density of the conventillos surveyed in 1925 was 56 residents, an average of 3.32 persons per room, with a maximum density of 8 people in a room.[46] These figures seem low, however, compared to numerous other accounts that decried the conditions of conventillo life. Although rooms averaged about 20 square meters in 1907, workers nonetheless crowded the tenement rooms to save on rent, which led, on occasion, to actual suffocation of residents.

Despite frequent complaints and municipal legislation to regulate living conditions, most of Santiago's workers had no choice but the urban slums for housing. The most concerted effort on the part of the state to deal with this problem was the creation in 1906 of the Higher Council on Housing (Consejo Superior de Habitaciones). This council oversaw the construction of 396 homes for workers between 1906 and 1925, but this number pales compared to the 3,246 residences built by private landlords in the same period. The council was more effective in ordering the closing and destruction of uninhabitable rooms, declaring 2,216 units inhabitable, finding 1,720 unhealthy, and ordering the demolition of 1,626.[47]

One of the principal complaints about conventillo housing was that workers paid too much for too little. In fact, working-class families selected for Labor Office studies between 1911 and 1925 reported spend-

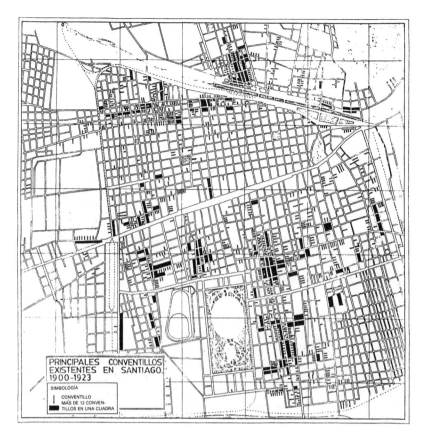

PRINCIPALES CONVENTILLOS
EXISTENTES EN SANTIAGO.
1900-1923

SIMBOLOGÍA

CONVENTILLO
MÁS DE 12 CONVEN-
TILLOS EN UNA CUADRA

3. Santiago's *conventillos,* 1900–1923. *Source:* Isabel Torres Dujisin, "Los conventillos de Santiago (1900–1930)," *Cuadernos de Historia* 6 (July 1986): 69. Courtesy of *Cuadernos de Historia,* Universidad de Chile.

ing between 7 and 16 percent of the family income on rent (see table 3). In comparison with the 60 percent of income reported spent on food, such rent expenditures would seem relatively modest. The perception, then, that conventillo rents were inordinately high was probably the result of other factors: rents in Santiago were twice those charged in other cities,[48] and working-class organizations, considering landlords usurious, joined popular efforts to regulate rental prices in 1914 and 1925.[49]

Women's economic importance to working-class family economy is widely evidenced in qualitative sources but very difficult to quantify, because Labor Office inspectors usually selected families supported by a male wage earner. Workers living alone or without families, as well as

Table 3 Average Family Expenses as Percent of Family Income, Santiago, 1911–1925

Expenses (Sample Size)	1911 (16)	1914 (20)	1921 (20)	1925 (6)
Food	59.9%	69.3%	59.3%	65.6%
Clothing	13.2	12.4	9.3	9.7
Fuel and Light	5.4	13.1	11.0	9.5
Rent	15.9	7.4	11.3	14.5
Various	7.7	6.6	13.9	7.7

Sources: BOT 12, no. 18 (1922): 97; *BOT, Anexo Estadístico* (1926).

women heads of household, were intentionally excluded from Labor Office surveys.[50] In the 1921 survey of twenty working-class families, for example, women reported their own income in only six cases, in which the male heads were bringing in less than 240 pesos per month. In those six cases, the income of the wife was roughly equal to the conventillo rent, representing anywhere from 9 to 22 percent of the total family income. Families without skilled, fully employed male workers at their head would indeed have found that conventillo rent consumed a much greater share of their income, as women and children typically earned less than half of a typical male wage.

Working women—with or without male partners—were in fact highly visible participants in conventillo sociability, because they both out-numbered men as residents and frequently conducted their work in common areas.[51] Chilean authors placed women and their precarious existence in the conventillos at the center of working-class novels about the period.[52] Although statistics that recorded the sex of residents are scarce, a 1925 survey of twenty-four conventillos in Santiago registered the presence of 375 men, 498 women, and 471 children.[53] Municipal inspectors' reports and news and literary sources, on the other hand, closely associated the conventillos with female poverty: "The problem [of the conventillos] becomes even more complicated when we consider that sizable group of people, especially the women, who live from some manual labor or run a small industry—such as the laundresses, fruit-sellers, and seamstresses—who take refuge in the conventillos because they cannot find cheaper housing anywhere else, but who are also very unfortunate in these dens."[54] In fact, the conventillo was an important site for female wage labor; laundry, commerce, prostitution, and sewing

4. Laundrywomen in a *conventillo,* circa 1900. *Source:* Augusto Orrego y Cortes, ed., *Chile: Descripción física, política, social, industrial y comercial de la República de Chile* (Santiago: Librería "C. Tornero y Cia., 1903), 93.

made working-class "homes" the very workplace of many of Santiago's women. A typical description recounted how "the women, tattered and disheveled, work and quarrel amidst a harsh uproar."[55] In a 1922 speech at a Catholic Social Week event, health inspector Aníbal Aguayo complained that rent costs forced women to work: "She spends the whole day washing to help pay for the room and has not been able to tend to herself or her little room."[56] Such descriptions of working women's plight were repeated endlessly as sympathetic observers despaired at the living conditions of the urban poor.

Problems that plagued these urban slums were predictable enough—water shortages, nonexistent or open sewers, accumulated garbage, and general filth—and were the source of constant petitions and complaints to municipal authorities, but to no avail.[57] All of these elements, combined with the overcrowding and ill health of Santiago's poor, made the conventillos ripe for disease and death, so much so that historian María Angélica Illanes has dubbed her history of this period "the history of the death of the people."[58] General mortality rates rose from 31.6 per thousand in 1886 to 37.6 in 1891, when a cholera epidemic swept the city.[59] This mortality rate alarmed the city's elites, including those who owned and rented city properties to the poor, who blamed the squalor of conventillo conditions alternately on their owners, the futility of state regulation, and the habits of the poor themselves. Surrounded by the poverty of urban workers and witness to their increasingly rebellious outbursts, Chilean elites were constantly reminded that the modernization that had brought them such wealth was threatening to destroy the working-class families who produced it.

Conclusions

This chapter has examined how changes in the national economy shaped the course of Santiago's demographic and industrial growth, emphasizing those elements that bore most directly on changing forms of working-class life and work in Santiago. Faced with fundamental shifts in the organization of the economy, working Chileans responded to the changing panorama of possibilities in gendered ways. Patterns of rural to urban migration, the organization of urban housing, and the composition of the urban workforce were shaped by men and women who faced different possibilities and obstacles for survival in the city. The accelerated migration of women to urban centers in the late nineteenth century made women's wage income even more crucial to their own and their families' survival, which in turn further modified gender relations and family strategies.

Although much of women's paid work was carried out in the home, where they washed, sewed, and cooked for their families and for income, their visibility on the streets and in conventillos of Santiago became widely acknowledged symbols for the evils of Chile's socioeconomic transformation and, most important, moral degeneracy. Largely because of the more public nature of women's urban work (and impoverishment), debates on the social question and the reforms it spawned came to be fundamentally gendered as well. Reformers also readily defined women's wage work as a key element in the larger social crisis. As these debates gained momentum during the Parliamentary Republic, the image of the working woman of Santiago as the hapless victim of "social progress" took on ever greater significance and became a central justification for efforts to produce social reform or revolution.

Before turning to a closer examination of the various initiatives designed to ameliorate the effects of women's urban wage labor, the following chapter offers a detailed examination of the subject of those reforms: the female workforce. Despite the limitations that inhere in relevant sources, it is possible to extrapolate from them a rough picture of female participation in the urban economy over this forty-year period. The resulting interpretation illuminates women's crucial contributions to the development of urban manufactures and services and provides a starting point for incorporating gender analysis into the history of the Chilean urban proletariat.

2

Women at Work in Santiago

As the contours of Santiago's population, geography, and industrial infrastructure changed at the turn of the century, the opportunities and necessity for women to work for wages in the city increased as well. In addition to their more traditional and informal activities such as domestic service, sewing, food preparation, and vending, women were recruited to staff the newly established clothing, food, leather, and textile factories of Santiago and Valparaíso after 1900. Although working-class women experienced a slight diversification of employment options in this period, as well as the commercialization of their traditional service activities, their wages and working conditions remained piteously poor, which made working women the object of constant public scrutiny under the Parliamentary Republic. Working women's presence was notable not just because there were more women working for income at the end of the century, but also because that work was more thoroughly documented and increasingly performed in public (and therefore dangerous) places. As Luís Sanz commented in "The Seamstress," a piece published in a 1906 anarchist newspaper: "The proletariat is not only made up of the mason, the blacksmith, the mechanic, the carpenter, etc., who are the only ones we acknowledge; it is necessary to speak and act on behalf of women workers—the mothers, partners, sisters and daughters of those masons, blacksmiths, mechanics and carpenters— who are forced by their *comfortable living conditions* to invade factories and workshops and to comb the streets of *our city* heading for the job registry and shop that wants to rent their labor at the price fixed by the fief. Hunger demands adaptation!"[1] Similarly, referring to the industrial statistics published in 1913, Senator Juan Enrique Concha urged his elite female audience to promote social reform because of the dangers inherent in women's manufacturing employment.[2] Across the political spectrum, from anarchist journalists to conservative senators, observers agreed that the scourge of female industrial employment offered new challenges for the whole of Chilean society. But what changing realities for working women lay beneath such dramatic critiques of the urban labor market? This chapter reconstructs the forms and levels of female workforce participation in Chile between 1895 and 1930, with particular emphasis on urban industrial employment. It then examines the concentration of female employment in several key "female" occupations and the sexual division of labor within the manufacturing sector itself to illustrate the prevailing continuities in "women's work" and the value assigned to it.

This chapter also examines the limited panorama of urban women's employment in terms of wages, hours, and working conditions, particularly in Santiago factories. Even as women provided essential labor for the expansion of industry and supplied many of the services necessary for the city's survival, they were treated as a secondary workforce, in part because of the widespread perception that women's wages only contributed to—rather than sustained—their working-class families. Despite the prevalence of employers' self-serving assumptions about the need for female wages, women's entrance into the growing urban industrial and service sectors over this period troubled the waters of the prevailing social consensus about the sexual division of labor, provoking widespread discussion on the propriety of women's work outside the home. Although most observers agreed that poor women had to work for their survival, where, how, and for how much money were issues widely disputed in public discourse.

"Mothers, Partners, Sisters, and Daughters"

Chile's census has regularly served as the starting point for the quantification of women's work in the early twentieth century. According to the first national census that differentiated occupation by sex, in 1854, almost a third of Chilean women engaged in some form of paid work, thereby constituting 38 percent of the national workforce. By 1895, although over three hundred thousand women reported an occupation, census figures showed that female participation in the workforce had shrunk to 24 percent of women and 32 percent of the total working population. Census data from subsequent years suggest the shrinking proportions of working women as a percentage of the economically active population.[3] According to the figures from the 1930 census, the percentage of the female population defined as "active" had shrunk to 13 percent, and only one out of five workers counted in the census was female. After steady increases through 1907, female employment dropped off and the female share of the total workforce declined by almost 1 percent each year.[4] The most dramatic change in female employment was recorded between the 1920 and the 1930 census: the number of women workers shrunk by 76,000 (21.7 percent), whereas male employment increased by 88,000 in the same time period (a 6.5 percent increase). By 1930, both female participation and share of active workforce had apparently sunk to levels lower than those recorded in the nineteenth century and today.[5]

Somewhat surprisingly, this interpretation of women's declining participation in the workforce at the turn of the century has gone unchallenged, as previous authors have generally not used the critical methods applied to other historical sources to assess quantitative data about female employment.[6] These positivist readings of the published census draw a misleading picture of high levels of female employment in the nineteenth century and a mysterious and sudden decline in women's work between 1920 and 1930, which was already apparent by 1907 in the industrial sector (see table 4).[7] Some women may in fact have withdrawn from the workforce during this period; others simply "disappeared" as the twentieth-century censuses became more detailed and restrictive in categorizing occupations.[8] This statistical decline in female employment, which seems to contradict a wide variety of contemporary observations about women's *increased* presence in the Chilean workforce at the turn of the century, raises important questions about how accurately the census can measure trends in female wage employment. By the late nineteenth century, census officials readily acknowledged the inadequacy of their statistical tools, even for producing a basic demographic count.[9] Although this was not the official intention, the progressive modernization of census methodology modified what kinds of women's work would actually be registered in the national census. Paradoxically, as more rigid definitions of employment and occupation were instituted, these changes actually decreased census takers' ability to account for women's work.

Historical as well as social scientific studies have repeatedly found that female activity is concentrated in precisely those areas of the economy where the labor of all workers, male and female, tends to be underrepresented in statistical surveys: informal trades, outwork, part-time or domestic labor. An accurate representation of the nature and level of women's wage work therefore requires a critical use of sources, especially those, such as the census, that have often been considered systematic and objective.[10] In the Chilean census of the nineteenth century and 1907,

Table 4 Women Active in the Chilean Workforce, 1895–1930

Year	Total workforce	% Total workforce	Women Total number	Women Number employed	Women % employed
1895	1,025,549	32	1,355,200	327,250	24
1907	1,246,716	28	1,625,058	354,851	22
1920	1,343,373	26	1,887,972	349,991	19
1930	1,355,537	20	2,164,736	273,986	13

Sources: Thelma Gálvez and Rosa Bravo, "Siete décadas de registro del trabajo femenino, 1854–1920," *Estadística y Economía* 5 (December 1992): 38–52; *Censo* 1930, vi–vii.

the simplicity of the survey conducted probably more than compensated for the exclusion of whole categories of female labor. Census takers were instructed to record the occupation of each person as he or she declared it, excluding only those who depended on others for their income or did domestic work only. Surveyors thus recorded occupations as reported, without imposing restrictions according to actual employment, number of hours, location of work, or skill level. The nineteenth-century census was also generous in its definition of occupation, because it included those who were unemployed at the time of the census and those who worked in family businesses. Those persons with more than one kind of income were instructed to declare to pollsters the trade that brought in the most money. This methodology favored the reporting of female employment whenever women were willing to declare it, regardless of where or how often they engaged in the work, which produced an occupational listing in which most women were grouped in traditional activities that involved sewing, laundry, and other services.[11]

Because many of women's wage-earning activities were in fact performed in the home or as a part-time extension of domestic tasks, their productive activity could easily be confused with women's domestic labor, depending to some degree on the surveyor's and the woman's own assessment of her contribution to the family economy. Illegal occupations such as clandestine prostitution also skewed census figures, for this activity went unrecorded or may have inflated reporting in certain occupations, such as the laundry and sewing trades.[12] In addition to such distortions, women characteristically moved freely among several employment options, making female occupational figures relatively unstable. Although the census could not measure this kind of mobility, other

PROFESIONES (Resúmen)

PROFESIONES	Número de clasificaciones	HOMBRES	MUJERES	TOTAL	Proporcion por 1,000 profesionales H.	M.	T.
Abastecedores...................................	7	2,361	205	2,566	20	4	15
Actores..	4	295	71	366	3	1.3	2
Agricultores	11	14,322	234	14,556	124	4	85
Artesanos, industriales i oficios varios...........	48	17,013	11,862	28,875	147	212	169
Artistas (Bellas artes).............................	5	220	....	220	2	....	1
Comerciantes..	7	13.122	2,128	15,250	114	38	89
Conductores de vehículos..........................	3	3,228	....	3,228	28	....	19
Diplomáticos (Ajentes consulares).................	1	10	....	10	0.1	....	0.05
Domésticos...	2	4,067	17,963	22,030	35	321	129
Eclesiásticos..	3	494	796	1,290	4	14	7.5
Empleados.......	8	11,286	1,880	13,166	98	34	77
Empresarios i contratistas.........................	4	158	....	158	2	....	0.9
Estudiantes...	1	7,214	3,963	11,177	63	71	65
Fabricantes...	3	465	24	489	4	0.5	3
Fleteros, lancheros i jornaleros....................	2	541	....	541	5	....	3
Gañanes..	1	25,171	151	25,322	218	3	148
Hoteleros i fondistas...............................	1	30	4	34	0.3	0.1	0.2
Marinos............	1	62	....	62	0.6	....	0.35
Mecánicos	6	1,377	5	1,382	12	0.1	8
Militares i policiales...............................	2	3,943	....	3,943	34	....	23
Mineros i canteros.................................	2	2,179	... .	2,179	19	....	13
Profesiones i artes liberales.......................	15	1,490	223	1,713	13	4	10
Profesores i preceptores...........................	3	368	559	927	3	10	5
Propietarios i rentistas............................	2	474	1,866	2,340	4	33	14
Sastres, modistas i zapateros......................	5.	4,904	13,549	18,453	43	242	108
Vendedores ambulantes............................	2	481	432	913	4	8	5
TOTALES......................	149	115,275	55,915	171,190	1,000	1,000	1,000

5. Census list of professions, Province of Santiago, 1885. *Source:* República de Chile, Oficina Central de Estadística, *Sesto Censo jeneral de la población de Chile levantado el 26 de noviembre de 1885* (Valparaíso: Impre. de "La Patria," 1889–1890), 188.

sources suggest the fluidity with which women moved between jobs— seamstress to prostitute, domestic servant to factory worker, laundress to sales clerk—in search of better wages.[13]

The major and, from a historian's point of view, unfortunate change in the method of 1907 census takers was the reduction in the number of categories available for classifying people's occupations. Thus the 1907 census introduced the criterion of skill as a prerequisite to having an occupation worthy of recording: "We have not classified the occupations as carefully as in the previous Census, above all those that fit under the general designation of artisans, if they do not require *a special apprenticeship.*" In 1907, census directors apparently considered a high level of differentiation unnecessary to describe the Chilean workforce and simply eliminated a wealth of occupations—such as weaver, wet nurse, embroiderer—that had enriched previous census listings.[14] One result of this change was that the figure for women employed in "various occupations" increased dramatically from about 5,000 in 1895 to approximately 45,000 in 1907. Although the 1920 census reintroduced a wider variety of occupations, this did not necessarily reinstate the simplicity of the nineteenth-century censuses that had favored the more detailed reporting of women's economic activities.[15]

In 1930, in an effort to provide a more accurate record of the population by economic activity, census takers began to distinguish between active and nonactive populations. This change reflected the new importance of defining who was a worker in official discourse and transformed the vision of the Chilean workforce. Instead of simply recording what people did when they worked, as of 1930 the census divided the population into classifications of their economic activities, which were further divided into two groups: the active population (professionals and unskilled workers) and the inactive (dependent family members, servants, and unemployed). Significantly, higher numbers of men than women appeared as "unemployed" in the 1930 count, and most "inactive" women were listed as "family members." Although this might, on the face of it, suggest that more women than men were dependents, it also suggests that women's "inactivity" was not considered "unemployment." This distinction encouraged census takers to classify women who may have worked but also reported relying on male income as "inactive," whereas before, these women would simply have reported their occupation regardless of the number of hours performed or income derived from it. Domestic servants, for example, were designated as inactive under this new rubric and listed as dependents in their employers' family groups. Given that more than one hundred thousand women were employed as domestic servants in 1930, calculations of the "active female population" that do not take that change into account have further distorted historical narratives about women's productive activities. Finally, the 1930 census also created a separate listing for "professionals." After determining that a person was actively employed, "one only noted the person as having a profession if he actually practiced it as something *really specialized"* at the moment the census was taken.[16] Although this definition of profession as a "skilled" activity introduced an additional subjective element in how work was registered in the census, it was an independent variable that did not necessarily affect census takers' calculations of the economically active population.[17]

The rise and fall of women's paid productive activities—and the potential link to perceptions of women's industrial labor—emerges even more dramatically in the census tabulations of the sectoral distribution of women workers (see table 5). Census officials in 1930 retrospectively classified the thousands of laundresses recorded in the 1920 census as part of the industrial workforce, further exaggerating women's industrial participation.[18] Further, the sharp drop in the number of economically active women between 1920 and 1930 (76,005, or over one-fifth of the female workforce) actually began much earlier in the industrial sector than in other areas. Women's participation in the industrial sector shrank to less than half of 1895 levels by 1930. Some of the 31,517 jobs lost by women in industry between 1907 and 1920 may have been absorbed in other sectors where female employment grew, such as in agriculture, commerce, and domestic service (employing 52,667 more women in 1920 than in 1907), but another 20,000 women seem to have disappeared from the census record. There is nothing in the simple comparison of census data that explains this supposed disappearance of women from the industrial workforce after 1895; in fact, census takers themselves noted in the introduction to the 1930 census that, surprisingly, the industrial workforce as a whole appeared to have shrunk between 1920 and 1930, but explained this as a result of the "perfection of mechanical techniques."[19] Although various historians have tied the decline in female employment to the impact of the world economic crisis of 1929, the fact that relatively few women were registered as "unemployed" in the 1930 census makes this explanation unlikely.[20] Rather, the slow erosion of female cottage industries, the slight masculinization of textile production, and factory owners' increasing reliance on homework may have contributed to the erosion of women's employment in the industrial sector. A more important consideration, however, is the transformation of census methodology in the early twentieth century, which contributed to the growing invisibility of women's productive activities in official records.

Despite these apparent fluctuations in female workforce participation, the census accurately records that the concentration of women

Table 5 Sectoral Distribution of Economically Active Women, 1895–1930

Sector*	1895	1907	1920	1930
Hunting, Fishing, Agriculture	19,708	22,020	48,181	25,307
Mining	9	0	449	639
Industry	156,549	135,251	103,734	70,627
Transportation	259	628	2,609	3,266
Commerce	9,951	13,176	22,651	28,183
Liberal professions	3,484	6,965	12,151	15,549
Public service	832	1,160	4,539	8,506
Armed forces	—	—	—	187
Domestic service	131,475	130,659	147,690	119,675
Various	4,983	44,992	7,987	2,047
Total	327,250	354,851	349,991	273,986

Source: Censo, 1895–1930.

* This and subsequent tables consolidate the following categories: for 1895–1920, liberal professions also include fine arts, teaching, and religion, and public service includes medicine; for 1930, transportation includes navigation, liberal professions include entertainment, and domestic service includes servitude, unclassified domestic service, and professional laundresses. In all cases, property owners and students have been excluded from the active population, and laundresses are included in domestic service, not industry.

workers in certain sectors of the economy remained fairly constant. Throughout the nineteenth and early twentieth centuries, most women who worked for wages were employed in the areas of industry, domestic service, and commerce. Not surprisingly, women predominated in trades linked to the early industrial economy in Chile, reaching a high point at over three quarters in 1907. Women's presence in industrial trades was significant: from 62.9 percent of the industrial workforce in 1895, female participation climbed to 73.8 percent in 1907, then fell to 38.2 percent in 1920 and 25.6 percent in 1930 (see tables 6 and 7). The feminization of industrial occupations peaked in 1907; at the same time, over half of the active male population was employed in agriculture through 1907, and only after 1920 did the balance for male employment shift to the industrial sector.

Although it hardly compensated for the jobs seemingly lost in industry, women's employment in other sectors seems to have grown steadily. Large numbers of women throughout the period found employment in

Table 6 Percentage of Economically Active Women Employed in Chilean Industry, Domestic Service, and Commerce, 1895–1930

Sector	1895	1907	1920	1930
Industry	47.8	38.1	29.6	25.8
Domestic service	40.2	36.8	42.2	43.7
Commerce	3.0	3.7	6.5	10.2

Source: Censo, 1895–1930.

Table 7 Feminization of Chilean Industry, Domestic Service, and Commerce, 1895–1930

Sector	1895	1907	1920	1930
Industry	62.9%	73.8%	38.2%	25.6%
Domestic service	86.7	87.3	82.8	85.2
Commerce	17.1	15.6	19.0	19.1

Source: Censo, 1895–1930.

two other growing areas of the urban economy: domestic service and commerce. More than a third of the women who were economically active consistently found work in domestic service, where they dominated the occupations of cooks, servants, and cleaners by more than 80 percent. As commercial activity grew steadily, so too did female employment in this sector, even though commerce remained highly masculinized: by 1930, almost thirty thousand women worked in commercial jobs. Although underreporting probably kept figures for female employment in domestic service and commerce low, neither sector encompassed female occupations that were redefined or reclassified as were those in industry. Domestic servants and saleswomen (whether fruit sellers or store clerks) conducted wage-earning activities that were unlikely to be confused with those of housewives at any point in the evolution of the census.

Despite its limitations, the census was also a good indicator of the diversity of female occupations, or lack of same. At the turn of the century, 73 percent of all women employed in Chile worked as laundresses, seamstresses, or domestic servants; in fact, many of those laundresses and seamstresses were working in the service of private employers and should, by modern standards, have been classified as domestic servants. Census surveyors, who often made their own calculations about an individual's occupation based on the amount and location of work, still may have provided the decisive opinion about how such work would be classified. Although significant numbers of women were employed as artisans (24,953), sellers (12,351), shoe workers (3,385) and day workers (11,748), the range of female occupations was considerably narrower than that which described male occupations. Women were classified in the 1907 census in 35 of the 48 available occupations, whereas all but one occupation (that of midwife) registered male participation (see table 8). However, female occupations did diversify slightly over the period, as women were registered in previously all-male trades such as tanning, tinsmithing, and bookbinding. Census takers commented on this "strange data," but asserted that they were probably the result of recording errors.[21]

Over the entire period, the most striking and dubious occupational change reflected in census figures was that of the seamstress. The sharp decline in women reporting to work as seamstresses after 1907 appears all the more dramatic because, according to the census, their numbers had been legion. There are several possible explanations for the 63,000 to 130,000 seamstresses registered in the nineteenth-century census. Salazar has argued that the importation of home sewing machines in the late nineteenth century provided the new urban migrants with an additional, independent source of income as they met urban elite women's demand for French-style fashions.[22] In addition to the prostitutes who might have said they were seamstresses (or actually plied both trades), early census figures probably included a generous count of housewives and daughters who took in some sewing work to contribute to the family economy. Factory homework, as well as cultural shifts that stressed working-class women's domestic responsibilities, all contributed to the underreporting of women's sewing work. As the Chilean census became more "modern" in the first decades of the twentieth century, official statistics transformed the nineteenth-century seamstress into an inactive dependent, dedicated to "homemaking" (*quehaceres de la casa*).

Although the critical examination of census methods and categories itself casts significant doubt on any positivist reading of female employment in Chile, other sources also substantiate the hypothesis that, if women in general were less likely to report part-time sewing, female participation in the manufacturing workforce remained constant in the early twentieth century. The following section explores the composition of the Santiago factory workforce in more detail to show how,

Table 8 Men and Women in Selected Occupations in Chile, 1907

Occupation	Women	Men	Total	% Female
Actor	75	228	303	24.8
Artisan	24,953	102,321	127,284	19.6
Artist	231	1,282	1,513	15.3
Baker	1,520	6,641	8,161	18.6
Businessperson	6	1,059	1,065	0.6
Civil servant	54	6,138	6,192	0.9
Dentist	10	453	463	2.2
Doctor	7	994	1,001	0.7
Domestic servant	67,682	18,910	86,592	78.2
Fisher	143	3,692	3,835	3.7
Hatter	505	634	1,139	44.3
Innkeeper	795	1,033	1,828	43.5
Laundry worker	62,977	108	63,085	99.8
Lawyer	3	1,944	1,947	0.2
Midwife	1,079	0	1,079	100.0
Musician	12	924	936	1.3
Peasant	5,849	62,930	68,779	8.5
Pharmacist	10	845	855	1.2
Printer	25	2,204	2,229	1.1
Religious	2,653	1,652	4,305	61.6
Salesperson	18,844	72,914	91,758	20.5
Scientist	11	671	682	1.6
Seller	12,351	66,139	78,490	15.7
Shoemaker	3,385	20,624	24,009	14.1
Tailor	88	4,921	5,009	1.8
Teacher	3,980	2,967	6,947	57.3
Telegraphist	609	1,537	2,146	28.4
Tram driver	19	17,439	17,458	0.1
Watchmaker	62	1,137	1,199	5.2
Other	946	1,305	2,251	42.0
Day worker	11,748	150,665	162,413	7.2
Unskilled worker	4,280	234,951	239,231	1.8

Source: Censo 1907, 1299–1300.

6. Seamstresses selling shirts, Santiago, circa 1910. *Source:*
Reginald Lloyd, ed., *Twentieth-Century Impressions of
Chile* (London, 1915), 113.

despite the reported decline in female industrial employment, women
continued to make up a significant portion of the factory workforce
throughout the period.

"To Invade Factories and Workshops"

It is no accident that sources other than the census that recorded wom-
en's work in this period measured precisely that of the woman whose
participation was most easily identified as work: the woman factory
worker. The women who received a factory wage—whether a piece rate
or a daily salary, work in the factory or outwork performed at home—
embodied the promise and the perils of Chilean industrial progress.
Industrial statistics show that, whereas female employment in what the
census defined as "industrial" occupations declined, the numbers of
women employed by Santiago factories increased by several thousand
between 1910 and 1925.[23] Even if, as many sources suggest, many of these
women performed their factory piecework at home, by 1910 women
employed by factories and workshops accounted for approximately one
tenth of the wage-earning women and almost one third of the manufacturing workforce of Santiago.

Table 9 Women Workers Employed by Santiago Factories, 1910–1925

Year	Number of factories surveyed	Number of women employed in factories*	Women as % of total factory workers
1910	1,066	7,738	31.5
1912	1,232	10,582	35.0
1917	814	8,509	35.0
1918	845	9,866	34.4
1920	900	8,756	33.5
1921	942	9,134	33.8
1923	1,064	10,720	33.5
1925	1,147	10,769	31.5

Sources: BSOFOFA 28, no. 11 (1 November 1911): 986; *AE* (Santiago: Sociedad Imprenta y Litografía Universo, 1912–1925).

* Tables 9–11 do not include male and female empleadas.

The proportion of women to men in the manufacturing workforce was consistently higher in Santiago than it was throughout Chile. According to industrial data from 1912 to 1925, between 20 and 29 percent of factory workers in Chile were women. In Santiago, where most manufacturing activity was concentrated, female participation in industry was consistently higher, ranging from 32 to 35 percent (see table 9). Census averages for women's industrial work were somewhat lower, but in 1930 the contrast between Santiago (29 percent) and the whole country (25 percent) was still evident.[24]

In the factories surveyed by the industrial census, women's manufacturing employment was concentrated in the food and clothing industries, where their activities ranged from small-scale baking and tailoring to factory-based work in the manufacture of shoes, crackers, cardboard, and paper. Women were numerically fewer than men or children in many of these factories, but they predominated in the areas of making dresses, corsets, shirts, sandals, wicker furniture, cardboard boxes, and wool clothing. Women also made up a significant number of workers in bakeries, and in cracker, sweet, soda water, shoe, pasta, empanada, and glass factories.[25] Clothing manufacture and repair consistently employed between one third and one half of female factory workers, and leather, textile, and food factories also employed significant numbers of women. About half as many women worked in textile manufacturing,

7. Women at looms, Gratry Textile Factory, Viña del Mar. *Source: Boletín de la Sociedad de Fomento Fabril* 25, no. 1 (1 January 1908): 394. Courtesy of the Chilean National Library, Serials Division.

most of them occupied in weaving wool and cotton, but they also dominated silk and sock-weaving production (see table 10).

The industrial survey data confirm the conclusions based on the national census with regard to feminization of certain occupations. Here the data are more meaningful, for they reflect the proportion of women working in manufacturing on a factory-by-factory basis. As table 11 demonstrates, women represented a majority of workers employed in clothing, textile, and tobacco factories between 1912 and 1925. About a third of the workers in chemical production and a fifth of those working in leather factories were women. Even in factories where women workers predominated, however, these workers were likely to have been supervised by men. Women managers were most likely to be found in textile (9 percent), tobacco (16 percent), and clothing (19 percent) factories, but they held only 7 percent of factory management positions overall in 1914.[26] The consistent levels of feminization in certain kinds of factories show that the decline in female industrial employment recorded by the census was not caused, at least in this period, by men replacing women in factory jobs. As other sources suggest, factory work remained an attractive employment option for thousands of Santiago's working

Table 10 Distribution of Women Workers in Chilean Manufacturing by Type of Factory, 1912–1925

Year	Rank			Total women
	1	2	3	
1912	Clothing	Leather	Food	
	10,968	2,141	1,932	20,409
1914	Clothing	Textiles	Leather	
	2,214	1,024	972	6,919
1917	Clothing	Food	Textiles	
	6,620	1,723	1,596	15,232
1918	Clothing	Food	Leather	
	7,704	1,723	1,690	16,787
1920	Clothing	Food	Leather	
	5,788	2,181	1,737	16,069
1921	Clothing	Food	Textiles	
	6,162	2,204	1,757	17,371
1923	Clothing	Textiles	Food	
	7,041	2,400	2,255	18,891
1925	Clothing	Textiles	Food	
	7,201	2,815	2,604	17,714

Source: AE, 1912–1925.

Table 11 Sectoral Feminization of the Chilean Factory Workforce, 1912–1925

Year	Clothing	Textiles	Tobacco	Chemical	Leather
1912	78%	67%	56%	28%	17%
1914	72	67	62	26	19
1917	79	63	66	33	20
1918	79	61	69	35	22
1920	80	59	71	33	20
1921	73	61	69	35	21
1923	79	67	74	34	13
1925	81	67	62	37	15

Source: AE, 1912–1925.

8. Packing department, Chilean Tobacco Company, Santiago, circa 1910.
Source: Reginald Lloyd, ed., *Twentieth-Century Impressions of Chile*
(London, 1915), 345.

women, despite the menial wages, long hours, and double workday that
it implied.

There is one more aspect of the female manufacturing workforce that
by all accounts was quantitatively important, but that contemporary
sources—especially quantitative—failed to disaggregate clearly. Homework (*trabajo a domicilio*), the Chilean equivalent of the English or
American "sweating system," was an important source of labor for factory production.[27] Though some accounts mentioned male homework,
sewing or shoemaking piecework was almost always a female activity. In
one Valparaíso clothing factory, for example, 26 male employees prepared the materials and packaged the final product, and 250 women
sewed the clothing in their homes.[28] This arrangement reduced employers' costs—because workplace, transportation, tools, and materials
were paid by homeworkers—and made it easier for employers to under-
pay workers or apply fines for lateness and poor work. After the passage
of a day care law in 1917, factory owners were accused of shifting women
to homework tasks to reduce the number of women on site and thus
escape the twenty-women minimum for applying the law. Homeworkers would therefore have continued to appear in factory-based industrial

statistics but might have "disappeared" in the changing categories of the census count, particularly because their employment was seasonal.

When homework was mentioned in newspapers or congressional debates, it was often proposed as a solution to the unwelcome presence of women in factories: by removing women from the morally and physically threatening factory environment and providing them with paid work at home, it was argued, women could maintain the home, contribute to the family income, and preserve their dignity as virtuous wives and mothers of working-class families. Evidently, the location of homework in the domestic sphere not only made it an ideal solution for those who objected to women's wage work outside the home, but it also masked women's productive activities by mixing these with the part-time (or overtime) activities they engaged in at home.

As proposals for a labor code, including provisions for women workers, began to develop in the 1920s, however, factory outwork came under increasingly critical scrutiny, revealing some of the contours of this crucial sector of female employment. In her 1924 law thesis, later labor inspector and feminist Elena Caffarena provided one of the first systematic, critical studies of homework in Chile.[29] In her work, Caffarena explicitly countered popular perceptions of homework as liberating for women and healthier for their children: "Unfortunately, this is not true. One only has to look through the window of a woman worker's home to find misery: women worn out by long work hours and at other times [you can see] children who are abandoned when they most need their mothers' care. This makes one think that homework, like Janus, has two faces and two names: one suggests pretty images; the other is summed up in the English term 'sweating system' or exploitation by sweating."[30] Caffarena based her study on interviews with homeworkers in their conventillos, and collected valuable data on homeworkers' wages and working conditions (see table 12). On the basis of her visits, Caffarena concluded that, in addition to the insufficient wages that characterized all female occupations, these women tended to work extremely long hours and under unhealthy conditions. Caught among domestic responsibilities, hunger salaries reduced even further by the costs of transportation and materials, and the instability of their employment, homeworkers were in fact worse off than their fellow factory workers, she argued. Another prejudice that Caffarena sought to undermine was the assumption that homework was essentially additional income for families supported by a male wage. She noted that, in her sample, "half of the women turned out to be the only ones supporting the family

Table 12 Women Homeworkers Interviewed by Elena Caffarena, 1924

Name	Work	Daily Hours	Monthly Wage
Sarela Leiva	sews shoe uppers	14	74
Lucinda Gamboa	sews shoe uppers	16	74
Olimpia Cruzat	makes vests	—	73
Laura Gutiérrez C.	cuts shoe soles	10	88
Ester Torres	makes pants	12	64
Carmela Soto	sews jackets	12	72
Eduvijes Espinoza	sews shoe uppers	14	84
Ana G. de Carrillo	sews pants	16	120
Trinidad Contreras	sews jackets	14	104
Ester S. de González	sews pants	—	104
María de Camoussent	sews pants	10	84+
Filomena C. De Gutiérrez	sews pants	—	up to 200*
Rosa Casanueva	sews shoe uppers	16	56
Guniercinda Guinea	sews mattresses	12	100
Adelina Casanova	sews shoe uppers	8	45
Basaura Salinas	sews jackets	—	68
Felicidad Anje	sews jackets	12	68
Aída Silva	sewing	—	68
Average hours and wages		12.8	79

Source: Elena Caffarena M., "El trabajo a domicilio," *BOT* 22 (1924): 104–7.
* With respect to Gutiérrez, Caffarena comments, "Here we see the other side of the coin: Filomena Gutiérrez is not exploited; rather she is the exploiter. All of the real work is done by two fifteen-year-old girls, whom she pays ten pesos a week!" (Caffarena, "El trabajo a domicilio," 106.) For the same reason, Gutiérrez's income is here excluded from the average calculation.

(consisting of four to six people, in most cases)."[31] Those homeworkers who could count on a man's wage tended to work fewer hours (e.g., ten hours daily).

Another characteristic of homework that troubled Caffarena was the seasonal nature of employment; the so-called dead period of the summer months reportedly meant that a "great number of women workers turn to prostitution." Caffarena attributed this tendency to the workers' inability to save their meager wages—in part a "racial defect"—but judged their fall to be economically necessary. Caffarena reported one woman's explanation that "the work is not steady; it falls off when summer begins and stops completely in April and May. In this period, she has to work as a prostitute to avoid starvation."[32] As in the case of the better-known factory workers, the problem of women's industrial homework linked concerns about female employment in these denigrating occupations with debates on urbanization, industrialization, and worker protection. Female participation in factory-based manufactures in particular—evident to the astute observer and substantiated by state and private statistics—ignited larger concerns about female morality and working-class family organization.

"To Rent Their Labor at the Price Fixed by the Fief"

The concentration of women workers in a limited number of highly feminized occupations—and in certain tasks within the factory workforce—corresponded to the poor wages women generally received for their work.[33] Even as the incipient labor movement began to mobilize around and achieve some advances on workplace issues, such as the length of the working day, accident protection, union recognition, and higher wages, the divide between male and female wages remained large. Employers succeeded in treating women as a secondary labor force, relegating them to the ranks of "unskilled" workers in most manufacturing activities. Both in and outside of the factory, women were concentrated in the lowest-paying service and commercial activities.

After 1906, the Labor Office diligently collected wage statistics, the most reliable of which were recorded in the area of factory manufacturing. These records show that not only were many Chilean factories highly segregated by sex, but also that this had predictable results for the wages awarded for the gender-linked tasks. Women usually held those factory jobs that were related to sewing, ironing, washing, and packaging the products, all of which paid considerably less than more "skilled" factory work. As was also typical of early industrialization elsewhere in Latin America, women's wages were considerably lower than those of men who worked in the same industries because women (and often children as well) were usually employed in what were considered low-skilled jobs that drew on a sizable labor pool.[34] Women not only performed, on average, lower-paying jobs, but were paid less in cases where their jobs were the same as those of male workers. Women working as fashion seamstresses or shoe factory workers might have made a modest wage of 5 to 9 pesos per day, but almost all of the lowest-paid jobs were held by women and by children under sixteen: ironers, laundresses, domestic servants, packagers, textile and other factory workers, cooks and confectioners, and so on.[35] On average, wages paid to women for manufacturing work were roughly half of those paid to men, both in Santiago and elsewhere in Chile.[36] This gendered occupational structure, so typical of early industrializing societies, would have important implications for the nature of female participation in the labor movement, and in turn on the kinds of demands that movement generated with regard to women's paid work. Contemporary observers, both working-class and elite, agreed that women were paid less *because* they were female. Manufacturers in textiles, clothing, and food industries took advantage of the sizable pool of nonunionized female labor to pay women considerably less than what they paid men, even if they performed the same tasks. Furthermore, whereas by the 1920s most male urban workers had secured daily wages, many female manufacturing tasks continued to be governed by piece rates or conducted at home, where labor inspectors rarely trod. A 1928 report by a Labor Office inspector, lamenting the illusory nature of the 1924 Labor Code's equal pay for equal work stipulation, showed that daily wages in a jam factory remained unequal: 6–8 pesos for men and 4–5 pesos for women.[37]

Although wage differentials persisted, factory work seems in fact to have offered women the most attractive income. On the one hand, women's work in any venue might be poorly paid; a 1906 Labor Office survey showed uniformly low wages among the women surveyed, and everyone from laundresses and seamstresses to textile workers reported earning between 1 and 2 pesos daily.[38] On the other hand, factory wages were higher than those found elsewhere: in 1918, a domestic servant typically earned 50 pesos a month (roughly the equivalent of a rural wage, the source notes), whereas 1919 wages for women factory workers were 60–80 pesos per month.[39] Numerous editorials in urban newspapers confirm that domestic service employers perceived factory jobs as the more attractive option for working-class women, provoking a hue and cry over the "servant crisis" in 1913. When more desirable manufacturing jobs were not available, a 1926 study indicated why women might turn to prostitution; although some prostitutes earned as little as 4 pesos a month, others reported earning as much as 60 pesos monthly for their work.[40]

Given the reformist spirit that pervaded public discourse in the "age of the social question," it is not surprising that a variety of observers denounced women's low wages throughout the press, from the conservative daily *El Mercurio* to newspapers designed for popular entertainment. In a manner consistent with Bravo Cisternas's editorials on Laura, the "Virgin of the Forest," *El Mercurio* columns regularly suggested that its elite female readers should avoid buying goods made with cheap female labor in order to end women's "hunger work and ridiculous salary."[41] *El Mercurio* editorials complained loudly and often about the misfortune of women's wages, attributing this injustice to social prejudices: "For now, we will just attest that the Chilean women workers' conditions are worse than that of her working companions, either because of their greater ignorance about life, for which they have not been prepared, or for the lack of respect with which their work is viewed, which makes it extremely unproductive work."[42] The fact that women were underpaid because they were women, whatever their trade, was here not exactly a denunciation of gender inequality, but rather an observation about the injustice of nature itself, which had left women so ill-equipped for economic survival. By 1918, perhaps inspired by debates on protective legislation, *El Mercurio* was sounding a more revindicative chord, explaining how low female wage levels had become the fundamental obstacle to women's—and the nation's—advance: "We have before us a reform that should raise the moral and physical level of the entire country. And this reform has to succeed here, as it has already succeeded in all of the more advanced countries."[43] As subsequent chapters show, women's wage work—and debates over whether to protect, promote, or discourage it—were central to reforms aimed at national economic progress at the turn of the century.

Journalists writing for other daily papers also penned a variety of sympathetic portrayals of women limited by social prejudice, including denunciations of lower pay for the same work. *La Opinión* reported on Lorenza Ampuero, who took over her husband's car repair shop after he died but was driven into poverty "either because [the public] mistrusted the repairs handled by a woman or because of the belief that women should be paid less than men, even if the work is the same."[44] When these prejudices were shared by employers (rather than clients), the effects were seen as more destructive: "One has to admit frankly that the main cause of the devaluation of women's work is the idea about women's capacity for work that is common among employers; it is believed that the woman cannot produce as much as the man, but in practice, this belief is false."[45] This editorial ended by advocating higher wages for women so that women could experience work as a source of pride and survival rather than as a burden. But this solution had its opponents, because presumably women were hired precisely because they could be paid lower wages. A 1920 editorial in *La Opinión* made this position very clear: "She has the advantage over her male antagonist that she demands less . . . in this sense, women's participation is one of the factors at the moment that tends to lower wages. . . . The day is thus not distant in which the woman who is content with less manages to expel many individuals of the opposite sex from the factory and the office; or, failing that, makes the cost of labor fall to the limit set by her scarce needs." Obtaining higher salaries for women is no solution, the author argued, because "if they try to demand as much as their male competitors, they could be excluded from their current activities because they would lose their only advantage, which is the low cost of their labor. Equal pay for both sexes would only prejudice the weaker sex."[46]

Although the majority of editorials and news stories on women workers criticized the inadequacy and injustice of female wages, a minority argued for the exclusion of women from wage employment on the basis of presumed male superiority. Provoked by a French pamphlet protesting unequal wages, "O. E." argued that women did not deserve pay equal to men's because they needed more physical rest and because women should not be permitted to take jobs away from men who worked hard and well for their employers. Even worse, the editorial argued, female employment, like the vote, could turn the domestic sphere into an arena for bickering between the sexes, converting women at the same time into "*viragos* who have given up [their role] not only as mothers, but also as women."[47] Although Chilean observers rarely addressed the issue in such a pointed fashion, the growth of female factory employment and the unchanging reality of their poor wages contributed to the rising public debate on what constituted appropriate work for women.

Conclusions

Urbanization in late-nineteenth-century Chile coincided with patterns of early industrial growth that relied heavily on female labor, requiring women to enter workplaces and relationships that disrupted popular norms about their domestic responsibilities. Although for a variety of reasons the census could not record accurately the real nature of this shift, it does reflect how women remained at the margins of what was regarded as productive activity, even as women came to play an important role in the manufacturing process. Factory employers' records, on the other hand, confirm the widespread perception of growing female employment in factory production, particularly in those areas or tasks where their "unskilled" labor could be bought cheaper than that of their male counterparts. Regardless of where their work was performed and whether it was acknowledged in statistical sources, women's employment options remained limited in the highly segregated urban workforce, further reinforcing industrialists' rationale for low female wages.

The apparent decline of female employment in the industrial sector cannot be explained simply through economic crisis or their replacement by male workers, for the proportions of women to men employed in factories remained almost the same over the period. In addition to the changing methodology of the census that first over- then undercounted female wage labor, the loss of female productivity in industrial occupations may have been the result of the growth of factory production of consumer durable goods for the domestic market. As textile, clothing, and food factories grew, they offered competition to female cottage industries such as weaving, food preparation, and needlework. The census's measure of female economic activity thus recorded the shift from small- to larger-scale production that, though providing some women with factory jobs, marginalized independent female wage activity in the home.

Although the gaze of statisticians, bureaucrats, and politicians involved in debates on women's work may have been sympathetic, even the most progressive agenda for labor reform relied on a fundamentally domestic construction of women's role in society, which increasingly identified men with paid work and support of the family. Thus, it was women's continuing presence in Santiago factories—and its relationship to the female life cycle and other employment options—that inspired the most controversy. Women factory workers are significant not only in numerical terms, but also because of the social and ideological changes that accompanied the growth of Chilean industry. Conflicts over the nature of industrial work—and women's capacity or suitability for it—show how these debates were fundamentally gendered. The chapters that follow explore how gender norms came to be contested and modified by a variety of social actors, all of whom claimed to act in the interests of working women, their class, and the nation as they struggled to stem the tide of social crisis.

3

"To Work Like Men and Not Cry Like Women"

The Problem of Women in Male Workers' Politics

As the public controversy over Laura, the "Virgin of the Forest," illustrates, the precarious position of women in the urban workforce raised troubling questions about the sexual division of labor, male control over female family members, and gender relations in the workplace. As diverse organizations for male workers took shape in the late nineteenth century, the problems related to women's paid work emerged as an important theme in working-class political circles. In addition to repeated calls for working-class women to rally in support of their male relatives, labor leaders used images of women at work to invoke the male prerogative to protect and provide for female family members. Particularly as women's presence in the factory workforce became a fact of life, however, workers' organizations also encouraged women themselves to organize and press for higher wages to attenuate the downward pressure on male industrial wages caused by the availability of a large pool of cheap female labor. With the important exception of the socialist feminists examined at length in chapter 4, workers' organizations perpetuated stereotypes about women workers as conservative and sexually vulnerable, bolstering the links between class identity and the attributes of working-class masculinity.[1] The admonition to male workers "to work like men and not cry like women" is just one example of how Chilean labor organizers relied on a language of sexual difference to diagnose and answer the obstacles to working-class mobilization. This discourse relied as thoroughly on the juxtaposition of male and female as on ideas about proper behavior for either sex.

Ironically, while many working-class leaders were busily sounding the alarm about women's "natural" passivity—as workers and potential militants—many women workers became active participants in the rank-and-file mobilization of industrial workers, where they joined mixed-sex trade unions, autonomous women's associations, political federations, and local strikes. Women also represented their organizations at workers' congresses and came to hold positions in national labor federations by the 1920s. This chapter, accepting for the moment the cultural construction of the "woman worker" as a woman engaged in some form of industrial labor, reconstructs this narrative of female participation in urban labor politics and organization. It then examines the gendered discourse of organized labor, arguing that many expressions of working-class identity and consciousness, and particularly working-class masculinity, were constructed on common assumptions about women's relationship to work, both paid and domestic. While the labor press repeatedly denounced the very real sexual harassment, poor working conditions, and low pay that women faced in the factory workforce, these representations of female vulnerability were also useful in the appeals that organizers made on behalf of male workers because they concerned the demands that male workers—with jobs to keep and families to feed—made as men. This chapter examines how many of the male voices heard in workers' associations and newspapers of the early twentieth century addressed the problems associated with women's work—from women's sexual vulnerability to their potential militancy—and how these positions reflected activists' larger concerns about working-class masculinity and the family of labor as a whole.

Women in Chilean Workers' Movements

From about 1850 through 1880, the most common form of worker organization in Chile was the society for mutual aid, which enjoyed legal status, advocated gradual reform of working conditions, and pooled worker resources for illness, death, education, and other immediate material needs of its membership.[2] Following the emergence of the first mutual aid society among artisans and unskilled print workers in Santiago in 1853, members of other crafts such as railway workers, tailors, and carpenters also formed stable mutual aid societies in the 1870s. DeShazo notes the diversity of forms evident in Chilean mutualism: "Many [mutual aid societies] were established along purely craft lines, other *socorros mutuos* admitted workers of several industries, served all the employees of a single establishment, or included only female or Catholic workers."[3] As industrial occupations became subdivided and increasingly deskilled after the 1880s, mutualist societies tended to reflect subdivisions within trades, prefiguring the union organizations of the early twentieth century.[4] Although mutual aid societies were in pur-

Table 13 Workers' Societies and Membership in Chile, 1870–1923

Year	Number of Societies	Membership
1870	13	—
1880	39	—
1890	75	—
1900	240	—
1910	433	65,136
1922	735	135,000
1923	1,114	177,711

Sources: Oscar Parrao, "La mutualidad en Chile," *BOT* 21 (1923): 13–25; Oficina del Trabajo, *Estadística de la Asociación Obrera* (Santiago: Imprenta i Litografía Santiago, 1910), 27–57; "Asociaciones Obreras en 1923," *BOT* 14, no. 22 (1924): 214–21.

pose and activity officially apolitical, the societies served as conduits for the dissemination of more radical labor ideology, which reached Chile primarily through European texts translated and published in Argentina.[5]

Mutualism expanded rapidly in Chile after 1883, increasing from 75 legally registered societies in 1890 to 735 in 1922 (see table 13).[6] As the functions of these societies expanded and other kinds of workers' organizations were also formed at the turn of the century, it becomes difficult to isolate the trajectory of mutualism. Data collected by the Labor Office in 1910, for example, included groups whose stated goals ranged from worker education, savings plans, and mortuary funds to political resistance. Statistical figures for mutualism, like those of other workers' organizations of the period, are shaky at best, as they reflect only those groups that had managed to obtain legal title.[7] On the other hand, labor associations frequently inflated their reported membership tallies, and Labor Office reports included members of unregistered societies in their estimates. Over time, mutual aid societies tended to get more involved in political activities, carrying to employers workers' petitions for wage increases, improved working conditions, and changes in management. Mutualism proved to be a particularly enduring form of organization, in part because the structure lent itself well to the spontaneous, local mobilization of workers that characterized the period. Mutual aid societies also collaborated with other unions through the Congreso Social Obrero (founded in 1903), La Gran Federación Obrera de Chile (founded in 1909), and the Congreso de Alimentación (1918). Mutualism provided

"To Work Like Men and Not Cry Like Women" 61

the organic underpinnings for more radical labor organizations after 1900 and remained a refuge thereafter whenever employer or state repression made anticapitalist mobilization impracticable.

At first, mutual aid societies were formed exclusively among male workers who shared a craft or a workplace. Historian Sergio Grez comments that women's exclusion from such organizations "did not happen because of explicit discrimination, but rather from a kind of unwritten, implicit convention, which led to a de facto segregation of [male and female] workers."[8] Mutualist forms of organization then spread to women, starting with the Sociedad de Obreras No. 1, founded in Valparaíso in 1887. In contrast to male mutualists, this and subsequent women's mutual aid societies organized working women of diverse salaried trades as well as women "without profession" in a single organization. Female mutualism was not centered around women's occupational identity or actual employment, but on their common identity as respectable, working-class women, hence the explicit prohibition of laundresses and domestic servants from their midst. Although male mutualists, in like fashion, excluded unskilled peons from their associations, women's mutual aid societies came to include domestic servants after a few years.[9]

One of Chile's earliest and most prominent women's mutualist societies was the Sociedad Protección de la Mujer, founded in Santiago in 1888 as La Emancipación de la Mujer. By 1910, the Sociedad Protección de la Mujer had become one of the largest working women's associations in Santiago, with five hundred "daughters of labor" (*hijas del trabajo*) registered as members.[10] Significantly, these early women's mutual aid societies enjoyed the support of the state, labor and daily news journalists, and movement biographers, who labeled all such women's organizations "feminist."[11] One workers' paper celebrated the founding of a mutual aid society for women shoe-stitchers, observing that "they must decide how legitimate the goals of feminism are, as well as specify the great program by which they will help men in the social renewal to which the most noble energies are today directed."[12] Like other mutual aid societies, most of the actions of the Sociedad Protección de la Mujer consisted of organizing mutual support among its members—such as night school, health and mortuary funds, savings programs, and occupational training—without directly challenging employers' prerogative to determine women workers' wages, benefits, and conditions. According to a 1910 Labor Office study, female mutualism grew to include twelve of sixty-six workers' societies in Santiago, representing approximately two thousand women members out of an estimated twelve thousand associates.[13] Although it becomes more difficult to ascertain the numbers of female workers' associations in Santiago after 1912, figures for other major cities indicate that women's associations represented 10 to 20 percent of workers' organizations: in 1917 there were 8 female worker associations in Iquique out of a total of 47 groups (1,001 women); in Valparaíso, 7 out of 89 (1,052 women); in Concepción, 4 out of 27 (480 women).[14] By 1922, women made up 80 of the total 735 mutual aid societies throughout Chile (18,000 women), and 47 out of 359 mutual aid societies were female in 1926.[15]

The nonconfrontational character of female mutualism changed after the turn of the century as women's associations, like male workers' societies, began to show the influence of anarchist rhetoric and tactics, increasingly turning to strikes and street protests to promote their demands. Women's mutualism also served as a training ground for women workers in union politics and fostered close ties with emerging resistance societies and the labor press. Even though political debates per se were not central to the functioning of mutual aid societies, women political activists (particularly of the Democratic Party) often began their political careers there and maintained their ties to mutual aid societies as their political involvement increased. Significantly, the founder and president of the Sociedad Protección de la Mujer, Juana Roldán de Alarcón, was the wife of Democratic Party founder Lindorfo Alarcón and a recognized activist in her own right.[16] Women labor leaders such as Roldán de Alarcón were often family members of prominent male activists, a fact that both secured male leaders' support and confirmed prevailing stereotypes of women's role as "helpmate" to the labor movement. The partisan activism of Roldán de Alarcón and the attention paid the society in the Democratic Party press shows that, even before women's resistance societies were founded, the Sociedad Protección de la Mujer represented one of the first attempts to organize Santiago working women for partisan and syndicalist objectives.

Developments in female mutualism corresponded closely to changes in workers' associations more generally around the turn of the century. Although male workers and their societies had participated in sporadic protests against protectionist measures and inflationary prices in the nineteenth century, movements based on workers' labor demands accelerated significantly only in the late 1880s. These were crucial years in terms of workers' political organization and representation, which culminated in two key events: the founding of the Democratic Party in

R

JUANA ROLDÁN DE ALARCÓN

«Pocos serán los que ignoraran los trabajos de la señora Juana Roldán de Alarcón, ella es quizás la única que en esta capital se ha conquistado el glorioso lugar que le corresponde, pues es una de las primeras mujeres que siempre se ha distinguido con orgullo, en todos los movimientos sociales. Siempre se le ha visto luchar por la emancipación del sexo al cual pertenece, cosechando de todos, los aplausos que merece».
(De *El Luchador.* —N.° 50. — Octubre 18 de 1908).

ROLDÁN DE ALARCÓN JUANA. — Nació en Santiago en 1851. Fueron sus padres Don José Dolores Roldán y Doña Dominga Escobar.

La obra de regeneración social y de la Educación de la mujer le debe a la Señora Roldán su iniciación y su progreso, habiendo principiado sus trabajos sociales en la Filarmónica «José Miguel Infante», se incorporó el 23 de Septiembre de 1883 juntamente con su esposo Don Jenaro Alarcón Pardo (véase Letra A, pág. 30).

La Comisión especial de Señoras, conociéndole su entusiasmo y su empeño por trabajar en bien de la institución, la nombró Presidenta, desempeñando siempre numerosas comisiones que le dieron mérito y renombre, y entre otras las «Conferencias sobre la instrucción de la Mujer».

La «Miguel Infante», reconocida a sus servicios, le dedicó el 31 de Agosto de 1885 un artístico diploma.

En la Sociedad «Filarmónica de Obreros», según el periódico *El Eco Filarmónico*, donde se publicó la primera Memoria— se fundó el 4 de Marzo de 1888 la primera sociedad femenina en Santiago, con el nombre de «La Emancipación de la Mujer». La Señora Roldán fué su iniciadora, la primera Vice-Presidenta, la que redactó los estatutos, la comisionada para el estandarte, mausoleo, etc.; puede decirse la que lo hizo todo hasta dejarla debidamente constituída. Actuó como Presidenta durante tres años, después cinco, como Vice; y luego otros seis años como Directora, no dejando de

9. Juana Roldán de Alarcón of Santiago's Sociedad Protección de la Mujer. *Source:* Osvaldo López, *Diccionario Biográfico Obrero* (Santiago: Bellavista, 1912). Courtesy of the Chilean National Library, General Collection.

1887 and the general strike of 1890.[17] These two episodes demonstrated the potential of worker mobilization and announced the arrival of a new, albeit still weak, political actor with which the Parliamentary Republic would have to contend.[18]

The growth of worker mobilization at the turn of the century was also significant—and thoroughly alarming to elites—because it showed that the tide of revolutionary ideology sweeping Latin America had crossed

Table 14 Literacy in the Department of Santiago, by Sex, 1885–1920

Year	% of men who can read	% of women who can read
1885	45	42
1895	54	53
1907	58	57
1920	67	68

Source: Censo 1895, 1: 187; Censo 1907, 428–29; Censo 1920, 304.

Chilean borders. This influence arrived later and in weaker form than in neighboring Argentina, where revolutionary movements had been bolstered by the arrival of large numbers of workers from southern Europe. Elite convictions and fears notwithstanding, foreign workers were relatively unimportant in directing Chilean labor organizations. More important in the dissemination of anarchist and socialist ideas were contacts between Chilean and foreign activists[19] and the growth of the Chilean labor press, which frequently published European writers in translation. Labor newspapers and periodicals provided a crucial vehicle for the articulation of local political expressions, given the relatively high literacy rates found in the Chilean urban population (see table 14).[20] This labor press not only gives us access to the meetings, rallies, and groups that composed the labor movement, but also testifies to the high priority accorded to propaganda and education in workers' societies of the period.[21] Further, the shifting networks of contributors and editors of the labor press, as well as their exchanges with foreign newspapers, have left us with extensive evidence about discussions of "the woman problem" in working-class political circles.

It was primarily through these periodicals—and the workers' societies whose activities they reported—that libertarian ideology made its deepest impression on Chilean workers' politics. In contrast with the flow of immigrants who brought Italian and Spanish anarchism directly to the shores of Argentina, Chilean anarchism was fostered primarily through anarchist writings that were often translated and published first in Argentina or Uruguay and later reprinted in the Chilean labor press. Alongside the articles and editorials produced by Chilean authors, for example, foreign anarchist texts littered and sometimes even dominated the pages of anarchist publications. Pieces by Bakunin, Kropotkin, Thackeray, Proudhon, Tolstoy, and Zola appeared regularly, as did those of Spanish and Italian anarchists such as Mir i Mir and Pietro Gori. This flow of anarchist ideology and news was facilitated by the vast exchange networks that flourished between domestic and foreign presses, which conveyed news to Chile from cities as distant as Madrid, Havana, Tampa, Montevideo, Buenos Aires, and Paris. This attention to foreign labor ideologies and movements testifies not only to the availability of European tracts, but also to the receptive and eclectic nature of working-class politics in Chile more generally.[22] Although a rough categorization of newspapers into anarchist, socialist, Democratic, and mutualist tendencies is possible, their heterogeneous, shifting ideological content provides further evidence of the permeability and flexibility of early labor radicalism in Chile.

The growth of the labor press reflected the increasing radicalization of workers' societies in Chile in the 1890s, despite constant employer opposition and periodic waves of state repression. Anarchist groups in Tarapacá precipitated the shippers' strike of 1890, which quickly grew into a national action. Using a strategy of "boring from within" existing mutual aid societies, anarchists urged workers to use illegal, direct action tactics against their employers. Correspondingly, the number of "resistance societies" and strikes grew dramatically after 1900 as anarchist societies led large and small walkouts and demonstrations, reporting on their campaigns in a wide variety of workers' newspapers.[23] Because of workers' widespread success in obtaining concessions—if not total victory—from employers through strikes, anarchist influence grew from its enclave among shipping and port workers to include other transport, tobacco, construction, and leather workers, as well as typesetters and other artisans.[24]

The spread of anarchist ideology throughout the labor movement, particularly in the urban sectors, changed the shape of working women's mobilization as well. With their emphasis on radical social transformation, the resistance societies founded in the first decade of the century encouraged women to take a more combative attitude toward their employers. The earliest evidence of explicitly nonmutualist organization among women workers dates from a 1902 letter from "a revolutionary hat maker" to her coworkers, urging them to join the newly formed resistance society in their trade. The letter, published in the anarchist *La Luz*, urged hat makers to lay aside competition over who was better skilled for the sake of the union: "Open your eyes to the light of reason and realize that your working conditions are really bad, your salaries are illusory, that they barely prevent us from dying of hunger, which is degrading treatment for our dignity as free women, and that if we try to make them understand our views, our exploiters just throw us out on the street."[25] Another of the earliest female resistance societies was the Valparaíso-based Federación Cosmopólita de Obreras en Resistencia, founded in 1903. Here the mixture of gender- and class-based demands was readily apparent in the group's statutes: "The moment has arrived for us to lay the basis for the 'emancipation of women workers,' to make the source of misery that runs through our sex disappear, since today we are considered society's useless beings, or the productive machines for those tyrants that we now call bosses. . . . The goals that we pursue are not only union, savings, and better and fair wages, but also the emancipation and improvement of our sex."[26] The seamstresses and shoe workers involved in the federation went on to state, "We are also trying to get woman to leave the narrow sphere of the home and take up, through her intelligence, the place that really belongs to her [in society] as well as a clear understanding of her rights and privileges."[27] This language of female revindication, as well as the institutional expression of women workers' common interests through resistance societies, embodied the emancipationist claims of early women workers' associations, which flourished in the working-class feminist movement discussed in chapter 4.

Women workers' increasing militancy after 1900 was most evident when they became involved in strike actions, which seemed to shock employers as much as it pleased male labor organizers. The evidence of female activism in this area is ample, shedding light on working women's capacity for public expressions of labor radicalism and organization. DeShazo found that women participated in about 23 percent of strikes recorded between 1902 and 1908.[28] Though women workers may have followed the male lead in mixed-sex factory strikes, women also led their own walkouts in solidarity with male strikers in other factories. Women's demands in these strikes were essentially the same as those of men: rehiring of fired workers, dismissal of abusive managers, pay raises, limits on hours, overtime pay, and union recognition.[29] Like their male counterparts, women workers benefited from the direct action tactics advocated by anarchists, forcing, for example, a successful negotiation with employers at the Corradi i Cia. Factory in March 1907. Although they achieved only 10 percent instead of the 30 percent salary increase they had sought, after the strike Sunday work was paid double and fines were abolished completely. Reports in the Democratic Party daily *La Reforma* expressed satisfaction with this example of women's militancy and with male solidarity with it: "We congratulate ourselves that in the trade of women weavers, a Federation has arisen that represents the interests of the workers. They have asked us to thank the unions of Tanners, Mechanics of 'Yungai,' and Bakers for their ready attitude in favor of solidarity with the *sisters of labor.*"[30]

It was also during this period of heightened strike activity that anarchist ideology and forms of organization exercised decisive influence over key leaders of the socialist Democratic Party, which had been founded in 1887 with the aim of using a workers' movement to break the political stranglehold of the Parliamentary Republic.[31] The central figure of Chilean socialism, Luís Emilio Recabarren, began his political career with the Democratic Party, first as secretary (1899) and then as director (1900).[32] A typographer and journalist by trade, Recabarren believed fervently in the labor press as a revolutionary tool and contributed extensively to the historical record through the various newspapers that he founded and directed throughout Chile.[33]

The Democrats succeeded in part by linking their electoral efforts to the organization of *mancomunales* or "brotherhoods" among nitrate workers in northern Chile in the 1890s. The brotherhoods, which typically federated workers' associations in a single city for the purpose of holding coordinated job actions against employers, quickly became the locus for the cultural and political activities of these mining communities.[34] As predominantly male organizations, the brotherhoods prescribed a supporting, subordinate role for women in the labor movement. One such appeal penned by Recabarren read, "We call women to our cause, educating them in the ideas of social demands; we contribute to forming the illustrious mothers who will raise our sons to know how to bring about the happiness of future generations."[35] The gender ideology of the brotherhoods, particularly in northern mining areas, reflected these communities' sexual division of labor and the lack of industrial employment for women; the idealization of women's domestic role and the patriarchal working-class family evident in the mancomunal movement presaged subsequent socialist positions on women's work, even as the Democrats shifted their attention to female unionization in urban areas in subsequent years.

Although Democratic leaders were unanimous in their resolve to break into the political arena and use legal mechanisms to improve the lot of the working classes, differences as to how this could be achieved split the party into two factions in 1906, the newest (the Partido Doctrinario Democrático) led by Recabarren and tinsmith Bonificio Veas.[36] One result of this split was that it freed Democratic associations to collaborate more closely with anarchist groups in the gathering momentum of urban protest prior to 1908. Particularly during this period of schism, the organizations and newspapers associated with Recabarren showed a clear affinity for anarchist teachings, even as some socialist leaders occasionally denounced anarchists' antielectoral strategies.[37] This temporary split in the Democratic Party, as well as the fluid appropriation of disparate ideological perspectives—from anarchist communism to patriotic nationalism—found its corollary in the instability of alliances and divisions formed among Chilean workers' associations more generally. Clear and consistent divisions between anarchists and socialists, for example, would not emerge until the political polarization brought about by the consolidation of Marxist political forces in the Communist Party in 1922.

It was precisely during this period of the Democrats' affinity for anarchism early in the century that Democratic organizers hoisted the banner of female emancipation and first provided material and rhetorical support to the cause of female emancipation through unionization. This movement for "worker feminism," discussed more fully in chapter 4, was nourished by a growing tide of journalistic invective against women's economic exploitation, and went hand in hand with the growing evidence of female militancy in Santiago and Valaparíso after 1902. By 1908, workers' society notices in the labor press recorded the stable existence of at least twenty-two female and mixed workers' associations in Santiago, many of which functioned as resistance societies during this period (see table 15). Whereas women activists began by forming resistance societies in those trades in which they clearly predominated (seamstresses, hat makers, etc.), their presence in mixed-sex factories led to their incorporation into existing unions in shoe, tobacco, and clothing preparation. In some cases, mixed-sex unionization pulled women workers away from existing all-female associations. In July 1906, more than one hundred women shoe-stitchers, some of whom already belonged to the all-female Asociación de Costureras, answered the invitation of male shoe-workers to meet at their headquarters and "hear long speeches by some comrades about the worrisome situation through which the women workers in this trade are passing."[38] The female stitchers then formed their own union (later joining the male shoe-workers in a mixed-sex resistance federation) over the objections of the head of the seamstresses' union, Esther Valdés de Díaz. Valdés de Díaz argued, "We are all sisters, we have the same needs, the same rights to defend, the same interests to support,"[39] which a male shoe-worker

Table 15 Women's and Mixed-Sex Workers' Associations, Santiago, 1906–1908

Asociación de Costureras Protección, Ahorro y Defensa

Ateneo de Obreras

Centro Ilustrativo Ambos Sexos Eusebio Lillo

Centro Social Obrero de Ambos Sexos el Arte

Consejo Federal Femenino de Empleados de Cocina

Federación de Resistencia de Zapateros i Aparadoras

Gremio de Sombreras "Resistencia de Sombreras"

Sociedad Protección de la Mujer

Sociedad de Abstinencia i Protección Mutua de Ambos Sexos por la Humanidad

Sociedad de Ambos Sexos la Fraternidad

Sociedad de Ambos Sexos la Patria

Sociedad Cosmopólita de Resistencia de Obreras en Tejidos i Ramos Similares

Sociedad Estrella Chilena

Sociedad Periodística *La Alborada*

Sociedad de Resistencia Daniel Pinilla de Cigarreros y Cigarreras

Sociedad de Resistencia de Lavanderas i Aplanchadoras

Sociedad de Resistencia Obreros de Fábricas de Ambos Sexos La Ideal

Sociedad de Resistencia de Obreras Sastres

Sociedad de Resistencia de Operarias de la Camisería Matas

Sociedad de Resistencia Tracción Eléctrica

Sociedad Socorros Mutuos La Aurora

Unión de Resistencia de Aparadoras

Sources: Oficina del Trabajo, *Estadística de la Asociación Obrera*; *La Reforma* (1906–1908); *La Alborada* (1905–1907); *La Palanca* (1908); *El Socialista* (Valparaíso, 1915–1918); *La Federación Obrera* (1921–1924).

dubbed "counter-propaganda" against their mixed-sex efforts.[40] This conflict illustrates the tension between all-female and guild models for organizing women workers: Were the common interests among women best defined by their female identity, or did the usual structural distinctions among trades also apply to women workers, requiring trade-based organizations? The division that ensued between stitchers and seamstresses, in this case, showed that the women stitchers opted for the latter, a guild model for worker organization.[41]

The mixed-sex shoe workers' resistance society that later formed be-

GALERÍA DE PRESIDENTES
DE SOCIEDADES OBRERAS

Srta. FRANCISCA QUEZADA M.
Presidente de la "Sociedad Proteccion de la Mujer"

10. "Gallery of Presidents for Workers' Societies," *El Obrero Ilustrado. Source: El Obrero Ilustrado* 1, no. 4 (15 June 1906): 1. Courtesy of the Chilean National Library, Newspapers Division.

tween female stitchers and male shoe-workers demonstrated the effective support that women workers lent to male workers through cross-gender solidarity. In February 1907, male shoe-workers issued a call for women stitchers to support their strike at San Agustín i Ancih; although there were complaints of women breaking the strike,[42] most reports celebrated the solidarity shown by the stitchers: "We must record the enthusiasm and self-denial of the *aparadoras,* who with this important attitude have faithfully demonstrated the value of female cooperation in workers' movements."[43] On its first anniversary, however, the stitchers' union was having trouble keeping up its membership. One member wrote, "*Compañeras*: you must not sleep, you must shake off this inertia and take care to strengthen our weapon of combat, which is union; let us save a little time to attend the meetings that are of utmost importance for our own progress."[44]

The increasing mobilization of women workers also produced female leaders who participated in local and national political events. At the Fourth Workers' Convention held in Chillán in 1905, for example, a number of distinguished female delegates spoke out in debates, expressing women's solidarity with male workers and pressuring for protective legislation for women (regulation of homework, the eight-hour day, minimum wage, etc.). Representatives of the Sociedad Protección de la Mujer also participated, calling for government funding for women's organizations and for increased attention to worker education in workers' associations.[45] Women attended and spoke at male congresses on issues of common interest; socialist journalist Carmela Jeria, in particular, was a favored speaker.[46] In the end, the Workers' Convention made a list of resolutions, a number of which would have had a significant impact on women workers if enacted. Most important from this perspective was a resolution to regulate piecework to secure a steady wage for homeworkers and to ensure a more even distribution of work.[47] Such protectionist strategies were consistent with Democratic initiatives in Parliament to enact social legislation and reflected the growing importance of "the woman question" in socialist politics in the first decade of the century.

By May 1907, however, the Chilean labor movement had peaked and began to lose its momentum, one of a number of periodic lulls in working-class organization in Chile. A combination of factors, including the fiscal crisis of that year, the failure of a national strike in June, and the government massacre of striking nitrate workers and their families at the Santa María de Iquique nitrate company, caused many workers to reconsider their political options. While employers crushed the resistance society movement by firing and blacklisting union leaders, the events of Santa María symbolized the brutal victory of the Parliamentary Republic over the nascent labor movement, discouraging significant new organization of workers for almost a decade.[48] After approximately eighty strikes in all of Chile in 1907, for example, 1908 witnessed only fifteen strikes; Chilean workers would not even approach previous levels of strike activity until the surge of activity after 1919.[49] Instead of taking to the streets to defend their demands, after 1907 many workers turned to less confrontational tactics and to mutual aid associations, enlisting in mutualist efforts such as the Gran Federación Obrera de Chile (GFOCH).

Originally founded in 1909 as a railworkers' mutual aid association—and much derided by socialists as a tool of Church and bourgeois manipulation—by 1916 the GFOCH could claim a membership of forty-five hundred, making it the only viable labor federation in the country.

The resurgence of Marxist labor organizing began when Recabarren, after two years of exile in Argentina and Europe, returned to Chile to found the Socialist Workers' Party (POS) in 1912. At the convention to establish the party in Tarapacá, tensions over women's role in working-class politics became evident: only one woman (northern activist Teresa Flores) actively participated in creating the party, and women workers present at a meeting to establish the party objected to the name Socialist Workers' Party on the grounds that nonworkers, particularly house-wives, would thereby be excluded; their counterproposal was defeated.[50] Although northern organization remained very weak due to economic depression and continued police intervention, Recabarren's stay in Val-paraíso reinforced the recovery of socialist workers' societies in that city. In 1916, socialist workers' councils gained important influence within the mutualist GFOCh, which Recabarren and other socialists began to praise as an example of "modern syndicalism."[51] The growth of the federation's socialist membership after 1917, particularly through workers' councils representing Valparaíso and Concepción, increasingly radicalized the federation, which in 1919 went on to elect Recabarren as its president and to announce its alliance with the POS. Thereafter, the (renamed) FOCh became the primary vehicle for Marxist labor organization in Chile. Although the federation's claims to represent the majority of organized workers in Chile may have been exaggerated, FOCh did succeed in mobilizing large numbers of textile and food-processing workers.[52]

The other source of continuing labor agitation in urban Chile by the late teens were the anarchosyndicalist unions active among Santiago and Valparaíso shoe workers, printers, and carpenters. Such unions led strikes, sponsored newpapers, and federated workers among several factories—keeping labor organization alive in the 1910s—and, like most unions, they suffered the trials of employer lockouts, blacklisting, and economic depression. Although anarchosyndicalist unions in shoes and construction frequently collaborated with both the FOCh and the newly established International Workers of the World (IWW, 1917), anarcho-syndicalists resisted incorporation into these larger federations and fought for their factory-based autonomy. Even after 1917, when FOCh made serious gains in mobilizing urban factory workers, anarchosyndicalist federations such as the Federación de Zapateros y Aparadoras (FZA) maintained a high profile as examples of effective, mixed-sex syndicalism.[53] Unionists' mobilization drive of 1917 to 1920 resulted in the significant strengthening of organized labor in Chile; it also led to ideological friction between Marxists and anarchists, which culminated in the vital splits of 1921, to the detriment of the anarchist forces.

In terms of female activism, increased competition between anarchist and socialist organizations drew many women workers already active in all-female or mixed-sex unions into the fold of the FOCH. Although the highly centralized IWW successfully united the (mostly male) workers in transportation and construction for industrywide strikes, FOCH's federative structure was more popular among (the predominantly female) clothing and textile workers, probably because it preserved the local autonomy of its member unions and allowed for sporadic, independent strikes at the factory level.[54] And although the IWW was weakest in the most feminized industries, the organization was not indifferent to female activism: female union representatives participated in the second convention of the IWW in 1921, and congress resolutions supported female unionization and equal wage demands.[55]

Similarly, the mutualist and, later, Marxist-led FOCH treated the education and mobilization of women workers as secondary—rather than central—goals of the organization. Whereas the GFOCH had made no reference to women in its original statutes (including the existing women's auxiliaries to the organization), the 1917 statutes of the FOCH advocated the "efficient promotion of the development of women workers' organization as a way of supporting the happiness of workers' homes."[56] Not until the Tocopilla Congress of 1919, however, was some version of women's emancipation revived as a goal for socialist revolution, a development that may have reflected the participation of women's organizations and their representatives in the congress. María Ester Barrera of the Consejo Femenino Santiago was elected secretary of the FOCH, and the resolution on women appeared in slightly modified form in the statutes: "To struggle for the development of women's organizations as a means of contributing to the integral emancipation of the salaried class."[57] In addition to a variety of other articles on social legislation, the 1919 FOCH convention recommended establishing the eight-hour day and a 4-peso minimum wage for women.[58] Convention delegates also supported prohibiting women from working in an advanced state of pregnancy and the institution of employer-sponsored day care for working mothers.[59]

Though the increased attention to working women's issues evident in the FOCH by 1919 may have reflected women's increased representation in the federation, the FOCH also moved to streamline female mobilization by creating local women's councils (*consejos femeninos*), which provided an undifferentiated structure for female participation. The FOCH women's councils apparently sought to organize greater numbers of working-class women by developing infrastructure that would incorporate housewives' activism and demands. For example, a women's group formed in Santiago's Mapocho neighborhood by Isabel Díaz in 1922 made the following appeal to working-class women: "All of the women who suffer today the stabs of abuse and see the figure of Hunger and misery hanging over their homes, those who watch their children go barefoot and ignorant, should take advantage of the call of their compañeras in pain, so that they can bring about better days for their homes."[60] Alongside the continuing activity of women's trade unions, women in the FOCH came to be organized along the lines of a women's auxiliary structure, regardless of their trade or economic activities.[61] This development of corporate organization for women within a federation of trade unions reflected Marxist leaders' growing concern to incorporate housewives—and their families—into revolutionary politics in the 1920s. The subsequent participation of women textile and tobacco workers in important strikes during 1923 increased the profile of women workers within the FOCH, leading to increasingly frequent portrayals of women workers as models of working-class militancy.

Although evidence of female leadership at the federation level is scarce, Micaela Troncoso and Isabel Soto were elected to the directorate of the FOCH 1921 convention, and Teresa Flores was appointed the Santiago representative on the Executive Council in 1922. Whereas almost eight hundred of the one thousand members that FOCH claimed for Santiago in that year came from the clothing trades, women's trade unions and FOCH women's councils constituted only about a fifth of the groups represented at national FOCH conventions. In 1925, these women's councils were renamed "women's propaganda committees" in response to a motion to promote "more propaganda for women's organization" approved at that convention.[62] This initiative resulted in the organization of a "women's week" planned for April of the following year. Organizers sought to make the "female element interested in its own well-being; this interest should be carried out in a week of intense agitation; as a prelude to the awakening of the Chilean woman, who is today perhaps the most enslaved [woman] of all the civilized countries of the world."[63] The list of women leaders involved in the initiative was impressive, as it included women who had been active in socialist politics for many years, such as Teresa Flores, Isabel Díaz, and Virginia Carvajal.[64]

The resurgence of Chilean labor organizations after 1917 had sustained a period of strikes, demonstrations, and ideological ferment in the labor movement that stimulated renewed employer organization and state intervention by the early 1920s. In addition, deep ideological polarization between anarchists and socialists had further divided the movement by 1921, and the FOCH suffered the loss of Recabarren (to suicide, in 1924) and the threat of state co-optation through the 1924 Labor Code. President Alessandri, who had been elected with labor's support, administered a brutal crackdown on organized labor in 1925 that rivaled the Santa María massacre in its dampening effect on organized labor. Finally, the climate of economic recession, internal schism, and failed general strikes in this period were compounded by the systematic and brutal repression of anarchist and communist unions, a crackdown ordered by General Ibáñez, first as Alessandri's minister of the interior and then as president. By the time Ibáñez took power in a military coup in February 1927, declaring war on communism and anarchism, the labor movement quickly collapsed.[65] With it, the struggle for gender equality in the workplace and the labor movement was postponed for another decade, when the resurgence of a feminist agenda within Popular Front parties would once again bring the objectives of worker feminism to the fore.

Defending the *Hermanitas Proletarias*

In the midst of the fluctuating, occasionally massive working-class mobilizations of the early twentieth century, it was perhaps inevitable that labor organizers should start to address the issues raised by women's presence in the factories of Santiago and Valparaíso. Women factory workers' visibility, as well as working-class leaders' awareness of the controversies broiling at home and abroad because of "the woman question," provoked expressions of concern from across the political spectrum. These writers, drawn primarily from Santiago's working men's associations, incorporated portrayals of working women into their analyses of capital, industrialization, and labor relations, revealing the underlying tensions in workers' movements about the changing roles of working-class women. Though these accounts reflect the very real exploitation that women workers faced in the industrial workforce, these texts also contributed to the construction of fictions about female victimization that served organizers' polemical, discursive strategies far more effectively than they exposed or advocated for women's interests in the workplace. This discourse was unmistakably patriarchal in perspective and strategy, as it exhorted male workers to provide for and protect the women of their class, whereas women workers were instructed (at best) to follow the example of their militant male comrades. Evidence for this emerging discourse, which in many ways contradicted the reality of women workers' ongoing agency in labor politics, can be found within the texts of workers' congresses, the labor press, and pamphlet literature produced after the turn of the century. Despite the ideological and strategic disputes among them, most socialist, mutualist, and anarchist writers struck a common chord of alarm when it came to analyzing the causes and effects of female industrial employment: from this anticapitalist perspective, women and children were the innocent fodder of greedy, unscrupulous employers who could no longer manipulate unionized male workers. The miserable living and working conditions of the factory seamstress, in particular, became a stock centerpiece for such texts; her plight dramatized capitalism's project to extract more profit, emasculate organized labor, and destroy working-class families. Significantly, this gendered paradigm of class exploitation drew on a broader social consensus—shared by Catholic reformers, liberal politicians, and the state's Labor Office—about women's fundamental unsuitability for industrial work. In the face of growing evidence of working women's agency as family providers and militants, the persistent paternalism of working-class leaders testifies to the importance of sexual difference for the definition of class identity and organized labor in early-twentieth-century Chile.

A dramatic illustration of how fundamental gender was to labor activists' understanding of class is how labor organizers described the nature of the problem posed by women's presence in the wage workforce. From about 1900 on, working-class writers stressed the depth of social crisis in Chile through the example of the increasing exploitation of women in modern industrial society. Not only were women at work in factories, they argued, but they received pitiful wages for their efforts, brought piecework home, slaved into the night to complete domestic tasks, and risked sexual harassment at work. Virtually all contributors who addressed the woman question described the problem in its far-reaching implications for both the domestic sphere and the heretofore masculine space of the factory. Although such expressions of alarm may in fact have reflected working-class journalists' sincere concern for the plight of women workers, they also drew on tropes of sexual exploitation as a paradigm for class inequality that were common to radical labor ideologies circulating in this period.[66]

What kind of women went to work in factories, and why, according to the labor press? The most common explanation for the growing female workforce was employers' search for ever cheaper sources of labor. Capitalist manufacturers were accused of draconian plans to increase profits and to sate their sexual appetites by exploiting women's lower wage expectations, more assiduous work habits, and moral vulnerability. Using a dramatic formula similar to but more vivid than that applied to male workers, labor journalists took aim at capitalism through the sights of the woman factory worker. In so doing, they also affirmed the immutability of the factory as a place of sexual danger, where women workers faced sexual harassment in addition to the physical overwork and psychological abuse typically inflicted on men.

One way labor journalists fashioned images of working women to serve labor's larger polemical ends was to emphasize women's inescapably desperate economic circumstances. Contrary to employers' portrayals of the factory girl as someone who worked only to supplement a family income or to become more independent, the labor press offered a more desperate vision of female motivation. One contribution, signed "A baker for love," tied women's need to work to the unfortunate decline in marriage among the working classes: "We must keep in mind that most women workers are not daughters of families or wives—because of this, women must learn how to earn a living."[67] Other accounts described orphaned girls or widowed women who were the sole support of other, weaker relatives, which at once stressed the necessity and absurdity of female economic independence. When Juana Olivares died of pneumonia during a shirt factory strike, she was eulogized in the labor press for her sacrifice: "Our heroine . . . returning from the demonstration to her cold home, where she found the two innocents she kept there—she was a widow—began to feel the first symptoms of deadly pneumonia, which devoured her in a few days, after the life-consuming factory had devoured her best years."[68] Tales of such women, bereft of family support and male protection, usually ended when women succumbed to disease, as they struggled against the odds of low wages and unhealthy conditions to provide for those even weaker than themselves. Even worse, capitalism was driving into the workforce even those women who should have been able to count on material support from their men. According to anarchist Luís Sanz's 1906 account, for example, female relatives were literally "invading the factories and workshops and combing the streets" to bring bread home to their unemployed menfolk: "Hunger demands adaptation!"[69] By describing female employment principally as an issue of sheer survival, however, most labor organizers downplayed women's agency in seeking to achieve, through work, better conditions for their families and greater independence for themselves, stressing instead the economic necessesity that drove women to work.[70]

The grinding poverty that drove women from their homes and into the workforce, according to the labor press, was exacerbated principally by the low wages they earned there, a reality that labor organizers regularly denounced. Capitalists underpaid a female worker "for the simple reason that she is a woman and her work is therefore worth less."[71] Labor organizers objected to this form of sexual discrimination because employers made their profits by employing women instead of men, but they also used such accounts to portray the basic inhumanity of factory bosses: "Would it not be more Christian and humanitarian to give her the pay she deserves, especially when she resorts to overtime, afflicted by misery?"[72] For dramatic and propagandistic purposes, therefore, the woman was capital's perfect victim: first economic necessity, then physical and intellectual weakness drew her into a "female martyrdom, which is even more abominable since the victim is so weak."[73]

In addition to the pernicious strategies of manufacturing employers, labor's central concern with women's factory work was the workplace itself. Juxtaposed against idealized portrayals of the "natural" working-class home, the factory appeared as the locus of a series of threats to woman's physical and moral health, which through her also threatened the health and well-being of her family. The physical dangers were constant (chemicals, disease, exhausting hours, and dangerous machinery), and their negative effects extended through the women themselves to the whole working-class community.[74] Recabarren summed up these dangers in a graphic speech to tobacco workers in 1915: "If you can learn all of this, and we are easily convinced, that in addition to the excessive and unhygienic work that hurts women physically, you have to add the bad living conditions, food and vices that complete the destructive work of labor on women's bodies; we can also be convinced that if you will always work under these conditions, your destiny will be to have rachitic, idiotic children, who instead of being our hope of support in old age, will only be what most workers are today: vice-ridden slaves, bad sons and worse husbands."[75] In texts such as this, the female body became the site of capitalist assaults on the working classes as a whole, and women who suffered this abuse quietly were likewise implicated. Although the socialist press praised several factories for providing excellent working conditions,[76] the factory was, in general, considered even more dangerous for women than for men because of women's responsibility for bearing and raising children. Moreover, factory work and industrial vocations were sometimes portrayed as fundamentally incompatible with women's physical and mental capacities. The traits necessary to exercise a vocation—though men acquired them through environment rather than at birth—were inaccessible, and certainly undesirable, for women: "It is undeniable that the physical constitution of woman is less resistant than that of man, thus she is exempt from gymnastic exercise and has the freedom necessary for her slow development, while the man develops in the environment of forced work, thereby educating his muscles for the sad odyssey of the struggle for bread."[77] What was worse, the process of industrialization and mechanization had perverted even those trades considered appropriate for women. The sewing machine, once promoted as technology that would lighten women's workload and give them an independent source of income, had become the instrument of their enslavement in the factory and workshop: "The bards who even yesterday sang of the virtue of work for their ladies; those who played the pitch-pipe of beautiful music, the poem of the needle, for the queens of the home; today fall mute before the sad seamstress, before the unhappy worker who destroys herself in her fifteen hours of work, making the machine turn and buzz, which the Mephistopheles of progress has placed in her hands. . . . Oh! machine, that emerged in the mind of the wise mechanic to alleviate the unhappy workers, you have been transformed from redeemer into the worst torture rack! I curse you, for your mockery of civilization and humanity."[78] At the same time that writers portrayed the factory environment as inherently destructive for women because of the limits of female nature, they objected that factory work reduced women to sexless machines (i.e., to mere workers), fundamentally violating the virtues of the female sex.

More than these physical dangers, labor journalists stressed the morally degenerate effects of female factory work for both women and their families. The ramifications of women's work for working-class families were grave, for the factory exhausted women and made them neglect their domestic duties. According to one observer, "the modern family" could be characterized by the competition and lack of affection among family members, which was caused principally by female and child employment: "What kind of a family is this in which the man, woman and child, working like mercenaries in a factory so as not to die of hunger, compete among themselves and only meet up at night, after spending ten or twelve hours apart?"[79] Competition among family members undermined both the security of male wages and the natural harmony of the working-class home, making more inaccessible the idealized, gendered separation between the worlds of work and home.

The most pressing concern of labor journalists regarding the theme of women's work, however, was female sexuality; journalistic attention to women workers, as to most women depicted beyond the scope of family protection, was fraught with references to sexual danger. Stories and news reports about sexual harassment shamed working-class men, who could neither keep their women out of the factory nor protect them from the harassment women received at the hands of foremen and employers. Sexual harassment was thereby constructed exclusively as an example of class exploitation and rarely implicated working-class men in the nightmarish depictions of working women's sexual vulnerability. Further, any woman who sold her labor traveled a fine line between honorable survival and the irreversible fall into prostitution.[80] Labor journalists regularly infused any situation in which a woman was driven to sell her labor with the suggestion that she might also sell her body. Complaints about women's working conditions thus also reveal anxieties about how female participation in the workforce threatened the exercise of working-class patriarchy, particularly in terms of men's control over female sexuality.

The almost inevitable slide into prostitution usually began with some account of how capitalism first destroyed male workers—through disease, workplace accidents, and repression—and then left women to fend for themselves, both economically and sexually. News stories and editorials about women at work, particularly in a factory setting, offered moralizing tales of the workplace as a threat to female virtue because it exposed women to sexual temptation, seduction, and coercion.[81] More than once, for example, the Chilean labor press printed excerpts from Argentine anarchist Juana Rouco's story of the seamstress, which described the tragic victimization of a virginal seamstress at the hands of her lascivious employer.[82] In other accounts, this seamstress was merely seduced by an employer, a neighbor, or a young man of the elite; in any case, the end result was a life of miserable prostitution. Many of these short stories and poems resemble a contemporary Argentine poem, "La costurerita que dió aquel mal paso," in which the seamstress daughter of a respectable working-class family is dishonored and leaves home, presumably for a life of prostitution.[83] But when young women crossed the line between amorous adventures and prostitution, responsibility was laid once more at the door of employers, whose greedy strategies made such activities necessary for female economic survival.

Despite journalistic consensus about the role of bosses in corrupting innocent seamstresses, a variety of interpretations emerged as to a woman's responsibility for selling her body. Although prostitution was presented as an option of last resort for women, assessments as to why and how women acceded to this pressure varied widely, revealing male workers' ambivalence about women's presence in the workplace. One account showed how Lucila Olea, a young woman driven by economic necessity to work in a tailor's workshop, was there seduced by her boss and tried to kill herself when he refused to continue their affair: "So it was that she met he who would win over her sensitive heart and emotions for great passion."[84] Lucila's plight, though regrettable, resulted from her emotional, unstable nature, demonstrating that the workplace was an inevitable source of sexual danger for women. At their worst, obreras who became prostitutes were "the bad feminine element . . . those girls who dress disgracefully and never work."[85] These kinds of stories buttressed working-class leaders' utopian vision of a future in which women sold neither their labor nor their bodies for economic survival.

Even more than the exploited, honorable seamstress, the obrera-prostitute symbolized the true inhumanity of capitalist exploitation. Though many of these tales implied the vulnerability of female virtue outside the home, employers and their factories were considered ultimately responsible for this form of female degradation. Capitalism reduced women to "a valued object that can be bought with the best offer,"[86] and employers were "those who want to exploit your strength at work, and your youth, beauty and virginity with false love."[87] Curiously, these accounts also sought to elicit readers' sympathy about the economic and/or romantic necessities that might drive a woman worker to have sex outside of marriage: "How is it possible that the fair sex, the mother of all generations, after being prostituted as the meat of pleasure, is vilely exploited; and if perhaps she gives herself to a man for love or necessity so that he might help her to better her lot, they charge her with disrespect, calling her WHORE."[88] This position emphasized the hypocrisy of employers, who were accused of first abusing women workers sexually and then using their dishonor to undermine women's status as workers. A prevalent complaint appearing in the labor press concerned employers' abusive language toward women workers, including insinuations that women workers were, by definition, also prostitutes.[89]

The flip side of this defense of female virtue involved a more complex justification of why women workers might engage in prostitution. Urban newspapers provide ample evidence that sexual harassment pressed women to surrender their bodies as well as their labor to employers and managers: "Perhaps those journalists [who write about white slavery] do not know that many factory owners have two aims in mind: from these [factories] they make women's lungs into blood and then they prostitute them with their miserable stalking."[90] Evidence of this reality is scattered throughout the periodical and archival sources of the period; in seasons of reduced factory or homework in women's trades, women turned to prostitution to survive.[91] In defense of women, observers argued that the factory and the conventillo conditioned women (and men) to the pervasive vice of prostitution.[92] By this account, prostitution was just one more example of capitalist efforts to undermine and further exploit the working classes, and the prostitute herself represented that community's desperate surrender in the absence of working-class organization.

For this reason, working women who turned to prostitution for economic survival were more often pitied than despised by labor journalists. Even though these authors were apparently deeply concerned with working-class women's virtue, labor's focus was really on employers and factories as instigators of vice, rather than on the character of women involved in prostitution. The anonymous "J.R." argued in 1902 that the inadequacy of women's wages had historically been the primary cause of prostitution:

> Taking a direct look at this real case, we see that the woman—the seamstress, ironness, etc.—this mute and obedient work machine, who both gives up her vigor and punctures her lungs in the work of her trade, enriching the capitalist for her ludicrous wages, gives herself over to the shameful, illegal commerce in an unfortunate moment of desperation and hunger, weary and despondent with the scanty and almost useless product she is awarded for her honorable activities. . . . Prostitution: is it necessary? . . . if the capitalists would increase the miserable wages that a poor woman can earn . . . this grave and disastrous element would be hugely diminished.[93]

Observers consistently pointed to the factory and capitalism as the principal causes of the growing population of prostitutes in the capital. From the perspective of workers' movements, prostitution was both a reality and a dramatic example: it reinforced the analysis of female exploitation as a by-product of industrialization and capitalist employers as the primary beneficiaries of working-class women's sexual vulnerability.[94]

Despite this primary emphasis on employers' combined economic and sexual exploitation, the perception that working-class prostitution was rampant challenged labor organizers to incorporate an analysis of sexual oppression into their accounts of class struggle. That is, one can see in several accounts and polemics on prostitution how women—as a group—were perceived to be dominated by men (of all classes), and how their condition as workers served only to further exacerbate this condition: "The crude macho is not content to exploit her at home and in the street, in the factory and the workshop, in the mine and in the field, but also—on the stage or in the brothel—he sullies her purity, degrades her instincts, dulls her instincts, clouds her mind. . . . To kill a woman, murderous cowards! To kill her, and claim that it is love that loads your weapon. You are lying, villains."[95] The above description was exceptional, insofar as it acknowledged that employers were not prostitutes' only patrons and likened workplace exploitation to domestic work. Other accounts portrayed working-class men who frequented or owned brothels as traitors to their class.[96] With the major exception of the worker feminist critiques discussed in chapter 4, however, few observers of the crisis of women's work explicitly discussed the possibility of working-class men's complicity in women's sexual subordination. Through their repeated emphasis on the factory as the site of women's exploitation and employers as the main perpetrators of sexual abuse, labor leaders represented women workers as vulnerable and helpless, perhaps in an attempt to justify and elicit male activism on their behalf.

The treatment of women's work and prostitution in the labor press contained two important elements that reflect the construction of female worker identity in the labor movement: first, women's economic and sentimental susceptibility to male domination; second, the way that employers and capitalism itself exploited this female vulnerability for pleasure and profit. On a symbolic level, female prostitution was a central metaphor for the degrading, dishonorable exploitation that factory labor foisted on working-class families. As an orphan in one dramatic monologue exclaimed, "How many orphans, like me, must have gotten sinful offers, and lacking the courage to reject them, have accepted these defeats and have besmirched the honor that their parents bequeathed to them!"[97] Consequently, the exceptional woman who chose death over the shame of prostitution was portrayed as revolutionary and exemplary for other women workers. In the story "The Rebel," for example, a poor woman whose lover was murdered was forced to look for work in the factory and as a domestic; in both cases, she was dismissed from work because she refused to sleep with her bosses. Homeless and destitute but with her virtue intact, she proclaimed to her listener, "I am worn out, mutilated, tormented . . . dead! But defeated? . . . never!"[98] With no status as a worker on which to base her struggle against capital, a woman alone seemed forced to choose between degradation (wage work or prostitution) and death. Into this breach stepped anarchist and socialist organizers, who would employ the language of female emancipation to incorporate women into the resistance societies of early-twentieth-century Santiago and Valparaíso. Before addressing these movements, however, we must examine the perceived obstacles to female activism that shaped the tactics and rhetoric of labor leaders across the ideological spectrum.

Gender and Mobilization in Labor Discourse

When they were not lamenting the sexual dangers of the workplace, many labor journalists of early-twentieth-century Santiago and Valparaíso addressed the problem of women's work primarily in terms of revolutionary strategy, because women's factory work was perceived to undermine the structure of work and mobilization for men. From the point of view of the male working-class leaders, the employment of women (and children) in factories drove down wages, augmented the population of potential strikebreakers, and furthered the deskilling of industrial labor. Although expressions of overt hostility toward women workers themselves were rare, the problem of how to educate, mobilize, and guide these women in defense of "the family of labor" perplexed and at times exasperated male working-class leaders.

The opinions expressed in the labor press about female militancy varied significantly according to authors' ideological perspectives and across time, yet the resulting proposals almost universally reflected the perception that both nature and environment had conspired to leave most women completely unprepared for labor militancy. That is, the same passivity or vulnerability to sexual and emotional manipulation that made women the ideal labor force for unscrupulous employers also prevented them from seeing the light of revolutionary wisdom and taking action in defense of their own interests. Some labor leaders evidently despaired, lashing out in frustration at female intransigence; others proclaimed optimistically the imminent dawn of female consciousness. Arguments for female participation ranged between two extremes, from celebrations of female strength and virtue to denunciations of their weak and corrupt essence, and sometimes the two perspectives appeared in the same argument. For most writers, however, woman's essential nature predisposed her to class solidarity (out of natural, loving impulse toward her male companion), but lack of education (or worse, religious beliefs) prevented her from assuming her place in the proletarian ranks.

An additional concern related to the question of female militancy was the widespread perception that women inhibited working-class mobilization both in the workplace and at home. Contributors to the labor press regularly complained that women, even those who worked outside the home, used their influence over male relatives and children to weaken working-class solidarity. Because a woman was considered the center of family life and education—which made her "the driver of the car of progress"—the ignorant woman could also inhibit male militancy at home: "Since the vast majority of our women are mostly uneducated . . . they join with a man with a ridiculous idea of life, not to be his compañera, but rather his hidden enemy in home life."[99] Women were sometimes held responsible for the failure of strikes, either for opposing male participation or for not joining in themselves: "So then imagine a compañera in this situation: If the man has to go to a strike, for example, she will encourage him, because she sees that if he wins there will be more bread in the house. But a woman who does not have this preparation, on the contrary, will discourage him and even oblige him to betray his comrades instead of encouraging him."[100] Female ignorance was usually blamed for this problem, but women were also portrayed as victims of clerical manipulation. Although Chilean labor movements were less consistently marked by radical anticlericalism than their counterparts elsewhere in the Southern Cone,[101] working-class leaders frequently couched their criticisms of female consciousness in terms of women's "enslavement" to the Church: "Woman, the slave of capital and made fanatical by the clergy, is now beginning to awaken from the lethargy in which she was sleeping, and the proof of this was given on the first of this month [May], accompanying her brothers of misery and protesting against the iniquitous exploitation of which she is a victim, where she is kept in ignorance."[102] Following the speaking tour of Spanish freethinker Belén de Sárraga in 1915, Recabarren published a speech on the pernicious effects of the Church on the female mind: "Woman has lived this way throughout history: courtesan of the Church, allied with it in all its crimes against humanity, against her own children. Kept in ignorance since savagery and barbarity for twenty centuries, it has been the woman, the mother of humanity, who is the very assassin of her children, because of the ignorance and mistakes to which the Church has subjected her." Recabarren went on to argue, optimistically, that education would release women from their enslavement to the Church, and "then the woman will be free, will bear free children, who are able to live free and respect the freedom of everyone."[103] Several Chilean anarchists of the 1920s, on the other hand, offered more scathing critiques of working-class women's misplaced trust in their priests: "If a noble idea occurs to you, you never try to act on it yourself, nor do you talk about it with your husband or compañero; rather you go to the priest, meek and obedient, to give yourself body and soul."[104] Although these writers disagreed about the permanence of women's association with the Church, they clearly considered it the primary source of female passivity and reactionary beliefs.

Women's nature was not just a domestic problem, however; men had to concern themselves with preparing women for labor activism to get them out on strike at crucial moments. It was up to male workers, then, to oversee the education and mobilization of their women. Once he had managed to "decatholicize his companion," for example, a man was advised to bring women to union meetings at least once a month, so that women might both prepare for activism and learn about where their men disappeared to all the time.[105] Presumably, only men had the necessary experience in organizing with which to guide women's awakening: "It is suitable, then, for the oppressed man to sit down and talk with the woman."[106] In fact, women were sometimes excluded from much of the daily political work of the mixed-sex unions they joined. The shoe workers' convention, for example, resolved that women members would be convened only periodically, "when it is considered suitable, [for] meetings in which a special lecture must be given to [that] sex and which would be of general interest to them."[107] The typographers' union had issued similar instructions to women workers to sign up, then delegate their representation to male coworkers, reminding them that, even without direct representation, they had already benefited from the work of the union.[108]

The most concrete representations of working women militants appeared in the recruitment efforts of unions involving both sexes, perhaps because women's potential to undermine male workers' pay scales and strikes was there a very real possibility. Calls to women workers to mobilize were usually based on the appeal of an already existing, successfully organized union of male workers, and women were exhorted to share in these benefits (and sacrifices) in the name of trade and class unity. A female member of the shoe workers' union of Valparaíso, for example, issued this plea to women stitchers in 1922: "Don't you find it just, compañera, that we should get together on our days off . . . to cast aside the sorrows . . . that we have to put up with . . . thus depriving ourselves from the many diversions that we, as workers, have the right to enjoy?" The logical answer to their plight, the author argued, would be to join the men of their trade in this association, who had already guaranteed them female representation on the directorate and ensured that their meetings would be held separately from those of the men. Female associates were also required to pay only half of what male union members paid in dues, in recognition of their lower salaries and to encourage their participation.[109]

Significantly, some anarchist texts appearing shortly after 1900 diverged dramatically from this widespread pessimism about female militancy in the labor press. Advocates of the "enslaved woman" hypothesis readily affirmed the possibility of women's mobilization in support of revolutionary goals. Anarchist writers argued that women's capacity to resist was sparked by their sexual oppression; their demands as militant women, then, were primarily shaped not by class identity, but by the indignities they experienced as women: "What will happen to the slave of all ages, that anonymous being, the meat of pleasure, the victim of society and, finally, the one who pays double tribute so that she will be allowed to live, banished as a slave to male egotism. . . . Tomorrow the women will answer you, as we have already seen they are preparing to achieve justice. Forward, fair sex; cede not a single step on the battlefield; laugh at the egotism of men and march on alone in pursuit of tomorrow, where you will cast Laws, marriage and religion into the abyss. . . . Hail!"[110]

The women of these early anarchist texts were archetypal: slaves until the moment of their sudden and glorious emancipation. This trajectory of women's enlightenment, activism, and emancipation thus illustrated the revolutionary potential of the *chusma*, any "lumpen" group whose imminent liberation was perceived to stem from the absolute misery in which they lived.[111] Revolutionary iconography also occasionally paralleled these abstract, metaphorical representations of female heroism; an illustration appearing on the front page of the confectioners' union newspaper shows an unclothed female Liberty, holding aloft a torch while clutching the Book of Revolution to her naked breast.[112] Some advocates of female emancipation thus inverted women workers' sexual and economic victimization to illustrate the revolutionary potential of even the most exploited members of society.

These pro-emancipationist visions of female militancy were not the only positions taken by Chilean anarchists, however. By the 1920s, a group of Chilean anarchist writers limited their comments on the subject to a few scathing observations on women's essentially counterrevolutionary nature. A contributor to the anarchosyndicalist bread workers' organ *El Comunista*, for example, depicted women as the irredeemable enemies of progress. One author wrote that a woman plays "the role of a lemon, which after having its juices squeezed out, is hurled into the garbage."[113] The woman not only meekly accepted her own oppression, he wrote, but also got in the way of labor organizing and was "a real martyr" at work. Anarchist author Aura was also unfailingly harsh in her lament about women's apathy: "Criminal! Murderer! With your apathy, with your mortal silence, you contribute to the corruption of your sons, you have lost your husband and your mother and the whole Universe! Now you cry, and if you suffer a lot, you deserve it! Roll around, wailing uselessly!"[114] In all the important meetings, moreover, "the female sex is the first to distinguish itself by its absence."[115] Aura advocated that women remedy this shameful condition by joining men in their anarchosyndicalist organizations and assuming an unspecified but militant role in revolutionary politics: "Only you women workers, women of the people, who have to work for the well-being of your own, who are the ones who suffer and, having suffered enormously already the cruel and ridiculous impositions of your enemies for thousands of years, listen now to the requests of your sister in struggle, who hopes to see you after today attending all of the cultural events of your respective neighborhoods, so that you can hear, along with the men, all that you must do to carry out the honorable mission that nature has assigned to you."[116] This kind of polemic, which usually disregarded the concrete issues affecting women in the workplace, was prominent among the few references to the woman question appearing in the anarchist press of the 1920s. Though this shift can be explained in terms of the declining influence of libertarian ideology in the face of Marxist-led unions, it is also true that these divergent assessments of female consciousness drew on dichotomous stereotypes about women's essential nature: enslaved/liberated, passive/catalytic, destructive/reproductive, and so on.[117] Furthermore,

El Obrero en Dulce

| Director: MIGUEL ESPINOZA
Administrador: ENRIQUE URIBE | Organo de la Unión Sindical de Confiteros,
Pasteleros y Anexos.—Aparición mensual.
Suscrición anual $ 2.00—Número suelto 20 centavos | Redacción y Administración: CASTRO 359
Casilla 5079 — Teléfono 2809 central |

| Año 1 | Santiago 1.º de Mayo de 1926 | Núm. 1 |

En este glorioso día de las reivindicaciones, los proletarios del mundo se estrechan las manos, y extienden a través del planeta la cadena de los corazones, a la luz de la antorcha del sindicalismo revolucionario.

Al entrar en la arena..

Con el presente número arrojamos nuestro primer grano de arena sobre el surco abierto para recibir la buena semilla.

Queremos también tener nuestro portavoz ante la opinión obrera, para hacer vibrar en él nuestras protestas y nuestras esperanzas. La Unión Sindical de Confiteros, Pasteleros y Anexos no debe permanecer en silencio dentro del concierto de las organizaciones obreras.

Y debe hacer oir también su voz en que se reflejan los sentimientos generosos de todo un gremio, que soporta todos los rigores de una explotación despiadada.

En esta voz palpita la esperanza de redención de este numeroso núcleo de trabajadores, que lucha desde hace veinte años por su mejoramiento.

Escrito por obreros, es probable que la crítica de los doctores o de los pedantes encuentre algunos reparos que formular a estas mal pergeñadas crónicas de dolor y de protesta; pero para nuestros hermanos que sienten arder sobre sus carnes los latigazos de la tiranía capitalista, nuestra palabra ha de ser escuchada con amor, porque ella expresa las ansias de redención que se levantan de nuestros corazones y los ideales de libertad que bullen en nuestros cerebros.

Con la visera levantada, de frente al sol, el pecho henchido de entusiasmo y el arma firme en el brazo que no tiembla, entra en la arena del combate este modesto paladín de las huestes libertarias.

Sabemos que no estamos solos. Defensores de una causa que apasiona a millares de hermanos nuestros de miseria y explotación, tenemos la convicción de que, al lado nuestro, hemos de contar con el refuerzo de otros luchadores, más vigorosos, más aguerridos, que lucirán más bruñidas armas que las que nosotros traemos aparejadas para el combate, pero que no desdeñarán —segur estamos de ello —el humildísimo contingente que venimos a ofrecerles, con débiles empujes, quizás, pero con ánimo levantado y sereno, y con ansias incontenibles del anhelado triunfo, que está próximo.

Hermanos de lucha y de esperanza, haced un sitio a vuestro lado al nuevo luchador.

11. Chilean Liberty, Confectioners' Union.
Source: El Obrero en Dulce 1, no. 1 (1 May 1926), 1.
Courtesy of the Chilean National Library, Newspapers Division.

such texts dealt with women's emancipation in abstract terms that symbolized the tensions inherent in workers' struggles. Unlike socialist leaders, who remained optimistic proponents of female unionization into the 1920s, these anarchist writers rarely concerned themselves with the day-to-day activities of women workers' unions, limiting their contribution to rhetorical inspiration.[118] Moreover, the fact that pseudonymous authors were the predominant "women's" voices in anarchist exchanges on the woman question further illustrates how completely this discourse originated in and addressed the class identity and concerns of male workers.[119]

Socialists' attention to striking women workers, by contrast, provided an alternative representation of female militancy: as examples of proper militancy for all workers. Journalists from *La Federación Obrera* clearly considered the textile workers of the 1923 Ñuñoa factory strike a wing of their own federation, using the weavers' strike as an example of socialist revolutionary spirit in action: "Our first impression upon arrival at the union local was of the order and culture that reigns among the 'strikers,' and we were impressed by the fact that almost everyone was busy reading 'social' books, which shows that woman is already an integral part of social struggles. These [women] workers who have gained consciousness of the importance of their strike are completely decided not to return to work as long as their union is not recognized, since they are not asking for higher wages but rather a more humane treatment, and to be considered workers and not a flock of sheep."[120] The journalist visiting the strikers' local held up the *compañeras tejedoras* as examples for all workers—including men—as the "the best representatives of the level of culture and social knowledge that some women workers have achieved in this, the most distant corner of the earth."[121]

Another way of using women's militancy to inspire adherence to the FOCH was for journalists to stress the bravery and "virility" of good socialist women. In one report, "Woman Worker Punishes a Sheep," textile worker Jovina Mesa severely beat Tomás Fuentes after he cursed her opposition to *cohecho* (vote buying) in the recent elections. His nose and mouth bleeding, Fuentes "presented himself crying to his masters to ask for the dismissal of compañera Jovina, because he feared that she would kill him with her fists!" The story ridiculed the "slave" Fuentes for his unmanly behavior and promoted Jovina Mesa as a brave example of workers' resistance: "The events that left the worker Jovina Mesa unemployed should teach all men and women workers that they should join the Workers' Federation in order to end these abuses."[122] Like the women of Colombia's 1920 textile strike who stripped male scabs of their pants, the story of virile women such as Jovina Mesa produced a temporary inversion of gender roles that was meant to inspire similarly virile behavior in both women and men.[123]

The story of activist Plácida Marín further illustrates the FOCH journalists' emphasis on the necessity of female worker resistance. An underpaid, then laid-off seamstress in Santiago (with a history of socialist militancy in Antofagasta), Marín refused to submit to her employer's will: "She sat down in the workshop and waited there, ready to upset this boss who liked to keep the products of the workers that she exploited and who at the same time abhorred the 'subversives.' At around eight at night when it was really dark, the exploiter came to cancel her debts and pay. Only this way did she get the worker [Marín] to leave the workshop."[124] Unlike the hypothetical "nonsubversive girl" ridiculed in the same article, Marín embodied the simple resistance of women workers on the principle of proper payment for their work. In another report, cigarette rollers in Talca went on strike to protest the insulting sexual innuendos of their employers: "These brave women declare that they would rather die than return defeated to work. . . . Thus they will achieve the triumph that will be our triumph."[125] What is striking about this tale is the absence of any reference to gendered resistance, as though the consciousness and militancy of women workers were no different from that of male workers.[126]

Such apparently sexless portrayals coexisted in the socialist press of the early 1920s with calls for women to shed the specifically feminine chains of indifference and join the mixed-sex trade unions affiliated with the the Workers' Federation.[127] Appeals to nonunionized women were most often couched in terms of how women, like all workers, were helpless without the protection of a union organization. In these stories, working women's sexual vulnerability could still be dramatized as a source of weakness for the family of labor as a whole, particularly when malevolent employers manipulated women workers to their antiunion ends. In one case, *La Federación Obrera*'s coverage of the 1923 hatters' strike at the Girardi Factory implied that the owners were using women workers to entice male strikebreakers to live and work in the factory: "All the employees got together and talked and joked, until there was an infernal party, and the men took advantage of the situation. Maybe some husbands haven't complained to their wives because they don't know this, just like some fathers whose daughters have passed several nights in the factory. For this reason, now the men just stay on, with pleasure, because at night there are real parties."[128] An eyewitness apparently corroborated this account, saying that "the men and women who stay in the factory drink a lot and at night there are big, repugnant scandals. There the women are degenerating as well as those of us who went to the factory in search of work."[129] The story of the Girardi strike served to illustrate the moral divide FOCh militants constructed between the women leading the strike and those who stayed in the dangerous space of the factory: the women workers inside the factory were deceiving their husbands and fathers, simultaneously betraying their families and their class.

In another example of attention to links between the sexuality and the militancy of working women, *La Federación Obrera* followed a dramatic story on its first page throughout June 1923: women workers at the Chilean Textile Company were humiliated by their employer who, accusing the women of stealing sewing scraps, forced them to strip naked and march down the street to the police station, clutching their clothing and the (admittedly) stolen goods. At first, the women "have to suffer the unspeakable outrage to their dignity and their sex, because they are women, have no protection, and more than anything because they are not organized." Within days of the women's declaring a strike and forming a union affiliated with the Workers' Federation, the employers acceded to all of their demands, thus demonstrating the importance of organization among the most helpless of workers.[130] Despite accounts of "virile" women, therefore, female vulnerability was also regularly invoked to demonstrate police brutality, such as when women participated in public demonstrations. Responding to a call from the women's section of the FOCh mining council in May 1922, a crowd of women gathered at the government palace to demand work for unemployed miners in the north. Following speeches by a representative of the railway workers' union and by Isabel Díaz (and sparked by an incident involving a man selling poisoned lemonade), police, according to FOCh reporters, unleashed their fury on the crowd "of defenseless women and children; of women and children who begged for work; of women and children who expressed their hopes quietly and freely; of women and children who, because they are weak, could not hurt anyone or endanger the public order. . . . This act alone carried out in a moment (of unconsciousness!) by the police who are men and as such have mothers, wives, sisters and children, suppresses civilization in one blow, destroys culture and attacks the most sacred, noble, and delicate part of humanity."[131] Reportedly, more than twenty women were wounded and one died in the melee. In reporting the story, the journalist invoked a gendered paradigm of women as helpless and dependent, one that existed in tension with the FOCH's own claims of women's revolutionary potential. Another commentary inspired by this riot claimed that women still had to be properly educated for labor militancy, referring to the women of the Russian Revolution as a prime example.[132] This kind of variety in the representation of working women's capacity for revolt demonstrates how FOCH militants employed multiple strategies to reach a variety of audiences in their drive to expand union membership in the 1920s, using gendered assumptions about women's capabilities to provoke both men and women to militant action.

Even in the variety of approaches suggested here, the problem of female militancy was a consistently gendered one; according to numerous working-class journalists and leaders, neither women workers nor housewives escaped easily from their weak, conservative characteristics. The persistence of these stereotypes of female passivity and intransigence, despite evidence to the contrary reported in the same newspapers, tips us off to the possibility that such discourse was something other than a transparent, objective reflection of reality. Because of the attributes of their sex, women as a group were likened to those male workers who, betraying their lack of virility, declined to participate in working-class associations or, worse, crossed picket lines. Women who defied these stereotypes—attending union meetings, walking picket lines, and speaking at rallies—were only exceptions who proved the rule of women's social "otherness" and who, through their inversion of gender stereotypes, reaffirmed the masculine character of labor militancy.

Complaints about women's counterrevolutionary or passive nature thus formed an important part of broader political rhetoric that instructed working-class men how to "fight like men and not cry like women"[133] and extended their duties as militants to raising revolutionary consciousness among their female companions and workmates. The resulting rhetorical bind for labor organizers may have been that the requirements of the female militant (bravery, self-interest, assertiveness) contradicted the very female characteristics considered essential to working-class femininity (sexual vulnerability, inexperience, physical weakness) and on which labor militants relied to inspire the male rank and file to action. In other words, how could women be militants if they were not, in the strictest (masculine) sense of the term, workers? Over the long run, the most consistent argument for female participation was one based exclusively on class solidarity, extending the call for revolution to women as wives, mothers, and sisters, and occasionally, perhaps, as workers. When they were not addressed simply as workers, women were usually invited to support sporadic labor actions as dependent members of working-class households.

Conclusions

On the face of it, the incorporation of women's organizations into the history of organized labor, however necessary, does little to alter the narrative of male workers' organizing in Chile. A closer examination of the discourse of labor organizers, however, reveals how the male-dominated labor movement relied on gendered paradigms, both implicit and explicit, to explain the existence of a female workforce and to rally male workers against their employers. The factory seamstress and her counterpart, the prostitute, became labor's favorite symbols for the perversity of capitalist domination. Capital had managed to enslave working-class women through factory work and prostitution, which implied that working-class men could no longer provide them with adequate sexual and economic protection. Not only did such fictions contain the potentially disruptive changes in working-class patriarchy initiated by women's widespread employment, but they also became effective rhetorical strategies with which to illustrate the extremity of capitalist injustice.

Given the undesirability of women's wage work from almost every angle, the central issue for organized labor that emerged after 1900 was what to do about the reality of women's factory work. Clearly, women's work more generally was not a major concern, because female employment in laundry, commerce, and domestic service was rarely addressed. Namely, women's presence in factory jobs became a pressing concern precisely because it threatened working-class patriarchy in significant ways: it put women almost on a level with men as wage earners; it literally placed women under the direction of men who were not family members in the male space of the factory; and their presence there increased the downward pressure on wages and, with some exceptions, threatened to undermine the "virility" of the labor movement. In response, some labor journalists repeatedly characterized women as unfit for manual labor and expressed their fundamental skepticism about female labor militancy, advocating in its place a kind of revolutionary female domesticity. These obstacles easily strengthened recommendations to increase male guidance and oversight to show working women the best way to lend support to their men. Even the symbolic and rhetorical models for female militancy that anarchists introduced into the labor movement at the turn of the century tended to reinforce the perception that women workers were intrinsically vulnerable and required male guidance. And, despite the contradictions that emerged at times between the real activism of women workers and the fictions that male labor leaders constructed about them, this juxtaposition reveals the "seamy underside" of Chilean working-class politics, in which stereotyped representations of working women as weak and victimized formed an integral part of masculine class identities and political strategies.[134] Because women were not expected to liberate themselves, the labor press also addressed the issue of how to create female revolutionary consciousness, relying in large part on women's roles as wives, mothers, daughters, and sisters to draw them into labor politics. What many of these campaigns failed to address, however, was the identity and consciousness of women as workers in their own right. The socialist movement for worker feminism that surged between 1905 and 1908 was one systematic attempt to do just that.

4

Somos Todas Obreras!

Socialists and Working-Class Feminism

"Our true emancipation lies within us," the typesetter and editor Carmela Jeria wrote in 1907, "and must be the work of women themselves."[1] In that paraphrase of Marx, Jeria articulated the close link between class struggle and gender emancipation that came to characterize socialist labor strategies in early-twentieth-century Chile. In the years after the turn of the century, explicit and sustained support for women workers' struggles came primarily from the newspapers and male resistance societies associated with the Recabarren wing of the Democratic Party in Santiago and Valparaíso. Articles in the Democratic press regularly profiled specific forms of female exploitation in the workplace—protesting their deleterious effects on working-class families and on the socialist movement—and union organizers actively sought to increase female union membership: Santiago's male shoe-workers, for example, urged female stitchers to join their union in 1906 by declaring, "Somos todas obreras!" (We are all women workers).[2] This convergence of female unionization strategies with the rhetoric of gender equality produced a kind of working-class feminism that represented one of the fundamental characteristics of Chilean socialism in the early twentieth century.

In their declarations of support for female emancipation, labor journalists, union activists, and key Democratic leaders—both male and female—described their response to the problems caused by women's paid employment as "worker feminism" (*feminismo obrero*): an analysis of society, labor struggle, and women's roles that promoted female emancipation through a strategy of active solidarity between male and female workers in union politics. Even though most of these activists, including female union leaders, agreed that women's wage work was intrinsically undesirable, they nevertheless embraced the goal of recruiting women workers into union ranks. Significantly, concepts of male and female in relation to wage work in turn shaped the worker feminist defense of women and their families in ways that were not always consistent with the more radical emancipatory claims of some worker feminists. Against male unionists' claims to support sexual equality, for example, worker feminists proffered evidence of male domination in working-class families and in the labor movement. Worker feminist discourse affirmed that women workers had legitimate demands of their own within class struggle, demands that mandated autonomous female organization and support from male workers in socialist politics.

This growing attention to women workers in the Democratic press also coincided with the founding of several newspapers and associations for women factory workers, which constituted a veritable worker feminist movement within Chilean socialism. The Democratic Party resources and propaganda directed to the cause of worker feminism effectively supported a dramatic increase in female unionization and journalistic expression between 1905 and 1908. As a result, female labor leaders rose to prominence in the socialist press and labor organizations for this brief period, fleshing out the rhetoric of working-class feminism in writing and in practice. This chapter begins by tracing socialist discourse about women's work and activism in the early 1900s to show how changing expectations about women, work, and activism conditioned the language and strategies of socialist politics in the first decade of the twentieth century. Even though Chilean socialism gave expression to radical demands for gender equality, this worker feminist movement and its leaders also drew on fundamental continuities with nonfeminist positions on "the woman question" in labor circles: the affirmation of the sexual division of labor, emphasis on female virtue, and representations of revolutionary motherhood. What was more distinctive to this expression of working women's rights was the participation and leadership of women labor activists, who grounded abstract calls for gender uplift in political practice for the first time in the history of Chilean workers.

Although socialist attention to the goal of female emancipation attenuated sharply after the last women workers' newspaper ceased publication in 1908, women remained active in these unions and in the FOCH through the 1910s, as Marxist unionism recovered some of its former momentum after 1917. Communist discourse of the 1920s only occasionally addressed "the woman question" as such, but FOCH congresses and newspapers increasingly emphasized the importance of female militancy in the FOCH after 1922, thereby offering an alternative

to competing anarchist characterizations of women as inherently passive and conservative. Even though the sustained militancy of women
workers constituted a potential threat to the patriarchal aspirations of
working-class men, socialist leaders consistently chose solidarity with
working women over the impractical ideal of keeping women at home
on male salaries. The strength of early working-class feminism among
Chilean socialists helped to make such a strategy politically appealing to
communist organizers of the 1920s because it joined short-term goals
such as preserving family income and broadening strike actions with the
longer-term ideal of gender equality, already a well-established principle in the rhetoric of Chilean socialism. This continuing support for
working-class feminism encouraged female activism and permitted the
partial erosion of the "oxymoron of the woman worker." In these circles,
obreras claimed occupational and class identifications that gave them a
new kind of footing in men's labor politics and permitted debates on the
meaning of sexual equality to flourish.

The Genesis of Worker Feminism

The types of feminism that have emerged in recent Chilean history are as
diverse as the political and social origins of groups that first popularized
the term at the turn of the century. Although liberal feminism can trace
its roots back to Martina Barros's 1873 translation of Mill's *The Subjugation of Women*, terms such as "feminism" and "women's emancipation"
came into currency among working-class authors at least a decade before
the emergence of feminist "conversations" among middle- and upper-
class women in the 1910s.[3] By the turn of the century, working-class
authors were using the term "feminist" to refer to women's class-based
activism, bourgeois women's campaigns to promote women's rights, and
suffrage movements in Europe and the United States.[4] Similarly, according to Chilean labor activists the "emancipation of women" encompassed a variety of social, political, and economic agendas for changing
women's lives. Anarchists tended to use the term feminist exclusively to
refer to (and to denigrate) bourgeois women; however, many socialists
embraced the term, appropriating its revolutionary connotations and
presenting feminism as the female equivalent of male labor militancy.[5]

   In the Chilean labor movement, the idea of female emancipation first
gained currency in anarchist newspapers and meetings, only later becoming popular among union leaders and journalists affiliated with the
Democratic Party. As elsewhere in the Southern Cone, anarchist writers

of the turn of the century identified the emancipation of women with the overthrow of all forms of social, economic, and political hierarchy.[6] Appearing in many of the short-lived anarchist papers published in Santiago after 1900, anarchist critiques of female subordination were predicated on the common theme of "the enslaved woman" or the historic tendency of men to oppress women, even as laws, technology, and education eroded the real differences between the sexes.[7] Although anarchists' radical critique of sexual hierarchy—manifest in women's subordination to the Church and to marriage—was not linked to any specific mobilization of working-class women, their analysis permeated the labor press across the ideological spectrum, in part because of the chaotic and undefined nature of Chilean workers' associations in this period.[8]

Though references to female exploitation were commonplace in Chilean political discourse of the period, the most consistent attempts to combat female subordination through unionization were championed by journalists and militants associated with the Democratic Party. The resulting rhetoric of "worker feminism" evolved in conjunction with the women's mutual aid and resistance societies associated with the Democratic Party. Although Democratic newspapers in most urban areas consistently addressed themes related to women, the printed campaign for working women's rights per se figured most prominently in the pages of urban newspapers such as *El Luchador* (1901–1907) and *La Reforma* (1906–1908), culminating in two papers edited for and by women workers: *La Alborada* (1905–1907) and *La Palanca* (1908).[9] Unlike the gamut of other anarchist, mutualist, and socialist publications that gave sporadic (and usually polemical) attention to women's issues, these papers reflected the participation and audience of unionized women workers, particulary seamstresses. The papers featured the writings of prominent female activists, printed announcements and reports from women workers' associations, and advertised women's clothing, medical services, and employment opportunities. The fact that the Democratic union activists of Santiago and Valparaíso used the labor press as a tool for education and mobilization of the working class may lead to an exaggerated picture of Democratic successes in mobilizing women workers, but because women workers themselves wrote for these newspapers, they provide a unique source with which to examine the experience of women in the labor movement. At the same time, these writings reveal just how deeply socialist gender egalitarianism was predicated on the ultimate ideal of the patriarchal working-class family.

Luís Emilio Recabarren became a key actor in the emergence of worker feminism in Chile, not only because of his leadership in Democratic politics as a whole, but also because he actively spearheaded the campaign to unionize women workers. Chilean women's historians have usually categorized Recabarren as a feminist, both for his texts analyzing women's condition and for his involvement in establishing women's groups in the Chilean north in 1913.[10] Although this reading, like much Marxist historiography of workers' movements in Chile, runs the risk of overstating Recabarren's impact, he did in fact explicitly encourage women workers to unionize and affirmed the crucial role of women—particularly working women—in Democratic politics. Writing primarily in the northern Democratic press, Recabarren drew on anarchist tropes of women's "double slavery" to argue for increased female participation and to elicit men's support for it: "Those of us who call ourselves socialists, who struggle for the liberty of the oppressed and enslaved, must take into account the fact that the woman suffers a double slavery, and so we should also try to liberate woman from this captivity. . . . If we love the woman as a mother, as a sister, as a partner, and as a daughter; if we respect her lovingly in those roles, we must also respect her when she is our friend."[11]

In subsequent articles, Recabarren reiterated the theme of women's economic and sexual slavery—"she endures the slavery in the home and the workshop, factory, store or office"—and dramatized women's victimization to drive his point home with readers: "Sad is the daily scene that a woman runs through in her most intimate thoughts; when the cold winter day breaks, she must abandon the gentle [embraces] of her lukewarm bed, or tear herself away from the loving lap of her sick mother to go and expend her little force in the brutal work of the day, which gives her a miserable wage that barely compensates for her miseries." When Recabarren then went on to recommend that women workers organize their own newspaper, he confirmed his personal support for women's activism: "If this [newspaper] is a good idea and is well received, we would not refuse to cooperate with sincere enthusiasm and actions to make it a success."[12] These brief texts testify to Recabarren's unequivocal support for the political activism of women workers, as well as the rhetorical similarity between anarchist and Marxist texts on the woman question prior to the 1920s. Although Recabarren himself apparently authored none of the articles that appeared in women's newspapers, he was nevertheless omnipresent, for those papers reported every detail of his travels, meetings, and speeches.[13] In later years, his involvement with the Centros Belén de Sárraga and writings on women's emancipation in

Soviet Russia confirm Recabarren's consistent commitment to improving working women's lot through political struggle.[14]

What this kind of emphasis on Recabarren's role as "Chile's first feminist" tends to overlook, however, is how working-class feminism became most pronounced in Santiago and Valparaíso (rather than the north, Recabarren's political base). Working-class movements in Santiago were probably more directly influenced by local papers such as *El Luchador*, edited by a father-son team active in Doctrinaire Democratic circles (PDD). Although the paper was edited by two men and was largely concerned with familiarizing readers with the goals of socialism, *El Luchador* also printed a variety of articles of a feminist nature, promoted the efforts of female activists, and involved several contributors who went on to play significant roles in the articulation of worker feminism. An early article briefly stated the paper's programmatic support for "the rights of the proletarian woman," and a 1903 editorial elaborated a more detailed and critical analysis of the sources of female oppression: "We must recognize that, if there have been few women who have achieved [distinction in arts and sciences], men are at fault, because they have always considered her a mere instrument, turning her into a docile domestic slave." The editorial then went on to advocate fairly traditional strategies—characteristic of mutual aid associations and liberal feminism—to solve women's ignorance and fanaticism: "We must try to develop her intelligence, this is the only way to achieve her complete emancipation."[15]

Unlike the vague and utopian promises elaborated by other advocates of female emancipation, however, *El Luchador* also highlighted the participation of a number of prominent female labor activists to demonstrate the viability of female agency and leadership in workers' movements. Like most Democratic publications, *El Luchador* lavished praise on the Society for the Protection of Women and its founder, Juana Roldán de Alarcón: "She believes that her work is not yet complete, and for this reason she takes every chance she gets to do what she can to ensure that her partners in sacrifice become educated so that they stop being slaves of fanaticism and of the caprices of their oppressors and executioners: the aristocracy."[16] The accompanying list of workers' associations that had benefited from Roldán's participation suggests the ongoing nature of female activism that papers such as *El Luchador* were beginning to recognize. The paper also introduced the first writings of Carmela Jeria, just months before she would begin to edit her own newspaper for women.[17] These brief references to women's activism mark the emergence of worker feminism in Democratic politics as a movement grounded in female agency and leadership.

The attention given to female leaders in the paper was consistent with the editors' support for female education and emancipation, yet it also reflected the ties of friendship and family that undergirded Democratic sociability more generally. When Lucrecia Campos de Díaz, wife and mother to the editors of *El Luchador*, died in 1906, for example, Jeria penned letters of condolence to the editors and published an emotional obituary in her own paper for women, *La Alborada*.[18] These social and political connections worked both ways, of course; in September 1905, *El Luchador*'s social announcements included this promotion of Jeria's forthcoming publication for women workers: "The distinguished and intelligent señorita Carmela Jeria Gómez will begin to edit a socialist newspaper in our neighboring port city on September 8. As far as we know, a very select group of worker intellectuals will participate in the paper. Of course, *El Luchador* sends the expected greeting to our new female colleague: we wish her great success in her campaign, just as we fervently congratulate señorita Jeria on her efforts to promote the emancipation of proletarian women."[19]

Jeria's opening editorial in *La Alborada*, which over the next two years would become the primary medium for worker feminist propaganda, similarly emphasized the wider organizational context for her new paper: "We are not seeking glory or gain: as we all know, every journalistic effort leaves only a bitter taste. We have no other resources for the publication of *La Alborada* than the firm convictions that animate us and the satisfaction that we feel when we support our brothers and tell them that their proletarian [sisters] are at their side to face the dangers of the struggle and [cry] 'Forward!'"[20] Jeria concluded this call for cross-gender solidarity by stating her expectation that men would surely rally to the feminist cause. In fact, women and men wrote for *La Alborada* in equal numbers, and the male editors of the Democratic daily paper *La Reforma* regularly declared their solidarity with women's journalistic efforts, which they claimed demonstrated "eloquently the frank spirit of comradeship that rules the hearts of worker journalists."[21] The circulation of news stories, article reprints, and contributors among *La Alborada* and other Democratic papers (primarily *La Reforma*, but including Democratic publications in the north) placed that paper squarely within a growing network of Democratic political activism.[22]

La Alborada was first published in Valparaíso on September 10, 1905, and was distributed bimonthly in major cities with only a few omissions

DIRECTORA
Carmela Jeria G

Casilla 1748
SANTIAGO

La Alborada

Número suelto
5 centavos

OFICINA
A. Prat 485

PUBLICACION FEMINISTA

APARECE LOS DOMINGOS

AÑO II. | SANTIAGO, DICIEMBRE 9 DE 1906 | NUM. 23

LA DIRECCION
DE
LA ALBORADA

suplica a todas las personas que se interesen por esta publicacion, se sirvan tomar algunos números para espenderlos en círculos obreros o bien entre sus relaciones.

Un bello triunfo
en perspectiva

La huelga forzada a que están sometidos los operarios mecánicos, fundidores, caldereros y torneros, nos hace entrever,—que si la gran familia obrera se une en estos momentos, con los benéficos lazos de la solidaridad,— puede obtenerse un hermoso triunfo en esta desigual lucha, que el elemento productor está sometido por la tiranía odiosa y despótica del Capital.

Pensamos, que la firme resolucion de los compañeros mecánicos, en no ceder a los caprichos de nuestros verdugos y la union jeneral de los diversos gremios arbitrando medios para ayudar a sostener a los compañeros faltos de trabajo, nos traería 'el mas hermoso triunfo obrero, de los últimos tiempos.

Triunfo, que a la vez de ser positivo y honroso para los compañeros sometidos a huelga forzosa, sería moral y de prestijio, para esta gran colectividad dispersa, que batalla afanosamente por realizar el comun y humanitario ideal.

* *

La guerra entre el Capital y el Trabajo!...

¡Que enjambre de tristes observaciones, sujiere en nuestro cerebro esta maldita frase, que cual estigma de oprobio y maldad, pesa sobre la honrada y noble labor del elemento productor!

¡Como siento oprimirse de dolor a mi piadosa alma, ahogarse en mi garganta las palabras y confundirse mis ideas, al pensar en el triste encadenamiento de miserias y dolores que habrá traido a los hogares de esos dos mil compañeros de trabajo, el simple capricho del esplotador de nuestras fuerzas y ladron de nuestro pan, el odioso y maldito Capital!

Y cosa estraña—mientras esos asesinos de nuestro qienestar declaran, sarcásticamente, que conocen la justicia de la peticion de sus operarios, al pedir un pedazo de pan mas, para su hogar, el abrigo y sosten necesario para la vida—ellos, los cuervos, declaran que al acceder a la razon que reconocen, obtendrían menos ganancias, *menos utilidades....*

Y ante la espectativa, de que unos cuantos pesos disminuya el oro de sus arcas, prefieren cometer el gran y cobarde crímen de dejar a dos mil familias sin abrigo y sin pan...

Como un torrente desbordado siento brotar de mi cerebro, miles de miles de santas maldiciones para esos crueles buitres, que gozan con el sufrimiento de tantos incentes que ajitándose en sus cunitas pedirán calor y pan...

* *

Y mientras los padres, hijos y hermanos, allá en el seno de la reunion, en que se infiltra la fuerza de voluntad para resistir el movimiento, sienten rodar por sus tostadas mejillas amargas lágrimas de rabia, que se secan en sus gargantas ávidas de pedir venganza, nosotras, las hermanas de esplotacion y trabajo, sacrifiquemos parte de nuestro jornal, para ayudar a nuestros hermanos a resistir los caprichos del enemigo comun.

Veinte o treinta centavos, entre dos o cuatro personas, nada representa, pero veinte o cuarenta centavos entre miles de bestias de carga que impasibles soportamos la mas vergonzosa e indigna de las esplotaciones, hará una suma que enjugará muchas lágrimas de esos tiernos e inocentes esclavitos, que impacientes en sus cunitas, se ajitarán pidiendo pan!...

No permitamos que por egoismo y falta de solidaridad se nos escape de las manos, un triunfo que nos es comun.

La *órden del dia* de toda sociedad de resistencia debe de ser: Proteccion a los valientes compañeros mecánicos.

De este modo apagaremos y ahogaremos con nuestra enerjía, la insaciable sed de oro de ese monstruo enemigo el Capital...

ESTHER VALDES DE DIAZ.

Santiago, Diciembre 6 de 1906.

Preparativos bélicos
ES INUTIL SOÑAR...

Por la prensa burguesa, nuestros buenos lectores se habrán impuesto del afan con que se discute en consejos de gabinetes, en sesiones secretas de la Cámara de Senadores y Diputados y aun en los salones de las casas particulares de la casta autócrata, el modo como poder distribuir un centenar de millones de pesos en la compra de grandes acorazados y una infinidad de elementos bélicos que necesitaría Chile para sostener una guerra internacional, o entre los mismos hijos de ésta tan abusivamente llamada república.

La clase dirijente de Chile y Perú, en beneficio propio quieren que se produzca un nuevo, acontecimiento sangriento, como en 1879, pero por desgracia, esos magnates no se han fijado en que el proletariado, o sea la carne de cañon, de éstas dos naciones, los une un formidable lazo de amistad; saben que son hermanos; saben que la guerra es un crímen cometido con premeditacion y alevosía; saben que es un negocio burgues; tienen el ejemplo de los veteranos del 79 y en fin han llegado a comprender que la patria es una farsa y que mientras ellos se devoran encarnizadamente, los oligarcas se rien *desenfrenadamente.*

En cambio, por felicidad, los pueblos de Perú y Chile se han instruido y educado; han llegado a comprender que solo pensar en ir a un campo de batalla es sentenciar a su familia con el hambre, con la miseria y con las miles felonías de que pueden ser víctimas de parte de esos ladrones de honras que se quedan en los pueblos, gobernando a mujeres, niños e imbéciles!

¡Cuántas familias han muerto por necesidades, mientras sus hombres, esos valientes del 79, andaban en el norte defendiendo un suelo que no les pertene!

Basta solo una rápida ojeada y un momento de pensar para cerciorarse de la conducta villana, de esa casta priviijiada, que no les importa ver correr un rio de sangre emanada del cuerpo del proletariado en cambio de poder acrecentar sus fortunas en algunas cantidades de dinero.

Tan inhumanos son los oligarcas chilenos, peruanos y los de las demas naciones, como lo eran los jesuitas, los inquisidores, que de jeneracion en jeneracion se vienen recordando con repugnancia, por los crímenes que cometian con la clase indijente.

¿Por qué Chile quiere robar a la fuerza bruta esa ostension de terreno que se llama Tacna y Arica?

Porque es un suelo de riquezas que para los oligarcas sería un pecado largarla, cuando con eso pueden reembolsar el dinero que derrochan en sus orjías, o en el tapete verde.

¿Por qué en vez de botar esa enorme cantidad de dinero, en compra de armas y otros elementos guerreros, no destinan una centésima parte a la ins·

---

12. Masthead of *La Alborada,* feminist workers' publication.
Source: La Alborada 1, no. 10 (9 December 1906): 1. Courtesy of the Chilean National Library, Newspapers Division.

until it ceased suddenly with the edition of May 19, 1907. In comparison with the numerous workers' papers that *aparece cuando puede* (publish whenever possible), the consistent appearance of *La Alborada* over a twenty-month period qualifies it as a relatively successful publication for its kind.[23] Similar in style to most papers published by workers' associations, the four-page paper included editorials, news notes, articles, correspondence, prose, drama, poetry, announcements, and advertisements. Founded on the principle that women should take a leading role in their own emancipation, *La Alborada* demonstrated "that a woman can also do redeeming work on behalf of her brothers through journalism,"[24] and sought to cultivate a female readership, particularly among women workers. Although *La Alborada* was clearly intended for a female audience, the paper's original masthead identified the paper simply as the "defender of the proletarian classes" and a "workers' social publication."[25] Editor Jeria did not turn her attention from Democratic political concerns to address explicitly the sexual oppression of women workers for almost a year: "When the daughters of the people find themselves free, completely free, of old worries, of stupid routines, then they will go forth resolved and serene, protected by their own intellectual forces, to conquer those rights that until today have been the exclusive monopoly of men."[26] Here Jeria implied for the first time that there were struggles particular to female workers, but her emphasis remained on the cross-gender solidarity necessary for class struggle.

Through editorials that described women's struggle to articulate and disseminate their views, *La Alborada* promoted a vision of female education and agency modeled after the paper's editor, Carmela Jeria; carpenter Ricardo Guerrero proclaimed that, "from the columns of her paper, *La Alborada*, [she] will convert her pen into a battering ram and make it the best feminist champion, the bravest defender of the oppressed."[27] The daughter of policeman Mauricio Jeria A. (a "worker intellectual" active in workers' societies of Valparaíso), Jeria reported that she was working as a typographer with the Litografía Gillet of Valparaíso when she founded *La Alborada*. Soon thereafter, according to Jeria, she was dismissed from her job for refusing to give up her political activities: "There was no other way than to choose the most honorable and noble way, in order to be able to take part freely in the crusade of regeneration in which the working classes are engaged today."[28] In reality, by 1905 Jeria was already well enough known to have served as a featured speaker at Democratic meetings and banquets, and in that year she also traveled as a delegate to the 1905 Workers' Social Convention in Chillán.

From the start, the paper's creators conceived of *La Alborada* as a weapon—almost in a literal, physical sense—for the defense of women workers. In one story published in the first edition of the paper, an obrera who had just been fired presented her boss with the (yet unpublished) paper, saying, "Here is *La Alborada* in which they tell the truth. If this happens again, I'll send you to jail bound and gagged."[29] The paper itself was often described as protector, comfort, and weapon for the woman worker. In the dramatic monologue "Sin madre!," for example, a young woman resisted the offers of a lustful young man by comforting herself with her mother's dying advice and *La Alborada*: "Books and this newspaper have nourished my mind with fine lessons that I will use to benefit my well-being and my happiness."[30] The paper's contributors clearly ascribed to the belief, then common among labor journalists, that revolutionary propaganda would strengthen working-class culture and promote revolutionary change by raising the individual and collective consciousness.

From the start, the paper's principal contributors affirmed their primary allegiance to the revolutionary cause, stressing their intention to incorporate women into a labor movement hitherto dominated by men, rather than to create a separate women's movement.[31] Writing for the paper in 1905, Juana Roldán de Alarcón protested the "incredible selfishness" of an all-male association that had refused to admit women arguing for the integration rather than autonomy of women: "We can call it this for now; well, it is inconceivable in these days that the [workers'] society men—who make such a big deal about women's progress and how necessary they believe it is, since they recognize women's rights as part of the natural and logical order of things—now refuse to make a place in their social order for the woman, even to a compañera of their own trade, to the woman who is or might later be the very compañera in their homes." Roldán scolded the unnamed, offending institution, arguing that although men may have meant well by telling women to form their own societies, "you have taken a step back in the praised social advance."[32] Correspondent Eloisa Zurita de Vergara, on the other hand, noted the paper's salutary effects on male workers, who "are already coming to our aid, those workers who love female emancipation."[33] In her regular news column, Zurita confirmed that the Democratic Party was intimately involved in supporting women's daily struggles by documenting the activities of women workers' societies, particularly the involvement of prominent Democratic leaders; she kept *La Alborada's* readers informed about Recabarren's travels, the marriages and widowing of prominent female activists, and the fundraising activities of northern women's associations.[34] These contributions reflect the perceived compatability between women's mobilization and Democratic politics (and sociability) that marked worker feminist discourse.

Worker feminism developed and deepened the existing analyses of female subordination and emancipation already evident in the labor press of various ideological orientations. For this group of socialist journalists, female subordination both in the workplace and at home was attributed, first and foremost, to the economic injustices of industrial capitalism.[35] Because women were typically employed in unskilled tasks, they noted, solidarity against employers was difficult to maintain in the face of available pools of unskilled labor. Moreover, mechanization had opened some jobs to women and decreased the pool of skilled jobs available to men: "Jobs that until recently required exclusively male efforts, quickly started to be worked by us [women]. Why? Because our condition offered more guarantees and benefits for Capital. Our bodies were more productive—we worked without complaining, more hours—and we accepted half the salary that a man would get: and also, we meekly accepted the hateful demands and caprices of Capital that man would not accept!"[36] Worker feminists recognized extreme economic necessity, either for self or family, as the primary motivation for women's wage work. Women's performance of this duty, which subjected them to conditions contrary to their natures and domestic obligations, were considered a temporary misfortune on the road to social revolution: "If it is not yet possible to get [the woman] out of the factory, because there she contributes mechanically to supporting the family, we will then seek the means to prevent her labor from being the fuel of exploitation and wasted energy."[37] But in this ostensibly temporary stage where women were forced to work for wages, women's ability to work in the "labors appropriate to their sex" also became their saving grace: "And the woman who has been left without her husband, her father, who does she turn to? To you, my needle! You relieve the soul, hold back the tears and provide the daily bread! You make it possible to scorn the promises made by lying lips: you dignify woman!"[38] These kinds of heroic and conflicting images of working women—as the embattled victims of capital, the shame of underpaid husbands and fathers, the saviors of their own virtue and guarantors of family survival—resurfaced throughout the worker feminist press, testifying to Chilean socialists' ambivalent, sometimes contradictory views on the identity of women workers.

For women to overcome their economic subordination, they first had to be instructed about the *multiple* threats to their well-being and learn how to fight them. Significantly, women were advised that they had to undertake their own liberation; men—because of ego, vice, or prejudice—could not do it for them: "If the men do not accompany us with sufficient sincerity, it is up to us to obtain our own well-being."[39] In this sense, Jeria and others were equally critical of women and men for the perpetuation of female subordination. Echoing a more widespread complaint about women's nature, several contributors deemed vanity to be women's most pernicious trait, because it allowed them to be manipulated by others. Selva, a regular, pseudonymous, ostensibly female contributor, emphasized that vanity made women complicit in their own subordination: "In my judgment, the origin of the slavery that oppresses us is not the ignorance that surrounds us, nor that we are unable to begin to share with man the problems that come up in his life, but rather and exclusively [the origin] is our unwise attempt to please them in their vanities and follies."[40] R. Gutiérrez R. concurred, arguing that if women were not able to eradicate their own vanity, men would always take advantage of them: "I do not believe, nor will I ever believe, that woman can emancipate herself from male selfishness and the boss's greed—no matter how much she studies and organizes in resistance societies—unless she manages to change her own habits. On the contrary, she will always be man's toy and the boss's instrument, men who take advantage of her ambition and vanity."[41] Such criticisms were usually accompanied by suggestions about how women could alter their sensibilities through socialist consciousness, and Jeria's own trajectory from typeshop worker to newspaper editor and Democratic activist was often cited as the best example of women's progression from ignorance to enlightenment.

Worker feminists' faith in the malleability of gender characteristics is most clearly evident in their consistent advocacy for female education, an emphasis this press shared with many women workers' societies as well as bourgeois feminists. Because women were the principal victims of "despotism and ignorance," worker feminists argued, they could best protect society from these ills through education and organization.[42] Baudina Pessini argued, for example, that ignorance was not a fixed characteristic of woman's nature: "They say that the woman is the eternal slave of the home because of natural law. . . . I do not think that this law is natural, because we [women] do not have enough freedom to educate ourselves." This characterization of women's subordinate position affirmed, rather than denied, women's intellectual and activist capacities. First, however, women must be allowed to educate and organize themselves: "The woman has just as much right as a man to enjoy complete freedom. Why then is the woman denied this natural disposition? Will we continue, as always, at the pace of a turtle toward the oasis of freedoms that belongs to each of us? Where is the equality that should exist between man and woman? Perhaps we do not also struggle for existence? Is it logical that the man should be free and the woman a slave? . . . Permit me to ask my sisters in slavery not to waste any effort to obtain a little education."[43] Significantly, contributors to *La Alborada* advocated female education not only to end women's slavery, but also to bring harmony and stability to working-class homes. Education in certain trades, for example, would enable women to gain better returns in the workforce: "The education of women should also extend to what is called the exercise of occupations and professions, since she is man's companion, she must be prepared to help him in supporting the home, because as they are equal in the narrow temple of the family, doubtless they have equal rights and duties."[44] Female education would also improve women's performance of domestic roles: "A young woman who is well-educated in school, who has good examples to imitate and is a good daughter, will be a model wife and unequaled mother."[45]

Worker feminists' discussions of the value of female education corresponded closely with their views on women's role in the home more generally. Even as worker feminists focused their attention on female exploitation in the workplace, their analysis of the sexual division of labor remained deeply traditional. Although the women writing for *La Alborada* were workers and activists themselves, they nevertheless articulated a vision of female employment that was justified only by family necessity, a necessity that would vanish in an ideal, postrevolutionary world of male-headed households. The paper's principal editor, Carmela Jeria, and later, Esther Valdés de Díaz, argued that the social revolution they promoted would return women workers to their "natural" position in society as guardians of the domestic sphere: beyond the struggle for class emancipation, women would find "purer satisfactions and teach the proletarian woman about her noble mission as daughter, wife and mother."[46] Like other efforts directed at women workers in the early twentieth century, the deep-seated emphasis in Chilean worker feminism on the emancipation of women from work itself—even as feminists struggled to organize and educate women workers—testified to the powerful pull of the "cultural paradox" of the woman worker in the labor movement, as elsewhere in Chilean society.

One of the most unusual aspects of socialist worker feminism relative to other working-class texts on the woman question, however, was some contributors' willingness to implicate working-class men—and even labor leaders—in the problem of female subordination. These authors, including several male contributors, argued that female exploitation also corrupted working-class masculinity. Capitalism had not only made men unable to keep their women at home, but had perverted their attitudes toward working women, who were, after all, the wives and daughters of other workers: "Authoritarian, pigs without any sanction, shrunken by debauchery and vices, without any healthy morals to limit their passions, it is natural that they do not see in the woman the angel of light who inspires the most noble sentiment; rather they see the fuel for their lasciviousness and evil passions, to which pursuit they dedicate themselves in order to sink her in the mire like a sport or recreation for their useless and onerous lives as workers."[47] Such failed, unrevolutionary men were also criticized (by other men) for squandering their meager wages in drink, gambling, and prostitution. The carpenter and prolific contributor Ricardo Guerrero dedicated several articles to this topic, lamenting the deterioration of working-class families because of male vice: "The evils are obvious: there are practically no happy homes; we have completely lost our good work habits of sobriety and savings, and we live in eternal merrymaking, without worrying about anything or anyone. . . . This is the result of what fathers teach their sons and it is no better if we examine mothers and the lessons they teach their daughters."[48] In response to a report from Concepción about a man who got drunk and beat his wife, Guerrero described this as shameful behavior for an enlightened man, and urged men to give up drinking and to treat their wives better.[49]

Part of the discourse of worker feminism, then, was an explicit mandate for men to understand and limit their power over women for the well-being of their families as well as for the cause of female emancipation. The arena for demonstrating this cross-gender solidarity was, first and foremost, the home, where mutual respect was touted as the key to domestic bliss: "The husband owes his wife the same consideration he wants for himself; even more [consideration], by the rights of her sex." In a rendition of worker feminism clearly directed at a male audience (and printed in *La Reforma*), men were exhorted to respect women and restrain their power over them: "No, gentlemen, you are not infallible gods; allow your wives to have every legitimate victory. They, like you, have souls that feel and minds that think." The author went on to urge women to show respect for their fathers and husbands: "You should *never* be demanding; you should always seem happy with what they can offer you with honor and dignity. Thus your care and presence will be compensated."[50]

Apparently, feminism was easier for socialist men to preach than to practice, and several contributors to *La Alborada* took unnamed male feminists to task for their hypocritical behavior. Commenting on his experience in the homes of several male labor leaders who espoused what he called feminist values, Nicolás Rodríguez reported "more than one case in which these ardent theorists of the integral development of women's rights conduct themselves privately in a way that contradicts what they preach on the stage or in the press. Their [female] companions have no rights, and are not given the respect they deserve, and do not get the instruction that their husbands advocate when they are outside of their own homes." Even worse, Rodríguez continued, male labor leaders often used feminism as a tool for seducing women: "The majority of the male heralds of feminism do not *feel* what they say, and the statements that they pile up for the honor and defense of women are in no way different in motive than those of any flattering lover to his darling." Rodríguez then went on to prescribe a dramatic reform in male behavior: "It is not possible nor logical that she should entrust her liberation to those who, full of old prejudices, think of her only as an instrument of pleasure or 'luxury furniture,' for anyone who can afford it to use. In order for man to truly help woman in her work of regeneration and natural recovery, he must clear the way of his own vices and raise himself in the moral order."[51] *La Alborada* and other Democratic papers thus provided a forum for some male activists to admonish working-class men not only for behaviors that were regularly described as "antisocial" (such as drinking, fighting, and womanizing), but also for their lack of consciousness about truly egalitarian gender relations.[52]

Such criticisms of male behavior, and of gender relations more generally, posed a potentially significant challenge to the socialist discourse of cross-gender solidarity because they publicly revealed the benefits that working-class men accrued through patriarchal control over female family members. Several ostensibly female authors went even further, beyond the criticism of male "misbehavior," to denounce men as a group. According to Selva, men were so accustomed to dominating women that they would never serve as proper allies: "That men should help us? . . . Sure, sure . . . ri-ight! . . . Not even! . . . They will eagerly hand us the tasty and disgraceful apple of the biblical Eden."[53] A. Calderón echoed this complaint about male domination by drawing a comparison between sexual discrimination in the workplace and in the home. Women workers, Calderón said, were constantly victimized by factory bosses, workshop managers, possessive fathers, and drunk husbands, but the worst was the continuing enslavement that was encouraged by their supposed allies, socialist men: "You revolutionaries, busy making and unmaking constitutions, how is it that you have not considered that all liberty will be a ghost while half of the human race lives in slavery?"[54] At times, this criticism of men in *La Alborada* was particularly scathing: P. P. Pretto lamented women's oppression by capital and "the absurd and fierce oppression by men, all the more tyrannical because it is so stupid."[55] Even the normally conciliatory Carmela Jeria remarked at one point on her encounter with male hypocrisy in the home of a supposed "advocate of women's liberty."[56] Such accounts conflicted with portraits most worker feminist writers drew of harmonious relations between working-class men and women, and questioned men's willingness to surrender their sexual privileges in the interest of female emancipation.

Esther Valdés de Díaz and Female Unionism

The fact that these discussions of male complicity were few and far between amid the plentiful news articles and editorials promoting cross-gender unity in class struggle suggests that these complaints were not, however, the primary concern of the paper's editors. Particularly during the first nine months of *La Alborada*'s publication, complaints about discrimination against women in the home and labor movement were often buried amid news of Democratic events, editorials on the virtues of socialism over anarchism, anticlerical diatribes, and flowery poetry. In her editorial marking the reopening of the paper in Santiago after an earthquake closed their Valparaíso offices, Jeria carefully restated the nonconfrontational position of her paper: "To present a paper to the proletarian woman produced by the efforts of her comrades [*compañeras*], so that she meditates and studies the best way to arrive at a level of true progress. . . . We don't want to be rivals with anyone, nor win laurels [for ourselves]."[57] Here again, Jeria rejected a separatist agenda for her journalistic project, insisting on the compatability between women's uplift and socialist revolution.

The most important result of the paper's relocation to Santiago was that it brought about increased attention to working women's issues and associations, particularly in Santiago. In this period, the paper broadened its pool of contributors to include working women such as Baudina

Pessini T., Esther Valdés de Díaz, and Blanca Poblete, all of whom provided substantive articles describing working women and their activism. In March of the following year the editorial staff of the paper even extended the following invitation to new contributors: "The women workers who are afraid or undecided as to how to organize their thoughts and suffer wondering whether or not their work will be published, must dismiss this doubt. This Staff will make it a duty to publish all works that denounce abuses and irregularities in workshops and factories."[58] The increasing attention given to working women's issues, which grounded feminist goals in the realities of women's factory work, also coincided with a surge of female mobilization spearheaded by resistance societies in Santiago. To the ongoing activities of the Sociedad Protección de la Mujer were added those of the Ateneo de Obreras and the Asociación de Costureras in July 1906. The female activism represented in these Democratic working women's societies became the nexus between an innovative social movement and the discourse of worker feminism.

Worker feminism and its corollary, solidarity between male and female workers, was the organizing idea behind the Women Workers' Club (Ateneo de Obreras), founded in July 1906 in the Democratic Casa del Pueblo. The club was considered part of the overall social revolution: "Since we consider it an indispensable duty of those of us who carry the banner in the social and economic struggles of the proletariat to promote women's campaigns to the greatest heights and successes, we comply with this duty by calling all of the women workers who are qualified and capable of doing so to attend the Club. Until now they have seemed a little indifferent in supporting this work. We make this call even to those male companions who . . . should attend in order to encourage the new promoters of that work."[59] Similar to male workers' clubs, the Women's Club called on female resistance societies to send representatives, or "female apostles," to "promote the intellectual development of the female sex."[60] The club began with a weekly lecture series and weekly classes in the Casa del Pueblo for women workers and their representatives. In August, the Ateneo collected funds for women affected by the Valparaíso earthquake, began to promote the organization of a union of laundresses and ironers "who have asked for our help,"[61] and called for mixed-sex organizations of the provinces to establish ties with the Ateneo.[62] As with other Democratic Party–affiliated organizations, one of the Ateneo's primary activities was to promote its publications: members of the group subscribed to *La Alborada* and distributed *La Reforma* every Sunday in the streets of Santiago.[63]

The most significant women's organization promoted in the pages of *La Alborada* was the Seamstresses Association (Asociacion de Costureras), founded shortly before the paper reopened in Santiago. On July 20, 1906, 120 seamstresses huddled together against the winter cold in the offices of *La Reforma*, definitively establishing their union as the Asociación de Costureras "Protección, Ahorro i Defensa."[64] Praised by *La Reforma* as "the awakening of feminism,"[65] the Seamstresses Association declared itself "an Association that will help us against the inhuman demands of capital which, represented by our bosses, exploits our forces like work machines, paying our labor with insignificant and measly wages." The directorate, led by seamstress and labor journalist Esther Valdés de Díaz, advocated social legislation to regulate work hours, institute Sunday rest, abolish night work, and provide just wages for working women.[66]

From the beginning, organizers lamented the union's inability to mobilize greater numbers of seamstresses. Significantly, Valdés de Díaz attributed this initial failure not to innate female passivity but to women workers' double duty at home and in the workplace. When not enough seamstresses arrived to convene the association for its first June meeting, for example, future president Valdés de Díaz noted that "our most glaring defect is not knowing how to distribute our time."[67] But later assessments of the union's slow growth were less forgiving; in a public letter inviting seamstresses to join the union, the new directorate lamented that "women's subordination is a sad and untold story that only we know and that has never come to light, because we do not have it in our character to complain, to protest in public, because we believe that we must accept the injustices of which we are victims as part of our situation." Even though this was one of the earliest resistance societies formed in Santiago, the directorate chastised seamstresses for being slow on the uptake: "Only we, the untiring needle workers, have boxed ourselves into the most punishable inactivity, into firm and apathetic indifference."[68] Nevertheless, by the end of its first year, the association had a membership of 350 seamstresses, had created a school and recreational center for members and their families,[69] and had attracted a sizable public to hear speeches from the seamstresses' leaders on its first anniversary.[70] The growth and activism of the Seamstresses Association, recorded in the pages of *La Alborada* and other Democratic papers, charts the mobilization of a small group of Santiago's obreras in the techniques of labor activism under the banner of worker feminism.

Once it reopened in Santiago, *La Alborada* quickly became Valdés

13. Asociación de Costureras "Protección, Ahorro i Defensa." *Source: El Obrero Ilustrado* 2, no. 29 (1 July 1907): 75. Courtesy of the Chilean National Library, Newspapers Division.

de Díaz's primary forum for promoting the Seamstresses Association, which she and others presented as a model for female organization at every opportunity. Like Carmela Jeria, Valdés de Díaz wrote that her involvement in labor politics had begun around 1904, when she began to read militant literature and attend mutual aid society meetings. Her stories about her own working experience dramatized her incipient rebellion: "When the madam forced me, along with my sisters, to keep working four, six, or more hours into the night, with the threat that if we didn't do it, we would be fired from her Workshop, my soul trembled with courage and bitter tears—precursors to what would soon be rebellion—moistened my throat, which was dry from the roughness of work and the fatigue that consumed my body."[71] Throughout her writings in *La Alborada* and speeches to the Seamstresses Association, Valdés de Díaz treated women workers' fears of labor unrest with great empathy, insisting on the formidable and multiple barriers to women's emancipation: "It is too bad to talk about this, but it is really true: the selfishness, cowardice and indifference that women workers show toward all of the ideas that would emancipate them from *the triple yoke* into which they are tied like a helpless mass. That yoke exploits their work, their ignorance, and their liberty . . . *in the home, the street, and the workshop.*"[72] In

14. Audience for the first anniversary of the Asociación de Costureras. *Source: El Obrero Ilustrado* 2, no. 30 (15 July 1907): 95. Courtesy of the Chilean National Library, Newspapers Division.

a heated exchange with J. Joaquín Salinas of *La Reforma,* Valdés de Díaz took the latter to task for his attack on women workers' passivity as "a condition of their sex." Women workers, she argued, stayed out of the labor movement because they had been conditioned to give in, mocked for their attempts to struggle, and denied the key to emancipation: education. Her own analysis of why women were not more active in their own defense was also negative, but more clearly implicated men in the formula of women's oppression: "Women's struggle and cooperation will be sterile while our protective compañeros conveniently fail to educate us to resist in this combat that is superior to the forces of men."[73] Evoking the principles of reciprocity and solidarity in the working class, Valdés de Díaz called for men to take the first step in undoing the much-derided "passivity" of women workers.

When she was not reporting on the activities of the Seamstresses Association or promoting female activism per se, Valdés de Díaz wrote extensively on the pressing need for protective legislation to ameliorate women's working conditions. In her series of articles entitled "Workers' Problems," published on the front page of *La Alborada* from March through May 1907, Valdés de Díaz advocated European-style social legislation to benefit women workers: regulation of work hours, equitable pay, prohibitions on child labor, Sunday rest, savings and retirement plans, and worker housing.[74] Significantly, one of her central appeals for an end to women's night work emphasized female sexual vulnerability: "We watch with sadness and bitterness how every day the wolves of lust lie in wait for their prey in the night shadows, and the defenseless sheep of a woman worker, treated like a beast in the workshop, finds comfort in the paradise that the pawing wolf describes for her simple, pure, and good imagination; she hears with pleasure and emotion the lying phrases of the false affect, only to weep tears of blood afterwards in the face of the consummated disgrace—seeing virtue brutally and intentionally profaned—before the ruins of the tranquility and happiness of a humble home."[75] Valdés de Díaz went on to chastise young male workers who went with prostitutes for participating in women's moral degradation.[76] These threats to female virtue could be brought to an end by state regulation of women's night work, which would prohibit employers the right to keep workers as late as they wanted. Like Carmela Jeria before her, Valdés de Díaz emphasized the importance of working-class women's virtue over—but not excluding—the defense of women's rights as workers.[77]

Valdés de Díaz's second argument for social legislation was that long work hours, like other abusive aspects of women's employment, wore women out and made them less inclined to partipate in associations. Here she portrayed employer avarice and antilabor strategies as the intrinsic will of "Capital," which "sees in [the woman] a precious tool for achieving its objectives; when the woman replaces the work of a male worker, she not only contributes to the reduction of men's wages, but also suffers the brunt of iniquitous exploitations, and her intelligence is trampled by the brutality of mechanical work, which prevents the ideal of social and economic well-being cherished by the proletariat from being achieved." In addition to state protection, therefore, Valdés de Díaz insisted on the importance of raising women workers' consciousness, maintaining that female participation in the labor movement was crucial for consolidating the gains already made by men: "If the woman does not fully understand the mission that corresponds to her in society and the home, is she not perhaps an unconscious enemy for the man to achieve his goals of improvement through union organization?"[78]

In a move that may have reflected the difficulty of continuing to publish the paper, twenty-two women met with Jeria and the staff of *La Alborada* (estimated at one hundred) to found the Sociedad Periodística La Alborada in January of 1907. In a report on that meeting, Jeria argued that the society "will give robust life to a newspaper that defends [women's] interests and those of the proletariat in general." The society set out to raise funds for the paper through social and political events, to organize conferences and classes for working women, and to establish a library "that will procure good and useful books so that the woman worker can easily start to work for her own emancipation."[79] The survival of the paper was here seen as a test of women's commitment to their own emancipation:

> La Alborada was established to amend these errors, but its languid life and small size clearly show that those who are favored by the paper do not give it the invaluable share of their support and care, and what is even more inexplicable, not even the monetary aid it needs to survive and to be rescued from failure and from dying along with the high interests it defends. This leads us to believe that because of the fair sex's own prestige, the continued existence of this brave champion will be assured; the contrary outcome would indicate that [woman] is happy with the humiliating role that man's selfishness assigns her in today's society.[80]

Ironically, and despite continuing expressions of support from contributors to La Reforma and other Democratic papers, La Alborada mysteriously ceased publication two months later, on May 19, 1907. Although the demise of the paper coincides precisely with the increasing fragility of organized labor during the months of May and June of that year, it is curious that the paper vanished without comment or protest from its supporters at La Reforma, which continued to publish regularly until August of the following year. With the disappearance of La Alborada, regular contributors such as Carmela Jeria, Ricardo Guerrero O., Selva, and Nicolás Rodríguez practically disappeared from the labor press, while Esther Valdés de Díaz continued to publish editorials on women's condition and reports on the Seamstresses Association in the pages of La Reforma.[81]

When Valdés de Díaz went on, in May 1908, to establish the newspaper La Palanca as the official organ of the Asociación de Costureras, she explicitly took up the reins of worker feminist publishing relinquished by Jeria: "The business we start today is not new: it is only the continuation of the interrupted work that our sister in struggle Carmela Jeria started the 10th of September of 1905 in Valparaíso with the publication La Alborada." A "feminist publication of emancipatory propaganda," La Palanca appeared only five times between May and September 1908, but it provided a forum to discuss and promote the

Seamstresses Association and report its rules and benefits to members. The paper's cover illustration reflected this renewed focus on women workers' emancipation: a seamstress used the stick of association, propped against the sawhorse of union and organization, to lift the boulder of ignorance, fanaticism, and slavery off the back of a wretched, chained young woman. Another woman stood with her chains broken, reaching out to the distant sunrise. The paper's opening editorial repeated the worker feminist analysis of female oppression, but again asserted the primacy of class unity in "the conviction that this struggle needs a considerable amount of bravery, action and energy, and now we have understood that the help of the proletarian woman will be decisive in the huge and unequal struggle."[82]

According to the paper's own reports, *La Palanca* was widely distributed in Santiago and throughout Chile, where it was both welcomed and reviled as a continuation of the worker feminist press. Isabel González, a reader in Chañaral, celebrated the existence of *La Palanca*, which "makes our sadistic exploiters see that the women of today are not as ignorant or as sheepish as they think; and that, just because they think we are production machines does not mean that we lack the intellectual energy and moral valor with which the personality of women is clothed."[83] Despite its positive reception in the Democratic labor press, *La Palanca* apparently provoked ridicule in the wider labor movement, as had *La Alborada* before it.[84]

La Palanca also addressed the issue of working-class sexuality, which had until that time received little or no attention in other labor newspapers, including *La Alborada*. For example, the June 1908 issue contained two articles on birth control, in which the authors argued that science had conspired with employers to deny this knowledge to working women. This situation had forced women to choose between criminal abortion and producing more slaves for the elite: "And consider, too, the criminal carelessness of scientific men, who do nothing to spread knowledge about normal and reasonable procreation among the people; they do nothing to make woman understand that she should control her body, that only she has the right to control it, to be a mother prudently, to the extent that her strength and her economic means allow it, choosing the proper moment."[85] This crime of omission was depicted as a conscious plan of elites to weaken the labor movement and swell the ranks of servitude in Chile. By insisting that only women and their enlightened male allies could be trusted to emancipate women, *La Palanca* continued to develop some of the more radical themes of worker

PUBLICACION
FEMINISTA
DE PROPAGANDA EMANCIPADORA

10 | REVISTA MENSUAL. ORGANO DE LA ASOCIACION DE COSTURERAS
Cts. | *Directora: Esther Valdes de Diaz. Redacción: Copiapó 782*

EPOCA SEGUNDA DE "LA ALBORADA"

AÑO I.   SANTIAGO DE CHILE, MAYO 1.° de 1908   N.° 1

EN EL PALENQUE

Henos aquí frente a frente al enemigo!

Años de vilipendio e ignominia han pesado sobre la noble personalidad de la Mujer.

Aun hoi, en pleno siglo XX pesa sobre los débiles hombros de la mujer la enorme mole de prejuicios, sujeta con férreas cadenas al poste de la actual sociedad imperante.

El hombre tras larga i árdua lucha ha conquistado medianamente sus libertades—pero la mujer ha quedado rezagada en el camino del progreso, i de la evolucion humana, i desorientada i sola—rechazada por el egoismo del hombre—hoi sordamente lucha, por desacirse de las cadenas que la oprimen, i ahuyentar el *fantasmon* que le oculta la luz de la verdad i la justicia.

Es verdad, que siglos de ignorancia i esclavitud han ido acumulando sobre nuestra jeneracion, espesas capas de inconsciencia i funesto letargo; i tan arraigada está en nuestra condicion de mujer, la creencia que nuestra esclavitud es cosa natural en inherente—que creemos tendremos que sostener ruda lucha, dentro de nuestro sexo, para convencernos de lo indigno i despreciable de nuestra condicion actual; i que debemos emplear toda nuestra enerjía, para llegar a conquistar en la Sociedad el puesto que por derecho natural nos corresponde.

A este noble propósito obedece que hoi un grupo de modestas mujeres den forma a un pensamiento largo tiempo acariciado.

15. Masthead of *La Palanca*, "A feminist
publication of emancipatory propaganda."
Source: La Palanca 1, no. 1 (May 1908): 1.
Courtesy of the Chilean National
Library, Serials Division.

feminism. The paper reprinted Sara Cadiz's polemic on the need for female organizing to combat economic and sexual oppression and reiterated that female emancipation was crucial to the achievement of social revolution. One female author argued pointedly that the labor movement had failed to advance precisely because male workers had ignored "this anonymous driving force; incomprehensibly abandoned, and on whose action the success of the struggle depends—this is Woman." "Do not be selfish," she continued, "opposing the spread of women's social education. Don't relegate her to the kitchen and the wash house!" She exhorted men to take responsibility for sharing their organizations and education with women, especially if women could not read for themselves.[86] At the same time, the Seamstresses Association acknowledged the support it received from some working-class men by naming two male militants as "advisory members" of the association.[87]

As the Seamstresses Association approached its second anniversary, it showed greater signs of vitality and infrastructural development. In addition to its own newspaper, the association had health and savings funds and provided members with access to the Labor Office's placement service. Study commissions had been established to survey workers' wages and hours and employer abuses for each work area, and the association had reportedly negotiated directly with employers on a number of occasions.[88] At the same time, many members of the association owed dues of six months or more because they were unemployed.[89] In Valdés de Díaz's anniversary speech of July 1908, she assessed the progress of the association in terms of female militancy (see appendix A). On the one hand, she celebrated that women had gained "that noble and valuable seal that imprints on all our actions the conscience that we know what we are and what we are worth"; on the other, she lamented that their work was just beginning: "The street actions achieved by women's organization have been few—one could truthfully say that the strike itself has not existed. . . . The relative gains in wages, work hours and the personal consideration of the woman worker has been achieved in some workshops and factories—in this category the Camisería Matas, the Fábrica de Tejidos and the Justiniano Military Workshop stand out, showing that the spirit and understanding of union organizing is slowly but surely making deep roots in women's trades."[90] Here Valdés de Díaz drew an accurate picture of the state of women workers' organizing around 1908; although educational and propagandistic efforts had resulted in the proliferation of resistance societies and popularized debates on feminism in the worker press, few associations had achieved a level of consolidation and legitimacy that would permit them to pry real concessions from employers. Further, the Seamstresses Association struggled—as did all workers' associations—against the declining popularity of labor activism in the face of economic hardship, employer blacklisting, and state intervention after 1907. The fact that the Seamstresses Association was one of six resistance societies still in existence by 1909 testifies to its remarkable vitality.

Like *La Alborada* before it, however, *La Palanca* suddenly and inexplicably ceased publication in late 1908 after only five issues, this time coinciding with the significant decline of all types of labor organization in Chile. In complimenting the paper for all it had done to promote female workers' consciousness, contributor Luís A. Mansilla warned against *La Palanca*'s demise in the paper's final issue: "When we let a labor publication that has appeared in journalism through the efforts of our compañeros and compañeras, bearing the emblem of education and freedom for all workers, die, we are doing ourselves a disservice."[91] When *La Palanca* indeed vanished, worker feminist activists—and the even limited debates on issues of gender and power in labor politics that they had generated—dropped largely out of sight. The subsequent demise of *La Reforma* and the great silence of Democratic politics in Santiago that followed also prevent us from tracing the actions and thoughts of worker feminist leaders in the years immediately after this date.

Over a three-year period, the worker feminist press had provided a space for writing by and about women workers. Clearly influenced by the more radical sexual egalitarianism proclaimed by anarchist fellow travelers, socialist writers in this press produced some expressions of working-class feminism that were considerably more critical of sexual hierarchy than elsewhere in the Democratic press. Despite these sporadic and more radical expressions, the essential thrust of worker feminist discourse remained one of cross-gender solidarity: female support for male leaders, male support for unionized women workers and respect for their own wives, and the affirmation of the female intelligence and agency made possible by revolutionary struggle. With some exceptions, worker feminism affirmed—rather than contested—the paternalism that the male Democratic leadership offered to women workers in their struggle for justice. When *La Palanca* ceased publication, this separate forum for the expression of (some) women's voices came to an end; thereafter, women militants would find their place within the broader forces of recovering Marxist labor organizing over the next decade. But continuing references to female subordination confirm that, as female mobilization flourished again in the 1920s, Chilean socialists continued to link the problems of working women to broader issues of sexual inequality and discrimination.

Women, Socialism, and Anticlericalism

In the years following the decline in resistance society activity and Democratic Party politics after 1908, women continued to participate in periodic strikes and workers' associations, but without evidence of the previous momentum or explicit references to worker feminism. The absence of newspapers directed specifically at women workers, which parallels the decreasing use of "feminist" propaganda in socialist newspapers, has made "women's voice" and female militancy itself more difficult to trace.[92] Although the sudden disappearance of Carmela Jeria and Esther Valdés de Díaz from journalistic circles after 1908 may exaggerate this shift, the distinctive rhetorical strategies employed by worker feminists—"the emancipation of women should be the work of women themselves"—were certainly not in evidence among socialists struggling to resucitate workers' organizations in the 1910s. Still, a latent concern with the woman question was evident in socialist and Democratic publications, and the theme recuperated significance in socialist circles of Valparaíso during Recabarren's stay there in 1915–1916. The recurring evidence of worker feminist themes, despite the absence of that movement's former leaders, not only contradicts existing hypotheses about the disappearance of worker feminism, but also suggests the gradual "naturalization" of the identity of the woman worker and her counterpart, the female labor militant in socialist discourse.[93] Although the culturally sanctioned figures of woman as mother, educator, and pillar of the home would never disappear altogether from the socialist labor press, the realities of female employment and unionization fostered and affirmed alternative images of women that carried forth the seed planted by those earlier, more explicit, campaigns for working women's rights under the aegis of worker feminism.

The drastic reduction in the size of the Democratic press throughout Chile after 1908 was the greatest blow to existing channels for the expression of working-class feminism. In contrast with the steady supply of daily news and editorials provided by *La Reforma*, socialist and Democratic Party publications in Santiago became sporadic, uncertain affairs. In those papers, attention to women workers and the woman question more generally was scarce. For example, the official organ of the Socialist

Group of Santiago in 1909, *El Socialista*, printed several articles on women and socialism, none of which dealt with women's role in labor politics. Instead, men were urged in abstract terms to educate women—and women, to educate themselves—in preparation for the achievement of a socialist future: "Socialist propaganda is very important in the heart of the family, in the worker's home. Inculcate your wives and daughters with the goodness of our ideas."[94] At the same time, these few articles show the continuing influence of worker feminist formulations in, for example, this criticism of sexual hierarchy: "No other party than Socialism is capable of granting guarantees to women; and these women want to free themselves from the tyranny not only of political laws, which have been so unfair to them, but also from men, who make women their slaves more than their partners, [and women] see in this ideal a new era of happiness for the human race."[95] The Democratic paper *El Trabajo*, edited by Evaristo Rios in Santiago between 1910 and 1911, returned to the theme of women's economic emancipation. Notably, the second issue of the paper contained a reprint of an article from *La Palanca*, "Women in the Economic Emancipation of the Proletariat," this time under the byline of Esther Valdés de Díaz.[96] Along with a news report about the Asociación de Costureras' acquisition of a new banner, the paper called for the organization of a women's auxiliary within the Democratic Party (primarily to ensure the proper education of children) and published a Ricardo Guerrero piece predicting the imminent union of men and women in a more just society.[97] But *El Trabajo* also included articles of a patently nonfeminist nature, such as the "Advice to Single Women" published in the Women's Section of the paper. The short piece, which caricatured the games of silly girls seeking to catch or avoid a husband, presented women as pretty objects and marriage as intrigue, a discourse diametrically opposed to the serious, emancipationist vision of socialist feminists.[98] Another short article, appearing in May 1911, also addressed women in the domestic context, urging them to support their husband's labor activism so that "you will be his wife a second time."[99] Although *El Trabajo* strove to continue the work of Democratic papers before it and reprinted articles of leading worker feminists to demonstrate those ties, editor Evaristo Rios appealed to readers' more condescending attitudes toward women—particularly daughters and wives—in the paper as well.

By 1912, socialist labor organizations had begun to regain their equilibrium in Chile, evident in the emergence of new workers' societies and publications in Santiago and Valparaíso and northern cities, where a

Recabarren-led convention founded the POS. The ambiguity of women workers' identity may in fact have been greater in the north, where female participation in wage work (particularly industry) was very small in comparison with Santiago and Valparaíso. At the same time, the apparent ambivalence over working women's identity as workers—and the evidently low representation of women in the founding of the new socialist party—also reflected the ways that a majority of Chilean socialists had come to view the woman question by the 1910s; on the one hand, continuing organization among urban women workers continued to strengthen the union movement in major cities, but on the other, the (presumably unemployed) wives and daughters of male workers became the source of greater concern. Hence we see the focus in socialist publications after 1912 placed not only on the mobilization of women workers, but also on the proper ideological instruction of women who stayed at home. In this vein, socialists readily perceived the primary obstacle to female enlightenment as the Catholic Church and increasingly urged male workers to exert their authority to pry women from the grips of "fanaticism."

One event that surely contributed to socialists' increasing anticlericalism was the 1913 visit to Chile of the Spanish freethinker Belén de Sárraga, who was conducting a speaking tour of Latin America at the time. Belén de Sárraga was received with great acclaim by both Radicals and Democrats, who between them hosted her speaking engagements in most of Chile's major cities. There she addressed Chilean workers' societies and political meetings with fiery rhetoric against the Catholic Church and speeches on science and social progress, reaching a wide audience of intellectuals, politicians, and workers. Her topics ranged from "woman as a social being" to speeches on evolutionary doctrine, the family, religion, and education.[100] Although she was much acclaimed in the political press as a champion of her sex, Belén de Sárraga said relatively little about women's rights or their political participation; interestingly, many news accounts and editorials about her visit barely mentioned the fact that she was female.[101] Not surprisingly, Belén de Sárraga's speeches also provoked conservative retaliation in the local press. For conservatives she was a prime representative of the twin evils—socialism and feminism—that threatened to disrupt traditional society.[102]

Like the socialist activists whom she addressed, however, Belén de Sárraga was a staunch advocate of the incorporation of women into socialist struggle. Denouncing authoritarianism in the family and calling for mutual respect between the sexes, she distinguished between the kind of feminism in which women organized themselves, which she claimed was too easily dismissed by men, and that which was initiated and encouraged by men: "On the other hand if you, men of progress who pass through this world without the heavy weight of prejudice; if you are the ones who cooperate and even take initiative in feminist affairs, if you declare in your political and social credo that woman is your equal, when she rises up—not against your will, but rather supported by your work—this hatred between the sexes (which is evident in some cases and that thinkers should devote more concern and study to than the hatred between the classes) will become pure and truly brotherly love."[103] Although Belén de Sárraga's analysis of female subordination (stemming from the noxious combination of religion and capitalism) and her strategy for overcoming it (unity between working-class men and women) echoed those of earlier worker feminists, her references to gender maintained a level of abstraction that elided discussion of women in the workplace or the labor movement.

For socialist organizers, however, the implications of Belén de Sárraga's visit for female mobilization were far from abstract, and her example and speeches fell on fertile ground where worker feminism had preceded her in the previous decade. Following a personal invitation for her to speak in Iquique and other northern cities, Recabarren and his then-companion Teresa Flores established Centros Belén de Sárraga in Antofagasta and Iquique and the Sociedad El Despertar de la Mujer in Valparaíso soon after her 1913 tour.[104] In contrast to the women's resistance societies that had previously flourished in Chilean cities, these groups were organized among women workers and housewives alike and gave a distinctly anticlerical cast to the project of female mobilization. According to Flores, the Iquique center was organized "in memory of and dedicated to the brave woman who has been subject to the ugly and abject attack of the clergy for preaching the liberation of conscience . . . [a place] where all the women who believe it is necessary and moral to fight the disastrous leprosy of arrogant and enslaving clericalism can gather."[105] Although the primary goal of the Centros Belén de Sárraga was anticlerical education, the societies were also concerned with more broadly defined women's issues, such as the 1907 Sunday rest law, prohibition, and women's emancipation. These groups became less significant after 1918, when declining nitrate production accelerated urban migration, and union and party organizations began to take precedence over smaller, local labor groups.[106]

Belén de Sárraga's speeches, distributed through political newspapers and collected in a volume published after her second visit, reached even further than her tour.[107] Perhaps because of her success, she returned to Chile for a second tour in 1915, where she was again well-received by fellow freethinkers. By then, Belén de Sárraga had found ample evidence of women's political involvement: "The Chilean woman, impassioned with her own destiny, has not shirked at these new directions of the feminine spirit. In addition to the very educated women of the capital, which includes a group who study the mind, there are societies of free-thinking women in Iquique . . . in Antofagasta, Valparaíso and else-where."[108] Following the political precedents set by worker feminists, Belén de Sárraga's tour also influenced the evolution of socialist positions on female emancipation.

What is striking here about Belén de Sárraga's visit is not, as previous scholars have claimed, that it stimulated the first expressions of female militancy in Chile.[109] Rather, and perhaps more important, Belén de Sárraga's anticlericalism contributed to the shifting strategies for female mobilization among Chile's socialist leaders. In his 1916 speech to FOCH workers in Punta Arenas, for example, Recabarren demonstrated the decisive influence of Belén de Sárraga on his thinking about women and socialism. In the speech later published as *La mujer y su educación*, Recabarren appealed to women not in their capacity as workers, but rather as mothers and educators of future generations: "For the Social-ists, the woman should be the freest Being, who knows how to educate her children, and so she should be better educated, enlightened, and wholly dedicated to the education of her children, if she has any."[110] In that speech, Recabarren made little reference to his previous concerns such as workplace mobilization and cross-gender solidarity, focusing instead on women's continuing enslavement to organized religion. Nev-ertheless, Recabarren's optimism for women's positive contribution to socialist politics was still in evidence. He argued that industrialization, which "cast the woman out of the home and enslaved her in work," had brought socialism and feminism with it, which in combination had the capacity to emancipate women and bring about revolution. The shift in emphasis from economic to moral issues reflected a wider tendency evi-dent among socialists in the 1910s—like mutualists of previous years—to address not only those working women directly affected by the rise of industrial capitalism, but also those women whose consciousness would shape working-class domestic culture and future generations of workers.

This trend was evident in the pages of *El Socialista*, a weekly paper founded by Recabarren in Valparaíso (where he lived between April 1915 and early 1916). The paper devoted an average of one article a month to some aspect of women and socialism, and Recabarren himself contributed a variety of signed articles in this vein. From the earliest of these articles, it is apparent that Recabarren had inserted himself in a community of labor activists who were familiar with the tenets of women's economic liberation.[111] In "A todas las mujeres," Recabarren addressed an assembly of women tobacco workers, where he denounced in familiar terms their economic, physical, and moral exploitation under the capitalist system, and urged them to struggle, if not for themselves, then for their chidren.[112] An editorial published a month later summed up Recabarren's view of women workers' motives for joining the workers' movement: "If a young woman loses her youth and beauty to brutal work; if a mother wants health and well-being for her children and at the same time hopes for a peaceful and comfortable old age; if a wife wants relief and a better life for hersef and her husband; if a woman of any condition suffers the evils that afflict us . . . Little women [*mujercitas*]: Come to man's side, as a sister in the struggle, to fight to make human life beautiful and happy."[113]

Further, in two articles published in early 1916, Recabarren continued to focus on the exploitation of women workers in a short series on "factory life," this time to shame both men and women into organizing to end these "inhumanities." After listing the physical dangers and poor wages suffered by women working in a Valparaíso glass factory, Recabarren complained that "workers of both sexes lament this disgraceful situation in which they work, but they do nothing to correct these evils. They only think about their vices and pursue these defects without concerning themselves with the aspiration to live better, with more comfort and health."[114] Similarly, he rebuked workers who put up with the abusive swearing of their employers and managers (who called women workers prostitutes, for example): "The working class is at fault, because it puts up with all of this indecent vocabulary. . . . When the workers, in unity and brotherhood, know how to get respect, we will no longer see bosses or managers using language to mistreat those who produce the wealth."[115] In these articles, Recabarren combined images of female exploitation—typically used to urge working men to protective action—with appeals to women workers to organize on their own behalf. They are distinctive in the corpus of Recabarren's writings on the woman question because they address specific groups of working women in a direct and noncondescending manner. In this sense, Recabarren's appeals to working women during his Valparaíso sojourn closely resemble those of the Santiago and Valparaíso feminists of the previous decade.

Once again, however, we must look farther afield than Recabarren's writings to trace the legacy of working-class feminism in Chile. Although no single author emerged as a regular contributor on women's issues, the systematic fashion in which contributors to *El Socialista* addressed the topic of women and socialism suggests that the editors saw female consciousness raising and mobilization as a vital socialist objective. Among the more prominent themes in this regard were women's education, the need for protective legislation, and the mobilization of women workers, all of which followed rhetorical patterns typical of earlier worker feminists.[116] The paucity of references to local unionization efforts among working women, however, and the regular employment of foreign developments in women's rights as examples suggest that the POS had relatively little local women's activism to celebrate.[117]

Significantly, a few articles even raised the specter of male workers' complicity with female subordination, holding men responsible for women's ignorance and resignation. This position was summarized in the epigraph to an article that outlined the history of prominent women: "For women, as a stimulus; for men, as a reproach."[118] An article by "Helle" even recalled Carmela Jeria's and Ricardo Guerrero's earlier rebukes of male hypocrisy: "Our women are ignorant. By modestly keeping her away from any free discussion about life's values and responsibilities, by carefully excluding her from every problem above those of daily contingencies . . . we have allowed her to invent her own world, according to the caprices of her confused instincts, [we are] satisfied that her passive and resigned obedience accords us all of the privileges that a boss gets from an inferior." Even if wife beating, the author continued, were a woman's "fault . . . eight out of ten times," men should still be held responsible for women's submission to it, which the author likened to women's submission to all of the injustices accorded their sex.[119] Speaking at a socialist gathering in Valparaíso, Soledad Zurriaga (of the association Despertar de la Mujer) reminded men that they had to incorporate women into their politics to obtain their support: "It is necessary to react against the custom of leaving women at home. Women should be in all the demonstrations where the men are, so that she gets used to the struggle and acquires a capacity for it." Zurriaga's closing statement reflected the persistent idealization of women's familial roles, so characteristic of earlier worker feminists such as Esther

Valdés de Díaz: "I congratulate you, socialist women, because you have provided the best example of what will be the woman of the future: the caring mother and the faithful companion. With women like you Socialism will bring days of happiness and good fortune to the world."[120]

Despite the continuity represented by Recabarren's participation and the familiar emancipationist rhetoric of many contributors, however, *El Socialista* also gave more expression than had the worker feminist press to concerns about sexual competition in the workplace and women's obstructionism in the home. Significantly, these writers emphasized working women's duty to struggle for increased wages not for their own benefit, but to support male industrial wages: "All this looks like a battle of the sexes. But that is not so. One can't benefit women and children without making the whole human race better and happier. When women organize and they refuse to receive low salaries and accept overwork, they will stop competing with men. Equal pay for equal work does a lot to improve men's salaries. . . . Little women [*mujercitas*]: men need you in politics and you need them to help you with your labor, the labor of protecting health and preserving life. . . . Women of the world, unite to achieve exactly the same rights as men, although you will have to justly accept all of the duties that go with it."[121] Another female writer put this more bluntly: "Women in industry are, as we see, an obstruction for the advance and economic situation of the working class." She then advocated that women organize, particularly in mixed unions, to improve their wages.[122] On the domestic front, socialists continued to advocate women's education, on the grounds that it would prevent women from obstructing male participation in unions. Not only would properly educated socialist women better understand their husband's situation and strive to provide a "pleasant" home life, but they would also encourage male activism. "So imagine a compañera under these conditions: if her husband has to go on strike, for example, she will encourage him, because she understands that if [the strike] is successful there will be more food at home, but on the other hand, a woman who does not have this education, instead of encouraging, will discourage him, even to the point of forcing him to betray his compañeros."[123] The theme of cross-gender unity, so central to the editorial position of earlier worker feminist papers, again eclipsed the feminist, emancipationist rhetoric in terms of emphasis. What had evidently "waned" or "disappeared" in the intervening years was not the discussion of women's rights itself, but rather the commitment among socialist activists to gender equality as a goal in its own right. These scattered references to women's participation clarify the socialist commitment to the sexual division of labor and the meaning of cross-gender solidarity that had already been evident in worker feminism; women's activism at this point was encouraged primarily to shore up male labor organization and bolster the male-headed household.

Despite the continuities in socialist rhetoric in support of women workers, however, a single article by Esther Valdés de Díaz that was published in Santiago's *Acción Obrera* in 1916, apparently for the first time, belies the appearance of cross-gender solidarity. In that article, Valdés de Díaz complained that workers' associations discriminated against women: "Whoever has taken a look at trade, mutualist and educational organizations will have confirmed that women barely play the smallest part in representing these groups and that, one way or another, separated or together [with men] they may take a different route, but their goal is the same and universal aspiration." Citing the predominance of all-male societies in Santiago (forty out of fifty), she urged that women be admitted to trade and mutualist organizations for typesetters, upholsterers, tailors, shoe makers, cigarette makers, and binders. Although she was primarily concerned with the representation of women workers in the labor movement, Valdés de Díaz also advocated the incorporation of women in their roles as wives and mothers: "If modern rationalism advises us to educate and involve women in all of the problems that develop in the life of humankind, and if women are the ones who educate, create and prepare [future] generations; it is also logical that, wherever there is a problem that concerns the interests of the home, the family or society, women should take a principal and effective part [in these organizations]." Although Valdés de Díaz here advocated for all women—and not just women workers—this single contribution to a new socialist publication expressed her "serious affirmation" that male organizations were continually impoverished by the lack of female participation. As in the example she set as head of the Seamstresses Association during the heyday of worker feminism, Valdés de Díaz urged men to welcome women into all levels of labor politics: "It is necessary and urgent that [men] share with women the school bench—a place in the lines—in the the directorate of the union or society—on the platform—in the [work of] propaganda and social action."[124] Writing a month later in the same paper, C. Alberto Sepúlveda seconded Valdés de Díaz's sentiments: "The participation of women in social action is as necessary as water in the desert, as air is to life."[125] Valdés de Díaz's complaints, registered near the end of this second, weaker cycle of socialist propaganda on the woman question, hint at the disappointing levels of female participation—and the possibility of gender discrimination—in labor politics during this period. The degree and nature of Valdés de Díaz's own participation, and that of her worker feminist colleagues of the previous decade, remain obscured by their almost complete absence from the labor press after 1908.

The Return of the "Enslaved Woman"

The emergence of a modified socialist position on women in labor politics—and the strengthening of socialist rhetoric and organization among women workers—eventually became more apparent with the resurgence of socialism under Recabarren's leadership in the FOCH after 1919. The official organ of that organization and the POS, *La Federación Obrera* (subsequently *La Justicia*), provides ample evidence for the continued mobilization of women workers in socialist unions, as well as socialists' changing discourse on the woman question.[126] Although *La Federación Obrera* and *La Justicia* reproduced elements of earlier worker feminism, several significant differences stand out. First, before 1923 *La Federación Obrera* enjoyed few contributions from women writers, an absence editors occasionally sought to remedy by profiling the activities of local and foreign women labor militants.[127] Second, although *La Federación Obrera* included regular news on women's unions, the FOCH Women's Council, and women's involvement in strike activities, until the middle of 1924 the paper made few explicitly feminist claims in addressing the problem of working women. Once the editors of the paper turned their attention to issues of social legislation and feminism in that year, however, the paper illustrates that the fires of worker feminism—nourished at times by contributions from anarchist authors—continued to burn in Chilean Marxist movements.

Some of the clues to the evolution of socialist positions on the woman question lie in how the FOCH represented female militancy in the course of its broader recruitment efforts. In the first years of the paper's existence, when women appeared at all their militancy was most often reported as simple fact, with little editorial embellishment. This perspective was amply demonstrated in press coverage of the three-month Ñuñoa Textile Factory strike of 1921. Sparked when the worker Laura Poblete refused to join the factory union organized by her employer's wife, the Ñuñoa strike received widespread support from other Santiago unions, including the FOCH Consejo Femenino de Oficios Varios No. 1, which announced the daily meetings of the strikers in *La Federación Obrera*: "All the compañeras should come to these assemblies, and also the parents of the members should give their daughters permission to come to the meeting hall at the indicated hour."[128] Male union leaders attended and spoke at strike rallies, and the employees of the Casa Ideal de Irmas Hnos. went on a solidarity strike.[129] The striking workers took refuge in the FOCh Women's Council of Ñuñoa, where they formed a soup kitchen, organized a boycott, and launched marches against the factory. The IWW also supported the strikers, taking charge of blacklisting workers who continued to work in the factory, and smaller anarchist unions supported the strikers with solidarity walkouts.[130] The effective solidarity of male workers apparent in marches and speeches during the strike demonstrated the cross-gender solidarity that worker feminists had promoted in practice.[131]

After 1923, however, *La Federación Obrera* gave space to editorial comments and women contributors who made a variety of appeals to women workers to join the communist cause, usually including the promise of greater gender equality. This was especially evident between March and May 1923, when the Weavers' Section of the FOCh Council of Manufacturing Industries sponsored an organizing drive among women weavers in Santiago, calling the "obreritas" and their families of the Yungay neighborhood to hear communist Congressional Deputy Luís Cruz.[132] Subsequent articles reminded women of their exploitation in the workplace, urging them in florid prose to educate themselves and join the ranks of the FOCh. While Amira M. relied on familiar rationalist tropes of the need for female education ("books are your best council"),[133] Isabel Díaz tried to rally support for the FOCh Women's Council by shaming women into action: "Have you ever thought about your emancipation and the rights you are due! Never: you are always the eternal slave, from birth to death, and you do nothing to liberate yourself and seek your betterment."[134] Calling women's education a priority because women educate future generations, Díaz invited her readers to sign up for the FOCh Women's Council, which seemed to become more active in May 1923. Although Díaz's direct appeal to working women was reminiscent of the inspirational worker feminist appeals penned earlier in the century, the angry tone and terminology more closely resemble anarchist tropes on women's double slavery, recently revived through the publication of Rene Chaughi's *La mujer esclava* in Chile in 1921.[135]

In subsequent years, and continuing into the publication of *La Justicia*, the various and sometimes conflicting positions of worker feminism were revived in the communist press, as the number of female contributors and editorial attention to the woman question increased. Editorials took particular note of elite women's efforts in this period to obtain legislation modifying the Civil Code and to grant women suffrage. On this issue, contributors were divided: some lauded bourgeois women's leadership and efforts to obtain women's political equality with men; others ridiculed their concerns and called for working women's independent action to obtain social and economic equality first. Both sides claimed to support absolute equality between the sexes: "Our revolutionary program considers the woman as a being to be equal in all senses to the man, with the right to be what she wants, to do what she wants, to have what she pleases without any limitations other than her own feelings, that is, absolute freedom, equal in every sense [to the rights] that man in his clumsy egotism reserved only for himself."[136] But a subsequent editorial derided women's efforts to obtain the vote, saying that "politics does not seem to preserve a principal role for women." Although this rejection of the need for women's vote might seem contradictory in a party newspaper that cultivated working women's political support, the editorial stressed the continuing need to incorporate women into social revolution to achieve class victory.[137]

Even as the editors of *La Federación Obrera* changed their tune on women's suffrage and bourgeois feminism, they included articles that addressed gender inequality in the most strident terms since the worker feminism of *La Alborada*. Several articles published in April 1924 pointed once again to the simultaneous oppression of women in the factory and in the home: "Compañeras, sisters of pain and misfortune, of sad and miserable lives, whether this is because you are chained to a salary, a workshop, or whether as a daughter or compañera in a present-day proletarian home."[138] The author then called on men of the FOCH to encourage women's education so that class unity would result. Puerto Rican anarchist Luisa Capetillo's article "La mujer" was also reprinted here, stressing women's continuing enslavement to men. Capetillo here lamented the way inequality poisoned family relations: "Because it is well known that an immense majority of men are little tigers inside their own homes; when he rounds the corner the children tremble and they hide when he arrives while the mother is frightened. And when this woman complies by granting or consenting to her husband's marital crime, she makes a sacrifice in which she yields her soul and crushes her heart, ending up in a terrible state of abuse, and when insemination happens in this situation, tell me what kind of children are produced by this union that is the antithesis of love?" If men would heed her admonition and women would find their "reason and conscience," "every home would be a school, a class, and fraternity would be the only law that would subject [their] hearts."[139] These more radical critiques of gender inequality, which dared to place working-class domestic arrangements in question, were not sustained in the communist press, and attention to feminist issues more generally attenuated in subsequent months.

There is therefore little evidence to support the hypothesis that, because "worker feminism" was less in evidence by the 1920s, women were actively excluded from socialist, then communist labor politics. On the contrary, their continued presence—and the need to mobilize them further—seemed self-evident and unremarkable, and militants in mixed-sex unions and the FOCH Women's Council sought actively to recruit more women to the revolutionary cause. What had in fact waned in Marxist propaganda was the degree of concern for the woman question, particularly working women, compared to other political priorities of the day. And with few exceptions, the radical feminist critique of discrimination within working-class homes and movements had disappeared. If women workers' political autonomy in early socialist organizing had been, in reality, quite limited, female organization under the FOCH was even more closely identified with the cross-gender cause of union mobilization. Rather than any explicit reassertion of male supremacy, this change corresponds to the strengthening of ties between Marxist labor movements and political parties that were most concerned with reaching male workers who could vote. The consolidation of the FOCH meant that, while women workers and housewives should be recruited to the socialist cause, labor's appeals were no longer explicitly or mainly built on the promise of women's emancipation "in the home, in the street, and in the workshop," but rather on the promise of imminent victory for the whole family of labor.

Conclusions

Worker feminism flourished during the first decade of the twentieth century because of women's visible presence in urban manufacturing just as radical worker politics were taking shape in Chile. The vigor of worker feminism was evident at several levels of socialist politics: the proliferation of all-women's resistance societies, the emergence of female labor leaders, and ongoing attention to women's issues and feminism in the socialist press. *La Alborada*'s clear institutional priority concerned encouraging women's support for Democratic leaders and organizations, but the paper also gave voice to radical interpretations of female subordination. These criticisms of male workers and their labor movement, along with increasing attention to working women's practical issues, made *La Alborada*, along with its sequel and affiliated associations, the key expressions of worker feminism in Chile.

Despite worker feminists' willingness to criticize gender inequality, however, their writings never developed a full-fledged theory of women's emancipation. Perhaps because of its narrow focus on the factory women who were their prime constituency, the paper neglected to address the situation and potential mobilization of important segments of the population of working women, including domestic servants, homeworkers, and prostitutes. Furthermore, because they viewed the exploitation of women primarily in economic and moral terms, worker feminists were unable to cope with, or uninterested in coping with, female subordination outside of the formal workforce in more than a superficial fashion; this would have required a substantially different reading of the nature and extent of women's domination by men, one more akin to contemporaneous anarchist tracts on "the enslaved woman." Worker feminist journalists likewise never challenged the idealized conception of woman as the pillar of domestic tranquility. Like the socialist leadership, contributors to Democratic, later communist papers resolved the conflicting goals of a militant female workforce with the domestic ideal by projecting these as sequential objectives. Once the class struggle was won, they argued, women would not have to work in factories or workshops and could return to their "natural" duties as wives and mothers. In the meantime, the tension between women's roles as wives/mothers and as labor activists was resolved in the adulation heaped on female leaders, whose "masculine" traits were praised by observers. In the liminal space of continuing labor agitation and accelerating organization, such exceptional female behaviors were tolerated and even presented as ideal for women workers.

Although the available sources offer no clear explanation for the decline of worker feminism as a mobilizational discourse after 1908, the immediate cause of its decline, like that of the broader Democratic Party movement, was the state's repression of striking miners in the Iquique massacre of 1907. Although women continued to participate in socialist politics after that date, the movement for worker feminism was transformed into sporadic references to female subordination, buried among strike reports and continuing complaints about women workers' vulnerability. Ironically, the relative inattention to working women's specific issues in the communist press of the 1920s may have reflected their successful incorporation into many of the political activities of the labor movement, even as female representation at the upper levels of union leadership remained scarce.

Drawing on available and sometimes contradictory tropes opposing sexual hierarchy and promoting working-class respectability, socialist worker feminism created the conditions for the incorporation of working women into first Democratic, then communist labor politics in Chile. Though not completely autonomous of male leaders' control and oversight, the women's newspapers and organizations associated with this movement aggressively carved out a distinctive role for themselves within Chilean socialism, one that went beyond the paradigms of helpmate or icon promoted elsewhere in the labor press in the period. Despite its clear moorings in the sexual division of labor and socialist paternalism, worker feminism rationalized and promoted women workers' militancy and laid the groundwork for more extensive critiques of sexual inequality on the left in the decades to come.

II

Women Workers and the Social Question

Given the changing urban landscape and increasing class conflict of the late nineteenth century, it is not surprising that most elite debates and actions concerning working women took place within the parameters of "the social question."[1] Historian Luís Alberto Romero has described this growing concern with the living and working conditions of the working classes as the "new gaze" of the elite, who "discovered that the popular sectors of Santiago lived in material and moral misery, even though they were not able to differentiate easily between them."[2] As they looked to Europe and the United States for solutions to the demographic and economic problems that accompanied industrialization there, Chilean elites relied on the rhetoric of the social question for discussions involving a broad set of concerns, including alcoholism, epidemic disease (including venereal diseases), prostitution, urban slum life, infant mortality, and political unrest.[3] The increasing organization of popular sectors provoked not only state repression, but also elite attempts to co-opt and discipline working-class discontent. To some extent, the emergence of the social question in national discourse owed less to actual changes in the socioeconomic status of the working poor than to their demonstrated organizational potential. Although striking male workers were the principal targets of private and state repressive actions under the Parliamentary Republic, Santiago's working women were consistently subjected to another sort of class discipline, one that solicited women's cooperation in the workplace as well as the home. The resulting elite projects sought to cultivate, improve, and thereby assure the compliance of working-class families with the advance of industrial capitalism.

Elite men and women controlled the terms of debate on the social question, which they discussed in the daily press, speeches to clubs and Parliament, and in studies and proposals of various government ministries.[4] These discussions of pressing social issues not only revealed ideological differences among social actors, but also produced conflicts over the proper behavior of working-class men and women. Liberal industrialists, well aware of the profitability of female and child factory labor, were among the first to challenge negative stereotypes of women workers. Recruiting young women from families headed by skilled male workers, industrialists and their state allies established schools to train women in industrial skills. Elite Catholic women, who had long supported private workshops and training programs for the poorest women, focused their attention on the shop and store floor, devising programs to aid and organize women factory workers and the growing population of store clerks through Catholic unions. Taking their cue from European legislators and local pressures to intervene in employers' relations with female employees, Chilean politicians also debated the merits of workplace protections for women workers, forging a consensus on female protective legislation that transcended the partisan conflicts of the Parliamentary Republic.

In each case, working-class women became the principal targets of campaigns to improve the health and productivity of the working classes. The social question was therefore a fundamentally gendered discussion; just as elites battled over the rights and responsibilities of male workers, they also designated women—the reproducers and caretakers of future generations of workers—as appropriate subjects of reform efforts. Elite Catholic women, moreover, appealed to images of working-class motherhood as they spearheaded some of the earliest such campaigns for working-class women. In this way, the definition of the social question was conceptualized and solutions were implemented in gendered ways, long before the state itself acted to intervene in labor relations in a systematic fashion through the labor code of 1924.

5

Womens' Vocational Training

The Female Face of Industrialization

Following the close of the Second War of the Pacific in 1883, Chilean industrialists and statesmen worked together to organize legislation and institutions that would stimulate the growth of Chilean manufactures, believing industry to be the key to national economic prosperity. Among other things, this project included improving the available pool of workers by expanding industrial education programs. This initiative stimulated proposals for vocational training for men and women, which its proponents claimed would produce "a working class that is ever more intelligent, ever more educated, with more needs and thus more laborious; that will contribute to the growth of our productive power and the country's general advancement."[1] The small Santiago Arts and Crafts School (Escuela de Artes y Oficios) had been training men as shop managers and mechanics since 1849.[2] This school served as a model for Chile's first Girls' Vocational School (Escuela Profesional de Niñas), founded in Santiago in 1889 to train more women to take their place in Santiago's growing factories and workshops. Over the next forty years, more than eighty thousand women would attend classes "designed to give women the vocational training suitable to their sex."[3]

On the face of it, this initiative for female industrial education seemed to contradict normative prescriptions for women's domestic roles: planners celebrated the high proportion of women employed in Chilean manufactures and set out to improve their skills, discipline, and earning power in the industrial labor market. Despite these egalitarian pretensions, however, the female vocational education movement merely transformed the modalities of the sexual division of labor and women's subordinate position in the labor force. Most of the Vocational School's curriculum focused on raising the level and quality of home production in clothing, food, and service industries, where women already predominated. Although daughters and widows might apply these skills in a workshop setting, industrial training was really designed for women tied to the home by domestic responsibilities. Women's increased vocational capacity would, in theory, be complemented by their skilled management of the domestic economy, which the schools improved through courses in home economics and morals. The Girls' Vocational School was thus a reform project that left untouched (and unquestioned) the sexual division of labor, the segmentation of occupations by sex, and unequal wage scales.

This tendency, already evident in early ministerial decisions about school curriculum, was further reinforced by the actions of female administrators and teachers, who came to control the schools in the first decades of the twentieth century and pursued more thoroughgoing objectives for working women than had the schools' founders. Between 1906 and 1918, ministerial officials and inspectors implemented aggressive reforms that transformed the Girls' Vocational Schools into moral and technical training programs for women's working-class domestic skills. In this period, many administrators found it necessary to justify the idea of training women as workers by showing how the schools improved their students in their roles as working-class wives and mothers. What were originally supplemental courses in home economics and morality thus became the central justification for continued female vocational training.

In a larger sense, the vocational training movement for both men and women formed one element in elite responses to the social crisis of industrialization and represented an attempt to control the occupational formation and moral habits of the working classes.[4] The Girls' Vocational Schools—and the controversies and reforms that beset them— clearly illustrate the gendered nature of the elite's project of social damage control.[5] Men had to be trained as better industrial workers, managers, and providers; girls had to be taught how to maintain, as well as contribute economically to, the stability of working-class families. Female industrial education came to encompass both the productive and reproductive skills of poor women, formalizing their subordinate position in both the home and the labor force.

Initiatives and Goals of Vocational Education

The impulse toward vocational education for workers formed part of the movement to stimulate and regulate national industry, which had been consolidated in the Santa María government's creation of SOFOFA in

16. Girls' Vocational School exhibit, Women's Exhibit. *Source: Actividades femeninas en Chile* (Santiago: Imprenta y Litografía La Ilustración, 1928), 40.

1883. The master artisans, industrialists, and politicians who made up SOFOFA uniformly assigned a leading role to industry as the key to national growth.[6] The society was responsible for formulating the principal industrial policies of the state, including government protection for domestic industries and selective foreign immigration, the development of the first industrial statistics, preparation of national industrial exhibits and publications, and administration of industrial schools.[7] Its strategies for industrial growth resembled national projects underway in other Latin American countries in this period, all of which looked to European and U.S. experiences as models for industrial growth. Unlike these precedents, as Kirsch has argued, Chilean capitalists preferred to place their money in short-term manufacturing investments such as clothing and food production, rather than developing a stronger industrial base in heavy industries.[8] In addition to promoting protective tariffs and inducing foreign immigration of skilled workers, SOFOFA sought to raise production levels by addressing what its members saw as the occupational deficiencies of the Chilean working population. In the creation of trade schools, SOFOFA and its state ally, the Ministry of Industry and Public Works, sought to modernize Chile's industrial workforce by providing "all the knowledge that gives [the working class] the ability to carry out its corresponding role in industry."[9] Moreover, the creation of new schools and the reform of old ones in the interest of industrial growth was not simply a technical project. While stressing the economic advantages to be gained by having a trained workforce, SOFOFA's advocacy for vocational education was permeated with references to the moral and disciplinary benefits that came with it. Work discipline and occupational specialization would, according to SOFOFA, assure that "the worker is civilized, and acquires more sober and orderly customs."[10] The whole tenor of proposals for industrial education resembled other reforms of the era insofar as training, work discipline, and moral supervision were considered to benefit the working classes and the nation as a whole.

The first attempts to implement industrial education in Chile were much older than SOFOFA; the School of Arts and Crafts had been established in Santiago in 1849 to "form educated and moral workmen who are capable of becoming workshop supervisors, and industrialists versed in the practice of the mechanical arts and electricity."[11] The original five-year curriculum was apparently too long, and was reduced to three years in 1894; by 1909, studies lasted two years for industrial workers and four for shop supervisors and skilled artisans. Nevertheless, the school suffered chronically low enrollment (about three hundred students per year), poor attendance, and low graduation rates. Although the curriculum contained obligatory courses on hygiene and religion, men's industrial training rose and fell on the technical aspects of their training: whether men could be disciplined enough to attend classes, be trained, and go to work in their chosen vocations.

From its inception in an 1887 SOFOFA proposal, industrial education for women was drawn up on the same model of national economic progress. In August of that year, SOFOFA presented its project for an industrial school for young women in a letter to the Ministry of Industry and Public Works, emphasizing the economic advantages of creating a female industrial workforce. Unlike the men's schools, the women's would raise the simple, low-capital-investment trades that were already considered "women's work" to an entirely new level. The women's schools should "teach and spread domestic industries that allow the participation of the entire family." The best way to do this, SOFOFA argued, was "to give women's industrial education a vigorous push by creating a school specially designed for that purpose, which is the method that is now universally recognized as the most appropriate way to achieve this goal."[12] National industry, they reasoned, would quickly reap the benefits of having a skilled female workforce that could replace expensive imported items with nationally produced ones.

Another justification for women's industrial education revolved around the commonly understood plight of poverty-stricken working-class families, and especially the daughters of those families. Without some kind of industrial training, educators argued, these girls had no alternative to prostitution, humiliating domestic service, or "the product of the needle in hands that are inexperienced, sometimes delicate, and sometimes, almost always, are too nervous for this sedentary occupation that frees the imagination and clouds the mind." The society elaborated on the considerable benefits that industrial education would afford the individual woman, "who, until now, lacked the necessary means to acquire, without sacrifice, industrial knowledge that would assure her a paying job suitable to her nature [*naturaleza*]."[13] Technical drawing, which would train women in fashion design and ornamental drawing, "opens up the horizon [for women], educates and guides their passionate, lively, and delicate imaginations; makes use of their abilities; impedes the temptation of vice and sloth; educates these uncultivated spirits in work and honor and directs their hearts, always good, along the broad and comfortable path of personal dignity and social respectability." With this training, women would presumably achieve higher wages, more interesting work and, most important, "an honorable position and the esteem of all honorable people."[14] Female vocational training, though conceived in the same spirit of modernization and progress as that of men, was justified in the crucible of women's honor.

According to SOFOFA's initial proposal, this "industrial school for women" would give only four to six hours of class a day to girls over fourteen who had completed their primary education. The proposed curriculum included ten skilled occupations that the society considered acceptable professions for women: commerce, sewing/tailoring, embroidery, glove making, artificial flower making, basket making, book making and leatherworking, charring, watch making, and weaving. These courses reflected the trades in which women workers already predominated, whether in a service or industrial context (see chapter 2). In addition, all students would be given classes in technical drawing, considered "an indispensable aid to the practice of any manual industry." This initial proposal detailed the important theoretical and practical training involved in each course that was to be the basis for the profes-

17. Machine sewing class, Girls' Vocational School, Curicó, circa 1925.
Source: Actividades femeninas en Chile (Santiago: Imprenta y Litografía La Ilustración, 1928), 292.

sionalization of women's trades.[15] The training would create a relatively permanent female industrial workforce for the sake of national progress and that of the women themselves.

The SOFOFA proposal distinguished between different kinds of women, however, projecting the simultaneous creation of an Occupational School for girls who would not make good industrial workers. According to SOFOFA, this school would teach washing, cooking, and sewing to the scores of girls in need of honorable work who could not be expected to learn industrial skills. Statesman Ramón Barros Luco explained: "It is understood that the women of our lower classes, whose capacities do not lend themselves to jobs that require some measure of refinement or good taste, would not take advantage of the education that could be given in these courses; and that there is an urgent need to develop the abilities they possess, which would benefit them because they would have an honorable way to earn a living, and industry and the country would also gain from the considerable forces that are now unproductive."[16] According to the society's proposal, this occupational school would function as an annex to the industrial one. The initial division of the female working population into two groups—one skilled and permanent, the other less capable, unstable, and subservient—

reveals the material, pragmatic emphasis of SOFOFA's initial proposal for female training for manufacturing jobs. Although moral improvement and domesticity were implied in their understanding of what made women into good industrial workers, girls' vocational training would focus primarily on their productive capacity, "delicacy," and preparation as workers.

The society's original vision did not hold for long; subsequent revisions and implementation of the project added a series of changes that ensured that women's domestic role would also receive substantial attention in the vocational school setting. Although the ministry's Council on Agricultural and Industrial Education responded favorably to SOFOFA's proposal, it dramatically reformed the proposed curriculum. Commercial sewing, cooking, and laundry were incorporated into the proposed Women's School of Arts and Crafts, but embroidery and glove making were eliminated, as those courses were already taught elsewhere.[17] As the SOFOFA bulletin later explained, the changes in the curriculum were made to adjust to a smaller annual budget: "It was necessary to cancel those sections that were considered less necessary and to make one school out of the two that had been planned."[18] Rather than eliminate one of the two projected schools, the ministry chose to combine women's industrial and service trades in the same curriculum.

The Women's School for Arts and Crafts opened for classes in March 1888, providing instruction to about 280 students in a rented building near downtown Santiago. Some of the students were migrants from the provinces, but the majority were probably daughters of Santiago artisans.[19] The name of the school was later changed to the Vocational School for Girls, apparently to distinguish the girls' school more easily from the men's School for Arts and Crafts.[20] The general regulations for the school issued soon thereafter established a schedule for grades on student progress and behavior, mandated a yearly exhibition of student work, set up a supervisory committee, and established fellowships for war orphans and distinguished students. Contrary to the founding decree, all students were responsible for paying about 5 pesos "as a guarantee of their attendance and good conduct," which ostensibly was to be returned when they completed their studies.[21] Students would be admitted in order of merit and had to be under eighteen years old, vaccinated, healthy, and literate. Moreover, the regulations excluded physical punishment for students, stating, "The students will be handled according to a rational discipline that will teach them to handle themselves with dignity. Thus, reprimands, detentions and expulsions will be the only punishments imposed on the students."[22] School administrators assigned students regular chores to maintain the school and schoolyard, and later controlled students' dress by prohibiting the use of the *manto* (a woman's cloak or veil used for mass or in public settings).[23]

After one year's operation, the school's budget had grown to 73,995 pesos and its curriculum had somewhat diversified. Embroidery classes were reinstated and new courses in box making and ornamental drawing were added. Significantly, almost all the school's teachers were European; only the flower-making and laundry teachers were Chilean. At the end of that year, SOFOFA considered the school to be a success, with average attendance at 248 out of 600 enrolled students. The society also extolled the fact that the school had already attracted the attention of a Swiss diplomat who wanted to visit the school: "This fact could not be more honorable and we are happy to have here a school that already has attracted attention in foreign lands."[24]

In the same year, school director Mercedes de Vivian filed a lengthy report with the Committee on Industrial and Agricultural Education, in which she detailed the operations and student body of the school. The first measure of the school's success, according to de Vivian, was the students' eagerness and success in finding employment: "Most of the students put the lessons that they receive in the school into practice every day. They wait impatiently for their diplomas to set up flower or clothing workshops in the capital or the provinces, to become teachers or to get a job; those who have small workshops hope to develop them better as soon as they acquire the necessary knowledge."[25] But the most popular course in the early years was that of commerce because graduates apparently found work as sales clerks and cashiers fairly easily.[26] De Vivian's report on the glove-making course shows how the school had to adapt to suit students from different sectors of the working class. The glove-making instructors found it necessary to pay the students directly for their work in class, or they would have had no students.[27] This arrangement apparently produced a dependency among the students, as there were no factories in Santiago where graduates could find employment. Because they could not be permanently employed in the school, the course was eliminated in 1891.[28] Administrators also made changes to accommodate students' limited resources and ensure their attendance: "In the sections of glove making, cooking, and laundry, students are paid a small amount so that they can attend the School regularly, because only the daughters of fathers from the lowest level of society dedicate themselves to these occupations, and they are usually the poorest."[29]

18. Commercial class, Girls' Vocational High School, Santiago, circa 1925. *Source: Actividades Femeninas en Chile* (Santiago: Imprenta y Litografía La Ilustración, 1928), 297.

At the other end of the spectrum, artistic embroidery was offered only to young women of some means, who could provide their own materials and who demonstrated an innate sense of good taste. Other courses in machine-woven cotton were offered after a Chilean industrialist traveled to Europe to study the technique; he observed that limiting the students' weaving to wool rendered them incapable of supporting themselves or making their own clothing in warmer weather (see table 16).[30] Other courses were subsequently added as machinery became available and administrators saw the need: linen embroidery was instituted in 1891; lingerie in 1895; hat and corset making in 1897; natural drawing and painting in 1899; and wood carving and modeling in 1907. The courses in fashion, lingerie, and drawing were significantly expanded in 1904 due to increased student demand.[31]

The most surprising observation offered in the 1889 report, however, was the fact that the Santiago Vocational School was attracting girls of higher social origins as well as women from the aristocracy. Noting the school's high enrollment, the director commented, "Not only have the

Table 16 Enrollment and Attendance in the Santiago Girls' Vocational School, 1892, by Area of Specialization

Course	Enrollment	Attendance
Artistic embroidery	57	27
Lingerie and Linen Embroidery	46	35
Flowers	27	25
Fashions	50	35
Machine weaving	27	24
Commerce and Calligraphy	30	42
Box making	11	9
Cooking	6	6

Source: AMIOP, *Consejo Enseñanza Técnica,* 1891–1892, vol. 420, list of students in the Girls' Vocational School, 1892.

daughters of the working classes rushed to enroll, but also a growing number of delicate young women who, some more accustomed to wealth than others, have come seeking nominal distraction and future well-being in work." Moreover, women over the age of eighteen were regularly accepted: "Ladies of 20, 30 and even 40 years of age; single, married, and widowed women have asked for a place to learn a profession." This flexibility reached its limit, however, and the administration barred further enrollment of aristocratic women in the school: "This has not occurred because the Council considers the school a safeguard against the immorality and poverty of the daughters who have lost destiny's favor."[32]

The director's report concluded with a reference to the need for additional courses for the mothers, wives, and daughters who "see in the school a source for their sex's healthy well-being, both material and moral." One such course, she said, would provide students with histories of the various industries and their benefits to individuals and to humanity: "I believe that the school thus would carry out its prized regenerative work more prolifically and would produce more abundant fruits and richer blessings."[33] This reality—class, age, and marital diversity among the students—quickly fragmented the vision on which the school was initially founded, that of a vocational school for the daughters of honorable but struggling working-class families. The society's initial project was further transformed by the interests and priorities of oversight committees and administrators, who would give increased curricular emphasis to home economics as the schools expanded.

Success and Expansion in the Girls' Vocational Schools

Compared to the small scale of male industrial education, the subsequent two decades saw the massification of industrial training for girls. While enrollment fluctuated from year to year, attendance in the first Girls' Vocational School (later known as the Vocational High School or Escuela Profesional de Niñas Superior) grew steadily from 248 in 1888 to 664 in 1902, and then fluctuated between 350 and 450 students per year from 1903 to 1909.[34] In 1902, about one third of the 664 students received diplomas after completing a three-year curriculum.[35] These were also years of national expansion, as twenty-eight more schools were established throughout Chile and a second, smaller school opened in Santiago. Accordingly, the infrastructure of the system grew to include a host of instructors trained at the Vocational High School and teaching in the provinces, school properties rented or owned by the state, oversight committees for each school,[36] and a tier of administrators responsible for directing and inspecting the schools. School administration was carried out largely by women, who inspected, directed, and taught the growing student body.[37]

Commentators at SOFOFA considered the first years of the Santiago Vocational School for Girls a resounding success, with lessons for male industrial as well as public elementary education. The principal improvement offered in the girls' schools, one author argued, was that in addition to giving proper vocational training and opening up new areas of work for women, the schools "discharged their proper role as a powerful support for our culture and the development of our population's principal and most widespread industries." Male education was apparently lacking in the preparation of sufficiently enthusiastic industrial workers, and should be reformed to "open new horizons to our workers' eyes, showing them higher ideals for their work, freeing their spirits from the fetters of routine by teaching them from the beginning about the new industrial arts and procedures, and how to perfect those that they already know."[38] Female industrial education thus indirectly reinforced planners' expectations that workers could be trained not only in skills, but also in work regimens and attitudes in such a way as to improve dramatically Chile's industrial production.

In 1893, in a report that applauded the initiation of cooking classes and the national exhibition of the schools' works, SOFOFA dubbed the Girls' Vocational Schools a triumph in social reform: "One might say, in conclusion, that this School has triumphantly opened the doors in Chile for women's vocational training, introducing a true revolution that is highly beneficial to the living conditions and morality of a large number of young women whose families lack sufficient resources to provide for their subsistence."[39] The success of girls' vocational training may have been limited to several hundred students, but SOFOFA considered it an experiment worthy of expansion and imitation. Despite its small size, the Girls' Vocational School was constantly promoted in the daily press, and the yearly exhibit of the school's works inevitably produced a flurry of favorable reviews from Santiago journalists. A typical review emphasized that women's economic participation was indispensable to Chile's industrial growth, and praised it as a "kind of Messiah that has to rescue us from the economic crisis we are facing."[40] The industrialists' trade journal in 1900 also applauded the success of the Girls' Vocational School and described it as a model for further expansion. The school's fame would reach as far as Buenos Aires, when a well-known journalist for *La Nación* went on a tour of the school. Factory and workshop owners were beginning to see the benefits of this training, "counting on women workers who are intelligent and are completely prepared for a diversity of tasks. For this reason, the most important factories and workshops prefer to hire them, thus assuring the future of all diligent students."[41] One of the keys to this success, the author continued, was the skill of industrial drawing that was applied in the diverse trades taught in the school. This skill, "the scientific and pedagogical basis for all industrial teaching," distinguished the Vocational School graduate from the common seamstress, embroiderer, and flower maker.

Because of the school's perceived success, administrators moved to establish a teacher-training program to staff future vocational schools throughout Chile. A course in teaching methodologies was added to the Vocational High School curriculum in 1899, preparing the top students to teach in the provincial schools after three years' training. This program was amplified in 1906, when courses in pedagogy, general methodology, home economics, math, Spanish, and gymnastics were incorporated into students' regular specialization. Upon completion, these students took a series of difficult exams[42] and were extolled as "models of dedication and good conduct" for the regular students.[43] The students who attended the Escuela Profesional Superior de Niñas at the corner of Avenida de las Delicias and Santa Rosa in the heart of Santiago's commercial district were drawn largely from nearby neighborhoods, suggesting either that they shared rooms in local cities and conventillos or were originally from families living in those districts.[44] By 1909, students in the Vocational High School also attended a new course in cooking and horticulture, in addition to linear and ornamental drawing and gymnastics: "The great number of students who seek to enroll here and the progress of arts and crafts suitable for young women has increased the number of courses, given new directions to others, and canceled some that originally functioned."[45] Weekly lectures in morals, domestic economy, hygiene, and urbanity were also required of all students.[46] Although some administrators viewed these classes with hostility, others saw in them an opportunity to reinforce the school and work regimen.[47] Noting that the speaker in morals and religion would do well to "oblige the students to pay better attention," the oversight committee advised him to "refer to the students' grades in the next class, and encourage them, as the director has, to increase their efforts to earn excellent grades always, in order to achieve moral progress and manual ability at the same time."[48] Insofar as it was even required of students, religion was apparently subordinate to the girls' technical training in the schools.

The success of the first vocational school inspired impassioned pleas for new schools in the provinces as early as 1889. A visitor to the Matas lingerie factory in Valparaíso, in which the workforce was almost entirely female (159 out of 173), complained that employers had to train their workers in every step of factory operations. The visitor, owner of another Valparaíso shirt factory, called for the establishment of a Girls' Vocational School in Valparaíso, "where they will teach the rudiments of the crafts that women usually execute, such as, in addition to cutting, sewing, washing and ironing linens, for example, the making of ladies dresses, shoe making, box making, etc.; and if they were taught commercial accounting, nobody would be better than women at selling behind a counter in the innumerable stores of Valparaíso."[49] A vocational school, the author argued, should complement industrial education at the elementary level to provide a skilled workforce for Valparaíso's lingerie and clothing factories. The Girls' Vocational School first opened in Valparaíso in 1897, and twenty-eight more schools were established throughout Chile over the next thirteen years. By 1910, female industrial education had grown to a national system of thirty schools, enrolling over four thousand students and graduating about six hundred of them every year (see table 17). Almost a third of these students attended the Vocational High School and Number 2 School in Santiago.[50] The provincial schools essentially copied the curriculum that had evolved in the Vocational High School; the distribution of class hours varied somewhat, ostensibly to meet the needs of local industries. Without excep-

Table 17 Founding Dates of Provincial Girls' Vocational Schools

1897	Valparaíso
1900	Concepción
1901 (6)	Tacna, Iquique, Antofagasta, San Fernando, Linares, Valdivia
1902 (3)	Talca, Chillán, La Serena
1905 (10)	Copiapó, Quillota, San Felipe, Rancagua, Curicó, Los Angeles, Traiguén, Temuco, Osorno, Ancud
1906 (6)	Rengo, Cauquénes, Taltal, Limache, Lebu, Angol
1910	Viña del Mar

Source: AE 1909, 437.

tion, the most important courses in vocational schools throughout Chile, according to number of class hours, were those offered in lingerie and fashions; tailoring and hat and corset making followed close behind, but were not taught in all of the schools (see table 18). The overwhelming majority of class hours in all schools in 1906 were thus dedicated to improving women's manufacturing and technical drawing skills, just as the schools' founders had intended.

Over the next twenty years, the girls' vocational school system continued to grow steadily, producing a steady stream of seven hundred to eight hundred graduates per year through 1927. Lingerie, fashions, and commerce continued to attract the most students and grant the most degrees in this period (see table 19). Finally, by 1926 a common curriculum had been established, which distinguished industrial, commercial, and teacher-training sections. In their first year, industrial students studied civics, Spanish, arithmetic, drawing and calligraphy, gymnastics, singing, home economics, and sewing; in the second, girls specialized in lingerie, fashion, hand weaving, children's clothing, applied arts, or home economics (including child education). Students had access to a medical clinic, grants-in-aid, and a cultural center for school alumnae.[51]

State funding, which had begun at a low 112 pesos per student per year in 1905, had increased ninefold by 1930. By comparison with other schools maintained by the state, however, the girls' vocational schools were still relatively inexpensive to operate.[52] By 1930, the Vocational Schools had granted roughly twenty thousand diplomas to Chilean women, and over eighty thousand women had enrolled.[53] According to one report, 50 percent of the schools' graduates went on to work in the home; 20 percent plied their trades in factories and workshops; 15 per-

Table 18 Weekly Hours of Instruction in Several Girls' Vocational Schools, 1909

Classes	Santiago Superior	Santiago Number 2	Valparaíso	Concepción
Lingerie	30	15	27	27
Sewing	30	30	27	27
Tailoring	—	15	—	27
Corset making	15	15	—	14
Haberdashery	15	15	15	13
Weaving	15	—	—	27
Flowers	—	—	12	13
Artistic embroidery	6	6	6	7
Linen embroidery	6	6	15	7
Drawing	15	15	15	21
Painting	15	12	12	6
Calligraphy	1	—	1	6
Home Economics	1	—	—	1
Math and Accounting	6	6	3	6
Morals and Religion	1	—	—	1
Hygiene	1	—	—	1
Gymnastics	—	—	1	1
Total hours	157	135	134	205

Source: AE 1909, 439.

cent worked independently, largely in the provinces; 10 percent worked in commerce; and 5 percent (about thirty per year) continued to study in order to teach in the industrial schools throughout Chile.[54]

By 1926, when the Vocational Schools were reviewed for the historic compendium of female education, *Actividades femeninas en Chile*, women's industrial education had apparently established a permanent foothold: "This year many vocational schools functioned throughout the Republic, developing industrial preparation and practice among the women who have to struggle for a living, attending to their own subsistence and that of their families. Thousands of students have passed through these Schools and thousands have benefited from their teachings, either through working in their own workshops, in commercial or industrial establishments, or applying their knowledge in the home, where they are educated wives and mothers, well prepared in domestic

Table 19 Number of Diplomas Granted in the Vocational High School by Area of Specialization, 1915–1924

Lingerie	777	31.7%
Fashions	405	16.5
Commerce	317	12.9
Embroidery	290	11.8
Weaving	201	8.2
Tailoring	85	3.4
Haberdashery	83	3.3
Home economics	62	2.5
Corset making	37	1.5
Painting	11	0.4
Flower making	9	0.3
Drawing	8	0.3
Various other	164	6.6
Total	2,449	

Source: AE, 1915–1924.

skills."[55] This review also reflects, however, the moralizing ideology of domesticity that had become firmly entrenched in the schools by 1926. As the schools and their administrations mushroomed after 1906, public attention subjected the gendered norms of the schools' mission to constant scrutiny. Thus, the mandate of the Girls' Vocational Schools was transformed into a project for reinforcing working-class domesticity, if not in deed then at least in word.

Domesticating Girls' Vocational Education

In 1909, Inspector General and Visitor of the Vocational Schools María Weigle de Jenschke initiated a campaign to regularize the school bureaucracy and standardize exams and grades to ensure that the schools' graduates would be of uniformly high quality.[56] Although the central content of these reforms concerned the mechanics of grading and exams, the inspector repeatedly emphasized the additional gains of such regulations, "since they are designed to complete the teaching given in those Schools, morally educating the students so that when they finish their studies, each one leaves *armed with a profession* and with *a moral personality* that saves her from life's contingencies."[57] She ordered, for example, that each student carry a booklet in which her attendance, progress, and grades would be noted by her teachers and signed by her parent or guardian.[58] Girls with unexcused absences would be dismissed, and the girls' work was to be graded on a scale of 0 to 6 (terrible to very good).

Most important, her detailed circular issued throughout the vocational school system signaled the emerging emphasis on moral education and domestic skills: "But manual teaching is not all that students should be given: they also need to be taught all of those fundamental principles that make up their moral personality, which are so necessary to going forth triumphantly in the struggle for life, so that they might be living elements of the country's moral progress at the same time."[59] The Weigle de Jenschke circular followed a ministry edict directing the head of the Vocational High School to enforce the general regulation rule that students receive a weekly talk on hygiene, urbanity, and home economics.[60] These talks included such topics as "duties of a well-educated girl," savings, the home, and cleaning:[61] "In these classes they try out many recipes to remove stains, clean furniture and home implements; they are taught to mend and darn used clothing; to prepare simple stews; to classify foods by their nutritive value; to avoid food decomposition through chemical procedures; to buy those foods; to keep accounts of incomes and expenses, inventories, purchase prices, etc., *which are indispensable to every woman.*"[62] By 1919, all but six of the twenty-nine Girls' Vocational Schools operating in Chile offered obligatory courses in domestic economy, morals and religion, and hygiene.[63] And in 1920, the Vocational High School began to grant degrees in the home economics specialty, granting sixty-two such diplomas in the next five years.

In December 1909, Weigle de Jenschke initiated another campaign, this time to toughen up the final exams in the industrial schools: "More than a few times, diplomas have been granted in the Vocational Schools to girls who are ignorant about the basics of the profession they have just studied."[64] On the other hand, she clarified, students who demonstrated comprehensive skills in their trades should be certified if they passed their exams after only one year. To graduate, students had to demonstrate their mastery of selected skills and undergo tests on theoretical materials that lasted several days.

Prizes for merit (usually a book of a technical nature) were distributed to students for best behavior, best attendance, and most distinguished in linear drawing. Six months after graduation, students gained access to their savings accounts, which consisted of 60 percent of the sale value of the items they had produced, plus savings prizes and 8 percent interest.[65] On that occasion, the director noted, "It is convenient in this distribution to read out loud the amounts that each one receives."[66] The most important part of the curriculum, according to one observer, was the way the school promoted "habits of savings, a problem of transcendental importance for the country."[67] In addition to having a profession, domestic skills, and good morals, Vocational School graduates were expected to be practiced in domestic thrift and savings.

The emphasis on practical domestic skills promoted by Weigle de Jenschke was apparently not popular among the students, who seemed to prefer courses on industrial skills and arts. The inspector general thus issued a circular in 1910 ordering obligatory, practical instruction in cooking (where possible), "darning, patchwork, stain removal, ironing, and everything about cleaning and repair of ladies' and gentlemen's clothing." Because most of the students came from low-income families, Weigle de Jenschke conceded that their paid labor was necessary for the families' survival, but argued that this was no reason to neglect their training in the practice of home economics. Her persistence in this matter was apparently encouraged by students' reluctance to take such courses: "I don't doubt, given the students' inclination to apply themselves with more enthusiasm to artistic and showy works, that this practice *that is obligatory for all students* will be a bit difficult in the beginning; but I believe that with a little zeal and firmness, the Director will quickly correct these difficulties and convince the students of its practical advantage."[68] School administrators—in contrast with the industrialists who proposed the schools—found instruction in domestic economy to be indispensable to proper vocational education.[69] Prior to these reforms, the delay in establishing cooking classes had provoked concern among inspectors, who considered cooking "indisputably one of the most important courses for girls who are educated here."[70]

The continuing tension between the schools' mandate to train industrial workers and its emphasis on preparing girls to be good housewives was also apparent in the school's 1912–1914 magazine, the *Revista Industrial Femenina*. "Dedicated to housewives and women's industries," the journal was prepared by teachers and alumnae of the Vocational High School and distributed in a printing of one thousand copies. Although the topic of women's work was never absent from its pages, the magazine was clearly designed to appeal to housewives: the *Revista* published recipes, sewing patterns, drawings, and domestic accounting advice, paying relatively little attention to women's paid work or the activities of the

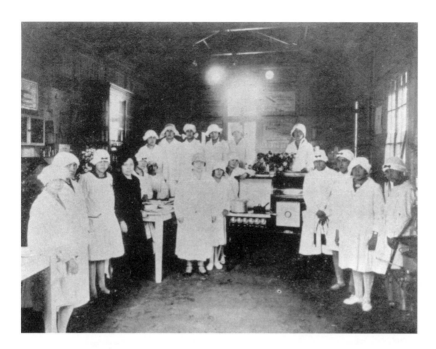

19. Primary school domestic economy class, Women's Exhibit, 1927.
Source: Actividades femeninas en Chile (Santiago: Imprenta y Litografía La Ilustración, 1928), 48.

school. In addition, the magazine highlighted poetry and essays by the Vocational High School's teachers and students on the virtues of motherhood and good housekeeping. This focus may have reflected their intended readership: not the poor women attending the vocational schools, but rather the middle- and upper-class señoras who were likely to use their services.[71]

The *Revista Industrial Femenina* also served as a medium to promote the public image and appeal of the schools to a wider public. In the magazine's second issue, the school's director argued that it was crucial to have a magazine that could elicit continued public support for the vocational schools, as well as provide housewives with access to the technical knowledge that abounded in the schools. The core of her argument, however, was that the vocational school movement represented a key to the moral and technical reform of women's professions, dignifying and legitimizing women's work: "The time has now come in Chile that work should be a sign of prestige, particularly for the female sex. . . . The poor woman who is educated for life and prepared for her profession is an important factor for the moralization of her profession, the base for putting together honorable families, disciplined for work and the common good."[72] Although the magazine was intended to provide housewives with useful information, she argued that "in no case should what I have said here be postponed." An important aspect of promoting female vocational education was for writers to emphasize the schools' image as a training ground for female morality and domesticity. One short fiction, for example, recounted the tribulations of a working-class mother whose daughter had become rebellious and refused to help around the house. A friend of the family urged her to send her daughter to the Vocational School because "moderate freedom does not harm good young women; hard work turns them away from bad ways . . . and he who carves out an honest future for himself by working with his hands, shuns the dangers in which the ignorant perish, and finally, I assure you that they demand a lot of morality from the students in this school."[73] The mother, fearful of sending her daughter out into the world, was apparently convinced that the combination of work and moral training would shape her daughter up while protecting her from the evils of the unsupervised workplace.

A third and apparently minor objective of the *Revista* was to stimulate girls' attendance and performance in the schools by publishing their testimonial contributions. Here, the training received in the Vocational Schools was extolled not as moral, but as economic salvation for young women. Filomena Sierra, a graduate of the Vocational School of Copiapó, wrote, for example: "I have seen my childhood ways extinguished and my childish dreams dissipated; I am now a young woman burdened with the social obligations and debts of my parents, of society, of the country and of humanity. . . . Today, I consider that I am happy and deserve to have the independence I have earned by struggling with advantage in the battles of labor, relying when necessary on the knowledge acquired to earn a daily living."[74] This view of abnegation and surrender to a life of brutal, but honorable, work also emerged in a letter written by a Vocational School alumna to her classmates, warning them of the trials to come in the real world of work: "The struggle for life is difficult, above all when in order to work, we have to abandon the home, where we leave a father and mother who love us, to go to another town where we have to complete the mission entrusted to us. . . . that will doubtless be the first suffering that you have had to endure."[75] References such as this to economic hardship were very few and contrasted sharply with the rest of the articles on femininity, domesticity, and scientific home management. Most stories were dedicated to the application of women's industrial skills in the home, which was stressed as the ultimate arena for all women's skills.

Despite Weigle de Jenschke's reforms and widespread praise of the vocational schools for the domestic and moral training they provided, home economics remained of relatively minor importance to the students' curriculum in terms of class time and number of special diplomas granted. This emphasis on domesticity in the schools' reports and outside observations may in fact be largely explained by the class position of administrators and elite women observers, who seemed to be more concerned about shaping female personality and shoring up working-class family values than stimulating the national economy through female industries.[76] Emphasis on domestic training in later years may also reflect a growing need to justify industrial training for women, who by 1920 were coming under increasing pressure to abandon formal, paid labor and tend to the home. Nevertheless, the theme of domesticity, especially the science of home economics, remained an important touchstone in public debate on the Vocational Schools throughout the period.

Debates on Gender, Work, and Education

Technical drawing classes notwithstanding, it was the Vocational Schools' effective combination of women's industries and home economics that reaped the most praise from observers of that movement. In the words of a 1909 *El Mercurio* editorial, the Vocational High School was especially laudable because, "at the same time that [students] master a waged occupation or profession, they acquire and begin to apply habits of order, planning, and economy in all work that belongs in the home and they become good wives of workers."[77] A few years later, a journalist writing for *Familia*, an elite women's magazine that offered the usual women's fare of recipes, cultural reviews, and fashion tips, visited the Vocational High School and came away with the definite impression that "the women's vocational schools pursue the double goal of forming women workers and women of the home." This project was primarily directed at working-class women, who, according to this author, would otherwise have been a massive drag on society: "The [schools'] goal is laudable: they train women workers, and particularly workers' wives (meaning wives in the broadest sense of the term), that is considering [women workers] to be just like all living beings that have to produce something in life, since now they do nothing but consume." She applauded the Chilean imitations of modernist education in France,

Belgium, and the United States that "today are rescuing women from the old and innate habits of their race."[78]

The success of the Vocational Schools inspired subsequent debates about whether such training ought not to be undertaken earlier, as part of primary education. The state could prepare poor girls for industrial work in elementary schools, common reasoning went, eliminating the need to subsidize their enrollment in the Vocational Schools later on. Teaching industrial skills to the young would, moreover, reinforce "practical" education in the elementary schools, where current curricula "inevitably depress our industry and produce an unquestionably excessive number of people working in the liberal professions."[79] Others argued against transforming elementary education into vocational training, because the Vocational Schools depended on solid training in the basics in elementary school and because industrial skills could only be properly taught at a higher level.[80] Officials in the school hierarchy opposed industrial instruction at the elementary level for these reasons, pointing out that "the girls enrolled in a Vocational School are already fourteen, and since it is not proper to make them work when they are younger, they should dedicate their studies first to reading, writing, arithmetic, drawing, etc., etc., courses that are indispensable so that a professional can take full advantage of an art or industry."[81] Whereas some cited the Vocational Schools as the quintessential example of the failures of liberal elementary education, those who viewed them as truly vocational—and not simply finishing schools for poor women—defended the autonomy of industrial education.

The Girls' Vocational Schools also served as an example for those who wished to promote the dignity of women's work—particularly that of poor women—in broader debates. In the ongoing discussions in the press and elsewhere about women's place in Chilean society, the issue of whether working for pay was suitable for women went to the heart of the motives of industrial education. With the success of the Santiago school, advocates for women's work could rely on a concrete example to debunk arguments for restricting female economic participation.[82] The industrial schools, both public and private, were often touted as the most effective means to female economic independence and survival, despite women's subordinate position in the labor market. With a lot of initiative and skill, it was argued, young women could become entrepreneurs and effectively stand in for absent or unemployed male family members. A 1912 editorial appearing in *El Mercurio* applauded the privately run Centro de Artes Domésticas, where girls quickly learned machine weaving, bought a machine together, and had plans to set up their own workshop. Another student, already established, told the reporter, "I tell you now, Sir: I support my mother and my brothers with my work. In our house I am the husband and the father of the family." This effort to train individual women had far-reaching effects: "To raise woman up, give her confidence in her own strength, teach her that she can achieve economic independence through honest work, is not only a work of charity, but also one of economic and social interest, because by getting the woman involved in production we regain unproductive economic forces and also moral strength to struggle against immorality and vice."[83] This particular editorial reproduced the original rationale for women's vocational education used by industrialists and politicians in the 1880s: vocational schools endowed women with skills that would spur national growth and moralize working-class families. Typical of this position was the revival of the idea of establishing a real school of female professions, where women could study to become gardeners, landscape architects, upholsterers and interior decorators, children's hairdressers, or nurses: "Many will ask themselves how one learns all this. One doesn't improvise landscape gardeners, upholsterers, or hairdressers. The needs create the means. Thus, as there are schools where one learns to embroider, to make corsets, and to cook, one would have to set up a women's trade school." However, the class background of the prospective students for the school was implicit in the description of their talents, derived from female socialization that would not have been available to poor women: a woman interior decorator, for example, "accustomed from girlhood to combine colors and arrange the folds of her dresses, would do this job perfectly."[84] Inspired by the French domestic training schools at a social service conference in Paris in 1929, Gabriela Mistral advocated that women also be trained for "new careers along the same lines of domestic education; housekeeper, hotel and bar manager, chambermaid, who at the same time is a hairdresser and masseuse, cook, nanny, etc."[85]

Many opinions expressed about female vocational instruction, however, seconded administrators' concern with female virtue in terms of the kinds and conditions of "women's work." The skills acquired in the Vocational Schools were consistently praised as the bulwark for protecting female virtue, as women "would not find themselves obliged by inability and ignorance to go about increasing ever more the numerous army of the wretched." Vocational education also allowed girls of poor families to avoid learning their trades in factory workshops, which were roundly denounced as "centers for vice and unfettered corruption." Moreover, commercial training in the Vocational Schools was undesirable both "because it takes woman out of the role for which she was created and because she has plenty of opportunities to work by simply joining the professions and occupations that are directly related to her sex," and because contact with male customers led inexorably to vice. Finally, the author criticized instruction in the decorative arts because students would only become accustomed to it and "will want to spend their whole lives among silks."[86]

This concern with the kinds of skills taught in the vocational school curriculum was also linked to the perceived "servant crisis" in Chile, particularly in Santiago, where "good help" was apparently getting harder to come by.[87] Many of the complaints published in Santiago papers between 1907 and 1911 blamed the shortage of good servant girls on the Vocational Schools. On the one hand, young women with vocational certificates were less inclined to serve in private homes, because in school they had been taught skills that made them "too good" for domestic service: "This lack of servants in Chile is one of the victories of progress, because the former candidates for servitude are now enrolled in school, where fifty different courses are taught—forty-five of them useless—which convert the former *china* [servant girl] with good muscles and a mane of hair into a señorita with fragile morals."[88] In short, "we are educating ladies and not servants."[89] On the other hand, vocational schools failed when they neglected to train young women as servants, "instruction that exists in the more advanced countries."[90] In an exchange printed in *El Ilustrado* about the wisdom of training programs for future servants, "A Housewife" argued that such training would only make domestic service more expensive, whereas J.E.S. pointed out that professionalization would make the occupation more desirable.[91] In this, as in other aspects of the so-called servant crisis, the debate hinged on authors' different assessments of the propriety of domestic servitude in a modern society; vocational instruction was here equated, for better or for worse, with "progress" away from the paternalistic relations of traditional Chilean society.[92]

Some critics argued instead that the emphasis of vocational schools should turn exclusively to domestic training, placing even less emphasis on wage earning or artistic skills: "It is necessary, in sum, to teach less fashion and more home economics."[93] Apparently inspired by reports of such schools in the United States and France, one author advocated that the vocational schools simply be changed into Escuelas de Dueñas de

Casa because the domestic economy courses were the most important for women anyway. The author suggested that a school for housewives would do well to imitate the pedagogy applied in the Instituto Superior de Educación Física y Manual. In that school, students role-played as housewives, servants, cooks, and bakers: "In sum, the girls do practically all the work of housewives. With one difference: they give reasoned and scientific explanations for everything they do."[94] This was commonly advocated as a logical course for Chile's progress, "to give to the future teaching of home economics the importance that it has already acquired in female education programs in more advanced countries."[95]

Another advocate of women's domestic education referred explicitly to U.S. and European domestic technical schools, which, "in the same way that the vocational schools aid the progress of the working classes by teaching them an art or a craft that will be useful to the ruling classes, ... seek this same progress exclusively for the use of the poor." The idea here was to separate industrial and vocational training from that of training respectable working-class housewives, who in turn contributed to national progress by providing male workers with healthy, well-organized homes: "The vocational school student will go on tomorrow to an almost certain wage-earning future. The student of the domestic technical school will go on tomorrow to direct, with modesty and certainty, her own home. The home of the people, managed by a woman with decorum, cleanliness, and economy!!! This is the only practical formula for the moral and material progress of the worker." Unlike the proponents of vocational education, who stressed the poverty of the students' families, this argument explicitly invoked the male family wage as the real solution to female poverty, making women's skilled work virtually unnecessary: "A worker who is skilled at his art or craft always earns enough to maintain his home." The key to successful working-class homes, according to this author, was the combination of effective domestic education for women and industrial education for young men: "Both works complement each other, and they are joined in the reasoned aspiration for the perfection of the working-class family."[96]

What at first had seemed an egalitarian-minded attempt to create a female industrial workforce to stimulate national industry had therefore become another normative strut in the continuing segmentation of the urban workforce. Not only did this fit with elite programs to stabilize working-class families under industrialization, but it rationalized and substituted for reform of unequal wage and occupational structures. Only rarely did commentary on industrial education refer to the problems in the structure of the labor market that prevented even Vocational School graduates from prospering in their work. One observer urged legislators to find ways to open areas for female employment, because most of these graduates "have to struggle for their lives since they are poor.... Our legislators have to think about how to provide work for the women who are educated in State schools, in order to avoid creating a new social problem someday that would be very hard to solve." Apparently, SOFOFA members had expressed the same concern, planning in 1915 to "establish more practical courses in the vocational schools that train the woman to earn a living more easily."[97] This was still a complaint in 1923, when Manuel Rivas Vicuña commented in *El Mercurio*, "There are many women without occupations and many jobs that have no personnel to do them."[98] Despite the glowing reports on Vocational School graduates' refinement, economic ingenuity, and housewifely skills, the schools remained the target of criticism from observers whose central concern remained the labor market, whether factory employment or domestic service.

By contrast, the silence of the labor press on the subject of female industrial education is significant. The only mention of the Vocational Schools was limited to announcements concerning graduation ceremonies and an occasional complaint about religious instruction in the schools.[99] This was not a sign of disinterest in working women's education, however; working women's associations frequently sponsored short courses in commercial sewing and other night courses for their members. Labor's apparent indifference to formal industrial education may have indicated a fundamental approval of the way such measures reinforced age and gender hierarchies in the labor market. Moreover, the increasingly domestic orientation of women's vocational education coincided with organized labor's enduring attraction to the respectability brought by domestic ideology and a proper gendered division of labor, even among more feminist-minded socialists.

Conclusions

In the midst of the supposed decline of female industrial participation around the turn of the century, the Girls' Vocational Schools produced a steady stream of certified seamstresses, tailors, artificial flower makers, sales clerks, and embroiderers for the labor market. The development of girls' industrial education in Chile, despite its limited impact, was emblematic of broader struggles in the state and society over the class and gendered meanings assigned to manual labor. Although this project began in the 1880s by acknowledging women's economic participation and trying to correct some of its deficiencies (while stimulating economic growth), the fact that this reform accepted and reinforced occupational segregation limited its potentially uplifting effect on women's employment, further training some women in trades already defined as "women's work." In addition, the reality of women's wage levels overwhelmed industrialists' optimism about female education's palliative effects; women's work would not provide them with sufficient wages, no matter how "skilled" the worker, because it was performed by women.

Moreover, the actual evolution of industrial education for women into a training ground for working-class housewives demonstrates how difficult it was for contemporaries to conceive of women's labor primarily in economic terms. Though work had the potential to dignify poor women and save them from vice, technical training for women had little meaning apart from instruction in the rules of proper conduct, service, and family management. Although working-class men, particularly those enrolled in the Escuela de Artes y Oficios, had also long been subject to the "moralizing gaze" of the elite, their vocational training did in fact prepare them to enter the labor market with skills that would garner them higher wages; no one argued that the men's school at the Quinta Normal should offer courses in butlering or home economics, for example. Women's training in the tasks of earning a living was, by contrast, still considered largely "unskilled" and was overshadowed by a curriculum that purported to refine women's domestic skills or prepare them to earn a living in the protected space of the home.

The available sources are far from conclusive on the reasons for this shift over time to an even heavier emphasis on domestic education in the Girls' Vocational Schools. Attempts to reform school curricula, instigated by ministerial decrees and individual administrators around 1909, seemed to stem from the growing concern evident in many sectors of Chilean society about the imperiled virtue of urban working women. Like politicians advocating female protective legislation or labor militants struggling to make women's employment unnecessary, vocational school administrators sought to encourage women's wage work outside of the factory setting, while at the same time increasing women's effectiveness as administrators of male workers' wages and behavior. Although the results of such training were apparently contradictory—preparing women for nonexistent employment while "spoiling" them for domestic service—the schools' claim to enhance women's domestic abilities clearly became an important factor in obtaining support from the schools' more well-off patrons, the probable employers of many Vocational School graduates.

The Chilean experience with women's vocational instruction in this period was hardly unusual compared to similar institutions created in Mexico (1871) and Brazil (1911). In both of those cases, women's technical education diverged from that of men insofar as it stressed women's training in nonfactory and domestic tasks, at least partially to elicit continued public and state support for the schools.[100] Likewise, in all three cases school administrators had to contend with the tension between the training students wanted—in marketable industrial and artisanal skills—and the information that their elite public wanted them to acquire.[101] If anything, compared to what we know of these schools in Mexico and Brazil, the increasing emphasis on home economics training in Chile in the 1910s and 1920s came about relatively more gradually and with evidence of continuing ambivalence about the purpose of women's vocational instruction.

The state and SOFOFA set out to modernize women's economic role and facilitate social adaptation to an emerging industrial economy. By professionalizing "women's work," elite sectors collaborated (on a small scale) to adapt women's economic performance to the demands and stresses of an increasingly industrial-based, capitalist economy; this adaptation aimed to increase individual women's capacity to perform manufacturing or service tasks in the home, where they would continue to be responsible for family unity, consumption patterns, and child care. Thus, despite the egalitarian promise of vocational training, the schools served to consolidate the segmentation of industrial work by sex (through the kinds of skills taught) and the sexual division of labor (by teaching domestic skills), just as work itself was increasingly defined as a masculine activity in many ways. Women certified by the Vocational Schools were expected to excel in the organization of productive and stable working-class homes. To what extent these women actually became experts in home economics is open to question,[102] but the promise of well-formed working-class homes, presided over by trained domestic managers, nevertheless became an organizing principle and important justification for Chilean vocational instruction as the century progressed.

6

Señoras y Señoritas

Catholic Women Defend the *Hijas de Familia*

With its burgeoning cities, militant and vociferous workers, and wide economic fluctuations, the early years of the twentieth century were clearly an alarming period for the Chilean aristocracy. Increasingly, public debates about the social question spread to the señoras and señoritas of the elite; the wives and daughters of Chile's senators and industrialists, steeped in the doctrines of Catholic Action and stimulated by the growing activism of aristocratic and middle-class women in public life, led some of the earliest systematic efforts to aid, educate, and organize working-class women.[1] Like women forging a public presence on national issues such as public health, women's legal rights, and the social question across Latin America, women of the Chilean elite enjoyed the education, resources, and political access that allowed them to bring their concerns into public discourse through newspapers, speeches, and publications.[2] Drawing, moreover, on decades of experience as patrons for the charitable associations run by the Catholic Church and private agencies, upper-class women were well positioned to design and oversee institutions that, in providing practical benefits for working women and their patrons, disciplined and organized working-class women in the fight against Chile's social and moral decline.[3]

The call to action spearheaded by elite women after 1900 was motivated both by the class fear engendered by the social question and by the economic shifts that were drawing non-working-class women into the workforce. This was not simply a continuation of debates on the social question from the previous decade. First and foremost, elite women's concern was sparked by the influx of the "deprived daughters of [good] families" (*desheredadas hijas de familia*) into the workforce, which affected even the most aristocratic homes. This situation—and the growing expectation that even women of means would have to contribute to the family economy—infused elite efforts to address the problems of working women with a new sense of urgency. The evolution of elite rationales in this period for educating, training, and organizing women workers reflected this move of respectable—married, middle-class, or simply educated—women into the industrial workforce.

At the same time, the expansion of clerical and sales jobs that accompanied the growth of Santiago as the country's administrative and economic center provided women with new occupational opportunities as *empleadas* (white-collar employees), from department store sales clerks to commercial accountants and telegraph operators. With more education and higher-class origins than their working-class counterparts, empleadas and professional women readily organized unions and issued propaganda in defense of their interests in the workplace. Further, the presence of "cultured" women and "daughters of good families" in the workplace reinvigorated debates on female employment, particularly over issues of femininity and social respectability. The new paradigm of respectable daughters at work challenged existing gender and class norms, which had traditionally dismissed such work as demeaning (i.e., only for working-class women) and unfeminine (i.e., only for men).

A third factor shaping elite women's response was their interest in countering the advance of socialism and corresponding forms of feminism in Chile. Alarmed by evidence of popular mobilization, particularly the growth of female resistance societies, aristocratic women struggled to reappropriate both feminism and worker organization by inscribing issues of female employment within a distinctively paternalistic framework. Under the aegis of Christian feminism, elite Catholic women now turned their attention to the mobilization of women workers, in so doing elaborating a rights-oriented discussion of women's work alongside the more traditional defense of working women's virtue. The result was a series of new protective, mutual aid, and union organizations, whose main concern was to defend the social benefits of women's work and to stop the advance of radical labor ideologies among working women.

Private Initiatives and Poor Women

Prior to the enactment of social legislation and the creation of effective state welfare structures in the 1930s, the task of protecting women from economic exploitation—and through them, protecting their families—was relegated to the realm of the private sector.[4] Individual industrialists, religious orders, mutual aid societies, and charitable organizations were thus the principal providers of social services aimed at, among other things, ameliorating the effects of women's paid work. Aristocratic ladies and the Catholic Church were long at the forefront of efforts to address social problems by setting up private initiatives to combat what they understood as an increasingly explosive social condition.

Catholic charities had long formed the basis of service provision to the poor in Chile. Inspired by the Social Action recommendations of the 1891 papal encyclical *Rerum Novarum*, elite Catholic women collaborated with religious orders to establish and maintain Church-owned factories, day care for working mothers, vocational training programs, and maternal health programs. One short-lived women's newspaper, proclaiming itself an "organ for the defense of women's rights," urged señoras to do good works for the poor and to rescue the "libertarian woman" from her immoral pastimes: "New wills soon will come together to construct the building of this precious ideal. It has a large, well-known and beneficial field [to develop] that intelligent and distinguished señoras will cultivate in their desire to rescue the Chilean and libertarian woman from the situation that currently degrades her moral being, helping her, if possible, break the silken chains which, regaling her vanity, tie her to a fatal system of spending her time wasting her graces and her money." After attacking the system of municipal regulation of prostitution and writing in defense of higher wages for women tram workers, the paper celebrated the selfless work of wealthy women among the most destitute: "There are wealthy women who have heart and they are not all false angels."[5]

Elite women were also closely allied with the institutions run by religious orders, which focused largely on aiding poor women; the services provided to poor women and children by the Hermanas de Santa Cruz and Sociedad San Vicente de Paul, for example, combined free education, medical services, and day care with occupational training.[6] The nuns of the San José Order were praised in a local newspaper for their work in 1903: "Mothers who need to earn a living with daily work, by the force of their own hands, but who also are busy raising their tender children, will find the help they need in the institution of the day care house. There the mothers can leave their little ones to the shelter and support of the daughters of Christian charity while they work during the day, labor in workshops, or help their husbands to earn their daily bread."[7] A broad network of services allowed nuns and aristocratic ladies to serve some working mothers and to protect children from neglect or the evils of the factory environment.[8]

Catholic women also joined in private efforts led by male politicians and professionals. Members of Chile's wealthiest landowning families, including Ramón Barros Luco and Santiago Intendant Enrique Cousiño, participated in the founding of the National Children's Foundation (Patronato Nacional de la Infancia) in 1901 to give aid to poor children.[9] The Children's Foundation programs manifested the founders' sense of scientific and moral urgency: "The National Children's Foundation has arisen from the needs of the people, and there was an urgent need to address the problem that until now had been consigned to the saddest fate: the poor boy in his home, the mother abandoned or ignorant of her duties and how to comply with them, materially and morally."[10] Most of their efforts were directed at poor mothers through a network of maternity wards, infant milk programs, and soup kitchens. These interventions included awarding prizes to mothers who nursed their infants to healthy childhood and a network of social workers who pressured mothers to legalize unions with the fathers of their children "in order to sanctify and legitimize the home."[11]

Most charitable efforts were designed to protect those who, because of disease, misfortune, or male abandonment, needed extra help to survive without turning to prostitution. The Protective Workshops for Women Workers (Talleres Protectoras de Obreras), for example, were founded in 1906 and staffed by 350 volunteers who worked on behalf of "the poor daughters of the people who live by working," teaching poor women laundry and cooking skills for future employment.[12] This effort was typical of private religious and charitable efforts, accurately reflecting elite assumptions about the inevitability of poor women's waged work. With the sponsorship of elite organizations such as the National Children's Foundation, prominent Catholic señoras participated actively in training working-class girls in the domestic and industrial arts. Like the state-funded schools discussed in the previous chapter, schools such as the Victoria Prieto Society combined home economics with moral instruction and occupational training: "The [Society's] goal is to reestablish the life of the home among the working and laboring people, preparing girls for this from their earliest years with a firm and solid physical, intellectual and moral education, under the safekeeping of religion, which we teach and inculcate in them as the basis for all moral perfection." Unlike the state vocational schools, however, classes in the three schools of the Victoria Prieto Society were taught by the señoras themselves, who also paid regular visits to students' families: "Similarly, we make home visits to the students' families, and try to maintain an

Table 20 Enrollment in Private Girls' Vocational Schools, 1909

Private Workshop/School	Enrolled	Attended
Escuela Técnica de Oficios Manuales Orden de Santo Domingo	103 boys 137 girls	115
Escuela-Taller de Santiago Apostol	480 girls	400
Escuela Profesional de María Auxiliadora	60 girls	53
Escuela Industrial de Niñas de la Calle Dávila	242 girls	—
Escuela Profesional de Niñas de la Calle Bascuñan Guerrero	166 girls	129
Talleres de obreras de la Calle Gay	68 girls	63
Asilo-Taller del Sagrado Corazón Misioneras Franciscanas	55 girls	52

Source: Adapted from AMIOP, *Escuelas Talleres Subvencionadas,* 1908–1909, vol. 2028, list of industrial schools funded, September 1909.

incessant moral contact between the the members of the society and the people who are favored by it, which among other things establishes a current of union and compassion between social classes that were completely separated before."[13] As Verba has observed, these "angels of peace and harmony" saw themselves and their working-class counterparts as the nexus of female cooperation that would heal the class conflict that had so divided elite and working-class men.[14]

Inspector Weigle de Jenschke, the indefatigable reformer of the state-run Vocational Schools, reflected on some of the key differences between those schools and the private, often Catholic-run workshops in her 1909 report (see table 20). As visitor to the Vocational Schools, Weigle de Jenschke also supervised privately run workshop-schools, the small institutions that were usually run by Catholic nuns and received some state funding. In her 1909 inspection report on private schools, Weigle de Jenschke criticized them for failing to train these girls in marketable skills such as domestic service. The Girls' Industrial School of Dávila Street, for example, was finally initiating courses in shoe making, cooking, and laundry, "some of the most important courses to train the kind of workers that are so needed throughout the country." Her visit to the Talleres de Obreras de la calle Gay also demonstrated "how difficult it is to teach these girls, who are from the poorest classes, to take interest in and love the jobs that are most necessary and, therefore, most practical for them . . . where can one find these days a laundress who knows how to work with the cleanliness and care that serves the family's interest?" So-called practical courses preparing girls as domestic servants were less appealing to students, presumably because they aspired to more skilled, better-paying jobs in manufacturing and commerce. On this score, Weigle de Jenschke also found the private schools lacking in theoretical training, "that is, the lack of a drawing course, which I consider very retrograde in the industrial Schools."[15]

Not surprisingly, these private vocational schools were the real strongholds for combined religious and industrial education. In these schools, vocational training and apprenticeship in domestic service were imbued with the moral and religious meaning of hard work for the poor. The speaker at the founding of the Escuela Profesional de Niñas de las Hijas de María Auxiliadora extolled that in the school the girls "receive an intellectual, moral, and physical education, based on the principles of the Gospel; where they learn manual labor, home economics, and a profession so that they will be able to earn a living . . . they form solidly Christian girls who will be useful to the family, to society, and to themselves; to teach them the lights of science grounded in Christian morality."[16] It was also in the religious school-workshops that the class of students was exclusively of the poorest, which helps explain why these schools emphasized training for domestic servants over manufacturing or artisanal skills. Like the orphanages and charities run exclusively for a clientele of poor women and their charges, the school-workshops were particularly paternalistic in expressing the purpose of their vocational training: "This workshop-asylum aims to give refuge to so many young women who, for whatever reason, are outside of the protection of their fathers' homes and are without resources, in order to keep them from being dragged down by vice and degradation, as happens in most cases . . . our institution exclusively benefits society's most helpless classes and it is not our intention to teach above the level of the social sphere to which our students belong. Our aspirations have been met when we rescue from hell people who can be useful to society, by giving them the means to earn an honest living, either in domestic service or small industry."[17] In other respects, such as emphasizing women's work as domestic industry and stressing thrift and moral development as integral to forming a working-class family, the religious school-workshops did not differ substantially from their public counterparts.

Another characteristic of Catholic women's charities was to emphasize the plight of the most needy women and the moral urgency of preventing their fall into prostitution. The most sustained effort in this regard was the White Cross (Cruz Blanca), a society founded in 1918 to provide housing for abandoned girls, single mothers, and prostitutes; to support legislation against the white slave trade; and to campaign against regulated prostitution at all levels of society.[18] Denouncing the inaction of the state against the "national shame known as the conventillo," President Adela Edwards de Salas explained that "we women of Chile, deeply moved by the evidence of the terrible plague that takes the defenseless daughters of the conventillo as its victims, have gathered together to find some remedy to the evil that we lament."[19] The White Cross remedy included extensive vocational training programs and industrial workshops, which by 1929 were netting over 60,000 pesos in yearly income for the institution.[20] Vocational and religious instruction for working-class women thus remained one of the main points of contact between aristocratic señoras and the poorest class of women workers, even as new mechanisms were developed to cultivate elite women's alliances with other sectors of the female working population. As the female labor force came to include better-educated and more organized women, moreover, elite women shifted their approach to include institutions that went beyond the provision of training and moral succour to the "daughters of the conventillo."

Women Who Had "Come to Less"

As even a cursory reading of prescriptive literature on women's work at the turn of the century will show, few of Santiago's elite men and women questioned the fact that it was the lot of poor women to work for wages, even if those wages were sorely inadequate. Some may have protested the excessive exploitation of women in industry, especially in those occupations that kept women from fulfilling their domestic labors, but the bulk of Catholic charitable efforts affirmed the expectation that if a girl was born to a working-class family, she would have to contribute to its sustenance. As in working-class circles, some Catholic reformers rejected women's wage work entirely, or accepted it only as a temporary remedy.[21]

In the second decade of the century, however, there was a noticeable

shift in elite women's assessments of women and work, seemingly provoked by material circumstances. Primarily through *El Mercurio* editorials and speeches delivered to the League of Chilean Women, elite
women displayed a special interest in what they saw as an alarming phenomenon: middle-class women performing sewing or other handicrafts
in order to contribute to family coffers.[22] In response to what the señoras
perceived as the plight of women "come to less," in 1912 the League
established the Women's Protective Workshops (Talleres Protectoras de
Mujer), in which volunteers sold the clothing produced by women in
their own homes in order to increase women's earnings and protect
respectable women from the shame of selling in public. The workshops
sold "delicate and artistic works such as embroidery, lingerie, dresses and
art objects at a relatively low price, thus benefiting women of all social
classes who, because of their needs, are forced to work."[23] Though the
workshop included the wares of working-class women, virtually all of
the propaganda for the workshops emphasized the need for aristocratic
solidarity with middle- (and sometimes upper-) class women. The
League's effort to support middle-class women in dire straits reflected
the increase of middle-class women in the needle trades—who were
clinging to respectability by staying at home—and called for a different
kind of support for them, because they could not be taken into existing
homes for poor women. A similar effort, the Abeja de Oro society, was
founded the following year in Valparaíso.[24]

The most distinctive aspect of the Protective Workshops was their
proponents' focus on the issue of social respectability, for the League
wished to help "the bashful lady: this phrase says it all. She deserves our
constant help, just like the wife and daughter of the worker."[25] Organizers and promoters of the workshops repeatedly emphasized that the
primary obstacle to the women they served was "the bourgeois and
middle-class prejudice against women's manual labor." Middle- and
upper-class women in need of income, they argued, "cannot appear in
public or sell [their goods] like workers and merchants to their equals,
their friends, even their close relatives."[26] It was necessary to illuminate
the specific nature of the respectable woman's oppression, advocating for
"the woman from a more elevated social situation who needs a certain
amount of independence and will not resign herself to being a slave to
earn her daily bread. There are clear and brutal forms of slavery that
humanity has abolished; but there are still others more silent, but no less
outrageous, that are mourned in secret and impose chains of shame and
sadness."[27] Above and beyond the exigencies of material necessity, the

workshops' proponents argued, respectable women were confined by social prejudice, which denied them their just remuneration and pride in their work.

According to reports in *El Mercurio*, the Women's Protective Workshops did very well in 1913 and 1914. Observers reported that their patrons were those women who overcame social prejudice to support the "invisible workers." Without their support, "what the shamefaced woman produces is not accepted as work but rather as an excuse to beg."[28] Aristocratic women who purchased from the workshops, proponents argued, also served to "improve the taste of our hard-working compatriots" by specifying the styles and fashions they wanted.[29] However, later reports in *El Eco* revealed that by 1915, the workshops could neither find enough products nor satisfy the demands of elite customers for inexpensive imported goods.[30]

The issue of shame in women's public work was also reflected in a pamphlet for the Academia Industrial Tejidos, a private Santiago school in machine weaving that trained women to work at home with new technology. The school sold its weaving machines, offered courses in their use, and received students in residence from the provinces. The pamphlet enumerated the problems facing respectable women who wanted to contribute to the family income or maintain themselves independently: "What can one do to make these dreams real when one doesn't have time to dedicate to a profession? Because it is not always possible to abandon the home for eight or more hours to devote oneself to a job, which is generally poorly paid and more demanding than the income earned. And what can one do when a Head of Household does not want his wife, daughters, or people under his care to spend the whole day out of the home? This is a problem with no solution in many homes. Industry in the Home. The Industry of machine-weaving is an advantageous solution to this problem." In addition to the promise of higher earnings, the school offered a way to combine waged activities with domestic duties for "a person of character." Scarcely acknowledging how home weaving might interfere with a woman's domestic duties, this propaganda was directed at women with time on their hands, who stayed out of the workforce only because of the social stigma of women's work: "And why do some active and intelligent people decline to take up some activity that falls outside of this mania for employment? Most because they fear failure. But what is failure? It is the consequence of a lack of WILL AND DECISION, even education, since there are still a lot of people who are swayed by prejudice and don't dare to work for fear of 'what people will say.' "[31] Promising that these skills would allow women to take advantage of "the growing demand for clothing textiles," the school promised to provide women with an alternative to the humiliation and exploitation of work outside the home. This vehicle to independent, mechanized home work for women of some means circumvented social prejudice by hiding women, and their work, in the domestic sphere. Similarly, Sara Perrin reported on dye artist Teresa Valencia's invention at the 1927 exhibition of *Actividades femeninas*: the "rat" was an attachment for Singer sewing machines that allowed women to carve wood and marble at home. "The señorita Valencia has with this invention given a great gift for many women who use the 'rat' to earn a living and, for others, to enjoy the pleasing solace of light work with beautiful results."[32]

Catholic señoras' insistence that honorable women must work only at home did not extend to advocating factory homework for middle-class women. Although weaving or sewing at home purportedly promised women safety from sexual danger and social opprobrium, it was well-known that homeworkers' earnings and working conditions were even worse than those of factory women. Moreover, supporters of the workshops noted that homeworkers were isolated from their fellow workers and were thus ignorant of the true value of their work on the market: "They form neither a trade nor a corporation . . . they don't have the option of associating to fix their prices, electing a common intermediary, or searching together for a solution to their misery." Like the legislators who later cited women's isolation and supposed "passivity" in their arguments for protective legislation for women workers, one author concluded that the homeworker's defenselessness qualified her for "the right to the protection of the upper classes, which they owe her as a debt to humanity."[33] The workshops, according to their sponsors, offered women the opportunity to earn more for their work without first organizing a union or legitimating their work in public opinion. The workshops thus represented a halfway point to Catholic unions, which would later be formed to more openly attack social prejudices against women in the workforce.

Perhaps the most full-fledged expression of the defense of respectable women's employment emerged following the massive exhibit of women's activities in Chile in 1927.[34] In the volume that accompanied the exhibit, Sara Perrin compiled a celebratory description of women's manual labor in Chile, focusing largely on artisanal training and production. All of the contemporary skills in which Chilean women excelled, she explained, reflected the natural evolution of women's domestic skills. She then cataloged how these skills were applied for aesthetic and economic purposes to tasks such as cooking, preserving, distilling, fabricating beauty aids, weaving, and clothing design and production. But modern times also forced women to adapt their skills to activities that were not in tune with their natures: "But life gets more difficult every day, and women must go beyond the applied arts to other areas [of employment] in order to obtain enough earnings to pull their own weight in society and often to support a whole family. Thus nobody is even surprised when they see a woman facing complicated chemical industries. . . . There are also brave women who fearlessly run factories and workshops placed in their hands by life's ups and downs. . . . Wherever we look we see the modern woman working tirelessly in small industry." Perrin's main concern was to defend the excellence of women's work, even if the conditions and kinds of that work were not optimal. In fact, although the triumphalist tone of the essay clearly precluded any objective evaluation of women's working conditions, Perrin accurately reflected the spirit of the Women's Exhibit when she lavished praise on this abundant demonstration of women's intelligence and creative potential: "This new century, called the century of lights, does not leave women in the shadows, and their hearts and minds, full of creative forces, are fully dedicated to work, and women obtain honor and benefits in industry."[35]

Also in the interest of celebrating women's achievements, the exhibit highlighted several factories owned and run by women, as well as individual artists whose products were displayed there. One of the factories represented was the Fábrica de Tejidos de Punto "La Standard," founded in 1921: "It is worth noting that the personnel that always work in this factory is made up of middle-class girls who have learned to earn a living in this unusual way that is, however, highly practical and beneficial. Moreover, this represents a great advantage to industry, since the works are done by people who because of their greater culture have more artistic taste and more responsibility for the products."[36] The fact that this factory was owned and operated by a woman, Virginia A. de Sander, no doubt contributed to Perrin's positive assessment, as did the kind of luxury goods it produced. She implied that eliminating the figure of the male boss or foreman did wonders for preserving the honor of the factory's women workers.[37] Here the implicit contrast between the value of middle-class and lower-class women is striking, especially as the work setting in both cases was the factory. Perhaps the most revealing rational-ization of middle-class women's manual labor to emerge in this period was that female participation in industry would improve the quality of production: "The work that comes out of these hands will bear the seal of the cultural milieu in which it is forged." Perrin and other essayists considered women of means to have innate aesthetic sense, which would serve as an automatic corrective for women's crafts and trades. Although Perrin went on to support the idea of female unionization, the defense of female employment was here dissociated from individual economic need and justified instead as a national good: "A suitable trade organization makes what is today a dawn . . . a considerable increase in national wealth, in both the material and moral sense."[38]

Further, Perrin went on to explain that the value of women's contribution to Chilean arts and crafts should really be laid at the door of aristocratic homes, where women made lovely things that, almost incidentally, brought them some income. Regardless of circumstances, Perrin argued, work was a noble activity, something that brought women together across class divisions: "It's very true that work is most noble in the hands of those who need it to live; but it is no less noble in these mansions, where it occupies many hands and minds in useful labors. The soft and distinguished hands are raised together with the hands of the working woman [*la mujer de trabajo*], [making] a single, grand hymn that lifts from the earth without pretense of sublimity, but that moves and animates with its notes of humanity and beauty."[39] Perrin's defense, like the Protective Workshops, sought to rationalize women's work primarily for women who were not working-class, attacking social limitations on female employment as unnecessary and counterproductive. The most dramatic example of Perrin's argument that "today the woman labors side by side with the man for the nation's wealth" was that of Gabriela Martínez Montt. An aristocrat whom "one day destiny looked upon with hostility," Martínez Montt learned leather working in the Girls' Vocational High School and went on to be an instructor there. In addition, she also owned and designed the furniture produced by the factory "Thelma." According to Perrin, Martínez Montt's aristocratic origins enabled her to employ her innate sense of good taste in the design and production of children's furniture: "In the workshop, Gabriela is the soul, everything there is the work of her genius: the pattern, the innovation, the coloring, the decoration, etc." Apparently bereft of other means of support, Martínez Montt was for Perrin "an example of what the will can do, when high goals and women's economic liberation have been achieved."[40]

As the contrast between the handiwork lauded at the 1927 Women's Exhibit and any contemporary description of working-class women's labors demonstrate, work performed by women of a certain class background was valued because of a series of characteristics—aesthetic beauty and female ingenuity among them—that were inconceivable in the goods produced by working-class women. This phenomenon was as much a sign of the concurrent discussion of women's access to education and professional jobs as the seeming recourse of otherwise respectable women to manual labor. Institutions such as the Women's Protective Workshops and the Women's Exhibit gave their sponsors the opportunity to promote the respectability of women's work (and make a profit from it), simultaneously reinforcing distinctions between those "poor daughters of the people" and the "daughters of family" who, despite their disparate origins, had to work to survive.

Women in Urban Sales and Services

Contemporary attitudes toward women workers and women's rights were also fundamentally affected in this period by the growing presence of women, better educated and usually unmarried, in a number of newer occupations that opened up for women in the city. Once the shopping public recovered from the first appearance of women sales clerks in Santiago department stores, the empleada became a fixture in the urban landscape. Sales apparently became an acceptable occupation for young women of middle-class origins: "Now it is more common and modest families are beginning to see the fact that their daughters work with less presumption."[41] Despite the proliferation of empleadas in Santiago, their image sparked a series of discussions on the propriety of such work and the morality and respectability of women who engaged in it.

The same kinds of women were also likely to seek work in the growing state sector, feminizing office work as well as mail, telegraph, and telephone services.[42] Especially in the growing commercial and public sectors, the gender characteristics associated with new jobs varied considerably, in terms of the motor skills, intelligence, physical strength, and interpersonal skills considered necessary for efficient performance. In the past, these criteria had been used to justify certain kinds of factory work for women; now such characteristics were linked to retail sales. Chile should, an *El Mercurio* editorial asserted in 1924, "reserve sedentary, prolific and patient work for women, since it is known that nature itself inclines women to it."[43] Moreover, the gender traits linked to women made them an attractive labor pool for store employers, as they had for factory employers before them: "In general the woman is more reliable and since her needs and temptations to squander are fewer than those of men, her needs are smaller and her honorable condition is more solid."[44] Elsewhere, *El Mercurio* editorialized on women's potential to work as teachers, typists, accountants, and government clerks: "They are in general more assiduous in carrying out their duties, more scrupulous and less demanding, now that a mountain of salaries is weighing down the state."[45] The fact that women could be paid less for the same work provided a recurring explanation for preferring women sales and service workers, and probably served as the most important factor in their recruitment for these newer jobs.

The character, work experience, and expectations of women working in the department stores (such as Gath and Chaves) were the subject of an extensive investigation and article by F. Santiván for *Pacífico Magazine* in 1913. Based on his visits and interviews with saleswomen and their employers, he lauded the estimated three thousand women sales clerks of Santiago for their independence.[46] By Santiván's account, the empleadas that were everywhere visible in Santiago stores and streets represented a new breed of worker: the young, single woman who contributed her wages to the tightly pressed middle-class family economy: "We are not referring here, of course, to the worker's home, whose condition is already well-known, but rather to the home of the so-called middle-class family, whose culture and habits are much higher than those of the low people [*bajo pueblo*], and whose needs, for the same reason, are much greater. The girls that we are referring to have been educated in secondary school, they like the social life, they feel the need to dress decently and correctly, and they have read some books and have more or less high aspirations." When empleadas married, they reportedly kept working, but usually retired when their first child was born. Their work in the large department stores, according to employers interviewed in the article, was stable and well-paid, especially in comparison with accounts of Parisian saleswomen. Inevitably, the supposed class and family origins of empleadas were used to justify their low wages. Because empleadas were considered "daughters of good families," employers argued, they did not need higher wages or work protections, for they were simply contributing to a larger family income. Employers interviewed by Santiván described their own role as paternalistic: "If a saleswoman feels ill? Well, she is allowed to sit down. If she gets really sick? She is granted a leave on full salary the first month."[47] As the union publica-

la ocupación. Una empleada parisiense, si no quiere morirse de hambre necesita recurrir a medios ilícitos para vivir; aquí, si alguna niña se pierde, es solo por que su temperamento y su inexperiencia la inclinan a ello, y lo mismo se comportaría aun cuando viviese bajo el te-

Una vendedora de Gath y y Chaves, anotando las ventas en su carnet.

En la Casa Francesa se encuentran las vendedoras muy bonitas.

cho paterno. Por estas razones, mientras en Europa se piensa ya en el problema del trabajo femenino, y se comienza a trabajar en pro de una legislación que impida los abusos, al mismo tiempo que se fundan sociedades que tienen por objeto protejer a la

20. Sales clerks, Casa Francesa and Gath y Chaves department stores. *Source:* F. Santiván, "La mujer que trabaja," *Pacifico Magazine* (March 1913): 389. Courtesy of the Chilean National Library, Serials Division.

tion of the 1920s later showed, empleadas frequently contested employers' assessments of the needs and difficulties of their "girls."

Part of the perception of the problems facing middle-class women in the workplace apparently stemmed from the application of class standards of material wealth and appearance, which even a young woman working as a sales clerk was supposed to uphold. This distinction produced a real separation in public discourse between working-class and middle-class women's employment, even when the object of discussion was labor legislation for all women and children: "The woman worker suffers in her way. . . . But the saleswoman suffers even more than the worker, whether this is because since she belongs to the so-called middle class, she has to maintain the huge expenditures that she needs in order to maintain the position she holds and that her social situation demands."[48] The author concluded by calling for women's civil rights and protective legislation, which together would supposedly allow women to maintain their class position, independent of male support. What for working-class women was an obstacle to economic survival, for middle-class women presented insurmountable social barriers: "The single woman suffers from innumerable problems; the married woman loses her personality and her patrimony."[49] This concern with women's civil status corresponded to ongoing debates on female suffrage and women's rights to their own income during this period.[50]

In Santiván's opinion at least, empleadas were caught between their lofty expectations and the reality of their employment. Though a few saleswomen reportedly appreciated the value of a good job, others were scandalized at the suggestion that they would want to keep working: "Stay here and remain single! How awful! Make an independent, honorable, and busy life, feeding the spirit with aspirations distant from love? They don't know what this means and how could they know! If in school and at home they have met no one who shows them other horizons that are more noble than that [of love, marriage] already mentioned?" Here Santiván blamed society for leaving young women unprepared to appreciate the virtues of their employment. Santiván reported that most saleswomen disliked their work and considered it a temporary condition, tiding them over until they could find a husband and raise a family. In fact, the reporter's potentially "indiscreet" questions about the young women raised suspicions that he might be a candidate for marriage. In the words of Santiván, empleadas knew how to "use flirtatious and forward manners when the male clients arrive, and accept the impertinencies of those with bad manners."[51] This kind of frequent characterization of saleswomen as flirtatious contributed to their image as husband hunters or, even worse, clandestine prostitutes.

The legitimacy of women's sales work was also bolstered by claims that such work was particularly unsuitable for men. Betraying more than a little distaste for any sign of male effeminacy, a number of Santiago editorials suggested that the state institute quotas for women in sales jobs, particularly in sales with a female clientele. An *El Mercurio* editorial objected to the employment of men in clothing stores and public offices: "They are full of people of the male sex who are employed in measuring cloth and belts, in selling rice powders, in copying documents or typing." The author went on to argue that in addition to giving women the work they needed to survive, men should be working in "establishments worthy of their sex." With adequate preparation in commercial institutes, "women will expel men from all work that does not demand virile force, because they make do with less pay, are more reliable, more patient, more sober . . . and do not practice drunkenness [*San Lunes*]."[52] Another debate on this issue—which spanned almost three years—had as much to do with concerns about what constituted "masculine" work as with providing work for women. A journalist's 1917 interview with Santiago Intendant Pablo Urzúa, for example, offered a strenuous argument for regulating male work in "women's jobs," such as street selling, lingerie sales, and cosmetics. Not only was virile energy wasted when men performed these tasks, but "if man snatches a woman's natural professions from her, he obliges her to thankless sewing, which barely gives her enough to live on." Preserving such jobs for the woman would "give her some independence . . . so that she earns enough to make an honest living."[53]

The Chilean Congress first took up the issue of gender quotas in commercial establishments in January 1919 in discussions of a legislative project that offered employers a 50 percent discount on their license if three-quarters of their employees were women. In the bill, Lorenzo Montt cited owners of "clothing, shoe, and toy stores, etc." and urged men to be generous in ceding their jobs to women: "It appears that many of the professions that until now have been carried out by men, could more properly be done by women, without men having to be jealous since they can use their labor in many other kinds of work, thereby giving their wives, sisters and daughters the opportunity to earn a living under conditions that suit their education and thereby producing a real relief for the home."[54] Newspaper commentary on the proposal went even further, scolding men who held women's jobs and calling this "a real shame for the male sex." This shame went to the definition of masculinity, which was apparently associated with only certain kinds of work: "As for the men, it would be good for them to use their energies, strength, and work in tasks other than that of selling silk skeins and balls of thread," such as mining and agricultural work.[55]

Another motive for this legislation was the continuing desire—expressed by legislators, educators, and señoras alike—to move women out of industrial workshops and into commercial settings, where their health and virtue could be better protected. The legislation was reintroduced in Congress "as concerning works or jobs that women can carry out easily and without the physical and moral dangers of other industrial jobs that are more suitable for men than for women."[56] This legislation apparently did not have the desired effect: in 1921 a representative from Valparaíso still complained, "We have seen healthy, strong men in many sales establishments and the like, selling belts, corsets and embroidery, work that is more suitable for women."[57] Cubillo Pareja proposed in response that, as it would violate individual liberties (i.e., male liberties) to actually prohibit male employment as sales clerks, stores should be pressured to prefer women as sales clerks. Stores that employed men in women's jobs, he argued, should be charged three times the value of their operating license: "I believe that this project would be enough, at least in part, so that those jobs that are improper for men be left for women."[58] Although this legislation to establish employment quotas in commerce never passed, the debate on the gendered nature of commercial jobs testifies to the contested arena of women's role in public employment: at the same time that various educational and legislative campaigns to restrict women's factory work were beginning to bear fruit, sales clerks were gaining legitimacy as honorable workers in the public space of the city, probably because they served a largely female clientele. In the midst of a diversifying urban economy, changing and emerging professions were contested areas where gender characteristics could be marshaled to justify the classification of a job as male or female domain.

Christian Feminism and Catholic Unions

As evidence of female labor activism increased in the early twentieth century, so too did attempts to discourage or distract women from radical labor politics. The most consistent efforts in this direction emanated from the Catholic women's charitable associations and clubs, whose

can provide great benefits!? If there ever was a profession that should be maternal, this is it; woman has special qualities for it; attention to detail, lively intuition, charitable forbearance, delicate procedures, etc."[62] As is apparent from the compendium of speeches from the congress, elite women's campaigns to Christianize feminism and protect women in the workplace had become mutually reinforcing projects. In this modernizing era, the idea that work could be ennobling and virtuous, especially for educated, respectable women, gradually acquired great currency in Catholic women's societies.

Several speakers at the Marian Women's Congress addressed the topic of women's social action by focusing on the issue of female unionization. The concerns that had traditionally dominated charitable activities— the living conditions of working women—were here expressed in terms of elite support for Catholic unions for women workers, which would ostensibly prevent them from joining resistance societies.[63] In her "Practical Manner of Organizing a Union," María Rosario Ledesma, president of the Argentine Centro "Blanca de Castilla," explained the ground rules for "women's Christian unionization" to her Chilean counterparts. She made explicit that Catholic unions were the only way to counteract "resistance societies; well, those are not really unions, the resistance societies go on supporting strikers, but they have neither employment services, job training, nor strike insurance. How can we let the extremist parties monopolize the women's union movement?" The union model differed from that of charitable societies in that it promised working women more say in matters: "Rather than being a charitable society, whose influence in favor of the workers is only passing, it will be the fruit of their own intelligence and work."[64] As she went on to describe several Catholic women's unions in Buenos Aires, another element of the model became clear: the leadership of elite Catholic women, especially wives of industrialists, in union activities. In this respect, she argued, the industrialist's wife could simultaneously fulfill her roles both as wife and mother to her family and as a Chilean citizen.[65]

The idea of Catholic unionization explicitly addressed the threat of resistance societies, which were described as immoral, parasitic, and deceptive. Eugenia Marín Alemany warned: "The idea of joining a 'resistance society' has been promoted a lot among the workers, a workers' society that leaves much to be desired from a moral point of view. These societies foster all kinds of vice and try to destroy faith among the workers altogether. Most workers have had to join the society in order to get work and good treatment from the other workers. Moreover, in these societies they entertain, sing, dance, recite, and if they have no other way to entertain themselves, they all get excited and have fun together. Recreational centers should be formed in order to try to distance women workers from such dangerous company."[66] Another speaker, Ema González, warned against "neutral or resistance societies, where all kinds of errors are taught." The way to overcome these errors was through the unity of workers with their women guardians (*sus protectoras*), so that they could struggle together in the conquest of women workers' "just demands": "The woman worker, whether she has family or not, is weak on her own, considered in isolation. She needs to associate with other workers in order to fulfill better and more tolerably the duties that work imposes; *to maintain morality, which is the basis of all force and of all righteous resistance;* to make up for the lack of income when there is no work; to reject the unfair demands of employers and also to recuperate health if she gets sick; and to live, if she becomes permanently disabled." The structure of Catholic unions outlined here took into account the practical effects of social distance between women workers and their elite protectors. The Catholic lady who wanted to organize a union, González counseled, had to overcome the independence and mistrust of the woman worker. This she must carefully do, offering moral guidance, religious education, and, if possible, financial assistance to the individual worker of "good reputation." Above all, González concluded, "it would be a great advantage for the Unions if the [female] owners of factories and workshops, as well as wives of factory owners and agriculturalists, were to figure among the lady protectors."[67]

Not all of the speakers at the congress drew such a rosy picture of women's cross-class unity, however. Marta Walker Linares, for example, included the figure of the "unjust and arbitrary boss" in her analysis of why female unionization was necessary. Here, the unionization, education, and mutual aid sponsored by the "lady protectors" was not enough; the Catholic union must also make workers strong enough to "impose conditions . . . on capitalist owners who have millions." Walker Linares proposed a model of corporatist women's unions, for she considered all working women to share the same essential interests: individual and collective contracts, regulation of hours and working conditions, wage controls, and Sunday rest, among others. She cited the combative posture of the union of Nuestra Señora del Carmen (see below) as an example of efficacious Christian unionism.[68]

Concern for working women also emerged as a central theme of the first convention of the Women's Catholic Youth Association (Asociación de la Juventud Católica Femenina), held in Santiago in May 1922. The convention attracted four thousand participants for four days of lectures and workshops, including women from the provinces and other Latin American countries. Following presentations on the most prominent themes of religion and family life, several speakers drew attention to the plight of women workers. Solutions to working-class living and working conditions focused on the need to educate women in home economics, to legislate social reforms and to sponsor Christian trade unions. The real discussion of women's work began on the fourth day of the convention with a woman worker's testimony. The press reported that the public received "with understanding and appreciation of its real value" Julia Jiménez's indictment of women workers: "She showed how, even more than asking for more salary for the woman worker, it was more important and viable to seek her perfection in every way. To teach her, and thus prevent her from spending the little she earns badly. She said, 'I have seen my friends who earn twenty pesos a week buy themselves a pair of socks that costs fifteen pesos.'"[69] In a somewhat more sympathetic presentation of the issue, Angelina Escobar Bahamonde spoke to the convention on "Women's Work: Its Nobility, Teaching, and Protection," exhorting young Catholic women to concern themselves with women's working conditions, social decay (including low male wages), and the spread of disease through factory homework.

Discussions of female unionization at this congress also reflected a concern to counteract the influence of radical trade unions among women workers. In her speech on "Salary and the Union," María García Ahumada "emphasized the danger of red unions and gave the example of the positive effects of Christian unions that have recently been established for saleswomen and office workers."[70] The trajectory of this Commercial and Office Employees' Union (Sindicato de Empleadas de Comercio y Oficinas) accurately reflected the kind of Catholic union advocated in the Marian and Catholic Youth Congresses. Originally an outgrowth of the factory union Sindicato de Nuestra Señora del Carmen (founded in 1905), the Sindicato de Empleadas became an independent trade union in 1916, declaring as its goal "the legal and extralegal defense of the economic and professional interests of its members," as well as providing them with professional training and access to consumer cooperatives. Even though the union continued to receive support and counsel from its religious patrons and was bound by its statutes to seek harmonious relations with bosses, the union declared that it would also "support the legitimate demands and complaints of [its members] with all the resources of the law."[71] Much like the socialist organizers who preceded them, the Catholic patrons of the union lamented the inexperience of their membership. Noting that the First Assembly of 1922 had been too quiet, the director commented, "How lovely it would be to hear the members express their ideas freely in these general assemblies and avoid later comments that only lead to division, which ruins the general progress of the Union."[72] The union's paper, *La Sindicada*, gave extensive expression to the moral issues that affected empleadas. By 1925, the Sindicato Señoritas Empleadas de Comercio y Oficinas took charge of the employment service for the Sindicatos Católicos Femeninos, which ran three placement services for employees, domestic servants, and obreras.[73] Another effort spearheaded by the señoras, the Sindicato "Aguja, Costura y Moda," moreover, functioned essentially as a mutual aid society for seamstresses, providing its several hundred members with lectures on social and union topics, tailoring classes, medical attention, and death expenses.

Elite Catholic efforts to stem left unionization among working women also found allies in the broader white union movement among male workers. *La Luz*, a Catholic union paper that called for a return to harmonious relations with employers, made a special appeal to women in 1922, warning them away from the tricks of "dishonorable" socialists: "Socialism is the most dangerous and brutal enemy of woman, which seeks a way to monopolize the union movement; it is necessary for women to learn to recognize this enemy and protect themselves from its tricks. The socialist program for free love would be their dishonor and disgrace and would make women fall under pagan slavery and become objects destined to serve and provide enjoyment for men."[74] Catholic women's unions, the author claimed, would protect the moral as well as economic rights of women factory workers. The proposed collective labor contract would guarantee adequate wages and better working conditions, but also "demand absolute morality from the workers in their relations with owners and bosses."[75] Similarly, union leaders of empleadas struggled to defend the image of the saleswoman from what seems to have been a recurring association with prostitution. Dismissing accusations that empleadas were just prostitutes, union leader Natalia Rubio Cuadra wrote that these rumors were "the fruit of the conduct of a few undisciplined [saleswomen]." She then exhorted union members to behave themselves and recognize that they had responsibilities as well as rights as workers.[76] In subsequent articles, Rubio Cuadra explained why immoral empleadas would simply be expelled from the union: "Those of

21. Sindicato "Aguja, Costura y Moda." *Source: La Sindicada* (August 1923): 11. Courtesy of the Chilean National Library, Serials Division.

us who proceed correctly in all our actions have to be satisfied with looking down on those in our trade who go astray and refrain from generously reaching out to lift them up and lead them along the right and honest path."[77] Although their behavior was unacceptable, she argued, employers were really to blame for choosing women of weak character, who then resorted to prostitution because their wages were too low. Even worse, clients solicited saleswomen with invitations to fancy parties, where "a hundred dirty old men, thieves of young honor," demanded saleswomen's sexual services. This string of editorials in defense of empleadas' honor suggests that working women's morality—both in image and in reality—was a central concern for this Catholic union: "I wish to always improve the good reputation of those of us who work in commerce, and so I attack head-on every attempt to ruin us."[78]

Despite the purported stability of sales employment, union leaders acknowledged that members often faced grim alternatives to unemployment in hard times. One suggestion was that the union form a sales cooperative for the products of unemployed workers because, apparently, even empleadas could sew when they had to: "For women, it is easy to exchange the pen for the needle, the store for the workshop, when circumstances demand it, without this meaning a demotion for anyone, since when God imposed the law of work on men, he did not divide them into categories."[79] Even as occupational categories for women were becoming more specialized, the assumption that women could always make a little extra with needlework—no matter what their class origins—suggested that saleswomen (like factory workers) often resorted to sewing or homework when formal employment opportunities declined.

Although the chorus of concern for the plight of women workers that echoed among Santiago's señoras increased with the rhythm of radical labor mobilization and urban change in the 1910s, the practical results must have been disappointing compared to the continuing socialist (and later, communist) influence among women workers. Both the empleadas' and seamstresses' unions survived, however, perhaps providing an alternative to radical labor organizations during periods of state repression in the 1920s. Regardless of their popularity, the female Catholic unions represented an important shift in how elite women conceived of their role in social change and their relations with working-class women.

Conclusions

This chapter has traced the emergence of elite women's concern for female employment, starting with the increased presence of the "daughters of [good] family" and extending, over time, to the "daughters of conventillos." Both types of activity reflected a change in the normative relationship of women to manual waged work in public discourse, albeit a limited and contingent shift. In addition to recognizing that middle-class and elite women shared many of the disadvantages that (they thought) poor women encountered in the labor market, these advocates defended women's right to work and promoted private sales cooperatives, unions, and protective legislation. At the same time, the transformation of some charities into Catholic union efforts through Social Action purported to unite women of different classes and directed elite attention to the systematic subordination of women in the workplace.

Although much of the historical literature on changing women's roles in the twentieth century has rightfully focused on the protagonism of the growing sector of middle-class, liberal feminism, it is time that we also recognize the impact, however contradictory from the standpoint of post-1970s feminism, of other forms of women's activism in Latin America. As Verba, Valenzuela, and others have shown, conservative women's movements in Chile were not indifferent to the gender discrimination and sexual harassment denounced by working-class feminists, but their solutions were very different and very much in keeping with the economic, religious, and social presumptions of their own activism. In fact, when we examine closely the many different claims made on behalf of women in these chapters, we can see that the position taken by the señoras and señoritas—in defense of female honor, labor protections, and a "living" wage—bears an important resemblance to the campaigns of their more radical counterparts, the worker feminists. Both sought, in one way or another, to dignify women's wage labor while working to eliminate the need for it.

Significantly, the rhetoric employed in defense of women's work incorporated elements that the señoras considered legitimate only when this work was carried out by middle- or upper-class women. In contrast with the industrialist, socialist, and anarchist discussions that had preceded it, the defense of the hijas de familia concerned two very different trends in female employment: the entrance of women into new sales occupations and the discovery of women of means in old ones, particularly in the sewing trades. One important factor that seemed to cut across texts on women at work was a value placed on work itself, which, depending on the economic class of the woman in question, always functioned in an ambivalent relationship to female roles. Essentially, this came down to the recognition that poor women's work was exploitive and destructive (for them and their family), whereas women of higher status could reap the economic and personal benefits of artisanal production and—under the proper conditions—do so with a minimum of gender or class impropriety. In each case, women were encouraged to struggle within the material limits of "honorable" work and elite women were called out in support of their efforts.

Little of this renewed concern would necessarily have been relevant to the lives and conditions of working-class women—who continued to struggle under adverse conditions to survive on their low wages—except that this discourse ultimately contributed to pressures to issue legislative protections to women in the workplace and shaped the resources and organizing alternatives available for working women outside of socialism. Moreover, emerging arguments in defense of female employment served as a key component in the suffrage movement and incipient middle-class feminism, where the limitations inherent in its class analysis and moralizing character would continue to present an obstacle for women's cross-class unity in Chile.

7

Women, Work, and Motherhood

Gender and Legislative Consensus

Despite the legislative inactivity that characterized the Parliamentary Republic, gender-specific laws were among the earliest legal mechanisms enacted to respond to the social question. In excluding women from heavy industries and night work, mandating factory day care, and enacting maternity leave by the 1920s, senators across the political spectrum demonstrated their agreement with the premise that women, particularly working mothers, merited the protection of the state. In the process, they articulated what distinguished working women from their male counterparts and why such differences merited the exceptional intervention of the state in the affairs of capital. The Chilean Parliament, though largely impervious to efforts to formulate a systematic response to the social question, nevertheless responded with limited legislative actions to the social crisis embodied in the figure of the woman industrial worker, debating and ultimately passing several pieces of protective legislation for working women prior to the decree-laws imposed by the military in 1924. A closer examination of these parliamentary projects reveals the development of political consensus about the state's obligation to intervene in *these* labor relations, a consensus that would later be extended to workers more generally in the Labor Code of 1931.[1]

Legislative response to the social question fell into roughly three positions: the noninterventionist school of conservative politicians, which assumed the active role of industrialists in preserving worker well-being; the socialist, pro-interventionist position that advocated the comprehensive regulation of labor relations; and the social Catholicism that stemmed from the 1891 papal encyclical *Rerum Novarum*, which favored a limited state role in protecting labor.[2] Despite the ample evidence of industrial conflict in strikes, the spread of workers' associations, and reports of the state's own agents, many legislators were reluctant to impose controls on the development of industry; however, where social problems seemed to threaten the productive and reproductive capacities of the working classes—as it did in women's industrial employment— even staunchly anti-interventionist politicians were more inclined to support an activist position for the state, arguing that nothing less than the health and productivity of *la raza* (the race) were at stake.[3]

Significantly, as legislators, newspaper editors, and other interested parties considered legal measures to address the social question, concerns about working-class maternity shaped their discussions about laws that might protect women in the workplace. A growing concern with eugenics and maternal health gave politicians from opposing camps common concern with infant mortality rates and other perceived ill effects of women's wage work. This consensus was possible only because factory work was seen as a threat to the health of children and women, the latter in their quality as mothers or mothers-to-be, establishing a rationale for protective laws that was fundamentally different from that applied to adult male workers. Whereas labor organizers and social reformers tended to stress equally the moral and physical vulnerability of *all* women entering the factory workforce, parliamentary proposals dealt almost exclusively with the protection of pregnant, birthing, and nursing mothers and sought to secure women's continued employment under conditions more amenable to child rearing. This focus on maternity not only coincided with social reformers' insistence on safeguarding children by protecting their mothers, but also served as a flashpoint of moral consensus for legislators across the political spectrum who were otherwise reluctant to interfere in labor relations. In this sense, Chilean politicians followed the lead of French rather than British or U.S. legislation; Chilean proposals sought to humanize and shelter working mothers, rather than to encourage their expulsion from the workforce altogether.[4]

In his now classic work on the social question in Chile, James Morris argued that the construction of an industrial relations system in Chile in the 1920s reflected a high degree of political consensus among political elites about the need for legislative solutions to the social question.[5] This chapter argues that such consensus was evident even earlier, embodied in the protective legislation directed at working women under the Parliamentary Republic. In spite of parliamentarians' adamant and repeated rejection of state intervention in *libertad de trabajo* (freedom of work), at a more fundamental level many socialists, liberals, and conservatives agreed that working women were already unfree and thus required legislative protection for the good of the nation. At once responding to the apparent decline of working-class families in Chile and to the protective legislation enacted by foreign states, Chilean legislators forged agreements across ideological lines to the effect that women merited exceptional state protection in the workplace.

Even once protective legislation had become a legitimate subject of parliamentary proposals and from there made it through numerous committees to become law, its impact on working women was delayed by the state's inability to regulate relations between women workers and their employers. Over these three decades, the promulgation of protective laws and their regulatory enforcement were confounded by the idiosyncracies of women's participation in the industrial workforce: working-class women's need to generate income—even at low wages, even while pregnant—was the principal factor in their exploitation, while state regulation threatened to undermine employers profits. Despite legislators' intentions, early protective legislation contributed to economic and social pressures that made women's industrial labor more informal and precarious over the course of the 1920s.

Arguments for Women's Protective Legislation

The Chilean industrial relations system remained formally undefined before 1924, subject only to a series of poorly enforced regulations on working conditions and accident compensation. Although social legislation was a source of constant debate among the voluble politicians concerned with the social question, in any practical sense the state played a minor role in regulating the relations of labor and capital in this period. In addition to legislators' general reluctance, this delay was due in part to the form of Chilean jurisprudence, in which laws and decree-laws were considered legally binding but unenforceable without accompanying regulatory decrees that specified regulating agencies and fines.[6] Despite the failure to implement the gender-specific legislation passed in this period, however, discussions about the state's obligation to protect working women anticipated and prepared the political elite for the eventual transition to an interventionist, paternalistic labor relations system by 1931.

Despite the long-standing concern with women's working conditions and persistent poverty evident as early as the 1880s, and with the exception of several local ordinances issued in 1891 and 1892 to regulate employment of women and children, the Chilean state remained a distant observer until well into the twentieth century. Welfare was left to private and religious charities—an important sphere of activity for elite women—or was restricted to providing services organized at the municipal level. Restructured by President Santa María in 1886, the Juntas de Beneficiencia supervised state charitable services and administration of hospitals, orphanages, insane asylums, cemeteries, maternity wards, and medical dispensaries.[7] The development of women's protective legislation in Chile was also hindered by the assumption, shared by many legislators, that industrialization itself offered great benefits to the working classes, and to women in particular. Sharing in the optimism that had shaped the charter for the Girls' Vocational Schools, industrialists and their political supporters argued that women's income was indispensable to working-class families' survival, and promoted the growth of industries that relied on women's labor. An 1889 report on the National Envelope Factory in Valparaíso, for example, stated that this new industry "gives honorable and lucrative work to a part of our working class that only now starts to take its rightful place as an active element in production: women."[8] Female industrial work—assuming employers shared this sentiment—gave women the opportunity to "bring into the home the food that is so often lacking, earned through work, which is always ennobling. The factories that employ women's services are here carrying out a work of transcendental importance: a moral work."[9] It was not that the poor didn't need or deserve help: industrialists' publications also examined foreign examples of private social services to working mothers, lamenting the fact that such programs were so scarce in Chile.[10]

Passage of social legislation in general, and gender-specific laws in particular, had to overcome the premise that industrialists would protect their own workers. Members of SOFOFA such as Senator Juan Enrique Concha initially hoped that modern forms of rural paternalism would solve the social question and that workers' legitimate needs could be met by reasonable employers.[11] Whether or not industrialists actually shared this expectation, their trade magazines regularly published reports of exemplary factories, celebrating the latest imported machinery, clean and spacious workshops, and worker housing and welfare. A reporter visiting the Puente Alto Fábrica de Tejidos de Punto in 1900 wrote approvingly that the owners had provided their roughly three hundred women workers with a church, dining rooms and kitchens, and housing, all of which had running water and electricity. Workers' lodgings consisted of five rooms off a central patio and were reportedly "clean, hygienic and beautiful."[12] A weaving factory in Viña del Mar reportedly provided a company store, bathrooms, and sixty-four units of worker housing, "with a kitchen, all for two pesos per week."[13] Social services granted by industrialists, particularly to women and children, were promoted by labor inspectors in the 1920s as examples of employer humanitarianism.[14] The limited scope of industrial paternalism in Chile, however, suggests that few employers assumed such costs voluntarily.

As might be expected, Chilean workers' associations took a variety of different positions regarding social legislation. On the one hand, many workers' associations, particularly those of an anarchist bent, seemed to prefer to negotiate directly with employers for benefits, and mutual aid societies already provided many of the social services their members desired.[15] On the other hand, socialist and mutualist congresses before World War I regularly called for state protection for women workers, in addition to hour limits, accident insurance, and benefits for all workers. The Convención Social Obrera, held in Chillán in 1905, for example, presented twelve demands to Congress via Democratic Senator Malaquías Concha, including prohibitions on night work for women and children and twelve weeks' maternity leave for pregnant women.[16] In the spirit of Bravo Cisternas's defense of Laura, the "Virgin of the Forest," and Esther Valdés de Díaz's series on protective legislation in 1907, the Marxist-led labor movement regularly used its labor press in the 1910s to promote legislative issues such as the campaign for the eight-hour day. And in 1913, a letter from the Sociedad de Artesanos "La Union" (read in the Chamber of Deputies) complained of legislative indifference, demonstrated by Parliament's inability to pass pending social laws, including accident protection, factory health codes, regulations for women's and children's work as well as laws regulating alcohol and tavern licenses.[17] Although Marxist labor leaders never argued that social legislation would supersede the need for revolutionary workers' organizations, they regularly intervened in favor of specific laws and joined anarchosyndicalists and mutualists in 1925 protests against the Workers' Insurance Law of 1924 (4054).[18]

Concern for social legislation was most evident within workers' associations affiliated with the Democratic Party, whose representatives introduced the first proposals for labor laws to the House of Deputies after 1901. The principal advocate of this type of broad social legislation was Deputy Malaquías Concha, whose unflagging commitment to legislating labor relations reflected his position within the reformist wing of the Democratic Party.[19] In 1901, Malaquías Concha outlined what at the time was considered a radical proposal for labor legislation, which

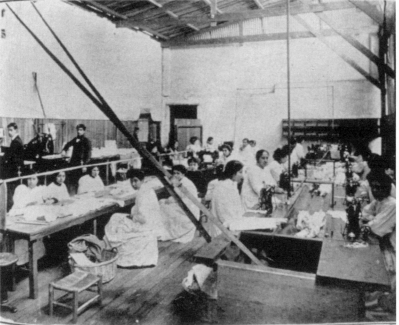

Una de las secciones de la Fábrica de Camisas de don Juan Matas, Quillota, (Chile)

22. Cover of industrialists' publication, *Boletín de la Sociedad de Fomento Fabril. Source: Boletín de la Sociedad de Fomento Fabril* 28, no. 7 (1 July 1911). Courtesy of the Chilean National Library, Serials Division.

included minimum wage laws, hour limits, and other worker benefits. The proposal was studied by various congressional committees and stripped down in successive years until only the limited Sunday rest and accident compensation provisions remained; even then, the laws approved by the Chamber of Deputies were tied up for years in Senate study commissions.[20]

Oddly enough, the most solid support for the spirit of Malaquías Concha's proposal came from Conservative Deputy Juan Enrique Concha Subercaseaux, the leading spokesman for social Catholicism in the Parliament, first as a deputy and then, in 1919, as a senator appointed to the Joint Committee for Social Legislation. Author of the first Chilean law thesis on labor, *Worker Questions* (1898), Concha faithfully represented the analysis of industrial relations outlined in *Rerum Novarum* and promoted by Acción Social in Chile, in which labor conflicts and the misery of the working classes were attributed to workers' and employers' joint moral failures. Reluctant to impose social reform through force of law—because individual behavior was considered the source of redemption—Concha viewed industrial employers as modern *patrones*, arguing that those who failed to protect their own workers should be held accountable through social laws.[21] Concha's "school of Christian democracy," as Morris calls it, pervaded progressive Catholic discourse in this period, evident in public fora such as the Catholic daily *El Diario Popular*, Concha's 1918 speeches to the Liga de Damas Chilenas, and a number of law theses and other manuscripts published throughout the period.[22] Typically, proponents of this school testified to the perceived contrast between a prior age of rural paternalism and the dehumanizing effects of mechanization and mass production, which transformed the worker into a mere machine for industrialists' profit. According to *El Diario Popular*, women's industrial work threatened female morality and health, "above all during the time when she is a mother."[23] This kind of analysis justified an increased role for the state in regulating labor and capital: "A reform legislation could serve to put a conciliatory and arbitrating force between these two rival forces; it could improve, as much as possible, the precarious situation of the worker with some small sacrifices from employers."[24] Although social Catholics in Parliament shied away from the Democrats' more comprehensive proposals for worker protection, Concha's active support for Sunday rest, and accident and women and children protections ensured that social legislation remained on the parliamentary agenda through the first two decades of the twentieth century.

Not to be outdone by the fervent parliamentary defenders of protective legislation, industrialists themselves contributed their own proposals to regulate working conditions, circumventing precisely those issues that most interested workers' associations, such as the minimum wage, hour limits, and severance pay. Employers argued, and lawmakers agreed, that state intervention in industrial relations was undesirable because it would restrict freedom of contract between bosses and workers. However, although SOFOFA might object to most of Malaquías Concha's proposal as violating "freedom of work," "the measures that have been proposed concerning women's work in industry seem appropriate to us."[25] In 1903, SOFOFA publicized its own counterproposal, which would have prohibited women's and children's employment in mining activities, night work, and work with dangerous machines; prevented women's employment in the four weeks before and after childbirth; and called on the state to implement guidelines for health conditions in factories and workshops, including prohibitions on female and child labor in particularly dangerous industries.[26] The society's position in support of specific types of social legislation was entirely consistent with industrialists' desire to highlight the modernity and paternalism of Chilean industry, even though many industrial employers would seek to undermine such legislation once it was finally passed.[27]

More important than industrialists' self-promotion or workers' protests in shaping the agenda of social legislation, however, was Chileans' familiarity with protective laws for women and children in other countries. Since the 1880s, international meetings had addressed the issue of women's protective legislation, most notably in several European meetings that mandated obligatory rest and partial wages for women before and after giving birth; a 1906 Bern accord prohibited night work for women; a 1912 meeting convened in Zurich to discuss the problem of industrial homework; and agreements about women's and children's work were formulated at the first meetings of the International Labor Organization in Washington, D.C. (1919) and Geneva (1920). Chilean advocates of reform were well aware of leading European and U.S. legislation and kept a close watch on international labor agreements. In defense of increasing the state's role, Malaquías Concha pointed not only to the progress of social legislation around the world, but also to maternity laws in particular: "A pregnant woman can not work four weeks before or after giving birth, and this is because the legislator seeks to reproduce and protect the country's inhabitants."[28] In another example, Labor Office Director E. Frias Collao wrote, in an official letter nominating the Chilean Ambassador to Belgium Jorge Huneeus to participate in the 1912 International Homework Congress, "This [Labor] Office thinks that it is advisable for countries like ours, which are passing through the first stages of industrial and economic development, to follow closely the development of modern ideas and the experience of countries that are more advanced in terms of social and labor legislation."[29] In addition to the examples they culled from U.S. and European laws, commentators acknowledged that neighboring Argentina was more advanced than Chile in the area of social legislation. The 1902 Santiago visit of Gabriela de L. de Coni, a municipal factory inspector in Buenos Aires, called attention to the elaborate protective laws then under consideration in the Argentine legislature.[30] Parliamentary advocates of social laws regularly cited foreign legislation and the principles of progress and modern science to support their arguments for legal protection to workers. A typical defense of the Sunday Rest Law proposed in 1907, for example, included the following admonition by Deputy Barros Errázuriz: "Finally, the Chamber must keep in mind that Sunday rest laws exist in all the civilized countries in the world, and besides these what is being proposed today is the easiest and simplest of all."[31]

Conservative opponents of such legislation, for their part, regularly dismissed social legislation as inappropriate to Chilean social conditions precisely because the proposals were based on foreign models. Most such arguments rejected the need for any social legislation, on the grounds that such laws were designed for countries more industrialized than Chile.[32] The tenor of these objections was best expressed in a 1907 editorial about hour limits that appeared in *El Mercurio*: "The problem in Chile is different. Rising wages, apparent in recent years, indicate the effective improvement of the living conditions of the working classes. In this country there are no great manufacturing centers, no plethora of workers, nor real proletarians, and consequently, the actions of the State should not go farther here than they have in those nations that have preceded us in accomplishing these kinds of social reforms." Although some aspects of the proposed eight-hour law were acceptable to the author, "others cannot be accepted without visible damage to the development of industry."[33] Echoing this objection in 1920, during the continuing battles over eight-hour legislation, Radical Party Senator Enrique MacIver observed wryly, "This law is born only in the spirit of imitation. Others did it, let's do it also, for reasons that are not reasons for us."[34] Further, MacIver argued, the "worker question" itself was nothing more than the result of the innate laziness of Chilean *mestizos*, and their complaining should not be rewarded with state charity. Opponents of social legislation also regularly denied reports that workers and their families lived under miserable conditions or that employers exploited their workers, arguing that such complaints were mere fabrications of their "honorable socialist colleagues." Underlying the arguments against social legislation was conservative politicians' deep suspicion of the working classes, particularly of male workers, which was only compounded by socialist advocacy for protective laws.[35] Although truly dismissive opinions were rarely expressed openly in congressional debates, the fact that Congress was unable to take effective steps in the area of social legislation suggests the unwillingness of its members to interfere with employers' jurisdiction over their labor force.[36]

Another important strut in the development of ideas about the social question in Chile was the academic and legal attention paid to workers' living conditions and legal status. The leading legislative and ministerial proponents of labor laws had themselves contributed a large number of the seventy law theses on the social question that were produced in Chile between 1895 and 1924. Typically, these theses reviewed in detail the development of foreign legislation and international agreements before making specific recommendations for Chilean legislation. In a 1918 law thesis, Luís Carcovich expressed the spirit of progress common to these tracts: "This aspiration [to material betterment and moral dignity] is founded in the essential character of the modern spirit—markedly solidarist—which is born naturally and as a result of social and economic evolution."[37] A great many of these authors, such as Malaquías Concha, Juan Enrique Concha, and Enrique Zañartu, went on to lead debates and policy proposals on social legislation.[38]

Concern for the social question was also increasingly evident in daily newspapers after 1900. Perhaps because the Labor Office and politicians provided information to journalists reporting on social laws, the daily press of the period contains numerous, detailed references to foreign laws and to Chilean legislative projects. Attention to these issues in social Catholic and workers' newspapers was predictable enough, but editorials in the business-oriented *El Mercurio* were also particularly attentive to projects for protective legislation for women workers. A 1905 *El Mercurio* editorial focused on the issue of women's and children's work to demonstrate that—despite the Democrats' much-touted defense of labor—social legislation was a bipartisan issue: "How can we believe that certain deputies have to make 'great efforts' to put a stop to child labor . . . that there is anyone in the Chilean Congress who is opposed to the youth having time to learn in the midst of his work, or that the woman be given a rest in the sacred period of motherhood?" Significantly, the editorial called protective legislation a sign of "a cultured and democratic modern society," but went on to oppose minimum wages and hour limits for adult, male workers as "impractical."[39] Another editorial contained all the images and dramatic argumentation that dominated congressional debates:

> Moreover, when the mother is unhappy, when the scene develops during the day in the pestilent workshop; when she wears herself out in the workday and wages are insufficient to bring the restorative and sufficient food to her lips; when all of these miseries converge on the poor mother of the people, all the energy of her being is not enough for the double expenditure of work and motherhood, and the "deficit" of her health takes its inexorable and brutal toll on her. And the consequences of this "deficit" are not delayed: the mother is destroyed as she surrenders herself to work, she is diminished or easy prey for sickness, and, as far as the fruit of her womb is concerned, [her child] bears the marks of the miserable "terrain" where the first roots of its life were sown.

In language that strongly resembled socialist rhetoric, this working mother came to symbolize the worst excesses of industrial capitalism, thereby justifying state intervention. Failure to protect these dependents, the editorial continued, implied that Chile was not a civilized or modern nation: "In civilized countries the Law, that is to say, the supreme expression of culture and social will, covers this unhappy mother with its protective wing and assures her the rest and wages for the last weeks of her interesting condition. Thus [the law] stops the *inveterately usurious businessman* from exploiting the misery of woman and the strength of the race."[40] *El Mercurio* editorials also argued that protective legislation was vital to the organization and morality of working-class families. Working women could not be counted on to prioritize "their sacred duties of motherhood. . . . It is thus a social duty to protect the life of the working mother, the life of her children and the happiness of her home, threatened by her long absences." Following a lengthy exposition on European legislation, the 1911 editorial concluded, "Concerning the preservation of woman's morality, which is the same as talking about the family's morality, they have taken the radical step [in Europe] of completely prohibiting her from night work."[41] By the 1910s, the "mainstream" press differed little from that identified with more radical movements on the subject of protecting women's labor.

Congressional and journalistic concern for the plight of women workers and their offspring was also influenced by the mounting evidence of a scientific connection between female employment and rising infant mortality rates. Elite concern over the living and working conditions of poor women had grown considerably after the turn of the century, as Santiago's infant mortality rate in 1903 reached a staggering 346 per 1,000 live births up to the age of one year.[42] Between 1906 and 1910, national infant mortality rates placed Chile far behind the worst European figures at 304.9 per 1,000.[43] Such figures were prime inspiration for the conferences, speeches, and newspaper articles on women and child health that proliferated as the century advanced. In a talk at the University of Chile in 1912, Dr. E. Croizet examined Chile's alarming infant mortality rate and pinpointed maternal health and education as the key to an organized response: "A principle that rules all infant hygiene during the first year of life is the following: whenever materially possible, the mother should nurse her child. It is the law of nature, which when it is broken leads too often to sickness and death. When she can, the mother should nurse her child, but she must also learn to nurse. Some believe, mysteriously, being a mother endows a woman with all the knowledge she needs. Nothing is more dangerous than this belief." The greatest threat to this "natural law," Croizet argued, was the growth of the market economy and women's industrial employment: "Without a doubt, the work that so many women do in the big cities and industrial centers is one of the greatest obstacles to maternal breast-feeding and one of the factors causing the higher infant mortality found in the cities compared with rural areas. *The woman worker is an affront to modern civilization, because this situation usually takes away the right to be a mother, in the accepted sense of the term.*"[44] Because neither wet nurse's nor cow's milk could substitute for mother's milk, the rest of Croizet's discussion involved urging private charities and the state to make it possible for working mothers to care for their infants. According to Croizet, private charities dominated efforts in the area, but because they lacked "medical standards, they are praiseworthy for their intention but [they have] results that do not correspond to that intention." Instead, he called for increased enforcement of state sanitary measures and the passage of labor legislation to correct workers' living and working conditions, arguing that "if we want to see robust children born . . . it is necessary to strengthen the mold in which they are forged." Most important, steps should be taken to provide child care education, paid maternity leaves, and support services for working mothers. In conclusion, Croizet reiterated the central rationale for implementing legislation and social services for working mothers in Chile: "The little ones have a sacred right that cannot be snatched away with impunity: that is the right to a mother's milk."[45]

Additional evidence of public concern for the eugenic implications of women's work is the First National Congress for Child Protection, held in Santiago in 1912. In a program of moral, medical, and legal talks that addressed the issue of infant mortality, Father Rafael Edwards addressed the need for social legislation for children, mothers, and pregnant women. He laid out his analysis of women's work as a social problem and called on the state to assume its true mission: "The State can and must intervene in those areas that are indispensable to making the rights of the weak respected. . . . Gone are the days in which the State had no more functions than those of a good policeman." Wishing to distinguish this mission from existing socialist projects, Edwards advocated social legislation that would support workers without alienating industrialists: "This supplementary mission cannot be extended further than necessary; it should excite private initiative and not suffocate it, seek indirect means over direct ones, and in no case disregard the facts, nor violate [anyone's] rights, even under the pretense of protection."[46] Edwards was careful to distinguish his proposal from socialist attempts to "suffocate" the rights of industry, but insisted that the burden of maternity be shared by women and their employers, mediated by the state. He then went on to formulate the congress's recommendations for social legislation in the area, which in many ways presaged the shape of Conservative proposals seven years later.[47] The project reflected several beliefs that were fundamental to Catholic social doctrine: that the greatest flaw of women's industrial work was the threat it posed to morality and child health, and that the state should regulate—though not direct—private efforts to ameliorate poverty and resolve industrial conflicts.

Finally, the widespread consensus about the need for protective legislation for women derived from the common wisdom that these workers, unlike men, could not be expected to organize on their own behalf. Male workers, however misguided by radical labor ideology, had proven their ability to organize in defense of their basic rights vis-à-vis employers. Women, on the other hand, were considered intrinsically vulnerable to the exploitation of avaricious employers, despite evidence that women had also been active in labor unions. Significantly, a common argument against labor's two most pressing demands in this period—minimum wages and maximum hour legislation—acknowledged that women and children required such exceptional protections, but adult men did not. Unhindered by maternity and physical weakness, men were expected to labor full time and negotiate with employers for a fair wage in accordance with their needs (single or married, etc.). Radical Senator Fidel Muñoz Rodríguez mused in 1913 that "the wage is the fair and equitable return for the work completed, and this return depends on an estimate based on the notion of law and justice, and not on a law of charity or aid."[48] As long as work was performed by men, other senators agreed, the state had no role in mediating labor's relations with capital. Such intervention could be justified only under extreme circumstances, and then only on behalf of subjects such as women and children who could not represent their own best interests. Whether advocates of protective legislation understood these "interests" to be violated by individual avarice or the capitalist system, their common perception of the deplorable exploitation of female and child labor allowed political opponents to forge a ready consensus about the need for state intervention, at least in this case.

From Project to Law: Implementing Consensus

While parliamentary action on most social legislation remained deadlocked until 1924, legislative attention to women workers went through three significant phases: 1901–1918, in which several basic international norms for protecting female and child labor were incorporated into Chilean law; 1919–1921, when the Conservative and Liberal Parties developed their respective labor code proposals, including considerable attention to the problem of maternity and industrial homework; and 1924–1931, when military decree-laws reinforced existing protective legislation and introduced new regulations for maternity leave. In the first phase, the Chilean Parliament debated, occasionally passed, but largely failed to implement a series of laws designed to protect *la raza Chilena* from the negative effects of industrial growth: in 1907, women and children (under sixteen) were absolutely prohibited from working on Sundays (men's Sunday rest was considered conditional); the 1915 *ley de silla* (literally, the law of the chair, or workers' rest law) ordered commercial employers to provide chairs and lunch breaks for their (predominantly female) employees; and a day care law passed in 1917 ordered employers of more than fifty women (over eighteen years of age) to install day care facilities in their factories and to allow women to nurse their infants for an hour a day. Given the mere weight of parliamentary inaction, as well as legislators' principled opposition to inhibiting "free" labor relations, the extension of legal protection to working women and children, even on paper, highlights the consensus by which women and children were regarded, unlike male workers, as helpless victims of industrial employers.

One law that survived from its inception in a deputies' committee to its approval by the Senate in 1907 was the workers' Sunday Rest Law, which stipulated obligatory Sunday rest for women and children and conditional rest for adult male workers. Significantly, debates in the Chamber of Deputies (as well as renewed debates in the Senate in 1917) focused exclusively on the clauses concerning male workers. Although Conservative Deputy Suárez Mujica tried to dismiss the law out of hand because Chilean workers already got too much "rest," the fact that the law would make women's and children's weekly rest "obligatory and unrenounceable" was never even challenged: "There is only one case in which rest can be established as an obligation: that of mothers and children under sixteen. It seems to me that no one can disagree with that. It is necessary to give a day of rest to mothers and minors who work six days a week, for reasons of morality and hygiene."[49] Arguing against Suárez Mujica's observation that Chilean men worked only two days a week to begin with, the law's authors pointed out that only those men who worked six days a week would be entitled to rest on Sundays. They argued strenuously that male workers also required a day of rest, but did so by constructing an image of hardworking, responsible men who had "earned" that right: "Most workers are men who are devoted to work, to their honored duties, models of seriousness and excellent heads of household."[50] In his lengthy defense of the law, Malaquías Concha pointed to the recent passage of the same law in Buenos Aires and to a plethora of foreign examples to illustrate the need for protective legislation for Chile's hardworking men: "With the same reasoning that is used to combat this proposal, one could ask tomorrow why the law protects children under twelve years of age and prevents them from going to the factories?"[51] Here Malaquías Concha tried to manipulate the apparent consensus for protecting women and children to include "workers," but he was only partly successful. The Sunday Rest Law enacted in 1907 left substantial loopholes for employers, who continued to operate their factories and stores on Sundays, claiming that male workers had missed work during the week or that their establishments had to operate continuously.[52]

That same year, the Chamber of Deputies debated and passed on to the Senate a proposal to "regulate the work of women and children" that essentially reproduced the articles suggested in SOFOFA's 1903 proposal, although articles were included to ensure the continuing education of children who worked. The 1907 proposal is significant not because it became law—in fact, this and several subsequent proposals never made it past the Senate committee charged with studying them—but because it was coauthored by Democrat Malaquías Concha and Conservative Party Deputy Juan Enrique Concha.[53] Here age- and sex-specific protections were combined in articles directed at young women between the age of sixteen and twenty, who were prohibited from working at night, on Sundays, for more than eight hours, and in mines, quarries, and other occupations "that are too painful or unhealthy." Although this proposal did not bar night work for women over twenty (as did most foreign legislation by 1908), it stipulated that women should not work past midnight. In addition to prohibiting women's work with "machines and powerful motors," the proposal contained a sweeping exclusion for women from "tasks or jobs that are contrary to good customs or lead to immorality."[54] The discussion of the project in the Chamber of Deputies is remarkable because of the only article that proved contentious: the deputies approved by a slim majority the article that granted women maternity leave, but could not immediately agree on how the dates of that leave would be determined. Although Deputies Barros Errázuriz and Puga Borne protested that "it is impossible to determine what the week prior to birth is" and "women can work up to the last day," Malaquías Concha's position of three weeks pre- and postpartum leave prevailed in the end.[55] Although this project to protect female and child labor was defeated in 1908, the ease with which the Conchas' project made it through the normally contentious Chamber of Deputies was a prelude to the consensus around the protection to working mothers that would emerge in both houses of Parliament in the 1910s.[56]

Although national legislation excluding women from certain types of work was not actually passed until 1924, attention to maternal health in medical and legal circles in the 1910s certainly contributed to the sympathetic reception of a factory day care law, proposed in 1916 and passed the following year as Law 3186. Stemming from a proposal formulated by the executive with input from the High Commission for the Protection of Children, the project was based on the scientific discovery that "mother's milk is the best guarantee of success in the care of infants."[57] The original proposal stipulated that factories with more than fifty women workers should provide an area for child care and give women an hour off each day to breastfeed their children. What ensued was a complicated debate on the logistics of aid to working mothers, the rights of industrialists, and partisan squabbling over workers' interests. Malaquías Concha, for example, rightly noted that the initial proposal restricted enforcement to relatively few factories, as most female factory workers labored in factories with fewer than fifty women employees. He used the project under consideration to propose a far more radical law: "Every factory that employs a woman who has children will have day care so that she can attend to them." When the law's sponsor, Zañartu, responded that the working commission wanted to avoid the outcome of seeing women with children denied factory work altogether, Malaquías Concha replied with exaggerated sarcasm, "Well, sir, it would not be excessive for us to take this kind of step that would keep mothers from working. According to Socialist principles, the woman should not work; only the man should work to support the needs of the family. The work of single women is accepted only as an exception."[58] Conservative Subercaseaux took this opportunity to swipe at the socialist—"This is a new Socialism, invented by my honorable colleague"—and the chamber had to be called to order.[59] The deputies then engaged in a heated debate about the implementation of the law under examination, that is, the size of factories that it would affect (employing fifty or thirty women over the age of eighteen), and whether women working in smaller factories could be allowed to nurse at home. Objections arose to home nursing on a number of practical counts: that women may not live near enough to the factory to make home nursing practical, that employers would refuse to hire pregnant women, and moreover, "These women workers who will be coming and going from the factory might bring alcohol or other things that make work more difficult."[60] Despite a few last-ditch arguments that the state should not intervene in what was essentially an economic relationship, the home nursing clause was added to the day care law in this session.

Significantly, debates on the day care law focused not on the principle that women workers should also mother actively; apart from the sarcastic aside by Malaquías Concha, all participants in the debate seemed to assume that some mothers would always work.[61] Rather, a good deal of discussion focused on whether certain forms of the law might discourage employers from hiring women, thus denying mothers the means to sustain their families. Democrats argued that, regardless of the cost to employers, mothers working in any factory, in any number, should have access to factory day care or the right to breaks allowing them to nurse at home. Opponents of this change, who favored instituting day care only in larger factories, argued that, by broadening the coverage of the law, Democrats would render it ineffective. Here the debate escalated into a partisan battle between Malaquías Concha and the president of the Commission on Social Legislation, Conservative Silva Cortes, over the desperately slow progress of social legislation in Congress. Silva Cortes chastised the Democrats for complicating the passage of social legislation by "presenting themselves as the only defenders or the principal representatives of the people," and Malaquías Concha called Silva Cortez "an ant on the burro's ear" and accused him of "claiming patrimony over" social laws proposed by the Democrats.[62] Although this nasty partisan exchange accomplished little in terms of the day care law—which was sent in amended form to the Senate, where the home nursing amendments were rejected—it illustrates that, despite deep political differences, the two parties fundamentally agreed on the legitimacy of state intervention in this instance. In fact, the deputies fought among themselves to champion the cause of working mothers. Beyond that, even on other issues of social legislation, the deputies found little ground for consensus.

Despite all this noble discourse, even legislation actually passed to protect working mothers was far from consistent. In what was an ironic counterpoint to the emerging consensus, women were systematically excluded from coverage under most general labor regulations prior to the late 1920s. In addition to the uncontested exclusion of domestic servants from all social legislation, certain predominantly female occupations were also explicitly excluded from the Sunday Rest Law of 1917. In most cases, these professions were singled out not because they were held by women, but because as service occupations they were considered to have continuous working hours. Among the affected workers were those employed in telephone or telegraph agencies; marketplaces; theaters "and the rest of the businesses of public spectacle and popular recreation"; hospitals, asylums, and the like; and many food, cigarette, soap, match, and paper factories. In the same project, domestic servants were excluded unless they worked in industrial or commercial establishments.[63] Once the principle of exclusion of certain work categories from the Sunday Rest Law was introduced, the capacity to expand the list of exceptions was great. In most cases—entertainment, public services, food and tobacco factories, transportation—women made up a significant share of the excluded professions, but this did not inspire separate legislation to ensure they would get rest, public outcry over protecting women and children notwithstanding.[64]

Despite the seeming public and legislative consensus about the need to regulate the work of women and children, such initiatives were largely ineffective in bringing about protective legislation before 1919. When they did, the executive decree necessary to regulate such laws rarely followed, and these laws went unenforced. For example, in 1924 the day care law was again amended to allow noncompliant factories to be closed down, but by 1926, 75 percent of factories inspected by the Labor Office still had failed to establish free day care for their workers.[65] Although these early laws had no apparent impact on the lives of working women, their passage inspired heated political debates and set some precedent for the elaboration of systematic social legislation and regulations in the 1920s.

A major turning point in the formulation of Chilean social legislation came between the years 1919 and 1921, when both the Conservative and Liberal Parties proposed comprehensive bills for regulating labor relations. Following the successive crises in nitrate production during the war and the resulting social unrest of 1917, legislators finally began to take more seriously the need for systematic state intervention in labor relations. The growing success of the Radical Liberal Alliance and Alessandri's populist-style candidacy also brought issues of working-class well-being to the fore, gathering public sentiment against oligarchic control of politics.[66] Populist pressure inspired conservatives and liberals alike to sponsor the presentation of projects to provide mediation and social benefits to workers in industry between 1919 and 1921. Although neither proposal made much headway in the stagnant parliamentary climate of the time, together they demonstrated the increasing scope of parliamentary consensus around issues of workplace protection for all workers, as opposed to women and children alone. Finally, these proposals provided the leaders of the 1924 military intervention with ready materials for their own decree-laws of that year, ensuring that Chile would finally enjoy a labor code, albeit a paternalistic one that helped to dismantle the independent labor movement.

The Conservative project was masterminded by Juan Enrique Concha and came to the floor of the Senate in June 1919 with the unprecedented support of the Conservative Party. Consistent with social Catholic positions over the previous two decades, this project argued that the solution to the exploitation of labor required industrial stewardship, religious education, and social legislation. Significantly, the project included comprehensive reforms such as a forty-eight-hour week, overtime pay, minimum wages, and the regulation of form and place of payment. Legally recognized industrial unions and government oversight would ensure that the "rights" of both parties in labor disputes were respected, and the project reiterated existing protections to women's and children's labor, including an unpaid forty-day maternity leave.[67] When the Conservative proposal reached the Senate, Malaquías Concha and Juan Enrique Concha again joined forces to defend its various articles; again the first article (which dealt with working conditions, including the work of women and children) was approved as a separate project, and the second and third (on legal unions and mandatory arbitration) provoked significant opposition.[68]

The Proyecto de Código del Trabajo i de la Previsión Social proposed by congressional Liberals in 1921 was the third project—counting the Democratic project of 1901—that sought systematically to regulate and reorganize labor relations in Chile. The proposal was marked by the influence of the renowned liberal specialist in social legislation Moisés Poblete Troncoso, who was also a personal friend of President Alessandri.[69] Throughout his copious writings on social legislation, Poblete Troncoso had demonstrated an ongoing concern with women and children in the labor force.[70] It should come as no surprise, therefore, that the Liberal proposal—which included labor contracts, minimum wages, insurance benefits, women's and children's labor, an eight-hour day, Sunday rest, hygiene and work security, professional associations, strikes, cooperatives and housing—dedicated considerable attention to the clauses on women's and children's labor. These were justified not only as modern and humane, but as measures that would guarantee women's role in the family and the survival of the race: "In like manner, the State has the right and the duty to protect the labor of the working woman; of course, by protecting the labor of woman, the health of her future child is also protected; and then *the woman is kept, as much as possible, in her proper place in the family*; which is an essential condition if you sincerely want to stop the dissolution and disorganization of the poor workers' homes."[71] The Liberal project introduced in 1921 incorporated the most progressive material on working mothers to date, including sections on women's and children's labor written originally in 1919 by Malaquías Concha and based on the International Labor Office's convention signed that same year in Washington.[72] In accordance with

Women, Work, and Motherhood 217

international trends, the project also contained elaborate plans for the institution of worker maternity (*maternidad obrera*). Articles 197 to 208 (Book II, Title II, Chapter IV) delineated the period of maternity leave at six weeks before and after childbirth; ensured job security for pregnant workers; created maternity insurance from a fund maintained jointly by employers and workers; mandated day care and nurseries in factories employing more than twenty women; and established rest periods for workers to nurse their infants. These clauses, according to one proponent, "put us among those nations with the most advanced legislation of this kind."[73]

The Liberal Alliance proposal, unlike the Conservative one, also addressed what many considered the most glaring excess of the industrial system: factory homework. Perhaps inspired by a wealth of shocking information generated in urban newspapers, law theses, and labor inspectors' reports, homework emerged as an important new concern in congressional debates on labor legislation in the 1920s. Senator Malaquías Concha had been, predictably enough, among the first to broach the topic of women's homework, "where, according to my own personal poll, one can find women who work more than twelve hours a day, earning one to one and a half pesos."[74] Similarly, several newspapers of different political perspectives all took up the issue of industrial homework in early 1921, consistently calling for state regulation to put an end to this particularly female form of exploitation. Numerous accounts showed homework to be the last recourse of the poorest women, performed in dark, insalubrious conventillos or workshops, and so poorly paid that women worked twelve to fourteen hours a day to survive. Moreover, as one observer writing in *El Ilustrado* noted, the isolation of homeworkers made it particularly difficult both to organize and to protect these women. He called on the Labor Office to carry out a study of working conditions, prices, and industry so that this form of work could be protected.[75] A review of the proposal in *El Mercurio* was optimistic about the prospects for regulating homework, as the state had already begun to regulate it indirectly, "either by prohibiting the sale of clothing made in conventillos or demanding that each article carry a tag that shows this."[76] In the same year, the FOCh-affiliated Obreros en Calzado proposed to abolish home- and piecework altogether, as it "makes it almost impossible to implement the eight-hour day" and "means that even the laborer or worker would reject that workday, for now, which is the goal of workers in all industries."[77]

While the Conservatives seem to have overlooked the problem of homework, the Liberal proposal of 1921 set the first minimum-wage levels and working conditions for homeworkers, stipulating that regulations would soon follow "to assure compliance with this law especially where it concerns women's work."[78] The Liberal code elaborated the following sections on homework (articles 51 to 74): employers should keep registers of workers and addresses; workers should maintain a booklet noting work, prices, and conditions; employers could fine workers for late or defective work; family workshops would be exempt from inspection, except where they used steam engines; and work was prohibited in disease-ridden environments. Significantly, other sections of the Liberal project specifically excluded homeworkers; accident insurance, for example, "defines the word worker to mean . . . he who carries out work outside of his home for someone else."[79]

Although the law was designed to apply "to both sexes without distinction," the focus on female workers was implicit in the occupational categories listed: "The production of suits and dresses, hats, shoes, lingerie, embroidery, aprons, pens, artificial flowers or any other work or manual occupation completed for someone else" (Article 51). Moreover, the process established for fixing minimum wage rates was premised on a female subject. Article 62 stipulated that the Labor Office would organize salary committees of equal numbers of employers and workers when asked to do so by a minimum of fifty workers. Once established, the committees would function for two years and would fix minimum wages by hour or by piece at the request of a member, the Labor Office, or "ten concerned workers." As one observer pointed out, "It seems that the petition can be made by workers of any industry, even if it doesn't occupy homeworkers, since the lack of associational spirit among homeworkers is well known."[80] Thus the proposal established protection for homeworkers under continued tutelage, on the assumption that because most were female, they would not independently invoke the law's enforcement.

The proposal also stipulated how the committees could arrive at a minimum wage (Article 66). By linking homework wages explicitly to the cost of living and wages of factory workers, this article was designed to transform homework from a poor woman's last recourse into a means of making a living. The wage committees were to take into account:

1. The nature of the work;
2. The current price of the clothing produced;
3. The minimum wage earned by workers in factories or workshops of the Department . . . ;

4. Local customs and prices of rooms and necessary items in the region or city where the industry or commerce functions;
5. The quotas that workers must pay in order to cover social security . . . ;
6. The value of the merchandise and tools the worker needs to complete the work.

Elsewhere in the proposed Labor Code, a wage hierarchy was introduced to differentiate between the individual and the family wage: "Minimum wage is understood as that which an adult, married worker needs to live and provide for the well-being of his family." Single men would receive 20 percent less than the minimum, and those under eighteen could receive 30 percent less, but throughout, "for the same work, men and women will receive the same wage."[81]

Like the Conservative proposal, however, Poblete Troncoso's master code ultimately died in committee, receiving surprisingly little attention or debate before the military intervention enacted its own Labor Code by decree in 1924. The Labor Office continued to pressure for homework and worker maternity legislation in the interim, however, by monitoring industrialists directly. Poblete Troncoso reported in 1923 that factory crèches had been established in 33 percent of Santiago's garment factories, and that "there are establishments which, through the intervention of this office, give their pregnant employees a month's leave with full wages, in addition to the medical aid and medicines that they need."[82] The Labor Office bulletin also kept the issue of worker maternity under discussion. In 1923, former Minister of the Interior Aguirre Cerda there introduced a project for protecting children and worker maternity. In this formulation, a woman would receive four weeks' rest before and after giving birth, supported by funds equal to half her wages from a proposed "working mother's support fund." Despite the "urgency to deal with this material as soon as possible and find the best way to protect the supreme interests of our race," nothing was legislated on worker maternity until the passage of the military code in 1924.[83]

Although both the Conservative and Liberal projects languished in Congress—even after a Joint Committee on Social Legislation provided a compromise proposal—these projects served, in modified form, as the basis for labor legislation imposed by the military junta in 1924. The history of social legislation in Chile in the 1920s is thus inextricably tied up with the crisis and downfall of the Parliamentary Republic, which was interrupted by military intervention in September 1924. In a somewhat inscrutable move,[84] the military government that ousted Alessandri proceeded to quickly pass seven pieces of labor legislation derived from a combination of the liberal and conservative proposals.[85] The 1924 labor laws incorporated a broad variety of regulations that affected both men and women in the workplace: work contracts, strike settlements, legal unionization, industrial accidents, minimum wage levels, the eight-hour day, and social security all came under the purview of the state. To the extent that this legislation was implemented, women also benefited from it. Women who held formal jobs in the manufacturing sector were thus covered, and strike demands and resolutions, as well as workers' petitions filed with the Labor Office, demonstrate little sex discrimination in this area.[86] In terms of maternidad obrera, the Obligatory Insurance Law (4054) passed that year stipulated two months' maternity leave for workers, including domestic servants, and medical expenses for the birth and the first eight months of the infant's life.[87] The law was not as generous as previous proposals in alleviating the economic hardship of pregnancy; pregnant workers were entitled to only 50 percent of their salary in the two weeks preceding the birth, and 25 percent until the child was weaned.[88] An additional decree-law (442) issued in April 1925 raised the maternal subsidy to 50 percent in the forty days preceding and the twenty days following a birth. The decree also extended the reach of existing factory crèche laws by including all factories employing more than twenty workers.[89]

Despite the elaborate plan conceived in the Liberal proposal, however, the sections on homework were apparently not included in the bills first passed by the military in 1924. In response to lobbying by Labor Office inspectors, Congress took up debate on a special clause on *female* homeworkers to be added to the Labor Contract Law (4053) in 1928. In arguing for the additional article, Deputy José Luís Sepúlveda focused his discussion explicitly on women homeworkers: "No one denies that there are thousands of women, widows, mothers with family, poor and needy, who have no alternative to the work of their own hands, who are real slaves to the machine and have no protection through our social legislation." The proposed amendment (Title VI of 4053) essentially reincorporated the 1921 proposal: factories should send the Labor Office a weekly list of homeworkers; the Labor Office should yearly fix rates for homework with input from employers and workers; and workers' homes would be subject to inspection for sanitary conditions by social workers.[90] The proposed amendment to the Labor Contract Law also provoked an appeal from the tailors' unions to have men's homework protected.[91] Accordingly, the next discussion of the amendment was entitled "Homework by Women and Men," "because it has been urgently demanded that we attend to all." In that session, Deputy Vergara read into the record the long history of the Federación de Sastres and their unsuccessful negotiations with employers for higher piece rates for homework. This account—full of strikes, negotiations mediated by the Labor Office, and so forth—contradicted the common assertion that homeworkers were, by the nature of their work, unable to organize a union. But it did demonstrate the effective resistance of employers to homeworkers' attempts to improve their wages.

In September of the same year, Deputy Sepúlveda proposed and got congressional approval for an amendment to Law 4053, establishing a minimum wage for homeworkers. The amendment established homework as an extension of factory operations that could be regulated by the state and subjected workers' homes to sanitary inspection and regulation. Unlike the 1921 proposal, however, this amendment established a baseline minimum "tariff" of at least 18 pesos (per forty-eight-hour week). Regional Labor Office inspectors would be responsible for setting the minimum wage levels in their region. The minimum wage issue raised obvious objections from senators skeptical of worker industriousness: "It is impossible to regulate the hours of homework. It is easy to regulate work hours in the factories and workshops; but in the homes it would be completely impossible to regulate them in order to fix a minimum wage." Deputy Cruzat Vicuña further observed that "with this article, the Director of the Labor Office could force the bosses to pay 18 pesos per week, even if [the workers] only work one or two days."[92] Despite these objections, the deputies did not oppose passage of the amendment.

Another aspect of the debate on regulating homework concerned the potentially negative effects of such legislation on workers themselves. Senator Edwards Matte argued strenuously, and apocalyptically, that the prohibition on homework in unhygienic conditions could condemn already miserable families to a worse situation: "The following phenomenon would result: The law, which tries to dignify poverty and see that work is carried out under more hygienic and humane conditions, to put it one way, the law becomes an aggravating circumstance in the same misery, since this family that lives badly, poorly, in an unhygienic house, not because they want to but because they cannot pay for healthy housing, would find its situation aggravated by this law that will stop the widow, the orphan, the poor woman from taking in sewing in order to partly alleviate her precarious situation." Or, alternatively, the minimum tariff set by a provincial Labor Office official could result in factory owners' simply closing their factories to homework: "Simply put, the manufacturing houses would not give out homework. And this would dry up the source of income for one sector, precisely the poorest and most miserable sector, of the social body."[93] Despite these objections, Deputy Edwards Matte stated that he could not bring himself to vote against the project.

In the course of discussion, it also became clear that the senators were talking about a form of employment that, because of the workers' sex and domestic workplace, was more difficult to regulate adequately. In response to those who naïvely insisted that homework benefited poor women because it allowed them to bring in money and tend to domestic responsibilities at the same time, Deputy Ayala observed that the form of work itself existed because it was cheaper for industrialists than paying factory wages: "The manufacturing establishments . . . send their work into the homes only and exclusively because they can pay less." If they were forced to meet a minimum wage, he argued, "soon they would find a way not to send work into homes" and these "benefits" to women would evaporate. Significantly, Ayala went on to mention that workers in two male professions that involved homework—tailors and shoemakers (tailors and shoemakers, not *costureras* and *aparadoras*)—would benefit from, not be hurt by, the legislation. He reasoned that these workers would not lose their homework, "since everyone knows that the tailors and shoemakers are absolutely necessary to their establishments." Given the benefits to be gained by this "large group of workers," and despite the possible ill effects for the remaining female homeworkers, Deputy Ayala gave his vote to the project.

Significantly, with the above exception, the homeworker was constructed as a feminine subject in these debates, an implicitly pathetic figure worthy of state protection. Although whole families of poor homeworkers figured in the discussion as senators repeatedly illustrated their deplorable working conditions, gender was the main obstacle to constructing adequate protective legislation: women, like children, were considered incapable of defending themselves; their "unskilled labor" was undervalued and if industrialists were forced to pay more for it, most women would be without work; the location of work in the home made it the obvious workplace for women, but simultaneously made it impossible to regulate.[94] Legislators' perceptions about this increasingly important area of women's work, and the fact that the deputies devoted considerable time to debating it, reveal that, even as most agreed on the need to protect such labor, the state was unable to protect women who labored for wages in the home.

Regulation and Reform

An important element in gathering information about working women and creating pressure for further regulation was the growth of the Inspection Department of the Labor Office after 1919. From the start, Director Moisés Poblete Troncoso had been a staunch advocate of social legislation in general and protective laws for women and children in particular. After the first officials were hired to collect statistics on labor in 1910, the Labor Office staff grew to provide unemployment services after 1914 and set out to enforce the 1916 Accident Law. In 1919, the Organic Law of the Labor Office created the Labor Inspection Team to review and enforce existing labor legislation, and a team of female inspectors was added to the office in 1926.[95] Inspectors' reports provide an important counterpoint to legislative debates and developments in the area of social legislation before 1927 because they record industrialists' attempts to circumvent such laws. Employers routinely ignored early protective legislation aimed at women and children, and in some cases manipulated the hiring and firing of female workers to avoid being subjected to the relevant legislation. By all accounts, fear of enforcement of women and child labor laws contributed to the growth of factory outwork in the 1920s, which may in turn have contributed to the undercounting of women workers in the population census.

The Labor Office inspectors embodied liberal optimism in the area of social legislation; the inspectors considered themselves the righteous arm of the state against resistant factory owners. The inspectors' reports show that they were interested not just in enforcing existing legislation, but also in providing scientific evidence of the need for further reforms. Significantly, Labor Office reports gave ample evidence of women's low wages in industry and suggested that women's economic participation could not be protected without addressing this situation: "In general, woman's work is very poorly paid in all the factories, so much so that if the workers lived only from their wages, they would vegetate in the most vile misery. This scarcity of wages injures, in our opinion, the workers' morality, especially if they are single or lacking family, which is often the case."[96] Labor Office reports consistently raised concerns about women's minimum wage and equal pay for equal work, but regulations for implementing existing statutes were still not in place by 1931.[97]

The central problem facing labor inspectors was the typical interval between social legislation and corresponding regulations. Regulations for the 1917 industrial day care law, for example, were not issued until March 1921. The existence of a law with no instructions for enforcement clearly confused a Valparaíso factory inspector, who wrote to the Labor Office, "I have observed that here they do not comply with the law, perhaps because regulations have not been issued yet, as article four of the law specifies. In order to write something about it, permit me to beg you to teach me about its regulation and compliance and other pertinent observations."[98] Employers also corresponded directly with the Labor Office in an attempt to clarify recent laws.[99] Prior to the passage of regulatory acts in 1925 and 1926, however, labor inspectors were limited to noting these infractions and encouraging industrialists to comply with social legislation voluntarily.

The labor inspectors' disappointment with this methodology was evident in the results of the Labor Office's report on visits to over 150 Santiago factories in 1922.[100] The two inspectors painted a gloomy picture in general: of unclean, unsafe industrial plants that failed to comply with a variety of health and labor codes. Perhaps because the factories inspected employed more women than men, the inspectors took special note of women's situation: "One could say that the pregnant woman has no protection. Shortly before becoming ill she abandons the factory to live painfully and miserably. If she gets better, sometimes she returns to the workshop, especially if she is married, and if she is single she never returns and hides her mistake from all her comrades. For the latter there is no day care nor law to protect them." The report went on to describe a variety of tactics used by employers to avoid compliance: "In practice we have observed that those who want to make this law impossible have placed a crib in a room, and believe they have complied."[101] On the other hand, officials were able to file only fifteen infractions of the industrial day care law because so few factories actually employed over fifty adult women. Apparently, most employers chose to evade the law by modifying their hiring practices: "Other factories, which because of the very industry they employ, are obliged to keep 100 or more women, prefer girls because they are outside of the reach of the law, in order not to comply with it, thereby leaving hundreds of mothers with families without a way to earn their bread. There are other bosses who are more humanitarian, dismiss their women factory workers, but give them work to complete in their homes." This report demonstrates the seeming ease with which industrial employers, congressional vitriol and the Labor Office's efforts aside, preferred to hire young, unmarried girls. Even when employers complied with the legislation, fear functioned to undermine the intent of the law: "The Day Care Law rules only in name; where they have been installed, they remain empty, since the workers cannot bring their children to work for fear of being laid off."[102] Women workers complained to the Labor Office in 1925 that day care legislation itself was the cause of their problems: "We are being victimized by the laws which you have passed with respect to day care . . . we women who have babies are getting fired."[103] Though social legislation provided them with mechanisms for filing a complaint, the results were apparently more negative than positive.

The strongest impetus for homework regulation came from the Labor Office inspectors, especially after women were incorporated into this office in 1924 and a women's inspection section was created in 1926. In addition to Alberto Hurtado's and Elena Caffarena's extensive reports on homework in 1923 and 1924, Labor Office inspectors routinely recommended the elaboration of special legislation to protect these workers because they were not included in inspectors' purview. Through homework, factory owners apparently frustrated inspectors' intentions with a conscious strategy for circumventing existing social legislation: "The General Labor Office should recommend as an absolute necessity that a law and regulation be written that deal with homework, both because today this class of work is slowly growing, and to bring down the employers' exploitative profits, thus ending how they can avoid the laws that protect workers (when work is done within an establishment)."[104] By the time such regulations were issued in 1928, concern about homework as unfettered exploitation had come full circle to focus on the plight of women and children in particular. In contrast with the genderless treatment of the subject in the Código del Trabajo y Previsión Social, in 1928 the debate revolved around the assumption (and apparent reality) that homework was a particularly female phenomenon. In that year, for example, the Congreso Social Obrero agreed to "ask the Supreme Government to pass legislation quickly on women workers' homework, fixing the minimum wage in factories or workshops of ready-made clothing, laundries, embroidery shops, etc., in order to improve a little the situation of these workers who now suffer the cruelest exploitation of their work."[105] Although in its original form Contract Law 4053 did not specifically exclude homeworkers, it apparently caused some confusion about how it applied to them. As in the initial phases of other social legislation, factory owners wrote to the Labor Office and other ministries to request clarification of the law. In March 1928, the Ministry of Social Welfare responded to an inquiry from the owners of the shoe factory Gorrino y Cía. that to comply with the spirit of Law 4053, they should make separate written contracts for homeworkers (solers and stitchers).[106] Labor Office officials corresponded with their Argentine counterparts and compiled lengthy studies of foreign legislation to strategize the best way to regulate homework in Chile.[107] The women's section of the Inspection Department also set out to gather systematic statistics on homework, issuing a circular requesting wage information from industrialists who employed women homeworkers.[108]

As the body of gender-specific legislation grew in the 1920s, women were added to the team of Labor Office inspectors, officially forming a special Women's Inspection Section in 1926. Female inspectors were charged with inspecting those factories that employed women and children and issuing the fines and reports relative to current legislation.[109] This work involved reviewing written contracts, posted work hours, and health conditions in the factories, which lawyer and inspector Elena Caffarena described as "very difficult."[110] Her colleague, the writer Elvira Santa Cruz Ossa (pen name Roxane), found it necessary to explain her calling as an inspector: "As you will understand, I accepted the work not out of monetary interest, but because I believed that in it I could carry out a social work, because I believed that, with all my might, I should protect the woman who works."[111] This growing team of labor inspectors contributed to the number of factory studies, legal theses, and journal reports that informed ongoing debates in Congress about the content and regulation of labor laws. By the close of 1925, the work of the women inspectors on maternity leave and day care infractions had swamped the Judicial Department of the Labor Office.[112]

The women inspectors reported that they were well received by their male colleagues but encountered stiff opposition from factory owners. In addition to numerous factory visits conducted by the Inspección Femenina in 1925, the female officials reported that they helped to formulate the Decree Law on Worker Maternity issued that year (see below) and recommended to the director that their section be reorganized to better oversee the day care, women's and children's labor, and maternity laws.[113] Inspectors Caffarena and Santa Cruz Ossa visited 672 factories in 1925 in an effort to oversee compliance with all labor legislation,

23. Elena Caffarena de Morice, Labor Office inspector, 1927. *Source: Actividades femeninas en Chile* (Santiago: Imprenta y Litografía La Ilustración, 1928), 433.

not just gender-specific laws. As table 21 demonstrates, in the absence of regulatory acts for most of the recent legislation, employers had been slow to comply with the law.

Although this report predated the creation of special investigators for gender-specific laws, Caffarena and Santa Cruz Ossa unapologetically focused their attention on the working conditions of women and children. Defiance of social laws was widespread and certainly not limited to women (only 3 percent of factories, for example, had the required written work contract), but small factories that employed women had especially bad working conditions; it was physically impossible for the inspectors to enforce maternity leaves (though they imposed thirteen fines); and only twenty-seven of the ninety-seven factories employing more than twenty women workers had free day care, some of which was deficient.[114] Nevertheless, the inspectors noted the growth of an "altruistic reaction among the industrialists who employ women," who "welcome gladly the dispositions of this law and have had the kindness to invite the labor inspectors to the inauguration of these rooms."[115]

One distinctive element of their report was the women inspectors' insistence on the fundamental importance of equal pay for equal work, stipulated in Article 23 of the 1924 decree-law on contracts. Noting the continued inequality of men's and women's wages, Caffarena and Santa Cruz Ossa wrote, "In many factories, women workers' wages do not exceed 1.50 or 2.00 pesos per day, which is even worse when in many cases the woman is the one who contributes the most to maintaining the home. It is absolutely necessary to issue a Regulation that indicates how to fix a minimum and equal wage." Equal and minimum wage laws,

Table 21 Compliance with Maternity and Day Care Law (DL 442), 1925

Type of Factory	Total Inspected	Failed to Comply
Textiles	32	22
Metals	1	1
Paper	5	5
Chemical	6	5
Food	4	3
Wood	1	1
Leather	30	25
Various other	4	1
Total	83	63

Source: Adapted from "Sinópsis de las inspecciones hechas en el año 1925 en Santiago," *BOT* 16, no. 24 (1926): 142.

according to the inspectors, would solve a number of far-reaching social goals: "On this point we could go on at length about the reasons that the working mother seeks work outside of the home and leaves the child to the premature abandonment of the School, which are poverty, the high cost of living, illegitimate unions, the vices of the natural head of the family, ignorance and lack of planning." In the same report, they argued for legal permission to obtain information about working conditions from workers themselves. Finally, in consideration of the large numbers of women working in industry without the proper legal protections, Caffarena and Santa Cruz Ossa argued for the creation of a Department of Inspection for Women and Children, which was created the following year.[116]

These first female labor inspectors also became significant actors in feminist politics in Chile, going on from that job to make more radical claims for state intervention on behalf of women workers. While still working for the Labor Office, Santa Cruz Ossa criticized the new labor contracts and their inability to protect women workers. Though she shared with authors of the legislation the belief that industrialization was destroying the family through women's work, she also made an equality-based argument for equal pay, typical of liberal feminists in the period: "If the woman abandons her home it is because hunger and misery oblige her to do so. Thus it is just that we get rid of the idea that her wages are just a complement for living or something like pin money. Even in the best-constituted worker's home, the high cost of living makes it necessary for the woman to work. For this reason, it is not fair to give the woman an unequal salary, since she contributes to maintaining the family just as the man does. The economic improvement of woman is one of the main factors for the well-being and salvation of the race." Here, as in reports to the Labor Office, Santa Cruz Ossa was careful to point out the moral outcome of the state's failure to enforce the law: "The scantiness of women's wages also produces immorality. The woman sees that she can win through prostitution."[117] For her part, Elena Caffarena went on to found the Movimiento Pro-Emancipación de la Mujer (MEMch) in 1935, which made equal pay for equal work one of its principal demands for bettering women's condition in Chile. Her involvement with working women's issues from her law thesis to the Labor Office made her a formidable advocate for women's economic rights, which also made MEMch one of the more successful feminist organizations in Chile in terms of cross-class mobilization.[118]

With the ever-present exception of those employers who upheld the more benevolent aspects of factory paternalism, there is little evidence that protective legislation had positive effects for women workers in the 1920s. Not only did maternity legislation effectively discourage some employers from hiring women of childbearing age, but day care requirements encouraged employers to shift production tasks into women's homes. Though increased homework may have provided increased opportunities for women unable to complete factory shifts, the intensive pace and physical demands of homework probably favored younger women who moved freely about the city to complete their factory-based tasks.

Conclusions

Although Chile's early social legislation was sporadic, limited, and full of loopholes for employers, such efforts testified to elite concern with the disruptive social effects of early industrial development. They also served as inviting topics for political squabbles between socialists and conservatives, as legislators struggled to champion "the cause of the people" in political debate. Like worker housing and sanitary laws, attention to labor legislation in this period testified more to elite anxieties about the menace of anarchism and superficial humanitarian interest than to any concerted effort to better the lives of Chilean workers. Both Democratic and Conservative proposals to protect workers were rejected in the first decade; by the 1910s, however, worker unrest and continued lobbying for more limited protections indicated the convergence of conservative and liberal views on the matter. Consistent with the prevailing consensus about the state of utter abandonment in which most poor women subsisted, Chilean legislators congratulated one another on their good intentions and debated how best to preserve the reproductive capacity and virtue of women workers, even if such laws were ultimately unenforceable. Significantly, more controversial issues such as contract negotiation and the right to strike were always discussed in terms of male workers, precisely because of the explosive pressure of organized male workers in key industries such as nitrate production and transportation.

As Lavrin has shown, Chilean legislators' attention to women's industrial homework and factory maternity policies in the area of social legislation was not unique to Chile; nor was the "problem of compliance."[119] After all, in Chile as in Uruguay and Argentina, advocates of women's protective legislation were acutely aware of international models and of the progress of each others' respective legislative projects. Chilean debates are particularly revealing, however, because of the particular challenge they offered—whether in liberal or social Catholic guise—to industrial employers' impunity, avarice, and failed paternalism. These prerogatives were challenged earlier and more directly in Argentina (by socialist politicians) and Uruguay (under the *Estado batllista*), as well as elsewhere in Latin America. In Chile, the public outcry over the exploitation of women and children in factories provided an important quota of legitimacy for political forces pushing for a more active role for the state.

Ironically, although women, like children, were singled out repeatedly as a category of worker requiring immediate and drastic state protection, most women worked in jobs that excluded them from such protections. This kind of exclusion deserves closer analysis, for, as Linda Gordon has observed, "Policy is as much constructed by denial of needs as by meeting them."[120] To begin with, important sectors of the working population, both male and female, were excluded wholesale from labor laws before a more detailed version of the labor code was passed in 1931: agricultural workers, domestic servants, and entertainers, among others. The exclusion of domestic service from such protective laws exacerbated the problem for many women workers because it meant that more than a third of them were not protected by contract, workplace conditions, or minimum wage laws until the 1930s. Because women working in service to another family were perceived to be performing necessary, "natural" duties, they were not protected by legislation designed to curb the exploitation of women and children industrial workers. Moreover, because legislative concerns arose from the perceived crisis of the working-class family—rather than gender inequality in the workforce—politicians focused exclusively on how industrial labor threatened female reproduction in lieu of developing strategies to regulate equal pay for equal work or to improve women's position in the labor market. Labor associations and female Labor Office inspectors were more critical of employers' discriminatory wage and hiring practices, but they also tended to consider domestics (and prostitutes) outside the purview of state labor regulation.

Debates on the aims and content of protective legislation for women also reveal the profound ambivalence among legislators about the role of women in industrial development. On the one hand, manufactures in the so-called women's trades relied on an underpaid female workforce, whereas women and their families relied on this income to survive. On the other hand, the perceived social crises associated with female employment—infant mortality and public immorality—required that the state intervene to preserve a minimum level of working-class subsistence. Gender-specific laws therefore usually were passed with a spirit of immediacy, even though their ultimate effect might have been to force women into an even more vulnerable position or exclude them from the manufacturing sector altogether. Women's protective legislation, therefore, offers some of the clearest expressions of elite attitudes about women's urban, industrial work in Chile during this period. Although thoroughly underregulated and insufficient in its provisions, maternity leave and pay legislation provided a precedent and institutional structures that would later evolve into the socialized motherhood of the Popular Front years.

Conclusion

Women, Work, and Historical Change

Would Laura Zelada, the "Virgin of the Forest," have faced a more acceptable range of alternatives for survival in the Santiago of 1930 than she did in 1903? Did the kind of outcry provoked by her case, and others like it, actually bring about change in women's position in the labor market and, consequently, their ability to survive without turning to "dishonest work"? Although many of the elements that had long characterized women's work in Santiago remained unchanged, including its marginal economic as well as social value, the parameters of public debate about women's paid work as a social problem were indeed transformed in this period. Various participants in these debates were willing to view women's manual labor as a virtuous necessity, but relatively few conceived of women's employment as desirable or "emancipatory" in any permanent sense.

An important exception to this generalization, and one that would exercise increasing influence over changing gender relations of subsequent years, was the emerging Chilean discourse of liberal feminism.[1] As female presence in the liberal professions increased, liberal women reformers turned their attention to the topic of the dignity of women's work, referring almost exclusively to white-collar professions such as teaching, journalism, and medicine.[2] From the liberal point of view of allowing women to work in suitable professional jobs, the tone of discussion turned sharply from issues of protection, virtue, and exploitation to the social and personal benefits of women's capacity to exercise a profession. In 1911, for example, "Bedel" wrote, "The woman who owes her situation to her own efforts, to the bravery with which she struggles for bread and to her well-directed talents, is something like a complete being and an economic element that contributes to the public's well-being. For this reason, the sight of women working in education, commerce, public service, journalism, and the liberal professions, gives an idea of independence and comfort."[3] In line with campaigns to improve female education and access to the liberal professions, prominent women educators and journalists spoke in their own defense. Elvira Santa Cruz Ossa (Roxane) was perhaps the most prominent exponent of middle-class feminism and its positive assessment of women's work.[4] She argued that "work, far from being a curse, was a promise of happiness that filled our life with something more noble and greater than futile and mundane affairs. . . . Work only brings joys; the hours robbed from sleep are never bitter, especially when the work corresponds to a vocation."[5] This vision of the value of employment and profession is almost unrecognizable next to contemporary debates on poor women, particularly about those women employed in the industrial manufacturing sector. As middle-class women's advocates increasingly turned their attention to women of their own class—and to their own political and professional aspirations—discussions of the problem of women at work were similarly bifurcated along class lines.[6]

In contemporary debates over the exploitation versus opportunity paradigms for female employment in offshore and export production, scholars and activists have struggled to resolve the seeming contradiction between gender-based discrimination in the workplace and the reality of many women's desire for (and even pride in) these jobs.[7] This historical study of women's manual labor in early-twentieth-century Chile has shown that, given that most aspects of working-class women's workforce incorporation were undoubtedly exploitative (as were those of many of their male counterparts), these activities are nevertheless significant because they represent the choices—constrained, coerced, or voluntary—that working women made according to their own needs and aspirations. My goal has been less to determine the relative "progress" of women's position in the labor market, than to examine how different social and political groups assessed the meaning of those changes, addressing the problem of women workers in the context of their own diverse political and class perspectives. Working women and those most concerned with their employment shaped public opinion, state policy, educational institutions, and the workplace itself in crucial ways.

The significance of Chileans' various assessments of the "problem" of women's work is reflected in the close relationship between the structural changes in the nature of women's urban employment and public awareness of—and judgments about—those activities. For example, the number of women participating in urban manufacturing did not decrease as dramatically in this period as census figures might suggest.

Although structural shifts in Chilean manufacturing from the late nine-teenth century to the Great Depression contributed to a decline in women's industry relative to men's, this decline has little conclusive meaning apart from a critique of the quantitative data on which it is based. The point here is not to discount the value of statistical data, criti-cally interpreted in a given historical context. Although some women may in fact have withdrawn or been forced out of the wage workforce, others certainly "disappeared" as the twentieth-century census became more detailed and restrictive in categorizing occupations. More impor-tant, the fact that assumptions about women and paid work changed over time—transforming the multitudinous seamstresses into "inactive" participants in the census, for example—also reflects how stricter defini-tions of paid work indirectly marginalized women from census calcula-tions. Industrial statistics can provide a more precise view of women's employment in the manufacturing sector, but the broader calculations of women's workforce participation presented here will require confir-mation through more detailed inquiry using municipal and factory rec-ords. Viewed through the census alone, statistics on female employment reveal more about the perspective of the census takers than anything de-finitively quantifiable about fluctuations in the female labor force per se.

Although neither census nor industrial records for this period allow us to examine the age structure of the female waged workforce, other sources confirm the diversity of that labor force in terms of women's family circumstances. With the exception of the younger vocational school students and the hijas de familia, Santiago's laundresses, textile workers, shoe stitchers, and seamstresses typically supported other fam-ily members, even if they were unmarried. Further, status as the wife or daughter of a working-class man clearly did not guarantee that a woman would not also need to seek work. In short, despite the efforts of a variety of social actors who sought to "speak and act on behalf of working women," the fundamental reality that tied industrial development and urban growth to the availability of cheap female labor and to women's continuing need for cash income confounded working-class and re-formist aspirations toward the bourgeois ideal of male-headed homes tended by full-time housewives.

Despite the growing evidence that women were indeed joining work-ers' movements at the turn of the century, existing paradigms that de-scribed their participation as exceptional or temporary proved to be very resilient. Although the attention of workers' associations to the problem of working women grew significantly after the turn of the century, labor discourse reflected both the diversity of ideological influences on workers' groups and male workers' continuing ambivalence about women's presence in the factory. Representations of women workers thus consistently served in labor rhetoric as the quintessential illustration of the perversity of capitalism, justifying the struggle of male workers against employers and the state. The conflation of working women's economic and sexual vulnerability in much of the working-class press represented an important foundation for a nostalgic vision of working-class domesticity, which included domestic gender hierarchy and a firm division of labor by sex. These kinds of accounts elided the practical issues relevant to working women—day care, higher wages, and workplace protections—and relied on tropes of female victimization that did little to address the economic situation of the many women working outside of the manufacturing sector, such as domestic servants, prostitutes, vendors, and laundresses.

Significantly, women workers active in labor politics were not deterred by their repeated representation in labor publications as victims (or, alternatively, as Liberty), and even appropriated some of the same symbols in defense of *their* "little proletarian sisters." Male and female socialists of early-twentieth-century Santiago and Valparaíso fused the demands of male workers with a discourse of female emancipation, borrowing much of the latter from the radical egalitarianism of anarchist fellow travelers. Worker feminists adapted working-class patriarchal expectations to the reality of women's employment and activism, aggressively recruiting working-class women for socialist unions. Unlike examples of male hostility to working women elsewhere, Chilean socialists (and later, communists) sought to incorporate working women into their movements, binding what they perceived to be women's interest in their own emancipation to the fate of the "family of labor." Although socialist strategies may have done little to undermine working-class patriarchal expectations—as evidenced by continuing feminist complaints of discrimination—socialist men and women in fact promoted working women's agency in labor politics and their struggle for a measure of economic and social equality.[8] The journalism and unionization associated with worker feminism therefore brought norms about gender and work into the contested terrain on which battles over the content of truly revolutionary socialism would be fought.

The fact that female participation in labor politics increased in tandem with worker feminist rhetoric suggests not only that women could achieve distinction as labor activists, but also that women workers responded favorably to a movement in which their work-related needs and problems had become a political priority. As Esther Valdés de Díaz and her contemporaries observed, women could be mobilized in the workplace, but it behooved leaders to acknowledge the particular obstacles that inhibited female militancy, such as social discrimination and time constraints. Where women workers responded to socialist mobilization efforts, they were rewarded with praise and male solidarity; where they did not, their passivity was attributed to the inherent weakness of the female sex or to the manipulations of Church and employers. Even where such mobilization was successful, however, socialist leaders explained women's activism in terms of paradigms that offered some continuity with workers' nostalgia for an effective patriarchal past and their aspirations for a revolutionary future. These aspirations help to explain the renewed appeal to women outside the wage workforce mounted by FOCh organizers in the 1920s; the wives and daughters of male workers once again became—as they had been in the 1890s—an important constituency for the political goals of workers' movements.

When union movements of the 1920s began regularly to promote female militancy as paradigmatic or unremarkable, we begin to see the unraveling of the paradox of la mujer obrera in workers' politics. In cases where the labor press celebrated female militancy, the story of Laura, the "Virgin of the Forest," provides an appropriate metaphor for the representation of women activists. Zelada's cross-dressing empowered her to struggle for survival in a man's world of work, and to a certain extent she was "masculinized" in Bravo Cisternas's account to illustrate the lengths to which a woman might go to overcome sexual discrimination. Although none of Zelada's supporters recommended that all women bereft of male support wear pants, they did attribute virility—manifest in women's unusual strength and courage—to those women who defended their virtue and their families through union activism. As other studies of male-led labor movements elsewhere have repeatedly illustrated, when women workers take prominent roles in labor activism, they challenge the gendered dichotomies between rationality and emotion, aggression and passivity, in ways that may seem "natural," albeit anomalous, to workers themselves.[9] Rather than leaving the mobilization of working women to male militants, which was not a viable solution in heavily feminized industries, the Chilean socialist press celebrated and promoted the extraordinary heroism of female unionists. Though the emancipation of women from the necessity of waged work remained the ultimate goal implicit in worker feminism, temporary measures such as female militancy (a kind of transvestism) also became acceptable in the short term. Although subsequent generations of historians and labor activists may have overlooked worker feminists' prominent role in urban workers' politics, communist militants still relied on their legacy as a tool to spur female participation in the 1920s.

Industrialists and politicians, by contrast, first addressed the problem of women's work in the closing decades of the nineteenth century by promoting women's role in industry, responding to an untapped female labor market with plans for vocational training. The remarkably unproblematic way that the Girls' Vocational Schools were designed and set in motion illustrates the flexibility of gender norms under the sway of arguments for national economic development. Parliamentary barriers involved the size of state subsidies for the schools, not the logic of training women for industrial trades. Once a cadre of female administrators and local supervisory committees took control of the schools after 1909, however, the training of women for manufacturing work increasingly took a secondary role to a curriculum that moralized working-class families through home economics instruction to poor women. In the interest of preserving women's traditional role in the family—and taking the "worker" out of the "woman"—administrators domesticated the Vocational Schools by reinstating a more conservative gender ideology in the 1910s, one that emphasized domesticity over vocational skill and creativity. The final result—industrial schools with a reputation for certifying working-class women to manage their homes and contribute a little something to family coffers—fell far short of addressing the real wage differentials and double workday that most women confronted in the workforce.

Significantly, administrators' efforts to domesticate vocational instruction coincided with both the modernization of the census, which redefined many women's activities as nonproductive, and the creation of protective legislation for working women. The fact that disparate groups of Chilean social actors moved to reinstate traditional paradigms of women's labor around the same time suggests that earlier attempts to define and legitimize women's paid work had reached their limit, forcing observers to seek alternative constructions to address the social crisis embodied in women's work. Though the interruption of worker feminist activism might also seem to reflect the above trend, this study has shown that the idea of worker feminism persisted as a viable supplementary strategy within the Marxist-led labor movement long after the disappearance of *La Palanca* in 1908. Despite socialist leaders' diminished attention to female emancipation per se, women workers remained a vital constituency for the recovery of union activism after 1917, both as symbols of rebellion and as actual strikers and unionists. With the exception of continuing female union militancy, politicians, industrialists, labor organizers, educators, bureaucrats, and elite women turned their attention in the 1910s to the protection of working women within the existing gendered division of labor, abandoning the promise of a more important role for women in Chile's industrial production.

The second decade of the twentieth century also marked the emergence of Catholic women's social action to protect poor women and dignify the work of women who had "come to less." Inspired by the influx of middle-class women into the sewing trades on the one hand and the development of clerical and service occupations for women on the other, elite women rallied to the defense of women's right to honorable work, transforming their charitable activities into advocacy for women workers. In defending their less fortunate sisters, Catholic feminists countered socialist versions of female emancipation with projects to improve working women's condition through moral vigilance and charitable commerce. Such efforts dovetailed with the projects of social Catholic politicians who sought to meet similar goals through legislative means. Whereas social legislation for most male workers had been roundly rejected in parliamentary circles, widespread consensus about the dangers of women's paid work led legislators to seek protections for women and children in the workplace long before the labor decree-laws of 1924. Once women inspectors from the Labor Office began to enforce that legislation, however, the negative effects of protection became evident: employers subverted protective laws by dismissing pregnant women and mothers and simply refused to establish adequate day care. Moreover, the increasingly stringent and contentious laws that regulated working conditions for men after 1924 were of little or no benefit for women, most of whom remained—by definition—outside the purview of the new labor codes. The rise of protective legislation also further reinforced the segregation of male and female economic activities into separate categories, much as census officials would do by introducing the concept of "inactive population" in the 1930 census. The bulk of the 1924 legislation did nothing to compensate for the negative effects of gender-specific legislation on women in the workplace and later contributed to the Chilean welfare state's emphasis on aid to women via their work in the family and to men as breadwinners. These crucial decades of legislative debate, which laid the groundwork for Chilean industrial relations, privileged protection to women and children in the workplace, at once providing employers with an incentive to exclude them and regulating the categories under which women's activity was considered "work." In short, women received their exceptional (and largely ineffective) protections on the basis of their capacities as mothers and not as workers, a paradigm that would prove fundamental to the development of industrial relations and the welfare state in subsequent decades.

Although the discursive and structural parameters of working women's options indeed shifted in this thirty-year period, no single analytical narrative can capture the interplay of contradictory perspectives and tendencies that are evident in this social transformation. The Chilean case does not, for example, unequivocally support the narrative of "modernized patriarchy" that Susan Besse has presented for Brazil in the interwar period.[10] Even as structural conditions assured that women's wage work would remain economically and socially marginal, Chilean labor organizers, reformists, and government bureaucrats addressed the perceived problems of women at work from a variety of perspectives, at times even promoting working women's increased economic autonomy. It is no coincidence, however, that their conflicting interpretations combined to strengthen the sexual division of labor and women's marginal position in the paid workforce; rather, this outcome testifies both to the strength of gender stereotypes and to reformers' and revolutionaries' proclivity for paternalistic solutions. The fact that working women's situation showed few signs of improvement is perhaps the best evidence that these many pro-woman advocates were in fact committed to their respective class and political projects more fully than to any egalitarian ideal. Only after 1931, and particularly under the Popular Front governments after 1938, did it become politically expedient for the state to pursue another type of solution to the problem of women's work through a labor code and social welfare policies that together reinforced the viability of male-headed working-class households.[11]

The social history of women workers in early-twentieth-century Chile further amplifies and documents our understanding of the forms and adaptations of patriarchy in modern Latin America. Rather than reproducing the tired stereotype of pathological *machista* domination, this study has shown how the changing contours of sexual hierarchy were inscribed within the material and discursive structures that framed working-class women's and men's lives. Although the prominent role that employers ascribed to women in the manufacturing infrastructure ensured a dramatic rupture in a more traditional sexual division of labor, it also limited that challenge by imposing material and normative limits on the advantages that women gained by participating in wage work. While bourgeois Chilean feminists blithely celebrated women's employment as access to the public sphere and independence from male control, working-class women actually faced competition for scarce desirable factory jobs, endured the hardship of poor working conditions and minimal wages, and contended with the competing demands of family and paid work. But these hardships, characteristic of so many forms of women's work across time and space, also increased the desirability of essentially paternalistic solutions to "the woman question," both for working women and for their self-appointed defenders. Denied access to the fruits of "modernity," Chilean working-class women had a lot to gain by lending support to the Democratic Party or to the señoras' Catholic unions, when and where these women in fact became politically active. The resulting picture of women in labor politics is not, then, one of domineering men who built class solidarity on the reification of sexual hierarchy, but rather one of working women and men who, for the most part, collaborated to this end because it reaffirmed powerful notions of working-class family, masculinity, and womanhood.

Given the variety of representations of working-class women and men explored in this study, it is worth noting that debates about women's work in early-twentieth-century Chile relied heavily on constructions of the symbolic opposition between male and female, and less so on the distinction between "good" and "bad" women according to standards of sexual virtue. Unlike the highly developed paternalism of the Braden Copper Company in Rancagua in the 1910s or of Medellín, Colombia, textile employers in the 1930s and 1940s, the development of Chilean manufacturing gave rise only to sporadic and incomplete expressions of industrial paternalism and kept moralizing forces such as the Catholic Church at the margins of, rather than within, the factory system.[12] Although industrialists' publications repeatedly illustrated and promoted the safety, orderliness, and productivity of female employment, workers' organizations and publications consistently portrayed the factory as a site of sexual and physical danger for women. In part, this critique of industrial relations, which was shared to a certain extent by state officials and private charitable associations, contrasts sharply with the success of paternalistic endeavors elsewhere; although some Chilean industrialists seemed eager to adopt such measures, there is little evidence that they dedicated the resources necessary to shape the factory as a "familylike" environment. This difference may explain the relatively scant attention to the virginity or marital status of women workers evident in public discourse.

Organized labor, for its part, relied heavily on the symbols of sexual difference to explain the norms of revolutionary behavior: if women workers were encouraged to be militant, *like men*, male workers could be no less so (hence the enjoinder for men to "work like men and not cry like women"). Where the need for women workers' mobilization became apparent, Chilean workers' movements drew on sexual dichotomies *and* adapted or inverted them to appeal to the various interests represented in their potential constituency. In this way, we see that working-class leaders challenged the representation of la mujer obrera as an oxymoron not only by drawing on radical notions of working-class womanhood, but also by acknowledging that the growth of a female manufacturing workforce had—at least temporarily—shifted the normative boundaries between the spheres of male production and female reproduction. Nevertheless, activists' ideas about cross-gender solidarity and gender hierarchy coexisted—and at times proved to be mutually reinforcing—within Chilean workers' movements.[13]

In recent decades, Latin American labor historians have been embroiled in a process of discerning new approaches to workers' lives and political behavior to address a wider array of categories of human experience. As others have noted, historians' renewed focus on "experience" also requires rigorous attention to the question of significance.[14] In the present study, the analytical focus on women workers, both real and "fictive," has allowed us to understand how that discourse shaped political movements and public policy in Chile. The fact that much of that history has, until recently, remained hidden has allowed Chileans to assume that women's incorporation into the workforce, and the increased female autonomy and rise of feminism associated with it, is a relatively recent phenomenon. Thus, observers and policymakers in today's Chile continue to reiterate the narrative of a social crisis created by women's work—the destruction of the family, female sexual victimization and promiscuity, the rise of feminism—that first emerged in the early twentieth century. As this study has shown, the "fictions" about women's wage work that emerged in response to the rise of women's factory work were instrumental to shaping women's choices in the wage workforce and the benefits they derived from employment. Contemporary debates on women's work, sexuality, and equality in today's Chile demonstrate once again how powerful such "fictions" can be in shaping public debate and state policy.[15]

It is thus vitally important today to remember Laura Zelada, Juana Roldán de Alarcón, Esther Valdés de Díaz, the empleadas, and others—as well as how others saw them—to appreciate how assumptions about working women operate in public discourse and how such norms are appropriated and contested by working women themselves. How might Laura Zelada fare in today's Chile?

Appendix A

Speech given by Esther Valdés de Díaz,
president of the Seamstresses Association, on the group's
second anniversary, Santiago, August 1908

Two years old! This is a cry that, in terms of the life and action of the Seamstresses Association, sounds something like a victory song, one of joy, deep satisfaction, and tenderness!

For those who follow every step in the development of modern workers' movements; for those who predicted that the organization of trade resistance societies would only last as long as the needs of the moment; for those who laugh sententiously, placing the success of women's organizations in quarantine; for all of those people it will seem strange, incomprehensible, and doubtful that the Seamstresses Association, organized and founded by women workers, should have arrived quietly, with slow but sure steps, at the end of two years of existence.

Actually, this might be the first time in the life of female organizing in the capital that a women's trade organization—discussed and attacked so much since its foundation—presents the beautiful spectacle of completing two years of existence. Don't be surprised if they say that it's strange that a society such as the Seamstresses Association should boast of entering a third year of life.

If we keep in mind the indifference and the almost complete lack of organizational spirit that characterizes women workers; if we remember that women resist everything that smells of violence and organized struggle; and then we note that in the actual case of the founding of the Seamstresses Association, the statutes call for economic improvement through energetic trade organization activity and the practice of the redemptive doctrines of solidarity and union (until recently, little known to our working compañeros); we will see that, in reality, the triumph of the Seamstresses Association's second anniversary is one of the greatest victories to be achieved in the recent years of trade organization. And we might add an important observation here: in these two years, working women have demonstrated their gifts of faith, action, and perseverance. And what is even more valuable, we see what these two years of organized existence have meant for us: women have shown their deep and rigorous discipline, and demonstrated their new consciousness of their worth and of their important and crucial productive potential.

The love and kindness of my compañeras, as well as my love for the cause we defend, have obliged me to remain until today at the head of this wonderful organization, which a handful of modest obreras started on June 24, 1906. Today, just as yesterday, I feel in my breast the beautiful and energetic longing for justice for the crushing and ill-paid work of the obreras, for these noble and bold collaborators of the increase of capital, who fuel employers' exploitation and luxury.

On the wings of memory I go back two years to examine the moral and physical state of my sisters of the workshop, comparing them with the women workers of today, who bear that noble and brave stamp that imprints on our acts the awareness that we know what we are and what we are worth. I see more self-assurance and energy in the formerly timid countenance of women workers, and as though to complement such a pretty picture, I find an atmosphere, a perfume of social solidarity that inspires all of their organized activities. These reflections are another valuable face of the victory that has been achieved with the spread of women's association and organization.

As for the rest, we all know about the change that has taken place in bourgeois practice and customs, in terms of the consideration and relative respect they now pay to women workers in the workshop and the factory. With a few brush strokes, we can paint a watercolor that shows the struggle and the victory that women workers have carried out during these past two years of female trade organizing. The street actions achieved by women's organization have been few—one could truthfully say that the strike itself has not existed. It would be more correct to say that a perfume—that powerful spirit of discipline, organization, and solidarity—has pervaded the proletarian environment and has caused women's action and energy to take its place in the economic struggle, a place that modern progress had reserved for it. The relative gains in wages, work hours, and the personal consideration of the woman worker has been achieved in some workshops and factories—in this category the Camisería Matas, the Fábrica de Tejidos and the Justiniano Military Workshop stand out—showing that union spirit and pressure are slowly but surely growing deep roots in women's trades. And the day is not far off in which the diverse and lost elements of women's organization will fuse together into one action and one force; and this occurrence will show working women the beginning of a dawn that will have no dusk, which will usher in an era of improvement and economic independence for working women.

The Seamstresses Association, rightly enough, has not been far from this slow but sure female awakening. One can say that because of the initiative, energy, and constant propaganda of the women workers who belong to those different workshops and factories (each of which contained members of the Seamstresses Association), the timid women workers—the classic and slavish meat of exploitation—one day rebelled and refused to be automatic machines any more; they took hold of the book and opened their hearts to the committed voices of their sisters, who want to save them from the opprobrious and bestial yoke of capitalist exploitation.

Oh! How beautiful! What a touching event! How our spirits move at the memory of such an important victory, the noble victory of freeing the spirit of our sisters! Ah! The awaited hour has come: that hour glimpsed by the *visionaries*, by those noble [women] fighters who sowed the seed of economic redemption in the midst of jokes and indifference. They have accomplished what the skeptics called *impossible*. These classic and legendary sheep evolved into wounded lionesses—modest and quiet, conscious and lofty—and demanded of their boss, that usurper of their well-being and energy, the fair and legitimate payment for the work they do for ten or twelve hours a day. The struggle did not last long. The furious and despotic boss laughed at the demands of the women workers and threw them out onto the street. Several days went by and the doors of the factory remained closed. However: the blindfold of pride and fatuousness that covered the avaricious eyes of the boss fell before the magnificent glimmer of ironlike female organization, and the boss of yore, who waited for the obrera to come begging for work, had to surrender before the evidence and recognize that the obrera of today had woken up and demanded what, as an agent of industry, corresponds to her.

Days went by and the Chilean obrera gave the most beautiful and noble example of union and social solidarity, perhaps for the first time. Union and force defeated the pride and gold of the despotic boss: he called his workers and made an agreement. "It is not possible," he said, "for me to give you all that you ask. This would ruin me. I will give you half and . . . afterwards we'll see if I can give you more. But you must promise me that no other boss will find out what I am paying you."

Here I have sketched the outlines of my talk, the work and triumph of women workers' organization. With victory attained singly in different workshops and factories, the value of women's trade organization has been recognized, at the same time that the organization moves toward a future and colossal collective victory.

It would be a mistake to sleep on our laurels, or to give in to the biased propaganda of our enemies, who spread the idea that women's trade organization has no purpose. It would be a crime to betray the work we have begun and have already set in motion with bravery and foresight. It would be cowardly and reprehensible to get left behind on the way. We must continue energetically and confidently to the end, even if we do so at a slow pace.

Like other human actions—the great causes, the struggles, the innovations, the very progress of humanity—this movement also has its painful aspects: deep sorrows, profound discouragements, which wound, demoralize, and destroy the warmest spirit. This has happened in the very bosom of our dear institution. It is painful to say this, but our mission is like that of the surgeon, who rips open living flesh to extract the pus that suppurates inside, and heals the wound with fire if necessary.

Not just a few, but many compañeras have deserted our ranks—why not say it?—discouraged by the antipropaganda that some members have blindly and treacherously carried out, lending credence to the rumors and slander that vent their fury on even the most noble and honorable things. This meant that we have had to carry out a mortal struggle within our own organization.

However, our enemies' propaganda against us have been countered in part by the constancy, bravery, and conviction of those courageous members, of those who have every day been like sentinels, watching over the future of our beloved institution. And today, in spite of viscissitudes and mishaps, in spite of the fact that the bone of contention has been sown in the very bosom of our Association, in spite of mistrust and even demoralization, our Association has stayed virile and lofty, challenging the rigors of the division that some have tried to sow there. Like those armies, destroyers of universal peace, who after combat and victory call the roll of the brave ones who have remained at the foot of the cannon, we today—after the innumerable tests through which we have passed in our short organizational life of two years—call the roll of the courageous ones who remain, the fighters who make up the vanguard of the proletarian women's army. We are few, perhaps, but we know that we are foot soldiers, seasoned and experienced in the field of battle, the anonymous proponents of the cause, who march unshaken to conquer the ideal that can be seen in the distance.

Appendix B

Excerpts from a speech given by Father Rafael Edwards
at the First National Congress for the Protection of Children,
Santiago, 1913

Notes, Observations, and Proposals on the Theme
Legislation of the Work of Children, Mothers, and Pregnant Women

The noble object of this Congress—the protection of children—cannot be fully achieved without reorganizing the family, which is the only organism capable of defending children against all kinds of dangers and is itself sufficient to assure the lives and well-being of children.

But we start by looking at what is, in fact, a sad situation: the family—and here I refer to the working-class family—is profoundly disorganized in Chile, and we could almost say that it does not exist. This is not the moment to enumerate the many causes that have aggravated and consecrated this destruction of what is the nucleus and the basis of all societies and races. This disorganization has many different consequences that continue to worsen and produce the most extraordinary and unexpected impact on this ailing body. A father in an urban working-class family has neither the authority to educate nor the ability to support his family.

The sad outcome of this situation is that women are converted into workers and proletarians; abandoning their homes, they go to the great market of labor, if not to the dark market of corruption, to look for what they need to survive. And this disorganization of the family, which displaces women from the home, is what casts children out into vagrancy, semi-vagrancy, or work. In this way, physically and morally weak beings are dragged toward an impetuous current that only the boldest can resist. For women, the workshop often precipitates their dissipation, and for children it is the school in which they learn surprising and deeply disturbing precocities.

All men who love social order and human progress must aspire to prevent both women and children from leaving home to experience the risks, the suffering, and the alternatives of a life of wage work. But this aspiration will not be realized for many years. Hunger has arguments that are much more effective than human theories and hunger is what pulls women and children out of homes and schools.

I might add in passing that I think that the phenomenon of truancy in Chile is essentially an economic phenomenon. Students lack many things and families need their children to work, which explains truancy better than children's supposed inclination to ignorance. Some people advocate piecework that women complete in their own homes as the great solution. But one has to be totally ignorant of the conditions under which such work takes place to believe that it will bring about women's economic redemption. Undoubtedly, from a moral point of view, homework, or working among family, is the best of all options. But from the hygienic and economic point of view, homework is carried out under the worst conditions, and it fosters *surmenage* [a sweatshop or household labor] and economic exploitation. We also should not hide the fact that the delivery [of the completed goods], especially for the seamstresses, is full of moral dangers. All of these drawbacks become worse and even more evident when they involve mothers. Mothers are forced either to abandon the home for long hours or to send their daughters to collect and deliver their work. This situation causes many dramas that bring an end to peace in the home. How many difficulties and dangers are implied by the work itself completed by pregnant women and mothers laboring at home? These dangers are certainly incomparably more grave when the work is performed outside of the home.

The moment will come in which the politics of nations will be an essentially social politics, in which the divisions and boundaries between parties will be drawn according to the different solutions that they offer to problems of social organization and of the relations between those who, with their capital or labor, contribute to a common work of progress. Among those questions that will group men together or divide them can be found that which is the basis of all social legislation: *How and in what form, to what point and with what limits can and should the State intervene in labor questions?* I will not get into a theoretical disquisition about this; suffice it to define the criteria by which I will adjust the proposals that I have the honor of submitting for this Congress's consideration.

I believe, first of all, that the State can and must intervene in those areas that are indispensable to making the rights of the weak respected, and that this intervention must be even more active and vigilant when the rights that it tries to protect are of great social importance. Gone are the days in which the State had no more functions than those of a good policeman. And thus, without converting the actions of the State into a universal rule or giving it any active function in the production or especially the distribution of wealth, it is necessary to recognize that the State plays a role that is a vital supplement to private efforts. The extent, the terms, and the means of this supplementary role can only be determined in view of, on the one hand, respect for the essential rights of human nature and, on the other, the actual conditions under which economic and social life take place: here and now, in a particular time and place. This supplementary mission must not be extended further than necessary; it should excite private initiative and not suffocate it, seek indirect means over direct ones, and in no case disregard the facts, nor violate anyone's rights, even under the pretense of protection. From this it follows that, when social and economic disorganization are extreme, the State's supplementary mission must also be carried out under extraordinary conditions.

Perhaps in no other order of things than this matter of social legislation has the old maxim that *no hay mayor enemigo de lo bueno que lo mejor* [There is nothing worse than improving a good thing] been proven with more precision. A strict legislation that favors workers without regard to sex, age, and condition, a legislation that does not consider the economic conditions of industry, could bring either a decline in salaries, a decrease in the demand for workers, or an industrial crisis that kills the hen that lays the golden eggs. Respect for the law; an exact knowledge of the evils that the laws must remedy; the situation of the patient to whom those remedies will be applied; an environment in which social and economic actions will flourish: these are the principal elements that any healthy social legislation must keep in mind.

The people concerned in the legislation that I study here are the most deserving subjects of protection from society and the State. There is no higher or more majestic mission than that of the mother; the mother embodies all the secrets of the greatness or decadence of any people. The mother carries out a mission on this earth that is divine, because she is a creator, and that is human, because she is the one who constitutes the very source of man's perpetuation on earth. Mothers give to the men they bear not only the blood of life, but also the seal of virtue, which is the only noble thing in life.

The nations care for the sources of their wealth, the basis of their growth, the resources for their future; but aren't mothers more qualified to be considered the source of wealth, the origin of well-being, and the promise of the future than the fertile ground, the mines of precious metals, and the waters that hold unending reservoirs of energy? Thus the mother and the woman, who is the temple and the workshop in which the Creator carries out the praiseworthy wonders of his blessings and his power, deserves to have society—and the State that represents it—uncover its head before her and recognize in her the source of life and the secret of the future.

And the child at the mother's side; the child before whom Origen's old father prostrated himself in devoted prayer and whose breast, temple of irrefutable saintliness, received the reverent kisses of that old man. The child is a deep secret, a terrible question, an unfathomable problem, an unknown quantity that the years start to reveal, but that is only solved with death.

The mother and the child, then, have a double and sacred right to social protection: because they are weak and because they are extremely important cells in the social organism. Work affects the child's future vitality not only because of what he suffers personally when he goes to work too early, but also for what he suffers when the one who will be his mother works, or when the woman who already bears the responsibility for a new life has to work. Thus, when the mother or the future mother is abandoned, the child is also abandoned; and if we protect the mother or the young woman who will be a mother—and this is the natural destiny of all women—the child will also be protected.

The organizing committee of this Congress has done well, therefore, to group mothers and children together when it proposes, for the exalted consideration of those gathered here, the indispensable legislative measures to protect the work of those who are as weak as they are kind, and are as worthy of protection as they are defenseless without it. . . .

Summarizing what I have said, we have established that the goal of social legislation and institutions must be to remove women and children as factors of industrial production; that this seems every day to be a more distant reality because of the growing needs of industry and the increasing disorganization of the home; that homework is not without difficulties and that it contributes to worsening the terrible conditions of worker housing; that protective legislation for mothers and children in industrial work must be such that it does not damage the economy of needy households; and that we should promote private initiatives, as long as these are effective, over the direct action of the State.

[Edwards goes on to detail the working conditions, wages, and seasonal unemployment experienced by women homeworkers, seamstresses, laundresses, and agricultural workers.] Woman's economic condition affects not only her physical well-being but also her moral life and social morality. The lower women's salaries, the wider the cancer of prostitution will spread in modern society. This is a law of the market that has been confirmed by reason and experience.

The awful problem of infant mortality is also intimately linked to the problem of women's industrial work. The greater the development of work outside of the home, the lower the birthrate and the higher the incidence of illegitimacy and infant mortality.

The work of children is no better. Women and children are at the mercy of a disloyal gathering, of a limitless exploitation, and of an unprecedented surmenage. And labor, which should be a source of honor and life for them, is the cause of dishonor, shame, sickness, and death.

I would have liked to have the time and the necessary information to study this grave question of women's and children's labor, but I have had to content myself with looking over some general ideas and sources of interesting information. But on the basis of what I have said and what we all know, there is enough to lay out the orientation of the future protective legislation for women and children.

These weak beings, in need of help from society and from the law, must often repeat the *timeo Danaos* [from *timeo Danaos et dona ferentes*: I fear Greeks, even when they come bearing gifts] . . . because, as I have already said, legislation that tries to prohibit, impede, or undermine the work of mothers and children will be a law of hunger if it does not establish a special protection to favor these same people, who might withdraw from wage work because of that law. It is easy to say that children should not be allowed in factories and workshops and mothers must be kept from working for a time before and for a month after birth. But we must also consider who will feed those children and who will support those mothers; this is why it is necessary to create public and private institutions that will provide for the needs of mothers and children. It is necessary to establish and to develop maternity hospitals and home visits for pregnant women, not only for the days after the birth but also during breast-feeding. We should also insist that female mutual aid societies not prohibit—through narrow and antisocial criteria—aid and support in the birth of a child. No statutes of a women's mutual aid society should be approved unless they include the right of the society's members to be protected during maternity. . . .

A pregnant woman needs to stop working three weeks before the birth and a month after it. Whether the worker or the boss wants this leave or it happens because of a particular law, the woman and her household continue to rely on her wages for fifty days. Once her work is suspended, we should come to the aid of the pregnant woman and her family by giving her some form of support that replaces the wages she no longer gets. This can be done by three principal means: first, through private charity; second, through women's mutual aid societies; and third, through public assistance.

Private charity will never be able to fund a problem of such great and extensive proportions: this is a beautiful area for social action, but charity's efforts cannot cover all of the cases, nor is it fair to leave such an important social need at the mercy of private charity alone. Charity is, in effect, a fountain of pure but intermittent and irregular waters: it is very powerful in cases of isolated disaster, but is almost impotent if a sustained effort is needed. Charity can alleviate this problem; it cannot solve it alone.

For now, women's mutual aid societies can be no more effective. The number of women mutualists in Chile is very small. There are about three or four thousand in Santiago and some others outside of the capital, and only about half of these are married women. Obviously, at this point the action of the societies in the area of maternal protection is not very effective. But the mutual aid societies make a contribution that is worth keeping in mind.

Let us turn to the third source, that of public assistance. This can be based either on the labor contract itself or on a special institution funded together by the State, industry, and the women themselves. Nothing solid can be done based on the labor contract because of the economic reasons we have already given, and because of the extreme mobility of our working men and women; this makes it impossible to base any system of protection on the labor contract, because in reality the contract does not and cannot effectively exist.

We are left, then, with the only solution: a National Maternity Fund destined to provide support to pregnant women. The money for this fund would be gathered through support from the State and the Municipalities; through a special license paid by all the industries and businesses that give work to women; and through a part paid by those who wish to have access to the fund's benefits.

Without a doubt, these last two sources alone cannot cover the costs of forming the necessary capital for the creation and stability of the fund. If the industries or businesses that give work to women were to see themselves as seriously injured by this situation, women's work would enter into a crisis and women would be replaced in industry by children and men. Nor can we expect that the services offered by the fund would provide sufficient incentive for the workers to want to pay a big portion of the cost. This fund could be managed by Public Welfare and could offer special deals to the women's mutual aid societies.

Employer oversight—that is, to leave these services to the bosses—would, in theory, be a good solution; but in practice it would not bear results because of the same economic and social reasons I have given, especially because women receive low wages, have unstable employment, and are mostly employed in small workshops.

For child workers, we should first determine the age at which they can begin to work and the age at which they should no longer be considered children in terms of the protective legislation. This work should be regulated in a way that addresses the needs of children's moral and physical development, and they should be prohibited from all kinds of harmful and dangerous work. Their working hours should also have a special limit and night work should be prohibited.

. . . The first thing that a worker can demand of a legal system that oversees labor is that justice be done quickly and easily. What the State should guarantee to all workers, it should much more readily offer for the benefit of mothers and children, who are the least capable of obtaining justice if it is not administered in a rapid, simple, and economic way.

Straight away the mother and child will have the right to have access to work that is not harmful, in terms of their natural weakness, their age, and their propriety; these injuries allude not only to age and physical condition, but also and more importantly to moral life and preserving and developing the good inclinations of the soul. Children and mothers need more ordinary rest and more periodic rests, which the education of the former and the responsibilities of the latter make indispensable.

Industry prefers the work of children and women because of their moral condition and the lower salaries they receive. The same industry that takes advantage of this workforce consequently must take responsibility for the special needs of those workers; industry should contribute to children's education and to meeting mothers' demands.

The natural institutions for the protection of women and children are primarily homes, schools, and charitable societies. The State ought to regulate industry's contribution to the preservation, establishment, promotion, and development of those institutions.

No one can ignore or forget that Religion and the Church are the most important citadels of workers' social redemption and world peace, and that this is especially true for the children and mothers.

Conclusions

The Congress for Children *proposes, with respect to the legislation of the work of children, mothers, and pregnant women:*

First. The creation of a permanent Council that is charged with studying the conditions under which children and mothers work, proposing the legal and administrative mechanisms that are necessary to protect these social elements, monitoring the execution of those laws, improving social awareness of this problem, and promoting public and private initiatives that are most conducive to its solution.

Second. The formation of *tribunals of good men* in all population centers and especially where there might be factories or workshops that employ women or children. These would be charged with ruling quickly and summarily as a jury on labor questions that arise between bosses or businessmen and their women or child workers. Parties in these disputes can include the father, the husband, the guardian, the Juvenile Advocate, the District Attorney, and the parish of the charitable foundations.

Third. That every workshop or industry that employs children under fifteen years of age should demand to see a certificate showing that they attend a public or private primary school, except for those who have a certificate showing they have carried out studies up to the second year of high school in a public or private school. The same workshops or industries, if they employ more than ten children and if there is no public or private school within a kilometer, should be obliged to have a school for those children (of whatever sex that the industry employs) that functions at least twenty-four hours a week.

Fourth. That mothers should not be made to work for any reason for more than fifty hours a week, before eight in the morning, after six in the evening, nor during vacation days. That the working conditions for mothers who breast-feed their children should be specified. That women's work outside of the home should end by midday on Saturday.

Fifth. That the proper separation of sexes should be established and that children should not work among the adults, although they should be monitored [by adults].

Sixth. That a special tax should be imposed on the factories, which will be used to promote charitable, aid, educational, and maternity and child assistance institutions, and that the factories should be made by indirect means to provide housing for the families it employs.

Seventh. That a National Maternity Fund be created to provide assistance and subsidies for working pregnant women during the twenty days before the birth and thirty days after it. That this same Fund should support the charitable and mutual aid societies in proportion to the number of pregnant women that they assist.

Eighth. That it should be determined what are the harmful, dangerous, and heavy jobs and that women and children be excluded from those jobs. That it be defined what special hygienic conditions should be maintained in workshops and industries that employ women and children.

Ninth. That vocational education should be promoted and regulated, as well as the hours, working conditions, and minimum salary that correspond to each student (male or female); the salary should be deposited in the Savings Fund and can only be withdrawn by the student after studies have been completed.

Tenth. That a special penalty should be established for those who contribute to the corruption of working women and children or who tolerate attempts against their morality.

Eleventh. That a group of women inspectors be created for women's and children's work. These positions could be given to employees from the primary schools and be carried out on a consultancy basis so they would not interfere with the employees' regular jobs.

Abbreviations

ADGT	Archivo de la Dirección General del Trabajo, Santiago
AE	*Anuario Estadístico*
AMIOP	Archivo del Ministerio de Industrias y Obras Públicas, Santiago
BOT	*Boletín de la Oficina del Trabajo*
BSOFOFA	*Boletín de la Sociedad de Fomento Fabril*
Censo	República de Chile, *Censo de Población*
CNCD	Congreso Nacional, Cámera de Diputados
CNCS	Congreso Nacional, Cámera de Senadores
FOCh	Federación Obrera de Chile
IWW	International Workers of the World
MEMCh	Movimiento Pro-Emancipación de la Mujer Chilena
POS	Partido Obrero Socialista
SOFOFA	Sociedad de Fomento Fabril

Notes

Introduction

1 Agustín Bravo Cisternas, *La mujer a través de los siglos: Historia de lo más importante que la mujer ha realizado en el mundo y reformas de que deben venir en pro de ella* (Valparaíso: Imprenta El Progreso, 1903), 173–205. I would like to thank Ericka Verba for unearthing and sharing this source with me. Unless otherwise noted, all translations are mine.

2 "Cuestión de pantalones," *El Diario Popular*, 29 November 1903.

3 "La mujer-hombre: Exijencias de necesidad. La filosofía de este suceso," *El Chileno*, 29 November 1903.

4 Reports of women dressing as men appeared periodically in the years following the Zelada case, usually provoking similar reflections on the theme of female oppression. See "Una mujer vestida de hombre," *El Diario Ilustrado*, 20 June 1906; "Aprehensión de una mujer," *El Diario Ilustrado*, 15 January 1910; and "La mujer hombre," *El Mercurio*, 7 February 1916. Similar cases were reported in the Brazilian press in the same period: see Margareth Rago, *Os prazeres da noite: Prostituicão e codigos da sexualidade femenina em São Paulo, 1890–1930* (Rio de Janeiro: Paz and Terra, 1991), 115–16.

5 Bravo Cisternas, *La mujer a través de los siglos*, 202.

6 Henry W. Kirsch, *Industrial Development in a Traditional Society: The Conflict of Entrepreneurship and Modernization in Chile* (Gainesville: University Presses of Florida, 1977), 8; Peter DeShazo, *Urban Workers and Labor Unions in Chile, 1902–1927* (Madison: University of Wisconsin Press, 1983), Table 1.1, 4. Nineteenth-century workers' movements—predominantly urban and male—have provided a rich area of study for social historians in recent years. See Luís Alberto Romero, *La Sociedad de Igualdad: Los artesanos de Santiago de Chile y sus primeras experiencias políticas, 1820–1851* (Buenos Aires: Instituto Di Tella, 1984); Sergio Grez Toso, *De la "regeneración del pueblo" a la huelga general: Génesis y evolución histórica del movimiento popular en Chile (1810–1890)* (Santiago: DIBAM, 1997); Andrew L. Daitsman, "And the People Shall Be All: Liberal Rebellion and Popular Mobilization in Chile, 1830–1860" (Ph.D. diss., University of Wisconsin, 1995).

7 Historian Gabriel Salazar calls these women "the abandoned ones" (*las*

abandonadas) and credits them with creating and sustaining much of the popular culture of the period. See Gabriel Salazar Vergara, "La mujer de 'bajo pueblo' en Chile: Bosquejo histórico," *Proposiciones* 21 (December 1992): 98–101, and *Labradores, peones y proletarios: Formación y crisis de la sociedad popular chilena del siglo XIX* (Santiago: Ediciones Sur, 1985), 256–322.

8 DeShazo, *Urban Workers*, Table 1.6, 16; Kirsch, *Industrial Development*, 108.

9 Gendered ratios of factory workers based on República de Chile, Oficina Central de Estadística, *Anuario Estadístico* (hereafter *AE*) (Santiago: Sociedad Imprenta y Litografía Universo, 1912–1925). Estimate of female factory work force, author's calculation derived from *AE*, 1912–1925 and República de Chile, Dirección General de Estadística, *Censo de la Población de Chile, 1895* (Santiago, 1895), 2: 186; *Censo 1907*, 467; *Censo 1920*, 45; *Censo 1930*, 1: 52.

10 Despite their other merits, most of the now classic works of Chilean labor history, both rural and urban, have restricted their scope to the beliefs and activities of male workers, giving only passing attention to the role of women in the workforce and the labor movement. See Alan Angell, *Politics and the Labour Movement in Chile* (London: Oxford University Press, 1972); Arnold J. Bauer, *Chilean Rural Society from the Spanish Conquest to 1930* (Cambridge, England: Cambridge University Press, 1975); DeShazo, *Urban Workers*; Julio César Jobet, *El partido socialista de Chile*, 2 vols. (Santiago: Editorial Prensa Latinoamericana, 1971); Brian Loveman, *Struggle in the Countryside: Politics and Rural Labor in Chile, 1919–1973* (Bloomington: Indiana University Press, 1976); Michael Monteón, *Chile in the Nitrate Era: The Evolution of Economic Dependence* (Madison: University of Wisconsin Press, 1982); Hernán Ramírez Nicochea, *Historia del movimiento obrero en Chile, siglo XIX* (Santiago: Austral, 1956); Hobart A. Spaulding Jr., *Organized Labor in Latin America: Historical Case Studies of Workers in Dependent Societies* (New York: New York University Press, 1977); Luís Vitale, *Historia del movimiento obrero* (Santiago: Editorial Por, 1962); Peter Winn, *Weavers of Revolution: The Yarur Workers and Chile's Road to Socialism* (New York: Oxford University Press, 1986).

11 This has also been true of U.S. labor history in the past. See Mari Jo Buhle, "Gender and Labor History," in *Perspectives on American Labor History: The Problem of Synthesis*, ed. J. Carroll Moody and Alice Kessler-Harris (De Kalb: Northern Illinois University Press, 1989), 55–79.

12 The pattern of sexual segregation and discrimination in the period of early industrialization has been carefully documented elsewhere: Theresa M. McBride, "The Long Road Home: Women's Work and Industrialization," in *Becoming Visible: Women in European History*, ed. Renate Bridenthal and Claudia Koonz (Boston: Houghton Mifflin,

1977); Joan Wallach Scott, "La mujer trabajadora en el siglo XX," in *Historia de las mujeres en Occidente, Tomo 4 Siglo XIX*, ed. Geneviève Fraisse, Michelle Perrot, and María José Rodríguez Galdo (Madrid: Taurus, 1993), 405–35; Ava Baron, ed., *Work Engendered: Toward a New History of American Labor* (Ithaca, NY: Cornell University Press, 1991); Milton Cantor and Bruce Laurie, eds., *Class, Sex, and the Woman Worker* (Westport, CT: Greenwood Press, 1977).

13 Some of the principal Chilean works in this line include Mario Garcés Durán, *Crisis social y motines populares en el 1900* (Santiago: Ediciones Documentas, 1991); Grez, *"Regeneración del pueblo"*; María Angélica Illanes, *"En el nombre del pueblo, del estado y de la ciencia (. . .)": Historia social de la salud pública, Chile 1880–1973 (Hacia una historia social del Siglo XX)* (Santiago: Colectivo de Atención Primaria, 1993); Julio Pinto Vallejos, *Trabajos y rebeldías en la pampa salitrera* (Santiago: Editorial Universidad de Santiago, 1999); and Salazar, *Labradores, peones y proletarios*.

14 Joan Wallach Scott, "On Language," in *Gender and the Politics of History* (New York: Columbia University Press, 1988), 60.

15 Emilia Viotti da Costa made this important observation in "Experiences versus Structures: New Tendencies in the History of Labor and the Working Class in Latin America: What Do We Gain? What Do We Lose?," *International Labor and Working-Class History* 36 (fall 1989): 17.

16 See Elizabeth Faue, *Community of Suffering and Struggle: Women, Men and the Labor Movement in Minneapolis, 1915–1945* (Chapel Hill: University of North Carolina Press, 1991); Nancy A. Hewitt, " 'The Voice of Virile Labor': Labor Militancy, Community Solidarity, and Gender Identity among Tampa's Latin Workers 1880–1921," in *Work Engendered*, ed. Baron, 142–67; Christine Stansell, *City of Women: Sex and Class in New York, 1789–1860* (Urbana: University of Illinois Press, 1987).

17 For example, see the attention to women's work in Grez, *"Regeneración del pueblo,"* 134–43, 598–604. Although Grez includes female subjects in the few pages dedicated to women workers and female mutual aid societies, for example, he ignores the implications of women's position in the labor movement and how gender might have shaped the formation and structure of working-class men's political activity in the nineteenth century. Similarly, DeShazo's otherwise thorough social history of labor in the early twentieth century fails to consider the significance of the strike statistics and union rosters that testify to, and help to explain, female marginalization in workers' associations and activities (*Urban Workers*, 244, 251).

18 DeShazo, *Urban Workers*, 3–87; Alberto Edwards, *La fronda aristocrática* (Santiago: Editorial Universitaria, 1982); Julio Heise González, *Historia de Chile: El periodo parlamentario 1861–1925*, 3 vols. (Santiago: Editorial Universitaria, 1982); Illanes, *"En el nombre del pueblo"*, parts 1,

2; Kirsch, *Industrial Development*; Brian Loveman, *Chile: The Legacy of Hispanic Capitalism* (New York: Oxford University Press, 1979), chap. 7; James O. Morris, *Elites, Intellectuals, and Consensus: A Study of the Social Question and the Industrial Relations System in Chile* (Ithaca, NY: Cornell University, 1966).

19 Women's and children's labor legislation is mentioned only in passing in two of the major works that discuss the development of industrial relations in Chile. Morris (*Elites*) considers such laws relatively marginal to ideological disputes over the social question, and DeShazo (*Urban Workers*) interprets most social legislation, including protective legislation for women, as irrelevant to workers and workers' politics prior to 1927.

20 In her study of the class discourse of elite women's groups in Santiago from 1915 to 1920 Ericka Verba has shown that the categories of class and gender can together be fruitfully employed to illuminate further the significance of the social question: Ericka Kim Verba, "The *Círculo de Lectura* [Ladies' Reading Circle] and the *Club de Señoras* [Ladies' Club] of Santiago, Chile: Middle- and Upper-Class Feminist Conversations (1915–1920)," *Journal of Women's History* 7, no. 3 (fall 1995): 6–33, and "Catholic Feminism and *Accion Social Femenina* [Women's Social Action]: The Early Years of the Liga de Damas Chilenas, 1912–1924" (Ph.D. diss., University of California at Los Angeles, 1999).

21 Four recently published anthologies testify to the increasing attention to women's history in Chile: Lorena Godoy Catalán, Elizabeth Hutchison, Karin Rosemblatt, and M. Soledad Zárate, eds., *Disciplina y desacato: Construccion de identidad en Chile, siglos XIX y XX* (Santiago: SUR-CEDEM, 1995); *Nomadías* 1, monographic series (Santiago: Editorial Universidad de Chile, 1999); Diana Veneros Ruíz-Tagle, ed., *Perfiles revelados: Historia de mujeres en Chile siglos XVIII–XX* (Santiago: Editorial Universidad de Santiago, 1997); Sergio Vergara, Paulina Zamorano, and Zvonimir Martinic, eds., *Descorriendo el velo: II y III jornadas de investigaciones en historia de la mujer* (Santiago: LOM Ediciones, 1999).

22 These early works in Chilean women's history include Paz Covarrubias, "El movimiento feminista chileno," in *Chile Mujer y Sociedad*, ed. Covarrubias and Rolando Franco (Santiago: UNICEF, 1978), 615–49; Edda Gaviola, Ximena Jiles Moreno, Lorella Lopresti Martínez, and Claudia Rojas Mira, *"Queremos votar en las próximas elecciones": Historia del movimiento femenino chileno 1913–1952* (Santiago: CEM, 1986); Julieta Kirkwood, *Feminismo y participación política en Chile* (Santiago: FLACSO Working Paper no. 159, 1982), and *Ser política en Chile: Los nudos de la sabiduría feminista* (Santiago: Editorial Cuarto Propio, 1990); Felícitas A. Klimpel, *La Mujer Chilena: El aporte femenino al progreso de Chile, 1910–1960* (Santiago: Editorial Andrés Bello, 1962);

Asunción Lavrin, "The Ideology of Feminism in the Southern Cone, 1900–1940," in *Latin American Program* (Washington, DC: Wilson Center, 1986); Lucia Santa Cruz, Teresa Pereira, Isabel Zegers, and Valeria Maíno, *Tres ensayos sobre la mujer chilena, Siglos XVIII–XIX–XX* (Santiago: Editorial Universitaria, 1978); María de la Luz Silva Donoso, *La participación política de la mujer en Chile: Las organizaciones de mujeres* (Buenos Aires: Fundación Friedrich Naumann, 1987).

23 Chilean women's historians have tended to present their studies as primarily compensatory—filling in the gaps of male-centered history— whereas many North American scholars, by applying gender analysis, have also examined working-class masculinity and framed their studies in terms of larger narratives about sexuality, state formation, and labor politics. For an exploration of the epistemological and theoretical distinctions between scholarship on women in the United States and Latin America, see Teresita de Barbieri, "Sobre la categoría género: Una Introducción teórico-metodológica," in *Fin de Siglo: Género y Cambio Civilizatorio* (Santiago: Isis, Women's Editions no. 17, 1992), 111–28; Elizabeth Quay Hutchison, "Feminism, Gender Studies and Trans-National Dialog in Post-Authoritarian Chile," paper presented at the Council on Latin American History Chile–Rio de la Plata Roundtable, Washington, DC, 9 January 1999; Amy K. Kaminsky, *Reading the Body Politic: Feminist Criticism and Latin American Women Writers* (Minneapolis: University of Minnesota Press, 1993), chap. 1; Sonia Montecino, "De la mujer al género: Implicancias académicas y teóricas," and Loreto Rebolledo, "Balance del desarrollo de los estudios y investigaciones sobre mujer y género en las universidades," both in *Mujer y género: Nuevos saberes en las universidades Chilenas*, ed. Sonia Montecino and Loreto Rebolledo (Santiago: Universidad de Chile, 1995); Victor Toledo, "Historia de las mujeres en Chile y la cuestión de género en la historia social," in *Huellas: Seminario mujer y antropología. problematización y perspectivas*, ed. Sonia Montecino and María Elena Boisier (Santiago: CEDEM, 1993), 51–64; Teresa Valdés, *El Movimiento social de mujeres y la producción de conocimientos sobre la condición de la mujer* (Santiago: FLACSO Working Paper no. 43, 1993).

24 This turn to working-class women's history in Chile was first signaled in the late 1980s by the publication of Cecilia Salinas's *La mujer proletaria: Una historia para contar* (Santiago: Literatura América Reunida, 1987), and Asunción Lavrin's "Women, Labor and the Left: Argentina and Chile, 1890–1925," *Journal of Women's History* 1, no. 2 (fall 1989): 88–116. More recent scholarship includes Catalina Arteaga A., "Oficios, trabajos y vida cotidiana de mujeres rurales en San Felipe, 1900–1940: Una reconstrucción a partir de causas criminales del Archivo Judicial de San Felipe," in *Perfiles revelados*, ed. Veneros, 197–216; Alejandra Brito, "Del rancho al conventillo: Transformaciones en la iden-

tidad popular femenina, Santiago de Chile, 1850–1920," in *Disciplina y desacato*, ed. Godoy et al., 27–70; Rebeca Conte Corvalán, *La mutualidad femenina: Una visión social de la mujer Chilena, 1888–1930* (Thesis, University of Chile, 1987); Janet L. Finn, *Tracing the Veins: Of Copper, Culture, and Community from Butte to Chuquicamata* (Berkeley: University of California Press, 1998); Lorena Godoy, " 'Armas ansiosas de triunfo: Dedal, agujas, tijeras . . . ': La educación profesional femenina en Chile, 1888–1912," in *Disciplina y desacato*, ed. Godoy et al., 71–110; Thomas Miller Klubock, *Contested Communities: Class, Gender, and Politics in Chile's El Teniente Copper Mine, 1904–1951* (Durham, NC: Duke University Press, 1998), chaps. 7, 8; Marcela Tapia and Gina Inostroza, "La mujer popular en el trabajo independiente: Concepción-Chile (1895–1905)," in *Perfiles revelados*, ed. Veneros, 141–70; Heidi Elizabeth Tinsman, *Partners in Conflict: The Politics of Gender, Sexuality, and Labor in the Chilean Agrarian Reform, 1950–1973* (Durham, NC: Duke University Press, forthcoming).

25 Corinne A. Antezana-Pernet, "Mobilizing Women in the Popular Front Era: Feminism, Class, and Politics in the Movimiento Pro-Emancipación de la Mujer Chilena (MEMCh), 1935–1950" (Ph.D. diss., University of California at Irvine, 1996); Susan K. Besse, *Restructuring Patriarchy: The Modernization of Gender Inequality in Brazil, 1914–1940* (Chapel Hill: University of North Carolina Press, 1996); Marifran Carlson, *Feminismo! The Woman's Movement in Argentina from Its Beginnings to Eva Peron* (Chicago: Academy Chicago Publishers, 1988); June Edith Hahner, *Emancipating the Female Sex: The Struggle for Women's Rights in Brazil, 1850–1940* (Durham, NC: Duke University Press, 1991); Asunción Lavrin, *Women, Feminism and Social Change in Argentina, Chile and Uruguay, 1890–1940* (Lincoln: University of Nebraska Press, 1995); Francesca Miller, *Latin American Women and the Search for Social Justice* (Hanover, NH: University Press of New England, 1991); K. Lynn Stoner, *From the House to the Streets: The Cuban Woman's Movement for Legal Reform, 1898–1940* (Durham, NC: Duke University Press, 1991).

26 For a related discussion about the need to historicize women's "progress" in the modern period more generally, see Elizabeth Dore, "One Step Forward, Two Steps Back: Gender and the State in the Long Nineteenth Century," in *Hidden Histories of Gender and the State in Latin America*, ed. Elizabeth Dore and Maxine Molyneux (Durham, NC: Duke University Press, 2000), 3–32; Maxine Molyneux, "Twentieth-Century State Formations in Latin America," in *Hidden Histories*, 33–84; Besse, *Restructuring Patriarchy*.

27 Lavrin's comparative approach provides a nuanced analysis of the emergence and influence of progressive feminist demands for legislative and political change (*Women, Feminism, and Social Change*).

28 Besse acknowledges the diversity of feminist orientations in the section titled "Other Feminisms" (*Restructuring Patriarchy*, 178–98). Important new research on conservative feminisms includes Christine Theresa Ehrick, "*Obrera, Dama, Feminista*: Women's Associations and the Welfare State in Uruguay, 1900–1932" (Ph.D. diss., University of California at Los Angeles, 1997); Sandra McGee Deutsch, *Las Derechas: The Extreme Right in Argentina, Brazil, and Chile, 1890–1939* (Stanford, CA: Stanford University Press, 1999), 304–25; Verba, "Catholic Feminism"; Patience A. Schell, "An Honorable Avocation for Ladies: The Work of the Mexico City Unión de Damas Católicas Mexicanas, 1912–1926," *Journal of Women's History* 10, no. 4 (winter 1999): 78–103; Erika Maza Valenzuela, "Catolicismo, anticlericalismo y la extensión del sufragio a la mujer en Chile," *Estudios Públicos* 58 (autumn 1995): 137–95.

29 Ann Farnsworth-Alvear, *Dulcinea in the Factory: Myths, Morals, Men, and Women in Colombia's Industrial Experiment, 1905–1960* (Durham, NC: Duke University Press, 2000), chap. 2.

30 Daniel James, " 'Tales Told out on the Borderlands': Doña Maria's Story, Oral History, and Issues of Gender"; Mirta Zida Lobato, "Women Workers in the 'Cathedrals of Corned Beef': Structure and Subjectivity in the Argentine Meatpacking Industry"; Barbara Weinstein, "Unskilled Worker, Skilled Housewife: Constructing the Working-Class Woman in São Paulo, Brazil"; and Theresa R. Veccia, " 'My Duty as a Woman': Gender Ideology, Work, and Working-Class Women's Lives in São Paulo, Brazil, 1900–1950," all in *The Gendered Worlds of Latin American Women Workers*, ed. French and James.

31 Deborah Levenson-Estrada, "The Loneliness of Working-Class Feminism: Women in the 'Male World' of Labor Unions, Guatemala City, 1970s," in *The Gendered Worlds of Women Workers*, ed. French and James, 211.

32 Other examples of working women's strategic and perceived "virility" can be seen in Hewitt, " 'The Voice of Virile Labor,' " 142–67, and Ann Farnsworth-Alvear, "The Mysterious Case of the Missing Men: Gender and Class in Early Industrial Medellín," *International Labor and Working-Class History* 49 (spring 1996): 73–92.

33 The Chilean labor press has proven to be a valuable resource for students of Chilean labor politics who have classified these working-class newspapers and journals and analyzed their impact on workers' movements during this formative period. Important information about the labor press can also be found in Osvaldo Arias Escobedo, *La prensa obrera en Chile* (Chillán: Universidad de Chile, 1970); Jorge Barría Serón, *Los movimientos sociales en Chile, 1910–1926* (Santiago: Ed. Universitaria, 1960); Patrick Edward Breslin, "The Development of Class Consciousness in the Chilean Working Class" (Ph.D. diss., University of California at Los Angeles, 1980); Ximena Cruzat and Eduardo

Devés, eds., *Recabarren: Escritos de prensa, 1898–1924*, 4 vols. (Santiago: Terranova Editores, 1987); DeShazo, *Urban Workers*; Salinas, *La mujer proletaria*; Claudia Aranda B. and Ricardo Canales A., eds., *Páginas literarias de los obreros socialistas (1912–1915)* (Santiago: Editorial ICAL, 1991).

34 Linda Gordon, ed., *Women, the State and Welfare* (Madison: University of Wisconsin Press, 1990); Dore and Molyneux, eds., *Hidden Histories*.

I Working-Class Life and Politics

1 Vicente Espinoza, *Para una historia de los pobres de la ciudad* (Santiago: SUR, 1988); María Angélica Illanes, *"En el nombre del pueblo, del estado y de la ciencia (. . .)" Historia Social de la Salud Pública, Chile 1880–1973 (Hacia una historia social del Siglo XIX)* (Santiago: Colectivo de Atención Primaria, 1993), 22.

1 Gender, Industrialization, and Urban Change in Santiago

1 Brian Loveman estimates that less than 10 percent of the 1875 population belonged to these more privileged sectors: *Chile: The Legacy of Hispanic Capitalism* (New York: Oxford University Press, 1979), 167–68.

2 Henry W. Kirsch, *Industrial Development in a Traditional Society: The Conflict of Entrepreneurship and Modernization* (Gainesville: University Presses of Florida, 1977).

3 Cristobal Kay, "The Development of the Chilean *Hacienda* System," in *Land and Labour in Latin America*, ed. Kenneth Duncan and Ian Rutledge (Cambridge, England: Cambridge University Press, 1977), 103–40; Arnold Bauer, *Chilean Rural Society from the Spanish Conquest to 1930* (Cambridge, England: Cambridge University Press, 1975).

4 Salazar notes that although young men obtained access to land and commerce near cities prior to the 1830s, they later found better opportunities by heading to mining areas or out of Chile altogether. See Gabriel Salazar, *Labradores, peones y proletarios: Formación y crisis de la sociedad popular chilena del siglo XIV* (Santiago: SUR, 1985), chap. 2.

5 Julio Heise González, *El período parlamentario, 1861–1925* (Santiago: Editorial Universitaria, 1982); Loveman, *Chile*, chap. 6.

6 Loveman, *Chile*, 234.

7 Marcelo Carmagnani, cited in Peter DeShazo, *Urban Workers and Labor Unions in Chile, 1902–1927* (Madison: University of Wisconsin Press, 1983), 11.

8 Kirsch, paraphrased in Oscar Muñoz, *Estado e industrialización en el ciclo de expansión del salitre* (Santiago: CIEPLAN, 1977), 25.

9 J. E. Vargas, "La Sociedad de Fomento Fabril, 1883–1928," *Revista Historia* 13 (1976): 5–53.

10 Muñoz, *Estado e industrialización*, 14, 33–35.

11 Ranked in terms of production, the leading Santiago industries between 1917 and 1927 were food, clothing and footwear, wood and wood products, beverages, tobacco, leather and rubber, and textiles. See De-Shazo, *Urban Workers*, 14–15.

12 Kirsch, *Industrial Development*, 8.

13 DeShazo, *Urban Workers*, Table 1.1, p. 4.

14 Quoted in Luís Alberto Romero, "Urbanización y sectores populares: Santiago de Chile, 1830–1875," *Revista EURE (Revista de Estudios Urbanos Regionales)* 7, no. 31 (October 1984): 59.

15 Armando de Ramón, *Santiago de Chile (1540–1991): Historia de una sociedad urbana* (Madrid: Editorial Mapfre, 1992), 221.

16 Salazar, *Labradores*, 254.

17 Carl Solberg, *Immigration and Nationalism: Argentina and Chile, 1890–1914* (Austin: University of Texas Press, 1970), 35.

18 Ibid., 38–39.

19 Montserrat Palmer Trias, *La Ciudad Jardín como Modelo de crecimiento urbano: Santiago 1935–1960* (Santiago: Facultad de Arquitectura y Bellas Artes de la Universidad Católica de Chile, 1987); Patricio Gross, Armando de Ramón, and Enrique Vial, *Imagen Ambiental de Santiago, 1800–1936* (Santiago: Editorial Universidad Católica de Chile, 1984).

20 Romero, "Urbanización y sectores populares," 62–63.

21 Census analysts attributed this disequilibrium to the lack of rural employment and growth in urban domestic service opportunities for women. See *Censo* 1907, xviii–xix.

22 DeShazo, *Urban Workers*, 3–4.

23 Alejandra Brito, "Del rancho al conventillo: Transformaciones en la identidad popular femenina, Santiago de Chile, 1850–1920," in *Disciplina y desacato: Construcción de identidad en Chile, Siglos XIX y XX*, ed. Lorena Godoy, Elizabeth Hutchison, Karin Rosemblatt, and María Soledad Zárate (Santiago: SUR/CEDEM, 1995), 30–40.

24 The term *roto* was also used to describe (and degrade) manual laborers of any profession; it was, and is, an epithet that suggests the indigenous and working-class origins of an individual.

25 Romero, "Urbanización y sectores populares," 60–61.

26 Gabriel Salazar, "La mujer de 'bajo pueblo' en Chile: Bosquejo histórico," *Proposiciones* 21 (December 1992): 66.

27 Romero, "Urbanización y sectores populares," 60–61; Luís Alberto Romero, *La Sociedad de Igualdad: Los artesanos de Santiago de Chile y sus primeras experiencias políticas, 1820–1851* (Buenos Aires: Instituto Di Tella, 1984).

28 DeShazo, *Urban Workers*, 12.

29 Another 42 percent of industrial workers were employed in firms of 11 to 100 workers (Kirsch, *Industrial Development*, 108).

30 DeShazo, *Urban Workers*, 13.

31 Ibid., 15.

32 1895 Industrial Census, cited in ibid., 12.

33 De Ramón, *Santiago de Chile*, 198.

34 Thelma Gálvez and Rosa Bravo, "Siete décadas de registro del trabajo femenino 1854–1920," *Estadística y Economía* 5 (December 1992): 16.

35 Brito, "Del rancho al conventillo," 30–37.

36 *El Ferrocarril*, 28 April 1872.

37 De Ramón, *Santiago*, 225–29.

38 Brito, "Del rancho al conventillo," 33.

39 Benjamin Vicuña Mackenna, *Transformación de Santiago* (Santiago: Imprenta El Mercurio, 1872), 34–35.

40 ADGT, *Varios*, 1923, vol. 94.

41 Brito, "Del rancho al conventillo," 33.

42 DeShazo, *Urban Workers*, 62.

43 Isabel Torres Dujisin, "Los conventillos de Santiago (1900–1930)," *Cuadernos de Historia* 6 (July 1986): 79–80.

44 Cited in DeShazo, *Urban Workers*, Table 3.1, p. 60.

45 Torres, "Los conventillos de Santiago," 70.

46 *BOT, Anexo de Estadística*, 1926.

47 Brito, "Del rancho al conventillo," 66 n. 2.

48 A Labor Office survey compared conventillo rents in Santiago and Arica in 1922: rents were twice as high in Santiago, yet average industrial wages were only 10.28 percent higher (ADGT, *Varios*, 1923, vol. 94).

49 Vicente Espinoza, *Para una historia de los pobres de la ciudad* (Santiago: SUR, 1988), chaps. 2, 3.

50 All of the twenty families selected by Inspector Luís A. Rojo in 1921 contained a married couple, and in only six of those families did the wife report having income. As Rojo explained in his report, he had selected "as much as possible, those families made up of more than two people, which are the families that now suffer most the difficult consequences of the economic crisis afflicting the country." See *BOT* 12, no. 18 (1922): 88.

51 Salazar, *Labradores*, 254. Brito's and Salazar's assertions about the predominant female presence in the city center are based on their readings of municipal inspectors' reports and period literature on the urban environment.

52 Alberto Romero, *La viuda del conventillo* (Santiago: Ediciones Ercilla, 1932); José Santos González Vera, *Vidas mínimas* (Santiago: Empresa Letras, 1933); Nicomedes Guzmán, *Los hombres oscuros* (Santiago: Zig-Zag, 1961).

53 *BOT, Anexo de Estadística*, 1926.

54 *El Mercurio*, 9 June 1910, 4.

55 Daniel de la Vega, "Miseria," *Revista de la Habitación* 4, no. 13 (1924): 191–92.

56 Aníbal Aguayo, "La vida en el conventillo," *Revista de la Habitación* 2, no. 19 (1922): 424.

57 Brito, "Del rancho al conventillo," 34–37.

58 María Angélica Illanes, *"En el nombre del pueblo, del estado y de la ciencia, (. . .)": Historia Social de la Salud Pública, Chile 1880–1973 (Hacia una historia social del Siglo XIX)* (Santiago: Colectivo de Atención Primaria, 1993), 22.

59 Ibid., 77.

2 Women at Work in Santiago

1 Luís M. Sanz, "La Costurera," *El Alba*, 15 March 1906, 8.

2 Juan Enrique Concha Subercaseux, *Conferencias sobre economía política*, 270, cited in Ericka Verba, "Catholic Feminism and *Acción Social Femenina* [Women's Social Action]: The Early Years of the Liga de Damas Chilenas, 1912–1924" (Ph.D. diss., University of California at Los Angeles, 1999), 257–58.

3 Although census administrators did not yet conceptualize their data in global terms, such as "economically active population," since the 1930s census data have regularly been manipulated to permit this calculation and allow for comparisons across time. See Thelma Gálvez and Rosa Bravo, "Siete décadas de registro del trabajo femenino, 1854–1920," *Estadística y Economía* 5 (December 1992): 1–52; Elizabeth Quay Hutchison, "La Historia detrás de las cifras: La evolución del censo chileno y la representación del trabajo femenino, 1895–1930," in *Historia* (Santiago), 33 (2000): 417–34; and Anne Pérotin-Dumon, ed., *El género en historia* [online] (Santiago: Universidad Católica, 2000, available from http://www.hist.puc.cl/genero.html).

4 Lucía Pardo, "Una revisión histórica a la participación de la población en la fuerza de trabajo: Tendencias y características de la participación de la mujer," *Estudios de Economía* 15, no. 1 (April 1988): 54.

5 The census of 1990 recorded that 22.6 percent of adult women were economically active, and women made up 25 percent of the total labor force. See *Mujeres Latinoamericanas en Cifras* (Santiago: Instituto de la Mujer, 1992).

6 Edda Gaviola Artigas, Ximena Jiles Moreno, Lorela Lopresti Martínez, and Claudia Rojas Mira, *"Queremos votar en las próximas elecciones": Historia del movimiento femenino chileno 1913–1952* (Santiago: CEM, 1986), 22–26; Peter DeShazo, *Urban Workers and Labor Unions in Chile, 1902–1927* (Madison: University of Wisconsin Press, 1983), 16–

22; Isabel Zegers and Valeria Maino, "La mujer en el siglo XX," in *Tres ensayos sobre la mujer chilena, Siglos XVIII–XIX–XX*, ed. Lucia Santa Cruz, Teresa Pereira, Isabel Zegers, and Valeria Maino (Santiago: Editorial Universitaria, 1978), 247–55.

7 When they have tried to explain this pattern, some authors have resorted to gendered assumptions about women's preference for traditional domestic roles, asserting that women withdrew from the workforce because of the relative prosperity of the 1920s or the impact of the 1929 economic crisis. Zegers and Maino argue that women "abandon the home" to work only in times of war, economic crisis, or industrialization ("La mujer en el siglo XX," 249–50).

8 Felícitas Klimpel was the first to point out that changing census categories distorted measurements of female employment trends. See *La mujer chilena: El aporte femenino al progreso de Chile, 1910–1960* (Santiago: Editorial Andrés Bello, 1962), 150–54.

9 As the director of the census commented in his introduction, "The general result of the 1895 Census is, in my judgement, far from being a real numerical reflection of the Republic's inhabitants . . . in some rural areas, TWO THIRDS of the inhabitants were not noted in the Census sheets" (*Censo* 1895, ix). The census of 1907 was considered so faulty at the time that it was almost left unpublished.

10 Similar approaches can be found in Edward Higgs, "Women, Occupations and Work in the Nineteenth Century Censuses," *History Workshop Journal* 23 (spring 1987): 76–77; Joan Wallach Scott, "A Statistical Representation of Work: La Statistique de l'industrie a Paris, 1847–1848," in *Gender and the Politics of History* (New York: Columbia University Press, 1988), 113–38.

11 Census officials themselves acknowledged that the figures for *costureras* (seamstresses) might be inflated by daughters reporting their sporadic needlework as an occupation, but did not, apparently, exclude such women from census occupational listings (Gálvez and Bravo, "Siete décadas," 4, 13).

12 There has been no historical investigation to date that would provide more than a rough estimate of the numbers of women working as prostitutes in this period. The archives of the Hygiene Office revealed some information, but so far no comprehensive register of prostitutes— like the one discovered by Donna Guy for Argentina—has been located. For a review of the rough numerical estimates, see Alvaro Góngora Escobedo, *La prostitución en Santiago, 1813–1931: La visión de las élites* (Santiago: DIBAM, 1994), 33–42.

   Many women who reported to census takers and police that they were seamstresses or laundresses may have actually practiced some form of prostitution. Contemporary sources also suggest this interpretation;

noting the seemingly incredible number of seamstresses and laundresses recorded in the census of 1854, census officials suggested that women might claim these occupations "in order not to report professions that might damage delicacy or modesty" (cited in Gálvez and Bravo, "Siete décadas," 13).

13   This mobility is further substantiated by Prunés's 1926 list of prostitutes' former occupations: Luís Prunés R., *La prostitución: Evolución de su concepto hasta nuestros días. El neo-abolicionismo ante el nuevo Código Sanitario de Chile* (Santiago: Imprenta Universo, 1926), 111.

14   *Censo* 1907, emphasis added; cited in Gálvez and Bravo, "Siete décadas," 7.

15   See the complex instructions to census takers in *Censo* 1920, xxiv–xxvii.

16   *Censo* 1930, xvi, xvii; emphasis added.

17   In fact, a greater proportion of the economically active female population was classified as professionals (35 percent) than were men (28 percent). However, only 24 percent of professionals recorded in the census were women.

18   Here, following the lead of Gálvez and Bravo in "Siete décadas," I have moved laundresses to the domestic service sector and kept seamstresses in the industrial category (including those who might have sewed at home), because seamstresses represented the quintessential expression of the woman worker in contemporary sources. Although female employment confounds the sectoral categories established with reference to male workers and national production, this adjustment more accurately reflects contemporary observations and is consistent with current labor classification methods.

   Different interpretations of these two most explicitly female activities as "work," furthermore, provide an excellent illustration of how statistical interpretation can function to reinforce gendered definitions of work. Peter DeShazo, for example, created a new sectoral division called "other service," composed predominantly of laundresses and seamstresses and including jewelers, watchmakers, barbers, butchers, tailors, embroiderers, bootblacks, and midwives. DeShazo thus excluded 141,468 women and 13,067 men from the industrial sector altogether, providing him with figures that isolated male industrial workers, who are the subject of his study. However legitimate that calculation for DeShazo's purposes, it made the elision of women from his study of "urban workers" a foregone conclusion (DeShazo, *Urban Workers*, 17–18).

19   *Censo* 1930, viii.

20   On female unemployment caused by World War I, see *El Mercurio*, 10 October 1914, 3, and *BOT* 5, no. 10 (1915): 32. The world depression hit employment in the nitrate sector hardest, but seems to have had a

lesser impact in either the service or manufacturing sectors, where most women worked. On the masculinization of the textile and clothing sectors, see Gálvez and Bravo, "Siete décadas," 20–28.

21 "Some figures may seem strange, such as women bricklayers, stone-cutters, blacksmiths and others, but these have been verified against the census papers, so if there is a mistake, it would have to have been made by the census taker" (*Censo* 1930, vol. 3, xvii).

22 Gabriel Salazar, "La mujer del 'bajo pueblo' en Chile: Bosquejo histó-rico," *Proposiciones* 21 (December 1992): 101.

23 The annual industrial survey, conducted first by SOFOFA and then by the National Statistics Office from 1910 to 1925, provides a different kind of measure of women's work than that of the census. These statis-tics were designed to measure—and applaud—the structure and effi-ciency of Chilean industry as evidence of modernization and national progress. Although the detailed classification of workers by task, sex, and nationality suggests the basic contours of the factory workforce, industrial statistics may be less comprehensive and objective than the census figures. The number of factories surveyed varied considerably, suggesting the somewhat random nature of the sample. Further, data were collected on the basis of questionnaires filled out by factory owners, who may have misrepresented the size and composition of their workforce to avoid official scrutiny or sanctions. Despite the ran-dom and unverified nature of these industrial statistics, they offer more detailed information than the national census on the proportion of male to female factory workers, the degree of feminization in different factories, and the segregation of management positions by sex.

24 *Censo* 1930, vi–vii, xii.

25 *BOT* 10 (1915): 32–65.

26 *AE* 1914, 30; this was the only year in which the management category was disaggregated by sex.

27 Furthermore, the designation trabajo a domicilio seems to have had ambiguous meaning as late as 1920, when census officials used it to refer to a seamstress who did work in the homes of various patrons. But by and large, and certainly in the protective legislation discussions of the mid-1920s, homework referred to piecework that factories farmed out to local women (*Censo*, 1920, introduction).

28 *BOT* 9, no. 12 (1919): 128.

29 Rafael Edwards's speech to the National Congress for Child Protection (1912), Jorge Huneeus's reports on the Labor Office on the Second International Congress on Homework in 1912, and Alberto Hurtado's 1923 study, *El Trabajo a Domicilio* (Santiago: Imprenta "El Globo," 1923) also publicized the plight of homeworkers. None of these ac-counts offers the kind of fieldwork-based insight found in Caffarena's work, however.

An excerpt of the thesis was also published as "El trabajo a domicilio," *BOT* 22 (1924): 97–107. Caffarena's academic advisor for this work was Moisés Poblete Troncoso, then head of the Chilean Labor Office and a staunch advocate of female protective legislation. In 1928, Caffarena joined the newly formed division of female inspectors in the Labor Office, and went on in 1935 to become a founding member and secretary general of the Movement for the Emancipation of Chilean Women (*Movimiento Pro-Emancipación de la Mujer Chilena,* or MEMCh). A recent biography of Caffarena elucidates her professional trajectory from law student to lawyer and national feminist leader; see Olga Poblete Poblete, *Una mujer: Elena Caffarena* (Santiago: Cuarto Propio, 1993). See also Corinne Antezana-Pernet, "Mobilizing Women in the Popular Front Era: Feminism, Class, and Politics in the Movimiento Pro-Emancipación de la Mujer Chilena (MEMCh), 1935–1950" (Ph.D. diss., University of California at Irvine, 1996).

30 Caffarena, "El trabajo a domicilio," 98.

31 Ibid., 100.

32 Ibid., 102, 107. Rather than abolish homework, however—the solution advocated by some labor organizations—Caffarena concluded that if homeworkers could be protected through state regulation, they would be better off than factory workers. "The Law is the only thing that can fight efficaciously against the 'sweating system,'" according to Caffarena, because the isolated nature of homework makes it impossible for women to unionize, and because charity work and consumers' leagues provided only limited responses (107–8).

33 Peter DeShazo's survey of newspaper and Labor Office sources revealed that the bulk of lowest-paid jobs—less than 5 pesos a day, in 1925 pesos—were performed by women: "ironesses, laundresses, domestic servants, packagers (female), most female factory labor, child factory labor, lowest-paid male factory labor, most textile factory workers, lowest paid food-industry workers" (*Urban Workers*, 32–33).

34 See Marysa Navarro, "Hidden, Silent, and Anonymous: Women Workers in the Argentine Trade Union Movement," in *The World of Women's Trade Unionism*, ed. Norbert C. Soldon (Westport, CT: Greenwood Press, 1985), 180–81; June E. Hahner, "Women and Work in Brazil, 1850–1920: A Preliminary Investigation," in *Essays Concerning the Socioeconomic History of Brazil and Portuguese India*, ed. Davril Audin and Warren Dean (Gainesville: University Presses of Florida, 1977), 107–9.

35 DeShazo, *Urban Workers*, 30.

36 Ibid., Table 2.1, p. 31.

37 ADGT, *Archivo*, 1928, Labor Office report, 21 January 1928.

38 ADGT, *Estadística de Trabajo*, 1906, vol. 1, Worker survey, 27 November 1906.

39 On domestic service wages: ADGT, *E. Frías Collao: Estudios y Trabajos,* 1918, vol. 48, "Población, actividades, ingresos totales, montos de los sueldos, etc."; on factory wages: *La Opinión,* 20 August 1919.

40 Prunés, *La prostitución,* 112.

41 "El trabajo de la mujer," *El Mercurio,* 26 September 1906.

42 "La mujer obrera," *El Mercurio,* 10 March 1908.

43 "Protección al trabajo femenino," *El Mercurio,* 11 December 1918.

44 "Una mujer que sigue el oficio de mecánico," *La Opinión,* 16 July 1915.

45 "El trabajo de la mujer," *El Chileno,* 4 May 1918.

46 "El trabajo femenino y la cuestión social," *La Opinión,* 22 March 1920.

47 O.E., "Sofismas Feministas," *El Mercurio,* 12 August 1907.

3 "To Work Like Men and Not Cry Like Women":
The Problem of Women in Male Workers' Politics

1 Organized labor's identification of skill, strength, and militancy as male attributes is not, of course, a uniquely Chilean phenomenon. See Nicholas Stargardt, "Male Bonding and the Class Struggle in Imperial Germany," *Historical Journal* 38, no. 1 (1995): 191.

2 María Angélica Illanes has argued that these societies provided a model for health and worker plans elaborated by the state after 1924. See *"En el nombre del pueblo, del estado y de la ciencia, (. . .)": Historia social de la salud pública, Chile 1880–1973 (Hacia una historia social del Siglo XX)* (Santiago: Colectivo de Atención Primaria, 1993), 35–50.

3 Peter DeShazo, *Urban Workers and Labor Unions in Chile, 1902–1927* (Madison: University of Wisconsin Press, 1983), 89.

4 Sergio Grez Toso, "La mutualité aux origines du mouvement ouvrier chilien (1853–1890)," *La revue de l'économie sociale* (1992): 175–76.

5 DeShazo, *Urban Workers,* 89–91.

6 Oscar Parrao, "La mutualidad en Chile," *BOT* 21 (1923): 13–25.

7 In 1890, for example, only 75 of a probable total of 150 mutual aid societies were actually recorded (Grez, "La mutualité," 178).

8 Grez elaborates that, although the prohibition on female membership was not explicit in mutualist statutes, "this phenomenon can be explained by the mutualists' simple adhesion to the morals and dominant norms of the Chilean society in that era, which excluded women from many areas of social activity." See Sergio Grez, *De la "regeneración del pueblo" a la huelga general: Génesis y evolución histórica del movimiento popular en Chile (1810–1890)* (Santiago: DIBAM, 1997), 598 n. 1751.

9 Ibid., 602, 604 n. 1769; Rebeca Conte Corvalán, *La mutualidad femenina: Una visión social de la mujer chilena, 1888–1930* (Thesis, University of Chile, 1987), 169–73, 190.

10 Oficina del Trabajo, *Estadística de la Asociación Obrera* (Santiago: Im-

prenta i Litografía Santiago, 1910), 27. Membership in the Santiago society was limited to workers (*obreras*), and excluded tram fare collectors and domestic servants.

11   The daily press regularly published notices for the Society's social events and night school, which received 1,500 pesos in state support annually: *El Obrero Ilustrado*, 15 June 1906. On this point, see Grez, *Regeneración del pueblo*, 604.

12   "Sociabilidad Femenina," *El Obrero Ilustrado*, 1 August 1906, 103.

13   Oficina del Trabajo, *Estadística de la Asociación Obrera*, 27–29.

14   ADGT, *Nómina de Sociedades Obreras*, 1917, vol. 37, responses to worker societies' poll.

15   Oscar Parrao, *La mutualidad en Chile* (Santiago: Imprenta Ramón Brías, 1926), 13–25; Moisés Poblete Troncoso, *La organización sindical en Chile y otros estudios sociales* (Santiago: Ramón Brías, 1926), 74.

16   Roldán de Alarcón was one of the seven women leaders written up in the 1912 *Diccionario Biográfico Obrero*, where she was lauded as "this exemplary woman who, together with her husband, has managed to struggle resolutely and challenges the attacks of those on high and the gossip and ingratitude of those below." See Osvaldo López, *Diccionario Biográfico Obrero* (Santiago: Bellavista, 1912), R3.

17   On the 1890 strike, see Sergio Grez, "La huelga general de 1890," *Perspectivas* 5 (December 1990): 127–67.

18   In his comparative study of labor mobilization in Latin American export sectors, Bergquist argues convincingly that the Marxist labor movement that emerged from the northern nitrate companies was unique in its capacity to shape the politics of twentieth-century Chile. See Charles Bergquist, *Labor in Latin America: Comparative Essays on Chile, Argentina, Venezuela, and Colombia* (Stanford, CA: Stanford University Press, 1986), chap. 2.

19   For example, the principal figure of Chilean labor organization (and later founder of the Communist Party), Luís Emilio Recabarren, hosted the visits of anarchist Pablo Gori in 1901 and anticlerical feminist Belén de Sárraga in 1913, among others. During his exile in Argentina and Europe in 1907 and 1908, Recabarren met with Alfredo Palacios, Juan Justo, Pablo Iglesia, Francisco Larguo Caballero, and Jean Jaurès.

20   Illiteracy at the national level reached 72 percent in 1895. See María Angélica Illanes, *"Ausente, señorita": El niño-chileno, la escuela-para-pobres y el auxilio. Chile, 1890–1990* (Santiago: Junta Nacional de Auxilio Escolar y Becas, 1991), 32.

21   Against Monteon's criticism that illiteracy impeded the impact of the labor press, Bergquist argues that workers probably read the papers to each other and that the papers also served as a crucial tool for networking and institution building in the early labor movement (Bergquist, *Labor in Latin America*, 51–52).

22 Julio Ramos notes the tendency of Puerto Rican anarchists to paraphrase freely from foreign texts, which were also often translated and read aloud to workers long before they became available in printed editions. See Julio Ramos, ed., *Amor y anarquía: Los escritos de Luisa Capetillo* (Rio Piedras, Puerto Rico: Ediciones Huracán, 1992), 27.

23 According to DeShazo's strike data, worker mobilization prior to 1927 reached its peak between 1902 and 1908. Resistance societies participated in 67 percent of the recorded strikes, as compared to the 23 and 10 percent participation registered by brotherhoods and mutual aid societies, respectively (DeShazo, *Urban Workers*, 270).

24 Although labor historians have typically stressed the Marxist roots of the Chilean labor movement, DeShazo has shown that anarchist groups were crucial to the mobilization and leadership of Chile's most concerted strike waves of the early twentieth century (1905–1907 and 1917–1919) and that many of the leaders and rank-and-file members who were later incorporated into socialist and communist union movements of the 1930s had started out as anarchist militants (ibid., 260–61).

25 "Una sombrerera revolucionaria," *La Luz*, 1 February 1902.

26 Letter to *El Trabajo* (Tocopilla), 6 December 1903, cited in Salinas Alvarez, *La mujer proletaria: Una historia para contar* (Santiago: Literatura América Reunida, 1987), 34–35.

27 Letter from Clotilde Ibaceta to the Tocopilla brotherhood, *El Trabajo* (Tocopilla), 14 February 1904, quoted in Cecilia Salinas, "Antecedentes del movimiento femenino en Chile: Tres precursoras (1900–1907)," *Cuadernos del Instituto de Ciencias Alejandro Lipschutz* 4 (March 1986): 10.

28 Of a total 371 strikes DeShazo recorded from 1902 to 1927, women struck alone only 16 times, although women participated in at least 135 other instances (40 percent of all strikes). *Urban Workers*, Table A.6, p. 268. From these figures, DeShazo concluded that "*obreras* did show themselves to be willing strikers once their male counterparts decided to take action" (115), an interpretation not borne out by contemporary accounts of how women themselves initiated many strike actions.

29 Based on author's review of strike petitions, ADGT 1906–1930.

30 "Las obreras en tejidos: Hermoso movimiento de solidaridad femenina," *La Reforma*, 4 April 1907; emphasis added.

31 Democratic leaders were essentially drawn from two groups: professional or white-collar politicians and worker or mutual aid society representatives (DeShazo, *Urban Workers*, 91).

32 Antofagasta also elected Recabarren as representative to Congress in 1906, but Congress refused to seat him because he would not take the customary Christian oath.

33 See, for example, Recabarren's writings in the compilation by Ximena

Cruzat and Eduardo Devés, *Recabarren: Escritos de Prensa 1898–1924*, 4 vols. (Santiago: Terranova Editores, 1987).

34 These cultural activities included sewing classes for women family members of the brotherhoods (Bergquist, *Labor in Latin America*, 49). On working-class mobilization in the nitrate sector, see Bergquist, chap. 2; Brian Loveman, *Chile: The Legacy of Hispanic Capitalism* (New York: Oxford University Press, 1979), chap. 6; Elias Lafertte Gaviño, *Vida de un comunista: Páginas autobiográficas* (Santiago: Austral, 1971); Miguel Monteon, *Chile in the Nitrate Era* (Madison: University of Wisconsin Press, 1982); Julio Pinto, *Trabajos y rebeldías en la pampa salitrera: el ciclo de solitre y la reconfiguración de las identidades populares (1850–1900)* (Santiago: Editorial Universidad de Santiago, 1998); Hernán Ramírez Necochea, *Historia del movimiento obrero, siglo XIX* (Santiago: Taleres Gráficas Lautaro, 1956); Julio Cesar Jobet, *Luís Emilio Recabarren: Los orígenes del movimiento obrero y del socialismo Chileno* (Santiago: Editorial Prensa Latinoamericana, 1955); Luís Vitale, *Historia del movimiento obrero* (Santiago: Editorial POR., 1962).

35 Raul Canebreris R. [Luís Emilio Recabarren], "Un feliz acuerdo," *El Trabajo* (Tocopilla), 22 November 1903. Clotilde Ibaceta was one of the few women recognized as a member of the mancomunal of Tocapilla.

36 The issue at hand in the 1906 schism within the Democratic Party was the presidential campaign then underway. Ironically enough, the labor faction of the party broke off in support of oligarch Pedro Montt, and the Malaquías Concha faction supported Democratic candidate Fernando Lazcano.

37 For example, Recabarren chided Argentine anarchists for centralizing workers' societies in the Confederación General del Trabajo, thereby excluding socialists; see March 1907 speech cited in David Viñas, *Anarquistas en América Latina* (México City: Ediciones Katún, 1983), 167–68.

38 *La Reforma*, 7 August 1906.

39 *La Reforma*, 3 August 1906, 2.

40 *La Reforma*, 4 August 1906, 2.

41 *La Reforma*, 29 June 1907.

42 *La Reforma*, 8 March 1907.

43 The same report noted the solidarity of the Sociedad Cosmopólita de Obreras en Tejidos with the strike (*La Reforma*, 17 March 1907). In the same strike, "We should note that on this occasion the women have shown great enthusiasm. Their attitude has given spirit to the strikers, who do not flag in their just demands" (*La Reforma*, 19 March 1907). Women stitchers expressed solidarity with striking male shoe-workers in Valparaíso (*La Alborada* 2, no. 26 [30 December 1906]: 3–4).

44 *La Reforma*, 29 June 1907.

45 Silvana, *La Alborada* 1, no. 1 (10 September 1905): 3–4.

46 Agustín Bravo Zisternas [*sic*], "La Mujer," *La Alborada* 1, no. 6 (1 December 1905): 1–2; "En el Ateneo," *La Reforma*, 5 July 1906, 1.

47 *La Reforma*, 28 March 1907, 1.

48 DeShazo, *Urban Workers*, 116–17.

49 These figures are drawn from statistical charts in ibid., 103, 136, 165, which in turn are based on the data compiled by Jorge Barría Serón in *Los movimientos sociales en Chile desde 1910 hasta 1926* (Santiago: Editorial Universitaria, 1960). Through DeShazo's painstaking reading of urban newspapers in Santiago, Valparaíso, Antofagasta, and Tarapacá, his figures confirm the basic fluctuations indicated by Barría's less critical and systematic calculations in 1960. For a detailed discussion of these discrepancies, see DeShazo, *Urban Workers*, 308–9.

50 Salinas Alvarez discusses this episode, as reported in *El Despertar de los Trabajadores* (Iquique) in *La mujer proletaria*, 86–87.

51 Ramón Sepúlveda L., "La Gran Federación Obrera," *El Socialista* (Valparaíso), 21 September 1917.

52 The FOCH's consistent overestimation of its membership has been the source of much controversy in the study of Chilean labor. Marxist historians long maintained the predominance of FOCH on the basis of the organization's own count of its members; as DeShazo and others have since pointed out, membership figures published in *La Federación Obrera* and reported in federation congresses rarely noted that many workers' councils had ceased to function and that many members did not pay dues or participate actively in the federation (DeShazo, *Urban Workers*, 153–54, 197, 245).

53 The FZA membership grew from five hundred to eight hundred men and women during the prolonged Ferrer strike of February 1917, which featured the active participation of women (DeShazo, *Urban Workers*, 150). A subsequent strike of the same factory involved 180 women and 70 men, who walked off the job to protest the suspension of two women workers for indiscipline. The thirty-three-day strike caused an estimated loss to Ferrer of 35,000 pesos, but secured most of the workers' demands, including a provision that employees treat women workers at the factory with more respect. See ADGT, *Formularios huelgas*, 1917, vol. 34, Santiago shoe factory strike, 6 July 1917, and *Formularios huelgas*, 1918, vol. 45, Ferrer shoe strike form and Ferrer letter to the Labor Office, January–February 1918.

54 Mixed-sex unions of typographers and shoe workers were perhaps the only significant exception to this trend, as those unions had been and remained the historic strongholds of anarchist ideology (DeShazo, *Urban Workers*, 153–55).

55 Barría Serón, *Los movimientos sociales*, 177.

56 Estatutos de la II Convención Nacional de la GFOCH (Valparaíso), 18 September 1917, cited in ibid., 115.

57 "Acuerdos de la III Convención de la FOCh," *Adelante* (Talcahuano), January 1920, cited in Barría Serón, *Movimientos sociales*, 123, 130.

58 In 1921, women's average daily wage in the industrial sector was 4.41 pesos, while the male average was 8 pesos, so as a demand, this minimum wage was remarkably low.

59 "Acuerdos de la III Convención de la FOCh," cited in Barría Serón, *Movimientos sociales*, 128. These demands were probably derived from those formulated by the Asemblea de Alimentación Nacional the year before.

60 "Una organización femenina," *La Federación Obrera*, 21 December 1922.

61 In 1923, the FOCh claimed seven women's (or mixed) groups in Santiago, among tram workers, window makers, weavers, cigar makers, telephone operators, hat makers, and various occupations. See "Asociación Obrera Femenina," *BOT* 13, no. 21 (1923): 184–92.

62 "Acuerdos de la VII Convención de la FOCH," *Justicia*, 23–31 December 1925, cited in Barría Serón, *Movimientos sociales*, 159.

63 "La Semana Femenina," *La Justicia*, 28 March 1926.

64 The full list includes Humilde Figueroa de Guzmán, general secretary; Isabel Díaz, secretary; Margarita Morales, treasurer; Esperanza Zamora, María Guzmán, Amanda Moscoso, Eulogia Román, Teresa Flores, Virginia Carvajal, Lucía Carvajal, Berta Carvajal, María Olivares, María de Hidalgo, Rosa Osorio, Catarina Rojas, Lucía Carvajal de Córdova, and Ida Osorio (ibid.).

65 DeShazo, *Urban Workers*, 241–42; Jorge Rojas Flores, *La dictadura de Ibáñez y los sindicatos (1927–1931)* (Santiago: DIBAM, 1993).

66 Dora Barrancos, *Anarquismo, educación y costumbres in la Argentina de principios de siglo* (Buenos Aires: Editorial Contrapunto, 1990); Michelle Perrot, "El elogio del ama de casa en el discurso de los obreros franceses del siglo XIX," in *Historia y género: Las mujeres en la Europa moderna y contemporánea*, Estudios Universitarios 38, ed. James S. Amelang and Mary Nash (Valencia: Edicions Alfons el Magnànim, 1990), 241–65.

67 This author concluded by proclaiming, "The right to work is a precious advantage for women, the security of her future emancipation." See Un panificador por amor, "Lo que deben hacer las mujeres," *El Panificador*, 4 August 1918, 2–3.

68 "Una heroina," *Numen*, 16 October 1919, 10.

69 Luís M. Sanz, "La Costurera," *El Alba*, 15 March 1906, 8. A fuller excerpt of this treatise can be found at chap. 2, n. 1.

70 Although middle-class feminist claims that employment was a virtuous and enriching activity for all women were certainly overdrawn, even the working-class press—as in the story of Laura—provided examples of the positive effects of women's wage work, such as supporting a family and

escaping the oppressive bonds of marriage. Mirta Lobato analyzes Argentine women workers' recourse to a language of "wage labor as 'necessity'" to explain their entrance into the meatpacking factories of early-twentieth-century Argentina, noting the flexibility of notions of "necessity" with which women, in retrospect, rationalized their decision to work for wages outside the home. See Mirta Zaida Lobato, "Women Workers in the 'Cathedrals of Corned Beef': Structure and Subjectivity in the Argentine Meatpacking Industry," in *The Gendered Worlds of Women Workers: From Household and Factory to the Union Hall and Ballot Box*, ed. John D. French and Daniel James (Durham, NC: Duke University Press, 1997), 58–61. See also Theresa R. Veccia, "'My Duty as a Woman': Gender Ideology, Work, and Working-Class Women's Lives in São Paulo, Brazil, 1900–1950," in *The Gendered Worlds*, ed. French and James, 100–146.

71 Una obrera, "La esplotación del trabajo de la mujer," *El Trabajo*, 25 November 1905, 3. See also "En la empresa de ferrocarril urbano," *El Martillo*, 6 April 1902; "A los tablaceros del consejo no. 2," *La Federación Obrera*, 11 April 1922, 3.

72 Luís R. Boza, "Por las mujeres del pueblo," *La Imprenta*, 26 April 1902, 4–5. See also Bravo Zisternas [*sic*], "La Mujer," 1–2.

73 Boza, "Por las mujeres del pueblo," 4–5.

74 After initially keeping her daughter at home because of the dangers of the workplace, a mother suffers the news that the girl has been sucked into a machine and injured at a clothing factory. See E. Muñoz C., "Mi hija! . . . ," *El Alba*, 19 December 1906, 3. One writer even speculated that factory work that involved sitting all day was unhealthy for female genetalia: "Because of this she gets lesions on her genitals . . . which increase when she uses a foot-operated machine" ("Hijiene: Hijiene de los diferentes oficios," *El Obrero Ilustrado*, 15 August 1907, 123–24).

75 Luís E. Recabarren, "A todas las mujeres," *El Socialista*, 21 August 1915, 2.

76 "Una industria nacional que progresa: The New England Fábrica de camisas a vapor, montada al estilo europeo," *La Reforma*, 3 September 1907, 2; *La Reforma*, 17 November 1906, 3.

77 Boza, "Por las mujeres del pueblo," 4–5.

78 El Loco Dario, "Aguja, máquina y tejidos," *Luz al Obrero*, August 1911, 3–4.

79 C. Malato, "La Familia moderna," *El Alba*, 1 May 1906, 2.

80 Elizabeth Quay Hutchison, "'*El fruto envenenado del arbol capitalista*': Women Workers and the Prostitution of Labor in Urban Chile, 1896–1925," *Journal of Women's History* 9, no. 4 (winter 1998): 131–51.

81 In one account, a storefront that was a clothing workshop by day became a "dance academy" by night, and young seamstresses were

pressured to stay after work and "dance" with patrons. See "Un Tipo especial y común de Academias-Filharmonicas: Va cayendo gente al baile," *La Federación Obrera*, 28 September 1923, 1.

82 Excerpts from Juana Rouco Buela's *Mis proclamas* (n.p.: [Lux], n.d.) appeared in a variety of Chilean papers, including "La Costurerita," *La Aguja*, 3 December 1924, 5; Manuel Ramírez, "La niña obrera," *Chile Obrero* 1, no. 3 (December 1911).

83 Evaristo Carriego, *La costurerita que dió aquel mal paso y otros poemas* (Buenos Aires: Torres Agüero Editor, 1977).

84 "Drama pasional," *La Reforma*, 22 June 1906, 2.

85 This criticism against girls who "worked" in dance halls (as prostitutes) appeared in a lengthy article in the communist *Federación Obrera*, in which dance hall owners, male customers, and prostitutes were reviled equally for their unrevolutionary betrayal of working-class virtue. See "Quienes constituyen la concurrencia habitual de las Academias-cabarets: Como las mujeres se van despenando hacia el abismo," *La Federación Obrera*, 27 September 1923, 1.

86 Luís Morales Morales, "Despertad, mujeres!," *La Luz*, 15 March 1902, 3.

87 Usbelia, "Compañeras," *El Obrero en Calzado*, 1 May 1923, 3.

88 Morales Morales, "Despertad, mujeres!," 3.

89 Srel [Luís Emilio Recabarren], "La Vida en las fábricas: El lenguaje," *El Socialista*, 25 March 1916, 3.

90 P.C., "Trata de blancas," *El Socialista*, 4 December 1915, 3.

91 Grimkel, "La prostitución i la sociedad moderna," *Lo Nuevo*, 15 June 1903, 228–40; see also chap. 2.

92 Articles appearing in *La Federación Obrera* indicated continuing concern with the scourge of prostitution and added the conventillo (August 1921) and bars (March 1923) to the factory as sources of working-class degradation.

93 Jota Erre, "Prostitución (1)," *El Martillo*, 6 April 1902.

94 Daily newspapers, by contrast, pointed to the *trata de blancas* (white slave trade) to explain women's misfortune; news stories repeatedly told how rural young women, enticed into the big city with promises of honorable work, fell into the clutches of pimps and brothel madams. See "La trata de blancas: Ecos de un proceso criminal," *El Chileno*, 6 March 1911; "La trata de blancas: Dos jóvenes secuestradas," *El Chileno* 19 December 1912.

95 Enrique Sastre, "La eterna esclava," *El Trabajo*, 5 August 1905, 2; see also Ricardo Guerrero O., "La Mujer: Ayer, hoi i mañana," *La Alborada* 1, no. 1 (10 September 1905):1–2.

96 In 1923, *La Federación Obrera* launched an excoriating campaign against a former Democratic activist and newspaper editor, Evaristo Ríos Hernández, for maintaining a brothel on Eyzaguirre Street in

Santiago. See "Quienes constituyen la concurrencia habitual de las Academias-cabarets," 1.

97 Luís T. Alvarado, "Sin Madre!," *La Alborada* 2, no. 24 (16 December 1906): 3–4.

98 Patricio Tovar, "La Rebelde," *La Protesta*, 1 July 1908, 3.

99 Efraín del Valle, "La educación de la mujer," *La Federación Obrera*, 22 August 1921, 4.

100 Gmo. Castro A., "Eduquemos a la mujer," *El Socialista* (Valparaíso), 9 September 1916, 2. See also "Al gremio de cigarreros, cigarreras y ramos similares: Salud!," *La Federación Obrera*, 14 January 1922, 3; Luís A. Pavez B., "Llamado a las compañeras tabacaleras," *La Federación Obrera*, 1 March 1922, 3.

101 Bergquist, *Labor in Latin America*, 50.

102 *La Reforma*, 4 May 1907, 2.

103 Luís E. Recabarren S., *La mujer y su educación* (Punta Arenas: Imprenta de "El Socialista," 1916), 10, 12.

104 Juan Levadura, "Tu eres como el limón," *El Comunista*, 6 August 1921, 2.

105 C. Alberto Sepúlveda, "La mujer en la acción social," *Acción Obrera* 15 (March 1916): 1–2.

106 L. Barcia, "La emancipación de la mujer," *La Protesta*, September, 1909, 3.

107 "La grán convención local de los obreros en calzado," *La Federación Obrera*, 19 November 1921, 4.

108 Pedro Pereyra, "Organización del gremio gráfico: Puntos capitales para su mejor organización," *La Defensa Gráfica*, 1 February 1914, 1–2; Pedro Pereyra, "La federación gráfica," *La Defensa Gráfica*, 1 March 1914, 2–4.

109 "Una aparadora federada," *Boletín Oficial de Obreros y Obreras en Calzado, Reorganizada* 1, no. 1 (March 1922): 1–2.

110 Luís Morales Morales, "Mujeres!," *La Luz*, 15 January 1902, 4.

111 Lily Litvak's study of the Spanish anarchist press emphasizes this pervasive "culture of wretchedness" ascribed to nonproletarian groups: youth, women, and the elderly. See *Musa libertaria: Arte, literatura y vida cultural del anarquismo español (1880–1913)* (Barcelona: A. Bosch, 1982), chap. 3.

112 Curiously, though not surprisingly, the *pasteleros* (confectioners) joining hands in front of Liberty are fully clothed, including their bakers' caps. In the same newspaper, a contributor called women to "our place . . . next to our comrades [*compañeros*]. Let us not leave them alone in the cold of battle, the roughness of the ascent, the bitterness of the trip. The bread that we win will be for everyone; the freedom we gain will also be for everyone. Because the condition of man and woman is the same before the exploiter; and they should also be equal

in struggle and victory" (Aída Salas, "Nosotras, también . . . ," *El Obrero en Dulce*, 1 May 1926, 2). Other anarchist publications featuring naked Liberty include *El Productor*, June 1913, 1; Rene Chaughi, *La mujer esclava* (1921); and Juana Rouco, *Mis proclamas* (1924).

113 Levadura, "Tu eres como el limón," 2.

114 Aura, "Mujeres, vuestros amores son mentiras," *Acción Directa*, 1 June 1922, 3.

115 Aura, "A mis hermanas," *Acción Directa*, 1 February 1922, 6.

116 Aura, "Mujeres, vuestros amores son mentiras," 3.

117 I thank Barbara Weinstein for this valuable insight, delivered in her comments on the author's "From *la mujer esclava* to *la mujer limón*: Anarchism and the Politics of Sexuality in Chile, 1900–1927," paper delivered at the Conference on Latin American History, American Historical Association, Seattle, WA, 8–11 January 1998.

118 The level of abstraction and pure rhetoric that characterizes these texts illustrates the distance between the anarchists' intellectual vanguard and the daily concerns of its rank and file. Maxine Molyneux argues that even Argentina's anarchist feminists, many of whom were themselves workers, also proved unable to bridge the gap between libertarian utopias and the realities of working-class women's lives: " 'No God, No Boss, No Husband': Anarchist Feminism in Nineteenth-Century Argentina," *Latin American Perspectives* 13, no. 1 (winter 1986): 119–45.

119 For a fuller discussion of the evolution of anarchist positions on "the woman question," see Elizabeth Quay Hutchison, "From *la mujer esclava* to *la mujer limón*: Anarchism and the Politics of Sexuality in Chile, 1900–1927," *Hispanic American Historical Review* (forthcoming).

120 "En la fábrica de tejidos de Ñuñoa," *La Federación Obrera*, 26 November 1921.

121 The reporter further lauded the efforts of the strikers: "We owe this to the dogged work of some compañeras who love the well-being of the proletariat and who, despite the mischief of a few weak spirits and lack of experience, continue to sow the living soil with the redemptive seed that will fertilize the workers' field" (L.R.B., "Solidaridad de hermanos," *La Federación Obrera*, 30 December 1921).

122 "La Fábrica de Tejidos Caupolicán: Una obrera que castiga a un carnero," *La Federación Obrera*, 10 June 1923, 3. Reports on other strikes were similarly littered with references to female valor: when striker Clara Garcia was attacked by police, she was described as "a valiant and committed striker who has stood out for her strength [*pujanza*] and arrogance [*altivez*]" ("Exhibiendo nuestras lacras sociales," *La Federación Obrera*, n.d. 1923).

123 Ann Farnsworth-Alvear argues that the "demonstrative transvestism" of such actions—and their prominence in working-class news reports—

served ultimately to obscure the diversity of women's (and men's) role in the strike, precisely because of their dramatic inversion of gender roles. See "The Mysterious Case of the Missing Men: Gender and Class in Early Industrial Medellin," *International Labor and Working-Class History* 49 (spring 1996): 73–92.

124 "Qué es una subversiva o un subersivo? Una lección objetiva," *La Federación Obrera*, 30 May 1922.

125 Luís V. Cruz S., "Correspondencia de Talca: Largo conflicto del trabajo," *La Federación Obrera*, 19 September 1922, 1.

126 Around the same time, *La Federación Obrera* published several news stories about notable women militants, including Lina Michel of Germany. See 8 May 1922; "La voz de la mujer," 25 July 1922; "Compañera prisionera," 14 September 1922; "Se apaga la vida de una luchadora," 18 December 1922.

127 For example, one letter directed to the women workers of the Compañía Chilena de Tabacos respectfully called on them to "fortify the ranks of our Consejo. . . . The door of our institution is wide open to receive you and the hearts of all the members are also open to show you our most honest sympathy" (Luís A. Pavez B., "Llamado a las compañeras tabacaleras," *La Federación Obrera*, 1 March 1922). See also "La Gran Convención Local de los Obreros en Calzado," 19 November 1921; "Al gremio de cigarreros, cigarreras y ramos similares: Salud!" 14 January 1922; "Un llamado a las obreras de Santiago," 16 June 1922; "Compañeras Tejedoras y Compañeros," 28 March 1923; Amira M., "Colaboraciones femeninas," 11 April 1923; "La Federación de Sastres," 20 April 1923, all in *La Federación Obrera*.

128 "La huelga de los obreros," *La Federación Obrera*, 17 February 1923, 1–2.

129 "El movimiento obrero de la Fábrica Girardi," *La Federación Obrera*, 3 March 1923, 2.

130 "Horrorosos abusos cometidos en la Compañía Chilena de Tejidos de la Calle Andes: La policía al servicio de los patrones viola siempre las libertades públicas," 21 June 1923, 1; "Las obreras tejedoras de la fábrica de la Calle Andes, se declaran en huelga," 22 June 1923, 1; "Las obreras tejedoras triunfan en su movimiento," 23 June 1923, 1; "Las incidencias en el movimiento de las tejedoras: Anoche a última hora salen las obreras que estaban presas," 24 June 1923, 2, all in *La Federación Obrera*.

131 "La policía contra las mujeres y los niños," *La Federación Obrera*, 29 May 1922.

132 "Los imponentes funerales realizados ayer," and "Las mujeres en la Revolución," in *La Federación Obrera*, 30 May 1922.

133 "Obrar como hombres, y no llorar como mujeres," *La Batalla*, 1 September 1914, 1.

134 Stargardt, "Male Bonding," 191.

1 Carmela Jeria, "Nuestra situación," *La Alborada* 2, no. 29 (27 January 1907): 1. Jeria certainly was not the first, nor the last, to adapt Marx's paraphrase in this way. See also Sara Cadiz, "La esplotación de la mujer," *La Reforma*, 6 July 1906, 1.

2 *La Reforma*, 28 February 1907, 3.

3 On the genesis of liberal feminism in Chile, see Ericka Kim Verba, "The Circulo de Lectura de Señoras [Ladies' Reading Circle] and the Club de Señoras [Ladies' Club] of Santiago, Chile: Middle- and Upper-class Feminist Conversations (1915–1920)," *Journal of Women's History* 7, no. 3 (fall 1995): 6–33. For a useful typology and discussion of feminism currents emerging in the Southern Cone in this period, see Asunción Lavrin, *Women, Feminism and Social Change in Argentina, Chile and Uruguay, 1890–1940* (Lincoln: University of Nebraska Press, 1995), chap. 1.

4 As scholars of feminist movements have frequently observed, "feminism" has had such a wide variety of meanings and applications in modern history that we can speak only of multiple "feminisms" and attempt to reconstruct those meanings in historical terms. See Nancy Cott, *The Grounding of Modern Feminism* (New Haven: Yale University Press, 1987), 1–10.

5 In addition to the pro-feminist anarchists and Democrats examined here, "feminism" also appeared throughout the labor press in reference to debates over women's fundamental equality with men. See, for example, the series "Feminismo" authored by "Un Obrero Socialista Democrático" in *El Socialista* between December 1901 and April 1902.

6 A more extensive discussion of Chilean anarchist discourse can be found in Elizabeth Quay Hutchison, "From *la mujer esclava* to *la mujer limón*: Anarchism and the Politics of Sexuality in Chile, 1900–1927," *Hispanic American Historical Review* 81:3–4 (2001). Other important studies of anarchism and gender include Dora Barrancos, *Anarquismo, educación, y costumbres en la Argentina de principios de siglo* (Buenos Aires: Editorial Contrapunto, 1990); Maxine Molyneux, " 'No God, No Boss, No Husband': Anarchist Feminism in Nineteenth-Century Argentina," *Latin American Perspectives* 13, no. 1 (winter 1986): 119–45; and Lily Litvak, *Musa Libertaria: Arte, literatura, y vida cultural del anarquismo español, 1880–1913* (Barcelona: Imprenta Clarisó, 1981).

7 Anarchist language and analysis of "the enslaved woman" was clearly influenced by French anarchist Rene Chaughi's *La femme esclave* (Paris: Temps nouveaux, 1908); excerpts of the work circulated widely in the anarchist press, and a Spanish translation of the work was published in Chile in 1921.

8 Unlike the anarchist feminists who published *La Voz de la Mujer* in Argentina in the 1890s, many Chilean anarchist writers on "the woman question" in the same period of Chilean history were male.

9 Although the single edition of *La Aurora Feminista* published in 1905 was "feminist" in the sense that it was written by and for women, it does not, as Lavrin has argued, belong to the family of socialist publications (*Women, Feminism and Social Change*, 20, 23). The paper's conservative orientation and audience are evident in its opening editorial: "The distinguished, intelligent and educated ladies have a huge, well-known and beneficent network at their disposal in the cultivation of their desire to rescue the Chilean and libertarian woman from her present situation, which degenerates her moral being" ("La Aurora Feminista," *La Aurora Feminista* 1, no. 1 [15 January 1904]: 1).

10 Elena Caffarena, "Luís Emilio Recabarren Feminista," *La Nación*, 15 December 1953; Edda Gaviola et al., *Queremos votar en las próximas elecciones: Historia del movimiento femenino Chileno 1913–1952* (Santiago: CEM, 1986), 31–32; Julieta Kirkwood, *Ser política en Chile: Los nudos de la sabiduría feminista* (Santiago: Editorial Cuarto Propia, 1990), 105–13; Cecilia Salinas, *La mujer proletaria: Una historia para contar* (Santiago: Literatura América Reunida, 1987), 79–88.

11 Luís E. Recabarren S., "Respeto a la mujer," *El Proletario* (Tocopilla), 23 May, in *Recabarren: Escritos de prensa, 1898–1924*, ed. Ximena Cruzat and Eduardo Devés (Santiago: Terranova Editores, 1987), 1: 147.

12 Luís E. Recabarren S., "Abandono femenino: Las mujeres inteligentes," *La Defensa* (Coronel, Lota), 26 May 1907, in *Recabarren*, ed. Cruz and Devés, 2: 127. The fact that Recabarren sent this statement from Buenos Aires, where he was living in exile, just a week after the first worker feminist paper *La Alborada* had folded, raises the question of exactly how closely Recabarren followed the worker feminist press in Chile.

13 While Recabarren certainly worked under pen names such as Raúl Caneberis and Srel, several observers have also speculated that he assumed female names in articles addressed to women. See Caffarena, "Luís Emilio Recabarren Feminista"; Gaviola et al., *Queremos votar*, 32.

14 Luís E. Recabarren S., "Belén de Sárraga," *El Despertar* (Iquique), 14 March 1914; *La mujer y su educación* (Punta Arenas: Imprenta "El Socialista," 1916); and *La Rusia obrera y campesina* (1922), in *Luís Emilio Recabarren: Obras escogidas*, ed. Julio César Jobet (Santiago: Editorial Recabarren, 1965), 133–39.

15 L.E.D.C. [Luís E. Díaz C.], "La mujer obrera," *El Luchador*, 22 November 1903, 1.

16 L.E.D.C. [Luís E. Díaz C.], "Dona Juana Roldán de Alarcón," *El Luchador*, 18 October 1903, 1.

17 Jeria here offered a literary piece that expressed her great disillusion-

ment with the world: Carmela Jeria G., "Fragmento de una carta," *El Luchador*, July 1905, 8. Another strange literary piece, this time dedicated to Jeria, also appeared in May of the same year: Armando H. González, "Muerte de Artista (A Carmela Jeria G.)," *El Luchador*, 1 May 1905, 4.

18 "Ecos del fallecimiento de la señora Lucrecia Campos de Díaz," *El Luchador*, 24 June 1906, 1–2.

19 *El Luchador*, 1 September 1905.

20 *La Alborada*, 1, no. 1 (10 September 1905): 1.

21 *La Reforma*, 5 October 1906, 2.

22 The Santiago Democratic daily paper *La Reforma* gave ample attention to women, both from an explicitly feminist and other perspectives. Worker feminists active in *La Alborada* occasionally contributed articles to *La Reforma*, and the paper regularly ran notices and reports on women's union activities. Perhaps most important, *La Reforma* opened its offices to activists from *La Alborada* when the paper moved to Santiago in 1906, providing them with space to receive mail, hold meetings, and print their newspaper.

23 According to Arias's survey of the labor press, only 53 of the 313 working-class newspapers published in Chile between 1900 and 1930 had press runs in excess of twenty months (17 percent). Newspapers of a longer duration, moreover, such as *La Federación Obrera* (1910–1924), sometimes transformed their editorial staff and their political affiliation in midstream, thereby obscuring what was really the creation of a new paper. See Osvaldo Arias Escobedo, *La prensa obrera en Chile* (Chillán: Universidad de Chile, 1970).

24 Silvana, editorial, *La Alborada* 1, no. 8 (1 January 1906): 2–3.

25 The paper's masthead was eventually changed to read "a women's publication," and then "feminist publication" when the paper relocated to Santiago after a massive earthquake struck Valparaíso in July 1906.

26 Carmela Jeria, "Tras el bienestar," *La Alborada* 1, no. 17 (15 July 1906): 1.

27 Ricardo Guerrero O., "La mujer: Ayer, hoi i mañana," *La Alborada* 1, no. 1 (10 September 1905): 1–2.

28 Carmela Jeria, editorial, *La Alborada* 1, no. 2 (1 October 1905): 1.

29 S.A.K.T., "Charlas," *La Alborada* 1, no. 1 (10 September 1905): 4.

30 Luís Alvarado T., "Sin madre!," *La Alborada* 2, no. 24 (16 December 1906): 3–4.

31 Most of Jeria's early editorials dealt with political issues and events that were not specific to women, such as the October 1905 Santiago meat riot, May Day celebrations, workers' death and prison sentences, as well as ideological debates current in Democratic circles.

32 Juana Roldán de Alarcón, "Egoismo increíble," *La Alborada* 1, no. 5 (15 November 1905): 2.

33 Eloisa Zurita de Vergara, editorial, *La Alborada* 1, no. 9 (1 February 1906): 3.

34 See "Notas desde Antofagasta," *La Alborada* 1, no. 4–2, no. 34 (1 November 1905–3 March 1907). Zurita de Vergara, herself acclaimed "the most important figure of worker feminism in Chile," had founded the first women's club and first society for women workers in Antofagasta in 1894. See Osvaldo López, *Diccionario Biográfico Obrero* (Santiago: Bellavista, 1912), 2: Z1. López was especially indebted to Zurita de Vergara for moral and financial support for his *Diccionario*.

35 In general, worker feminists blamed men's low wages for women's need to work, although individual men were also faulted for failing to fulfill their obligations: "Man must give subsistence, tenderness, and defense to woman; however, only some men understand these sacred duties" (Ariadna, "Infelicidad nuestra!" *La Alborada* 2, no. 26 [30 December 1906]: 1).

36 Esther Valdés de Díaz, "Despertar . . . Para el valiente adalid femenino," *La Alborada* 2, no. 20 (18 November 1906): 1.

37 Esther Valdés de Díaz, "Problemas obreros," *La Alborada* 2, no. 42 (19 May 1907).

38 Blanca Poblete, "A mi aguja," *La Alborada* 2, no. 37 (24 March 1907): 2.

39 Jeria, "Nuestra situación," 1.

40 Selva, "Como emanciparnos?," *La Alborada* 2, no. 29 (27 January 1907): 1–2. Contributors using female pseudonyms—whether male or female in reality—may have done so in order to increase the validity of their arguments about women. See Hutchison, "From *la mujer esclava* to *la mujer limón*."

41 R. Gutiérrez R., "Un eslabón de la cadena: Dignifiquemos nuestro puesto," *La Alborada* 2, no. 39 (14 April 1907): 1.

42 Baudina Pessini T., "Emancipación social de la mujer," *La Alborada* 2, no. 29 (27 January 1906): 2.

43 Baudina Pessini T., "Instrúyase a la mujer," *La Alborada* 2, no. 35 (10 March 1907): 1.

44 Vicente Acuña C., "La instrucción de la mujer," *La Alborada* 2, no. 12 (15 April 1906): 2.

45 Pablo Pedro Figueroa, "Misión suprema: Apostolado de la educación de la mujer," *La Alborada* 1, no. 4 (1 November 1905).

46 Esther Valdés de Díaz, "Despertar . . . Para el valiente adalid femenino *La Alborada*," *La Alborada* 2, no. 19 (11 November 1906): 2. Although Recabarren apparently shared this view of motherhood as women's natural state, he introduced an important qualification: "Even if it is beyond dispute that Nature has given a procreative and maternal mission to women (although not to all women), we cannot ignore the trends in present society that have obliged woman to support herself, violating natural laws, separating her from the mission that Nature has

given her." In his 1922 essay, *Worker and Peasant Russia*, Recabarren marveled at the ability of the Soviets to provide women with a full range of professional and educational opportunities, and maintained that, in the best of all worlds, a woman would be able to choose for herself between such activities and "the place that Nature and her vocation have truly entrusted her." In the meantime, equal rights for women would allow them to participate fully in the struggle to "normalize" a society that had perverted their natural roles: "One does not see that women's new situation has deviated them from their mission even more; on the contrary, one can justly think that in a deviant society, armed with rights equal to those of men, woman can set out to reconquer her natural state and contribute to the normalization of life's real conditions." Luís Emilio Recabarren, "La condición actual de la mujer en Rusia y sus expectativas para el porvenir," *La Rusia obrera y campesina* (1922) in *Luís Emilio Recabarren*, ed. Jobet, 133–39.

47 Guerrero, "La mujer," 1–2.

48 Ricardo Guerrero O., "Defectos educativos y sus malas consequencias," *La Alborada* 2, no. 29 (27 January 1907).

49 Ricardo Guerrero O., "Como tratamos a la mujer!," *La Alborada* 2, no. 20 (18 November 1906). This analysis demonstrates the cultural dichotomy between "good" and "bad" expressions of masculinity, or between a "real macho" and a "*machista*," examined in more detail in recent studies of Latin American masculinities. See Elizabeth Brusco, *The Reformation of Machismo: Gender and Evangelicalism in Colombia* (Austin: University of Texas Press, 1995), chap. 5; Alfredo Mirandé, *Hombres y Machos: Masculinity and Latino Culture* (Boulder, CO: Westview Press, 1997); Roger Lancaster, *Life Is Hard: Machismo, Danger, and the Intimacy of Power in Nicaragua* (Berkeley: University of California Press, 1992); Matthew Guttman, *The Meanings of Macho: Being a Man in Mexico City* (Berkeley: University of California Press, 1996).

50 Betsabe de Alarcón, "El Hogar," *La Reforma*, 9 January 1908.

51 Nicolás Rodríguez, "La Sinceridad en nuestras manifestaciones esternas [sic]," *La Alborada* 1, no. 7 (15 December 1905): 1.

52 Klubock has noted similar tensions over masculine behavior in the creation of a disciplined labor movement among El Tentiente miners in the 1930s and 1940s. The political mobilization of copper miners in this period relied on expressions of working-class virility (such as drinking, gambling, fighting, and womanizing), while at the same time promoting "respectable" forms of masculinity (such as maintaining a household and protecting dependents). See Thomas Miller Klubock, "Working-Class Masculinity, Middle-Class Morality, and Labor Politics in the Chilean Copper Mines," *Journal of Social History* 30, no. 2 (winter 1996): 435–63.

53 Selva, "Como emanciparnos?," 1–2.

54 Calderón also faulted the "men of faith," who "persuade women that their servitude is irremediable, make them adore their chains, feed their souls with beliefs destined to make their captivity eternal." She then tied this social domination to a sexual one, arguing that men destroyed women through their sexual demands; if women resisted, she claimed, they risked becoming victims of "crimes of passion" (A. Calderón, "La mujer," *La Alborada* 1, no. 14 [15 May 1906]: 3).

55 P. P. Pretto, "Para vosotras," *La Alborada* 2, no. 35 (10 March 1907): 1.

56 Jeria, "Nuestra situación," 1.

57 Carmela Jeria, editorial, *La Alborada* 2, no. 19 (11 November 1906): 1. The reopening of the paper also elicited another ringing endorsement from Ricardo Guerrero, urging women workers to support Jeria's efforts: "Oh! She more than anyone has to give [*La Alborada*] her heart, dedicate all of her energies, help the paper with all her resources" (Ricardo Guerrero O., "La Alaborada en Santiago," *La Alborada* 2, no. 19 [11 November 1906]: 1).

58 La Dirección, "Problemas obreros," *La Alborada* 2, no. 35 (3 March 1907): 1.

59 *La Reforma*, 28 July 1906.

60 *La Reforma*, 17 and 20 July 1906.

61 *La Reforma*, 17 and 23 August 1906; Carmela Jeria, *La Alborada* 2, no. 20 (18 November 1906): 1.

62 *La Reforma*, 9 August 1906.

63 Members of the Ateneo also contributed 1 peso per month to *La Alborada*: "We accept gladly and with honor a friendly relationship which the illustrious and self-sacrificing worker and writer of Valparaíso, Carmela Jeria, has offered us. By special invitation we will subscribe to her interesting fortnightly newspaper *La Alborada*" (*La Reforma*, 9 August 1906; *La Reforma*, 13 November 1906).

64 "Gremio de Costureras," *La Reforma*, 3 July 1906. How the Seamstresses Association for "Protection, Savings, and Defense" would finance the goals stated in this name, given that the first one hundred members were admitted free, was not addressed.

65 *La Reforma*, 24 July 1906.

66 Letter from the Seamstresses' Directorate to "women workers in general," quoted in Florencio Olivos, "Asociación de Costureras 'Protección, Ahorro i Defensa,'" *El Obrero Ilustrado*, 15 July 1906, 95. Olivos heralded the association as proof of "a new element of progress and the likelihood that at last, a happier day and more pleasing material and moral state will dawn for the workers of the fair sex."

67 Esther Valdés de Díaz, "Una nueva falanje (a mis hermanas de trabajo)," *La Reforma*, 6 June 1906.

68 Letter from the Seamstresses' Directorate, 95.

69 *La Reforma*, 5 July 1907.

70 "El 1.er Aniversario de la 'Asociación de Costureras,'" *El Obrero Ilustrado*, 15 July 1907.

71 Esther Valdés de Díaz, "Propaganda social: La asociación de costureras," *La Alborada* 2, no. 29 (13 January 1907): 2.

72 Esther Valdés de Díaz, editorial, *La Alborada* 2, no. 32 (17 February 1907): 1; emphasis added.

73 Esther Valdés de Díaz, "Al correr de la pluma," *La Alborada* 2, no. 27 (13 January 1907): 2.

74 Esther Valdes de Diaz, "Problemas obreros: Reglamentación de las horas de trabajo para la mujer obrera," *La Alborada* 2, no. 36 (17 March 1907): 1.

75 Esther Valdés de Díaz, "Problemas obreros," *La Alborada* 2, no. 40 (21 April 1907): 1.

76 Esther Valdés de Díaz, "Problemas obreros," *La Alborada* 2, no. 42 (19 May 1907): 1.

77 Previously, Jeria had editorialized in favor of regulating women's work hours, as "she is weaker than man, which is how Nature indicates that she should have more moderate work" (Editorial, *La Alborada* 2, no. 20 [18 November 1906]: 1). In an earlier controversy over municipal legislation that prohibited women from working in bars, Jeria supported the legislation, arguing that "it is preferable to withstand a few days of scarcity, rather than to keep corrupting one's morals" (Carmela Jeria, "Las mujeres en las cantinas," *La Alborada* 2, no. 24 [16 December 1906]: 1).

78 Valdés de Díaz, "Problemas obreros" (19 May 1907): 1.

79 Carmela Jeria, "La Sociedad Periodística *La Alborada*," *La Alborada*, 2, no. 34 (3 March 1907): 1.

80 Ricardo Guerrero O., "La mujer y *La Alborada*," *La Alborada* 2, no. 34 (20 January 1907): 1.

81 Esther Valdés de Díaz, "Un paso hácia la emancipación económica de la mujer obrera," *La Reforma*, 18 June 1907, 1; "Movimiento social," *La Reforma*, 11 September 1907, 2; "La prensa burguesa i el pueblo," *La Reforma*, 14 December 1907, 1; "Notas sociales," *La Reforma*, 18 April 1908, 2.

82 Esther Valdés de Díaz, "En el palenque: Hénos aquí frente a frente al enemigo!," *La Palanca* 1, no. 1 (May 1908): 1–2.

83 Isabel González E., "Voz de aliento," *La Palanca* 1, no. 1 (May 1908): 5.

84 One contributor complained that she was instructed by a male militant not to bother buying the paper because it was just an anarchist publication that copied European ideas. See Yedra, "Diatribas y cuchufletas," *La Palanca* 1, no. 3 (July 1908): 33–34.

85 Yedra, "Fecundidad, o procreación inconsciente," *La Palanca* 1, no. 2 (June 1908): 19.

86　R. S. de Z., "La mujer i la emancipación económica del proletariado," *La Palanca* 1, no. 4 (August 1908): 42.

87　*La Reforma*, 31 May 1907. *La Palanca* included only one contribution authored by Carmela Jeria, a strange, sad poem about loss: "Tarde de invierno," *La Palanca* 1, no. 4 (August, 1908): 43.

88　"Asociación de Costureras: 'Protección, ahorro i defensa.' Fundada el 26 de Junio de 1906," *La Palanca* 1, no. 1 (May 1908): 11.

89　Valdés de Díaz urged members whose contributions were in arrears to make arrangements to pay at least half of their debts so that the association could meet its obligations to its membership. See Valdés de Díaz, "Notas sociales," 2.

90　Esther Valdés de Díaz, "La celebración del segundo aniversario de la Asociación de Costureras," *La Palanca* 1, no. 4 (August 1908): 44–47.

91　Luís A. Mansilla, "La Palanca," *La Palanca* 1, no. 5 (September 1908): 58.

92　The bylines Esther Valdés de Díaz and Carmela Jeria rarely appeared in the labor press after the demise of *La Palanca*; none of the articles that do appear indicate their consistent participation in any journalistic effort thereafter, and some are reprints from the 1905–1908 period. See Carmela Jeria G., "La Mujer," *Luz y Vida* (Antofagasta) 4, no. 38 (November 1911): 3; Esther Valdés de Díaz, "La mujer i la emancipacion economica del proletariado," *El Trabajo*, 2 July 1910, and "Orientaciones," *Acción Obrera*, 15 February 1916. Salinas observes that an anarchist paper reported that Jeria was ill in May 1908, but no mention of her whereabouts appears in the labor press after that date (*La mujer proletaria*, 67).

93　Existing surveys of working-class feminism in this period (including previous articles by this author) have interpreted the disappearance of worker feminist newspapers in 1908 as a defeat for working women's interests within Chilean socialism, attributing remaining evidence of socialist organizing among women in the north to the efforts of Recabarren and his partner Teresa Flores. See Elizabeth Quay Hutchison, "La defensa de las 'hijas del pueblo': Género y política obrera en Santiago a principios de siglo," in *Disciplina y desacato: Construcción de identidad en Chile, siglos XIX y XX*, ed. Lorena Godoy, Elizabeth Hutchison, Karin Rosemblatt, and M. Soledad Zárate (Santiago: SUR/CEDEM, 1995), 277–79. Asunción Lavrin, "Women, Labor and the Left: Argentina and Chile, 1890–1925," *Journal of Women's History* 1, no. 2 (fall 1989): 98; Salinas, *La mujer proletaria*, 72, 90. On the basis of a broader examination of the socialist press in Santiago and Valparaíso, however, this chapter argues that modified forms of worker feminism continued to find expression in urban political movements after 1908.

94　"En el hogar," *El Socialista*, 7 August 1909, 3.

95　"Las mujeres socialistas," *El Socialista*, 10 July 1909, 3.

96 Valdés de Díaz, "La mujer i la emancipación económica del proletariado." This article was first printed under the same title in *La Palanca* (August 1908): 2 under the byline R.S. de Z.

97 "Sección obrera: La defensa del trabajo de costureras," *El Socialista*, 20 August 1910, 4; B. Pereda Arteaga, "La mujer i la democracia," *El Socialista*, 16 September 1910, 1–2; Ricardo Guerrero O., "El primero de mayo i la reivindicación femenina," *El Socialista*, 16 September 1910, 9–10. The Guerrero piece is striking for its extreme level of abstraction and lyrical style. After a lengthy column describing the "horrible proportions" of individualism and capitalist exploitation in present society, Guerrero concludes with a brief paragraph on women's role in social revolution: "And the woman, this sensitive being full of attractions, this angelic soul that we have so brutally shunted aside, will arise from the swamp like the most pure flowers, filling the life of her compañero with perfume and beauty." In this sense, the text is more similar to other odes to the First of May than to Guerrero's critical editorials appearing in the worker feminist press of the previous decade. Guerrero was still active in labor journalism and politics in 1915, when he joined the editorial society of *El Heraldo*, the organ of the Democratic Party and mutulism in Santiago. See Arias, *La prensa obrera en Chile*, 33.

98 "Sección Femenil: Consejos a las solteras," *El Trabajo*, 16 September 1910, 8. The article has more in common with the portrayals of women in the daily press.

99 "Consejo de un socialista a la mujer del trabajador," *El Socialista*, 15 May 1911, 7. Similar advice also appeared later in Sara B. de Armijo, "El socialismo y la mujer," *El Socialista*, 30 April 1913.

100 For a more detailed description of Belén de Sárraga's tour in the north, synopses of her speeches, and discussion of responses to her in the daily and labor press, see Salinas, *La mujer proletaria*, 68, 73–79; Luís Vitale and Julia Arévalo, *Belén de Sárraga: Precursora del feminismo hispanoamericano* (Santiago: CESOC, 1999); Lessie Jo Frazier, "Memory and State Violence in Chile: A Historical Ethnography of Tarapacá, 1890–1995" (Ph.D. diss., University of Michigan, 1998), chaps. 3, 4.

101 See, for example, Luís Emilio Recabarren S., "A Belén de Sárraga," *El Despertar de los Trabajadores* (Iquique), 22 February 1913; Nestor Recabarren V., "A la señora Belén de Sárraga de F.," and Salvador Barra Woll, "Para Belén de Sárraga," in *El Despertar de los Trabajadores* (Iquique), 8 March 1913. All are transcribed in Claudia Aranda B. and Ricardo Canales A., *Páginas literarias de los obreros socialistas (1912–1915)* (Santiago: Ediciones ICAL, 1991), 26–27, 37, 39.

102 Salinas, *La mujer proletaria*, 74–75; Ericka Kim Verba, "Catholic Feminism and *Acción Social Femenina* [Women's Social Action]: The Early Years of the *Liga de Damas Chilenas*, 1912–1924," (Ph.D. diss., University of California at Los Angeles, 1999), 359 n.23.

103 *La Razón,* 15 March 1913, cited in Salinas, *La mujer proletaria,* 79.

104 "Sociedad El Despertar de la Mujer," *La Defensa Obrera,* 15 November 1913, 3.

105 Letter from Teresa Flores, *El Despertar de los Trabajadores* (Iquique), 10 April 1913, cited in Edda Gaviola, Ximena Jiles Moreno, Lorela Lopresti Martínez, and Claudia Rojas Mira, "Evolución de los derechos políticos de la mujer en Chile (1913–1952)" (thesis, University of Santiago, 1985), 68.

106 Gaviola et al., *Queremos votar en las próximas elecciones,* 31–32.

107 Belén de Sárraga, *Conferencias* (Santiago: Imprenta Victoria, 1913).

108 Belén de Sárraga, *El clericalismo en América* (Lisbon: Tip. José Assis and Coelho Días, 1915), 307.

109 Both Gaviola et al. and Julieta Kirkwood have cited the Centros Belén de Sárraga as the first expressions of autonomous female mobilization in Chile, overlooking the prior movement for worker feminism altogether. See Gaviola et al., *Evolución de los derechos políticos,* 64–70; Kirkwood, *Ser política en Chile,* 105–13.

110 Recabarren, *La mujer y su educación,* 10.

111 *La Defensa Obrera* (Valparaíso, 1913–1915) occasionally addressed female emancipation in connection with the women's association El Despertar de la Mujer. See, for example, Daniel Cordova, "Eco de la velada de El Despertar de la Mujer," *La Defensa Obrera* (Valparaíso), 14 March 1914, 3.

112 Luís Emilio Recabarren, "A todas las mujeres," *El Socialista* (Valparaíso), 21 August 1915, 2.

113 LERS [Luís Emilio Recabarren Serrano], "Las mujeres deben luchar," *El Socialista* (Valparaíso), 4 September 1915, 3.

114 Srel [Luís Emilio Recabarren Serrano], "La vida en las fábricas: Las mujeres y los niños," *El Socialista* (Valparaíso), 11 March 1916, 2.

115 Srel [Luís Emilio Recabarren], "La vida en las fábricas: El lenguaje," *El Socialista* (Valparaíso), 25 March 1916, 3.

116 On education: Ivan Ardif, "A la mujer," 25 December 1915, 2; Laura E. Salfate O., "La educación de la mujer," 8 January 1916, 3; "Una gran fuerza," 16 May 1916, 3; Ana Gutiérrez, "Nuestros derechos," 2 September 1916, 2; Gmo. Castro A., Cincel [chisel], "Eduquemos a la mujer," 9 September 1916, 2; Ivan Ardiff, "Ecos de Viña del Mar: A la mujer," 21 August 1917, 2.

   On legislation: Helle, "Feminismo: Para la justicia y la dignidad," 22 April 1916, 2; Teresa Flores, "Día de porvenir," 29 April 1916, 3; Roberto Colombatti, Serrucho [handsaw], "El trabajo de las mujeres y los niños," 20 August 1916, 2; Carlos E. Laferrte, "La carne de la fábrica," 30 December 1916, 1; "Otra victima que el capital devora," 10 May 1917.

On mobilization: Julia Arévalo, "Voces femeninas: A las obreras, mis hermanas," 31 December 1915, 2; "Signos de progreso femenino," 12 February 1916, 3; Lidya Recabarren S. [Viña del Mar], "A luchar! A las mujeres," 15 April 1916, 3; Flores, "Día de porvenir," 3; "Una gran fuerza," 3; Redención, "Brotes femeninas: Carta íntima," 20 May 1916, 2; Luzmira Carril Osk, "A mis compañeras," 17 May 1917, 4; Carlos Flores U., "Nuestras savias proletarias," 8 October 1917, 1; all appearing in *El Socialista* (Valparaíso).

117 *El Socialista* regularly printed news stories and summaries from international socialist newspapers, usually highlighting the model activism of foreign women in defense of their rights and/or the socialist cause. See "Desfile sufragista" (from New York), 30 October 1915, 1; C. Loveira (Mérida), "La mujer yucateca: Contestación de Carlos Loviera a una encuesta, a proposito del primer Congreso Feminista celebrado en Mérida," 2 September 1916, 1, 4; "Estados Unidos: El trabajo de las mujeres," (from *El Universal*, Mexico), 30 December 1916, 2; "Carolina Muzzilli," 29 March 1917, 1–2; "En España: Una mujer socialista en la carcel" (from an interview with Virginia González by the Spanish writer Colombine), 25 September 1917, 4; "La entereza de la mujer" (letter from Concepción Calvo, Madrid), 10 February 1918, 2; "Las mujeres socialistas" (letter from the Women's Socialist Group, Madrid), 16 February 1918, 2; all appearing in *El Socialista* (Valparaíso).

118 A. de Guafra, "La mujer," *El Socialista* (Valparaíso), 18 September 1917, 2; continues 25 September 1917, 4.

119 Helle, "Feminismo," 2.

120 Quoted in "Una gran fuerza."

121 Grace T. Sims, "Mujeres de mundo unios!," *El Socialista* (Valparaíso), 14 August 1915.

122 Arévalo, "Voces femeninas."

123 Gmo. Castro A., "Eduquemos a la mujer," *El Socialista* (Valparaíso), 9 September 1916, 2.

124 Esther Valdés de Díaz, "Orientaciones," *Acción Obrera*, 15 February 1916, 3–4.

125 C. Alberto Sepúlveda, "La mujer en la acción social," *Acción Obrera*, 15 March 1916, 1–2. Sepúlveda's editorial emphasized the need for men to "decatholicize" their wives and invite them to at least one meeting per month.

126 Although *La Federación Obrera* has traditionally been used as a source on communist organization at the national level in the 1920s, more recent critiques have pointed to the paper's more limited regional base in the Santiago–Valparaíso area and the northern cities. For the purposes of this study, the paper remains the principal forum for the debates on Chilean socialism, including the woman question.

127 In July 1922, editors announced a new series on female militancy, "La voz de la mujer," *La Federación Obrera*, 25 July 1922.

128 "En la Fábrica de Tejidos de Ñuñoa," *La Federación Obrera*, 12 November 1921.

129 "En la Fábrica de Tejidos de Ñuñoa," *La Federación Obrera*, 3 November 1921. The strikers also received support from the Sociedad de Curtidores en Resistencia, Consejo 23 de Dulceros, Consejo 20 de Metalurgicos, Electricistas, Gasfiters, etc. "En la Fábrica de Tejidos Ñuñoa," *La Federación Obrera*, 25 October 1921.

130 On blacklisting, see *La Federación Obrera*, 8 and 27 November 1921. In December, the strike committee was broadened to include the Unión en Resistencia de Labradores en Maderas, Departamento de Oficios Varios de la IWW, Unión en Resistencia de Estucadores, Tejedores de Paños, Albañiles, Gasfitería i Hojatelería, Federación de Obreros y Obreras en Calzado, Unión General de Obreros Metalurgicos, and the Unión Local de la IWW. See *La Federación Obrera*, 15 December 1921.

131 See further reports on male workers' immediate solidarity with women strikers in *La Federación Obrera*, 12 September 1921, and "Como se esplota a la mujer proletaria," *La Justicia*, 28 April 1925.

132 "Compañeras tejedoras y compañeros," *La Federación Obrera*, 28 March 1923, 4.

133 Amira M., "Colaboraciones femeninas: Obreritas," *La Federación Obrera*, 11 April 1923, 4.

134 Isabel Díaz, "A mis compañeras," *La Federación Obrera*, 19 May 1923, 4. See also "A las obreras mujeres," *La Federación Obrera*, 30 July 1923, 4.

135 Rene Chaughi's *La mujer esclava* (Santiago: Editorial La Alborada, 1921) inspired the publication of a series of related articles on this theme in the anarchist *Acción Directa* in 1922 and *El Surco* (Valparaíso) in 1924.

136 "Levantemos la mujer," *La Federación Obrera*, 12 August 1923, 1. The editorial "Acción Feminista," published the following year, also supported the campaign for women's political rights, although it stressed that "it is necessary that the defense of those who work be a primary [concern]" (27 March 1924, 1).

137 "Los derechos de la mujer," *La Federación Obrera*, 11 June 1924, 1. A later news story on the Comité Pro Derechos de la Mujer reiterated this point, that "before political rights, [women] should recover their legal rights and the right to rule the home" ("Pro Derechos de la Mujer," *La Federación Obrera*, 8 July 1924, 2).

138 Herminia Cepeda, "La hora presente," *La Federación Obrera*, 17 April 1924, 1.

139 Luisa Capetillo, "La mujer," *La Federación Obrera*, 28 April 1924, 1. Capetillo's extensive writings are reproduced and analyzed in Julio Ramos, ed., *Amor y anarquía: Los escritos de Luisa Capetillo* (Rio Piedras, Puerto Rico: Ediciones Huracán, 1992).

1 The focus of public debate on "the social question" doubtless has various origins. Augusto Orrego Luco introduced the phrase itself into Chilean public debate in 1884, and by 1900 "the social question" had become a stock phrase in any discussion of the living and working conditions of the urban poor.

2 Luís Alberto Romero, "Los sectores populares en las ciudades latinoamericanas del siglo XIX: La cuestión de la identidad," *Desarollo Económico* 27, no. 106 (July–September 1987): 211.

3 Selections of the better-known expressions of alarm about the social question can be found in Christián Gazmuri, *Testimonios de una crisis. Chile: 1900–1925* (Santiago: Editorial Universitaria, 1979); Sergio Grez Toso, ed., *La "cuestión social" en Chile: Ideas y debates precursores (1804–1902)* (Santiago: DIBAM, 1995); Armando de Ramón and Patricio Gross, "Algunos testimonios de las condiciones de vida en Santiago de Chile: 1888–1918," *Revista EURE (Revista Latinoamericana de Estudios Urbanos Regionales)* 11, no. 31 (October 1984): 67–74.

4 For a detailed discussion of the social question, its evolution, and principal authors in Chile, see James O. Morris, *Elites, Intellectuals, and Consensus: A Study of the Social Question and the Industrial Relations System in Chile* (Ithaca, NY: Cornell University Press, 1966).

5 Women's Vocational Training: The Female Face of Industrialization

1 "La industria nacional: La fábrica de camisas i artículos de lencería de don Juan Matas, Valparaíso," *BSOFOFA* 6, no. 8 (August 1889): 372–74.

2 Juan G. Muñoz, Carmen Norambuena C., Luís Ortega M., and Roberto Pérez R., *La Universidad de Santiago de Chile* (Santiago: Universidad de Santiago de Chile, 1987), 15–63.

3 *AE* 1909, 436. The daily operations of the schools are examined in greater detail in Lorena Godoy Catalán, " 'Armas ansiosas de triunfo: Dedal, agujas, tijeras . . .': La educación profesional femenina en Chile, 1888–1912" (Thesis, Universidad Católica de Chile, 1995).

4 On discipline in the Escuela de Artes y Oficios in the nineteenth century, see Claudio Barrientos B. and Nicolas Corbalán P., "El justo deseo de asegurar el porvenir moral y material de los jóvenes: Control y castigo en las prácticas educativas en la Escuela de Artes y Oficios, 1849–1870," *Ultima Década* (Viña del Mar) 6 (January 1997): 163–93.

5 In his brief study of class relations under the Porfiriato, William E. French emphasized the importance of women's vocational training for understanding the construction of middle-class womanhood and, by extension,

Porfirian elite hegemony: "Prostitutes and Guardian Angels: Women, Work, and the Family in Porfirian Mexico," *Hispanic American Historical Review* 72, no. 4 (November 1992): 529–53. Other recent studies have examined the importance of women's vocational education for state and industrialists' modernization projects in the 1920s and 1930s: Patience A. Schell, "Teaching the Children of the Revolution: Church and State Education in Mexico City, 1917–1926" (D.Phil. diss., Oxford University, 1998), chap. 6; Barbara Weinstein, "Unskilled Worker, Skilled Housewife: Constructing the Working-Class Woman in São Paulo, Brazil," in *The Gendered Worlds of Women Workers: From Household and Factory to the Union Hall and Ballot Box*, ed. John D. French and Daniel James (Durham, NC: Duke University Press, 1997), 72–99.

6 Prior to 1920, industrialists were marginal to SOFOFA's operations and statesmen dominated, which Vargas argues "speaks to the conviction [the statesmen] have about the value of industry for a people's 'progress' and 'civilization.' This [conviction] was rooted in their basic interest in [industry] and not, as one might suppose, in any close connection with it." Industrialists' political and economic interests, as such, were better represented by the SOFOFA spin-offs, the Centro Industrial y Agrícola (1898) and the Asociación del Trabajo (1921) (J. E. Vargas, "La Sociedad de Fomento Fabril, 1883–1928," *Revista Historia* 13 [1976]: 20).

7 Henry W. Kirsch, *Industrial Development in a Traditional Society: The Conflict of Entrepreneurship and Modernization in Chile* (Gainesville: University Presses of Florida, 1977), 43–45, 129–33.

8 Ibid., 152–60. Kirsch argues that this investment pattern was what really limited Chilean development, rather than dependence on export income per se.

9 *BSOFOFA* 2 (1888): 105.

10 *BSOFOFA* 9, no. 11 (November 1892).

11 *AE* 1909, 400. The *Sinopsis estadística i jeográfica* also notes: "The School of Arts and Crafts trains our first-rate mechanics, and agricultural machines and locomotives are made in its workshops." See República de Chile, Oficina Central de Estadística, *Sinopsis Estadística i Jeográfica* (Santiago: Imprenta y Encuadernación Universitaria, 1894–1895), 185.

12 "Crónica: Escuela de Artes i Oficios para Mujeres," *BSOFOFA* 5, no. 1 (January 1888): 43.

13 Ibid.

14 H.E., "La enseñanza industrial," *BSOFOFA* 4, no. 5 (May 1887): 196–97.

15 Godoy notes that the model for enrollment and curriculum was based on French models for female vocational instruction ("'Armas ansiosas de triunfo,'" 82–83).

16 AMIOP, *Escuelas Profesionales de Niñas*, 1888–1889, vol. 279, letter from SOFOFA to Ministry, 10 August 1887.

17 Ibid., letter from Council on Agricultural and Industrial Education to Ministry, 14 and 16 December 1887. The official decree establishing the Women's School for Arts and Crafts also lowered the minimum age of students to twelve and specified that classes would be free. The decree also ordered that part of the earnings from the items produced by students be deposited in savings funds, to be turned over to the students upon graduation.

18 "Crónica," 43.

19 AMIOP, *Escuelas Profesionales Para Niñas*, 1888–1889, vol. 279, Director's annual report to the Oversight Committee, 18 March 1889. Although administrators made repeated references to the girls' poverty, enrollment records show that many came from mechanics' and carpenters' families. Also, the fact that young women were free from work to attend school and pay registration fees suggests the relative well-being of the girls' families.

20 Ibid., letter from Educational Council to the Ministry, 21 August 1888.

21 *AE* 1909, 437.

22 AMIOP, *Escuelas Profesionales Para Niñas*, 1888–1889, vol. 279, General Regulations for the Women's School for Arts and Crafts, 17 May 1888.

23 República de Chile, *Sinopsis estadística*, 1902, 314.

24 Ibid.

25 AMIOP, *Escuelas Profesionales Para Niñas*, 1888–1889, vol. 279, Director's annual report to the Oversight Committee, 18 March 1889.

26 The cooking classes proved most useful to "ladies and their servants." Servants were given classes in cooking separate from their bosses, about whom the director commented: "There was no one more present and enthusiastic than the ladies for the culinary arts classes." At this point, the school's supervisory committee did not consider cooking to be a priority for its students, hence the señoras had to pay extra for gas (ibid.).

27 "We have been unable to stop paying the students of this section for their work. . . . The teacher has had to do this because he would not have any students otherwise" (ibid.).

28 "Memoria del señor Ministro de Industria i Obras Públicas presentada al Congreso Nacional," *BSOFOFA* 8, no. 3 (March 1891): 222.

29 *BSOFOFA* 6, no. 10 (October 1889): 475–76.

30 "Correspondencia de la Sociedad: Industria de tejidos de punto," *BSOFOFA* 9, no. 3 (March 1892): 154.

31 *AE* 1909, 434.

32 AMIOP, *Escuelas Profesionales Para Niñas*, 1888–1889, vol. 279, Director's annual report to the Oversight Committee, 18 March 1889.

33 Ibid.

34 Ministry enrollment figures are always slightly lower than those given by SOFOFA or listed in the *Anuario estadístico*. This may have been

because school administrators calculated the actual number of students enrolled, whereas the latter figures may have included students enrolling in two courses simultaneously. See *BSOFOFA* 6, no. 10 (October 1889), 475–76; República de Chile, *Sinopsis estadística*, 1902–1907; *AE* 1909, 450–51.

35 "Length of study varies according to the specialization," according to the 1909 *AE* report.

36 The oversight committees were made up of concerned men and women of the elite and presided over by the Vocational School inspector: "The committee was in charge of supervising these services and was empowered to propose to the Ministry professors and administrative employees, new courses, and the creation of rules and general direction of teaching" (*Actividades femeninas en Chile* [Santiago: Imprenta y Litografía La Ilustración, 1928], 283). The schools were administrated by the Ministry of Industry and Public Works through 1926.

37 In 1910, only 39 teachers out of a national staff of 254 were male, and 29 of these were priests. Most of the teachers had certificates from the Vocational Schools, and in the Vocational High School, most had a master's degree in vocational training (*AE*, 1910).

38 "Escuela profesional para obreros," *BSOFOFA* 9, no. 11 (November 1892).

39 "Nuestras escuelas industriales," *BSOFOFA* 10, no. 5 (May 1893): 202.

40 "Escuela Profesional de Niñas: Esposición," *La Ley*, 8 January 1898, 2.

41 J.A.N. [Abelardo Nuñez], "Enseñanza industrial," *Revista del Centro Industrial y Agrícola* 3, no. 9 (1900): 100–101. Advertisements such as the following from Simon y Cía. did appear in the Santiago press on occasion: "We take the opportunity to remind you that we will always have a preference for the graduates of your School in our workshops of children's clothing, shirts, and men's clothing" ("La Escuela Profesional de Niñas y el comercio de Santiago," *El Chileno*, 4 January 1906).

42 An examiner's report to the Oversight Committee details the contents of these master's exams, which tested the students' knowledge about and skill at their chosen profession and the proper techniques for teaching it in the Vocational Schools. The test for technical and ornamental drawing, for example, contained the following questions for potential teachers: "[Write a] Drawing Curriculum for a Vocational School. Why should you emphasize decoration in a Vocational School? What fundamental ideas of linear drawing are needed for drawing forms? What are the main styles? Who are the few famous women in art history? How do you find the point of perspective of a room?" (AMIOP, *Escuela Profesional de Niñas Superior*, 1908–1911, Examining Commission report to the Oversight Committee, 27 December 1907).

43 *AE* 1909, 436.

44 In one of the few pieces of information available about the schools'

students, the enrollment lists for the first Girls' Vocational High School indicate the concentration of students on the streets San Francisco, San Isidro, Recoleta, Olivos, and surrounding streets. A large number of students apparently shared a residence at San Francisco 204, a location within blocks of the numerous brothels along Eluterio Ramírez street. See AMIOP, *Escuela Profesional de Niñas Superior*, 1908–1911, vol. 2025, "Matrícula correspondiente al año 1908."

45 *Actividades femeninas en Chile*, 286.

46 AMIOP, *Memorias*, 1909, vol. 2190, report on the Vocational High School.

47 A minister of industry asked to supply five hundred texts each in sacred history and catechism to the Vocational High School asked, "For what? These are lectures, not Catechism classes." See AMIOP, *Escuela Profesional de Niñas Superior*, 1908–1911, vol. 2025, letter from director of the Vocational High School to Ministry, 9 December 1907.

48 Ibid., vol. 2022, records of employee meetings, 25 June 1909.

49 "La industria nacional," 372–74.

50 The Number 2 School, established in 1906, was renamed the Escuela Profesional de Niñas Emilia Toro de Balmaceda in 1926 (*Actividades femeninas*, 300).

51 Ibid., 297–98.

52 This may have been because 40 percent of the sale revenues from the students' products was poured back into the school administration. These estimates are from República de Chile, *Sinopsis estadística*, and *AE*.

53 Estimate based on figures from the *AE* for the years 1909–1930 and *Actividades femeninas*, 303.

54 "Las Escuelas Profesionales," *Familia* (September 1911): 10. The reviewer's only criticism referred to the moral formation of the women in teacher training: because "it is well known that girls can acquire varied and more cultured habits by taking them out of the home for a time," these students should have been housed in the school and not in boardinghouses, where "they are not able to protect their morality, which is the basic foundation for the public life of a teacher and the basis for forming future society."

55 *Actividades femeninas*, 284.

56 Weigle de Jenschke had previously served as director of the Vocational High School (1891–1907).

57 AMIOP, *Inspección de Escuelas Profesionales*, 1909–1911, vol. 2182, circular no. 12, 26 August 1909, 6; emphasis added.

58 On the last point, she instructs that "the guardians or parents who do not know how to sign their names should return the booklets personally to the Director of the School" (ibid., 4).

59 Ibid., 1.

60 Ibid., letter from Ministry to Director, 5 June 1909.

61 AMIOP, *Actas de Sesiones de las Escuelas Profesionales de Niñas*, 1910–1911, vol. 2224, minutes of the Rancagua Girls' Vocational School, 7 April 1911.

62 *AE* 1909, 441; emphasis added.

63 These six exceptions were Iquique, Copiapó, San Felipe, Los Angeles, Angol, and Ancud (*AE*, 1919, 63).

64 AMIOP, *Inspección de Escuelas Profesionales*, 1909–1911, vol. 2182, circular no. 18, 1 December 1909, 1.

65 *Actividades femeninas*, 295, 298.

66 AMIOP, *Inspección de Escuelas Profesionales*, 1909–1911, circular no. 18, 1 December 1909, 6.

67 Students who continued to save two years after graduation were given additional prizes. "They have already acquired sufficient habits and motivation to want to create their own future that will give them a certain amount of independence, that we might call true female individuality" ("Las Escuelas Profesionales," 10). Night school and public lectures on the necessity of savings consistently depicted women as more motivated and effective at thrift than men. See, for example, Carlos Ibáñez, "El ahorro," in *Conferencias dadas en el año 1902* (Santiago: Imprenta Universitaria, 1902), 33–44.

68 AMIOP, *Inspección de Escuelas Profesionales*, 1909–1911, circular no. 25, 15 June 1910, 1, 3; emphasis in original.

69 An interview with the school inspector in 1916 revealed that the increasing emphasis on domesticity was part of the plan for setting the schools on "a more practical path . . . giving women not only knowledge of a manufacturing industry, but also domestic and agricultural instruction, making cooking classes and clothing repair obligatory, and introducing new classes in beekeeping, aviculture, agriculture, horticultural gardening, basket making, chandlery, etc." ("Enseñanza industrial femenina," *El Mercurio*, 29 February 1916, 12).

70 AMIOP, *Escuela Profesional de Niñas Superior*, 1908–1911, vol. 2025, letter from Director M. Guerrero Bascuñan and Secretary Elicenda Parga to Ministry, 15 September 1908.

71 Instructions for how to keep domestic accounts, for example, allocated 50 pesos per month for a servant out of a total budget of 500 pesos. See S.R., "Contabilidad del hogar," *Revista Industrial Femenina* 1, no. 2 (December 1912). Although it is not inconceivable that working-class families might have had some paid domestic help, the overall budget exceeded that of a well-paid male industrial worker several times over. See "Salarios corrientes en la ciudad de Santiago," *BOT* 1, no. 1 (1911): 90–100.

72 Ana Vial de Borquez, *Revista Industrial Femenina* 1, no. 2 (December 1912): 1.

73 "Novela de la vida," *Revista Industrial Femenina* 1, no. 2 (December 1912).

74 Filomena Sierra, "Fin de la jornada," *Revista Industrial Femenina* 2, no. 12 (March 1913).

75 Sara Araya, "Para mis compañeras del curso normal," *Revista Industrial Femenina* 1, no. 8 (August 1913).

76 On elite and middle-class women's views on "personality" in this period, see Ericka Kim Verba, "The *Círculo de Lectura* [Ladies' Reading Circle] and the *Club de Señoras* [Ladies' Club] of Santiago, Chile: Middle- and Upper-Class Feminist Conversations (1915–1920)," *Journal of Women's History* 7, no. 3 (fall 1995): 17–21.

77 "Escuelas profesionales de niñas," *El Mercurio*, 13 July 1909.

78 "Las Escuelas Profesionales," 9.

79 "Nuestras Escuelas Industriales," 202.

80 J. Abelardo Nuñez, "Enseñanza Industrial II," *Revista del Centro Industrial y Agrícola* 3, no. 10 (March 1901): 111–12.

81 AMIOP, *Escuela Profesional de Niñas Superior*, 1908–1922, vol. 2025, letter of General Inspector to Ministry, 2 March 1911.

82 In one such polemic against an essay that argued against public education for women, the author argued, "There are no indecent occupations, Madam, if they are honorable. . . . She who does not know, who has not suffered in the struggle for life, would be incapable of consoling anyone" ("Enseñanza artística de la mujer," *El Chileno*, 20 July 1903).

83 "El trabajo de la mujer," *El Mercurio*, 23 December 1912, 3.

84 Snow, "Trabajos para la mujer," *La Opinión*, 31 July 1916, 1. The author considered these occupations "more appropriate for [women], since they require little muscular strength and plenty of delicacy, patience and art."

85 ADGT, *Providencias*, 1929, vol. 199, Gabriela Mistral report on Social Service Conference in Paris, 4.

86 Lisamoberno, "La Esposición de la Escuela Profesional de Niñas No. 2," *Ciencia y Trabajo* 1, no. 2 (1915): 2–3. See also "Como crear un porvenir a la joven obrera," *La Opinión*, 3 May 1920, 1, 7.

87 The more humorous responses to the "servant crisis" included satirical suggestions that Chileans import cannibals to work as cooks—as long as their primitive instincts could be kept under control. See "Una solución . . . algo peligrosa a la crisis de los sirvientes," *El Ilustrado*, 29 April 1907. At least one *El Mercurio* article also suggested that monkeys be trained as servants: "Sirvientes," *El Mercurio*, 15 January 1911.

88 X., "Sirvientes," *El Ilustrado*, 7 January 1907. An *El Mercurio* editorial, also entitled "Sirvientes," also blamed the state for "regenerating and moralizing [the "china" population], and [now] they all want to be citizens and not servants. What is to be done?" ("Sirvientes," *El Mercurio*, 16 January 1911).

89 "Escuela doméstica," *El Chileno*, 4 November 1907. X. (quoted above) portrayed Vocational School graduates as uppity: At "many so-called instructional establishments the women graduate knowing little more than embroidery or something of the sort; and of course, no one who knows how to embroider sees herself taking a job as a servant" (X., "Sirvientes," *El Ilustrado*, 26 January 1908).

90 "Escuela doméstica."

91 Una dueña de casa, "Crisis de servidumbre," *El Ilustrado*, 10 March 1914; J.E.S., "Sirvientes domésticas," *El Ilustrado*, 11 March 1914.

92 Verba documents widespread Catholic complaints about the negative effects of vocational training on working-class girls. See Ericka Kim Verba, "Catholic Feminism and *Acción Social Femenina* [Women's Social Action]: The Early Years of the *Liga de Damas Chilenas*, 1912–1924" (Ph.D. diss., University of California at Los Angeles, 1999), 214–19.

93 "La enseñanza de la economía doméstica," *El Mercurio*, 22 October 1910, 3; "La mujer y la enseñanza profesional," *El Mercurio*, 18 October 1910, 3.

94 "El Instituto Superior de Educación Física y Manual. Su importancia, sus programas, L'Ecole de Ménagères. Escuela de dueñas de casa. Demás ramos," *El Chileno*, 18 June 1907.

95 "La enseñanza de la economía doméstica," 3.

96 "Por la familia obrera," *El Mercurio*, 24 July 1910, 3.

97 "Protección a la mujer," *El Chileno*, 12 October 1915.

98 Manuel Rivas Vicuña, "Educación profesional femenina," *El Mercurio*, 10 July 1923, 3.

99 See the short notices, such as "La Escuela Profesional de Niñas: La fiesta del domingo," *La Reforma*, 3 January 1908, 2. Anarchist Juan F. Barrera complained in 1916 that a girl enrolled in a Santiago Vocational School was told that she could not advance to the next level unless she went to confession "De Melipilla: Confesarse o no adelantar" (*La Batalla*, 1 January, 1916).

100 Weinstein, "Unskilled Worker, Skilled Housewife," 77–79; Schell, "Teaching the Children," chap. 6.

101 This tension is perhaps most poignant in the case of Minister of Education Vasconcelos's insistence that the Secretaría de Educación Pública change the cooking curriculum to stress Mexican dishes so that students would be able to prepare low-cost meals for their families. Teachers and students, well aware of the employment possibilities available to women who mastered the art of European cuisine, resisted Vasconcelos's cooking reform (Schell, "Teaching the Children," chap. 6).

102 Aside from the few admittedly problematic articles by students that appeared in the *Revista Industrial Femenina*, there are few sources that allow us to explore student perceptions of the schools and their curriculum. Student enrollments support the interpretation, also suggested by

inspectors' repeated observations, that home economics courses were less popular among students than those that taught marketable skills such as embroidery, fashion, and commerce.

6 *Señoras y Señoritas:*
Catholic Women Defend the *Hijas de Familia*

1   By referring to women of the elite as "señoras," I do not mean to suggest that working-class women were not, or did not view themselves as, señoras and señoritas in their own right. This terminology, rather, reflects elite women's exclusive identification of themselves as the guardians of respectable society. As Verba has shown, women of means referred to working-class women in a variety of ways—*mujeres del pueblo* and *mujeres de trabajo* were among the most popular—but understood the term señora to apply only to women of their own class. See Ericka Kim Verba, "*The Circulo de Lectura* [Ladies' Reading Circle] and the *Club de Señoras* [Ladies' Club] of Santiago, Chile: Middle- and Upper-Class Feminist Conversations (1915–1920)," *Journal of Women's History* 7, no. 3 (fall 1995): 6–33.

2   For a useful synthesis of women's activism in Latin America in this period, see Francesca Miller, *Latin American Women and the Search for Social Justice* (Hanover, NH: University Press of New England, 1992), chaps. 3, 4. Asunción Lavrin provides a more detailed examination of liberal and socialist feminist activism in the Southern Cone in *Women, Feminism and Social Change in Argentina, Chile and Uruguay, 1880–1940* (Lincoln: University of Nebraska Press, 1995). Christine Ehrick and Susan Besse take a broader approach to the multiple feminisms that evolved within Uruguay and Brazil, respectively, including significant currents of Catholic feminism, often overlooked by women's historians: Christine Theresa Ehrick, "*Obrera, Dama, Feminista*: Women's Associations and the Welfare State in Uruguay, 1900–1932" (Ph.D. diss., University of California at Los Angeles, 1997), and Susan Besse, *Restructuring Patriarchy: The Modernization of Gender Inequality in Brazil, 1914–1940* (Chapel Hill: University of North Carolina Press, 1996), chap. 7.

3   With the exception of the rather triumphalist narratives by Klimpel, Pereira, and Zegers and Maino, the topic of conservative women's activism in the early twentieth century has been largely neglected in Chilean women's history. The recent works below suggest the direction of some of this important new research: Erika Maza Valenzuela, "Catolicismo, anticlericalismo y la extensión del sufragio a la mujer en Chile," *Estudios Públicos* 58 (autumn 1995): 137–95; Diana Veneros Ruiz-Tagle and Paulina Ayala L., "Dos Vertientes del movimiento proemancipa-

ción de la mujer en Chile: Feminismo cristiano y feminismo laico," in *Perfiles revelados: Historias de mujeres en Chile, siglos XVII–XX*, ed. Veneros (Santiago: Editorial Universidad de Santiago, 1997), 41–62; Ericka Verba, "Catholic Feminism and *Acción Social Femenina* [Women's Social Action]: The Early Years of the Liga de Damas Chilenas, 1912–1924" (Ph.D. diss., University of California at Los Angeles, 1999). For an important treatment of conservative women's activism in recent Chilean history, see Margaret Power, *Gendered Allegiances: The Construction of a Cross-Class Right-Wing Movement in Chile* (University Park: Pennsylvania State University Press, forthcoming).

4 For detailed accounts of the Parliamentary Republic's inability to design or implement effective public health policies prior to the 1920s, see María Angélica Illanes, *"En el nombre del pueblo, del estado y de la ciencia (. . .)": Historia social de la salud pública, Chile 1880–1973 (Hacia una historia social del siglo XX)* (Santiago: Colectivo de Atención Primaria, 1993), chaps. 3, 4.

5 María, "La Aurora Feminista," *La Aurora Feminista* (15 January 1904), 1.

6 Illanes, *En el nombre del pueblo*, 97.

7 "Las casas-cunas," *El Diario Popular*, 17 December 1903.

8 The numerous private efforts spearheaded by women of means are listed in Felícitas Klimpel, *La mujer Chilena: El aporte feminino al Progreso de Chile, 1910–1960* (Santiago: Editorial Andrés Bello, 1962), chap. 8. The pervasiveness of charitable efforts is one of the reasons, Verba argues, that women of the Liga de Damas Chilenas, the señoras' flagship organization for *acción social*, opted not to implement programs for working-class mothers and families ("Catholic Feminism," 225, 229).

9 The Foundation should not be confused with the Protectora de la Infancia, a Catholic orphanage founded in 1894 by ladies of the aristocracy. On the latter, see *Actividades femeninas en Chile* (Santiago: Imprenta y Litografía La Ilustración, 1928), 530–37.

10 Ibid., 545.

11 According to the *Actividades femeninas'* report of 1927 (ibid.), the Patronato dispensed 22,304,000 infant feedings between 1915 and 1926; performed 309 home visits in 1926; served 100,596 lunches to nursing mothers; and distributed 196,564 pieces of clothing in fourteen years.

12 "Ricos y pobres: Una obra digna de toda alabanza. Talleres Protectores de Obreras," *El Chileno*, 17 August 1907; Pedro Sánchez, "Los Talleres Protectores de Obreras," *La Unión*, 23 July 1915.

13 Patronato Nacional de la Infancia, "Monografía de la Sociedad Victoria Prieto," in *Almanaque del Patronato Nacional de la Infancia* (Santiago: Balcells and Co., 1921), 301–3.

14 Verba, "Catholic Feminism," chap. 3, especially 205–13.

15 AMIOP, *Escuelas Talleres Subvencionadas*, 1908–1909, vol. 2028, inspec-

tor's report, 19 October 1909. Weigle de Jenschke's subsequent comments on the Limache vocational school (also private) reflect her emphasis on servant training: "Given the good standing of the School and the comforts that its large building offers, I believe that we could give it a more practical character, by broadening the cooking and laundry classes, introducing confectionary, preserving, and darning, etc.; in a word, all of those classes that contribute to the training of servants" (ibid., 21 October 1909).

16   "Escuela Profesional de Niñas de las Hijas de María Auxiliadora: Colocación de la primera piedra," *El Porvenir*, 27 January 1903, 3.

17   AMIOP, *Escuelas Talleres Subvencionadas*, 1908–1909, vol. 2028, letter from Director of Escuela-Taller del Asilo de la Misericordia to Ministry, 14 October 1909.

18   On the Cruz Blanca and Chilean abolitionist efforts more generally, see Álvaro Góngora Escobedo, *La prostitución en Santiago, 1813–1931: Visión de las élites* (Santiago: DIBAM, 1994), 207–47.

19   Adela Edwards de Salas, "La Cruz Blanca," in *Relaciones y documentos del Congreso Mariano Femenino* (Santiago: Escuela Tipográfica "La Gratitud Nacional," 1918), 319–27.

20   For a thorough account of the philosophy and accomplishments of the White Cross, see *Memoria de la Cruz Blanca* (Santiago: Palacios, 1929).

21   Verba, "Catholic Feminism," 239–55.

22   A paradigmatic tale of one woman's forced entrance into the workforce can be found in the memoirs of Carmen Smith, who, on her father's death, supported herself and her mother by making fashionable hats: *Mis memorias* (Santiago: Imprenta El Imparcial, 1936). I wish to thank Lucrecia Enriquéz for bringing this text to my attention.

23   "En defensa del trabajo de la mujer: Fundación de una nueva sociedad," *El Chileno*, 28 August 1913.

24   This society was frequently cited in urban newspapers, where proponents defended themselves against accusations that they charged fees to women to sell their goods, and pointed out that women enjoyed use of their restaurant and reading room. See "Noble protección. En favor del trabajo femenino. La obra que comienza y su desarollo futuro," *El Chileno*, 24 January 1914; V. de V., "La protección al trabajo de la mujer. Entrevista con la señora gerente de la sociedad. Los adelantos de la institución," *El Chileno*, 28 January 1914.

25   "Por el trabajo femenino y la infancia desválida," *El Mercurio*, 25 December 1912, 5.

26   "Obreras invisibles," *El Diario Ilustrado*, 30 May 1914, 3. The League's notion of the shame of manual labor was not universally shared; Smith recounts in her memoirs that she rejected the League's offer to sell her fine hats because she found nothing dishonorable in selling them herself (*Mis memorias*, 142).

27 "El trabajo femenino," *El Mercurio*, 6 December 1912.

28 "Por el trabajo femenino y la infancia desválida," 5.

29 "El trabajo de la mujer," *El Mercurio*, 2 November 1914, 3; "El trabajo de la mujer," *El Mercurio*, 23 December 1913, 3.

30 Verba, "Catholic Feminism," 290–95.

31 *Cursos rápidos, para señoras y señoritas, internado para alumnas de provincias* (Santiago: Academia Industrial Tejidos a Máquina "Rasco," n.d.).

32 Sara Perrin, "La mujer en las industrias," in *Actividades femeninas*, 648.

33 "El trabajo femenino," *El Mercurio*, 6 December 1912; "El trabajo femenino," *El Mercurio*, 15 May 1913, 3.

34 The Women's Exhibit commemorated the fiftieth anniversary of the 1877 Amunátegui decree, which granted women the right to earn a high school degree. The exhibit's organizers compiled reviews and photographs of the displays, as well as commissioned essays on the history of Chilean women's activities in charitable associations, literature and the arts, and education in the massive volume *Actividades femeninas en Chile*.

35 Sara Perrin, "La mujer en las industrias," 646, 647.

36 Ibid., 653.

37 This all-female arrangement—never viewed in such positive terms by working-class critics—was the explicit strategy of Catholic reformers in early-twentieth-century Medellin textile mills, who stressed the importance of segregating workers by sex. See Ann Farnsworth-Alvear, *Dulcinea in the Factory: Myths, Morals, Men, and Women in Colombia's Industrial Experiment, 1905–1960* (Durham, NC: Duke University Press, 2000), chaps. 5, 6.

38 Perrin, "La mujer en las industrias," 648.

39 Ibid., 647.

40 Ibid., 650. See her biographies of other women of means for examples of Perrin's appraisal of genteel industriousness.

41 Women were reportedly first employed as salesclerks in 1882 in Casa Pra, a Santiago department store, sparking controversy and curiosity among the buying public: "The ladies came just to look at the saleswomen like strange beings" (F. Santiván, "La mujer que trabaja," *Pacífico Magazine* [March 1913]: 396).

42 One observer lamented the dead-end nature of most of these service jobs: "The telegraph workers are numerous and persevering, but they have few expectations for their careers. Their work is one of rigorous compliance and of patience. Promotions happen slowly, while years pass" (C., "Telegrafistas mujeres," *La Opinión*, 24 November 1916).

43 "Shaping a future for women, one gains true liberation; one makes her more moral and dignifies her so that she will cooperate in the home and in society" (Alma, "Enseñanza comercial femenina," *El Mercurio*, 9 January 1924).

44 Santiván, "La mujer que trabaja," 395.

45 "Protección al trabajo femenino," *El Mercurio*, 11 December 1918.

46 Other estimates of Santiago's salesclerk population are difficult to come by: the 1907 census lists approximately eight thousand *empleadas*, some of whom presumably worked in retail sales. Unfortunately, the 1920 and 1930 census do not disagregate saleswomen from those working in commercial establishments that sold food, clothing, and so on.

47 Santiván, "La mujer que trabaja," 387, 394.

48 Eugenio Sepúlveda Arellano, "Legislación social: El trabajo de las mujeres y los niños," *La Opinión*, 18 March 1920.

49 "Feminism can be disputed in its political aspect; but in its other two aspects, the economic and legal, it has managed to become part of public consciousness throughout the world and in this country, which is evidence of its imminent realization" (Clarín, "La chilena, esclava de la ley," *El Mercurio*, 18 October 1921).

50 See Elena Caffarena Morice, "Situación jurídica de la mujer chilena," in *Actividades femeninas*, 75–86; Martina Barros de Orrego, "El voto femenino," *Revista Chilena* 1, no. 9 (December 1917), 390–99; Ricardo Salas Edwards, "La futura acción política de la mujer," *Revista Chilena* 3, no. 24 (March 1920), 337–51; "Una encuesta sobre el sufragio femenino," *Revista Chilena* 4, no. 31 (May 1920), 62–79.

51 Santiván, "La mujer que trabaja," 389.

52 "Trabajo femenino," *El Mercurio*, 23 October 1909.

53 Pablo A. Urzúa, "El trabajo de la mujer," *La Unión*, 11 April 1917.

54 CNCD, *Boletín de Sesiones Estraordinarias*, 14 January 1919, 2047–48.

55 G., "Nuevos horizontes en favor de la mujer," *La Union*, 16 January 1919, 2.

56 CNCD, *Boletín de Sesiones Ordinarias*, 15 June 1920, 196.

57 CNCD, *Boletín de Sesiones Ordinarias*, 19 August 1921, 1804–5. Significantly, several laws that restricted or prohibited women's employment were already on the books. See chapter 7 below.

58 Ibid. This admonition about masculinity was echoed in a 1923 article by author María Larraín de Vicuña, who urged her audience "to speak with the owners of clothing, rag, and tailoring stores, so that the employee positions that open up can be filled by women. Thus it would be easier for women to find work and one would not see virile lads selling boxes, belts and corsets. [We should also] demand that salaries not be lowered when women occupy the positions" ("Apuntes para la Liga de Madres: Feminismo cristiano," *El Mercurio*, 9 December 1923).

59 Elvira L. de Subercaseaux, *Estudios sociales: Trabajos leidos por señoras de la Liga de Damas Chilenas, en el Curso de Estudios Sociales* (Santiago: Imprenta Chile, 1916), 22.

60 See Sara Covarrubias Valdés, "Capacidad económica de la mujer," and Eugenia Marín Alemany, "Condiciones del trabajo de la obrera," both

in *Congreso Mariano Femenino* (Santiago: Escuela Tipografía "La Gratitud Nacional," 1918), 280–87. I would like to thank Ericka Verba, who
first brought the records of the Congreso Mariano Femenino to my
attention.

61 Rosa Rodríguez de la Sotta, "El Congreso Mariano," in *Congreso Mariano*, 1.

62 Ibid., 5. Her sentiments were also reflected in Larraín de Vicuña,
"Apuntes para la Liga de Madres." There, feminism was equated with
seignorial charity on behalf of "our less-privileged sisters" (*hermanas
menos priviligiadas*). Though Larraín de Vicuña opposed women's suffrage, she advocated social legislation and sex quotas in sales establishments to improve women's working conditions.

63 An article in *La Unión* celebrated the discussion of Catholic unionism
at the congress, "because it involves exercising rights and achieving
victories in an ordered way, with justice and reciprocal advantage" (X.,
"Sindicalismo femenino," *La Unión*, 3 January 1919).

64 María Rosario Ledesma, "Manera práctica de organizar un sindicato,"
in *Congreso Mariano*, 289.

65 Verba argues persuasively that the women of the Liga and congress saw
themselves as the prime channels for appeasement between working-
class men and their employers. On the one hand, the señoras appeased
working men by instructing and aiding their wives; on the other, the
señoras influenced their powerful husbands to consider the needs of
working-class families ("Catholic Feminism," chaps. 3, 4).

66 Marín Alemany, "Condiciones del trabajo de la obrera," 286–87.

67 Ema González M., "Manera práctica de organizar un sindicato," in
Congreso Mariano, 292; emphasis added.

68 Marta Walker Linares, "Sindicato femenino," in *Congreso Mariano*,
294.

69 *El Mercurio*, 21 May 1922, 31.

70 *El Mercurio*, 22 May 1922.

71 Teresa Ossandón Guzmán, "La acción social de la mujer en Chile," in
Actividades femeninas, 590. The employees' union was supervised by
elite ladies and priests, and Catholic Youth declared that it would pa-
tronize stores that treated the union and empleadas well. See Rubio C.,
"Ley de silla," *La Sindicada* (January 1924).

72 "La primera Asamblea General," *La Sindicada* (8 June 1922).

73 Most of this service involved placing women employees as defined by
Decree Law 216 (who they felt should be handled by the Labor Office)
and domestic servants. One report on the employment service notes
that there was little movement in the area of factory workers, where the
association did not get involved in contract negotiations (ADGT, *Varios*,
1925, vol. 112, Bolsa de Trabajo Sindicato Señoritas Empleadas de Comercio y Oficinas, 19 June 1925).

74 "Las mujeres deben reunirse en Sindicatos exclusivamente femeninos?," *La Luz* (Valparaíso), 15 January 1922, 4.

75 Lirpa, "La mujer obrera," *La Luz*, 1 December 1922.

76 Natalia Rubio Cuadra, "Lo que afea a nuestras jovenes en su trabajo,"
La Sindicada (April 1923).

77 N.R.C., "Como señalan otros, los peligros a que se exponen algunas
jóvenes de nuestra profesión," *La Sindicada* (July 1923). The article
sought to defend union members against the recent characterization of
empleadas as loose women in *Zig-Zag* and *Acción Femenina*, "in which
they allude to commercial saleswomen, presenting them as easy and
sure prey for those who corrupt bodies and souls, who take advantage of
how young people love the dance halls, the philharmonic clubs, etc."

78 Natalia Rubio C., "Avisamos a las incautas," *La Sindicada* (January
1924).

79 "Un problema difícil," *La Sindicada* (September 1923).

7 Women, Work, and Motherhood:
Gender and Legislative Consensus

1 The phrase "protection of women's and children's labor" became axio-
matic in newspaper titles and legal tracts in the early twentieth century.
Although the present chapter deals exclusively with women workers,
the question of child labor certainly deserves further study. For studies
that address children's work and education in this period, see María
Angélica Illanes, *"Ausente, señorita": El niño-Chileno, la escuela-para-
pobres y el auxilio. Chile, 1890–1990* (Santiago: Junta Nacional de Auxilio Escolar y Becas, 1991), and Jorge Rojas Flores, Cinthia Rodríguez
Toledo, and Moisés Fernández Torres, *Cristaleros: Recuerdos de un siglo.
Los trabajadores de Cristalerías de Chile* (Santiago: PET, 1998).

2 These three positions are proposed and analyzed in more detail in
Ramón Angel Díaz, *Del trabajo de las mujeres y los niños en la industria*
(Santiago: Imprenta y Litografía "Santiago," 1919).

3 This pattern is hardly unique to Chile. Jane Jenson has argued that,
because state protection and welfare for working mothers became well
established in France before the war, "the men could, and did, ride to
leisure on the skirts of the women." See "Representations of Gender:
Policies to 'Protect' Women Workers and Infants in France and the
United States before 1914," in *Women, the State and Welfare*, ed. Linda
Gordon (Madison: University of Wisconsin Press, 1990), 156. Renee D.
Toback also shows that the Massachusetts ten-hour law of 1874 and the
Brandeis brief of 1908, both of which recognized the state's obligation
to protect women workers, served as a wedge to gaining universal reg-
ulations for labor. See "Protective Labor Legislation for Women: The

Massachusetts Ten-Hour Law" (Ph.D. diss., University of Massachusetts, 1985).

4 The comparative literature on this point demonstrates the importance of perceptions of working-class womanhood to the construction of welfare states in Europe and the United States, although many authors disagree on the reasons for such disparate outcomes. See Jenson, "Representations of Gender," 152–77; Susan Pedersen, *Family, Dependence, and the Origins of the Welfare State: Britain and France, 1914–1945* (Cambridge, England: Cambridge University Press, 1995).

5 James O. Morris, *Elites, Intellectuals and Consensus: A Study of the Social Question and the Industrial Relations System in Chile* (Ithaca, NY: Cornell University Press, 1966).

6 Chile was one of the few Latin American nations that formulated the details of social legislation outside the purview of the Constitution. The Mexican Constitution of 1917 is a classic example of the majoritarian, systematic approach to sociolegal issues taken in most countries. See Moisés Poblete Troncoso and Ben G. Burnett, *The Rise of the Latin American Labor Movement* (New York: Bookman Associates, 1960), 35.

7 María Angélica Illanes traces the emergence of the *estado asistencial* in parts 1 and 2 of *"En el nombre del pueblo, es estado y de la ciencia (. . .)": Historia social de la salud pública, Chile 1880–1973 (Hacia una historia social del Siglo XX)* (Santiago: Colectivo de Atención Primaria, 1993).

8 "La industria nacional: La fábrica nacional de sobres," *BSOFOFA* 6, no. 8 (August 1889): 367–74.

9 Armando Arancibia C., "Fábrica Nacional de Impermeables de los Señores Velásquez Hnos.," *BSOFOFA* 21, no. 1 (1 January 1904): 17–19. The author further noted that the eight-hour workday in the factory he visited "resembles one of the ideals of Socialism . . . and this is just."

10 Adolfo Ortúzar, "La gota de leche," *BSOFOFA* 23, no. 1 (1 January 1906): 80–81.

11 Morris, *Elites*, 114.

12 "Descripción de la Fábrica de Tejidos de Punto de Puente Alto," *Revista del Centro Industrial y Agrícola* 2, no. 5 (1900): 59–60. A similar assessment of this factory appeared in "La Fábrica de Tejidos de Punto de Puente Alto," *BSOFOFA* 25, no. 1 (1 January 1908): 227.

13 "Fábrica de tejidos de algodón i de lino de los Establecimientos Americanos Gratry en Población Vergara, Viña del Mar," *BSOFOFA* 25, no. 1 (1 January 1908): 393.

14 One such case of exemplary paternalism was reported by a labor inspector in 1927 in his description of the social services of the Volcán Companía de Fósforos in Talca: "I questioned a number of course and they were only pleased and thankful with their bosses. In effect, in addition

to complying with Law 4054, the Company maintains two huge rooms for day care and a pharmacy." The day care center was complete with nurse and toys, and employers made provisions for worker housing, health and entertainment (ADGT, *Inspección General del Trabajo*, 1927, vol. 144, Inspector's report on Talca factories, 18 April 1927).

15 DeShazo notes labor's seeming indifference to regulating workplace conditions compared to their interest in campaigns for better work schedules and wage protection, but this interpretation applies more accurately to some anarchists and later the IWW, who rejected the political reformism of the Democratic Party and social legislation as a matter of principle. See Peter DeShazo, *Urban Workers and Labor Unions in Chile, 1902–1927* (Madison: University of Wisconsin Press, 1983), 40.

16 B.V.S. [Bonificio Veas], "La causa del pueblo: Lejislación obrera," *El Mercurio*, 22 October 1905.

17 CNCD, *Boletín de Sesiones Ordinarias*, 25 January 1913, 946–49.

18 Decree-Law 4053 was considered bad for workers because it mandated the creation of insurance funds based on a portion of workers' salaries and employer contributions; mutualists feared that the funds would replace their own services, and anarchosyndicalist and communist leaders insisted that the funds be supported by employer contributions alone. See DeShazo, *Urban Workers*, 219, 238–40; Jorge Rojas Flores, *La dictadura de Ibáñez y los sindicatos (1927–1931)* (Santiago: DIBAM, 1993).

19 Luís Malaquías Concha went on to make social legislation the subject of his law thesis, *Sobre la dictación de un código del trabajo y de la previsión social* (Santiago: Imprenta Cervantes, 1907).

20 The commission in charge of social legislation in the Chamber of Deputies, "desiring to facilitate the study and passage of the law," chose to separate the question of women's and children's work from the other issues brought to the commission by Malaquías Concha: factory health and safety, hour limits, and accident insurance. See CNCD, *Boletín de Sesiones Extraordinarias*, 1907–1908, 28 January 1908, 1840; "En bien de los obreros," *El Mercurio*, 4 July 1907, 12. In 1909 and 1910, Senator Eyzaguirre and Deputy Malaquías Concha repeatedly requested that their projects for accident protection and women's and children's labor, pending since 1907, be expedited in the Senate. See CNCS, *Boletín de Sesiones Ordinarias*, 1909, 648; CNCD, *Boletín de Sesiones Ordinarias*, 4 July 1910, 21 July 1910, 867.

21 For a more complete discussion of the evolution of legislative social Catholicism in Chile, including the central role of Juan Enrique Concha, see Morris, *Elites*, chap. 5.

22 Social Catholic writings on the social question are discussed at greater length in Ericka Kim Verba, "Catholic Feminism and *Acción Social*

Femenina [Women's Social Action]: The Early Years of the *Liga de Damas Chilenas, 1912–1924*" (Ph.D. diss., University of California at Los Angeles, 1999), 158–67, 280–84.

23 "Reglamentación del trabajo," *El Diario Popular,* 18 June 1903.

24 Díaz, *Del trabajo de las mujeres,* 8.

25 "Reglamentación del trabajo: Importante informe," *El Porvenir,* 23 January 1903.

26 The proposal also called on employers to indemnify workers injured in workplace accidents, "except when the event is the worker's fault or stems from the action of a third party" ("Reglamentación del trabajo: La responsibilidad de los patrones," *El Diario Popular,* 12 June 1903, 1).

27 In comparative terms, industrialists' response to social legislation seems to be closely linked to dominant views of development in their respective countries and associations. According to Marysa Navarro, Argentine industrialists' opposition to 1907 women's and children's labor legislation was overt: "They argued that . . . their losses would be great because women and children did not do essential work; they only assisted in the production of goods." See "Hidden, Silent, and Anonymous: Women Workers in the Argentine Trade Union Movement," in *The World of Women's Trade Unionism,* ed. Norbert C. Soldon (Westport, CT: Greenwood Press, 1985), 178. Among the Brazilian industrialists studied by Barbara Weinstein, however, opponents to social legislation were in the clear minority by the 1920s. See "The Industrialists, the State, and the Issues of Worker Training and Social Services in Brazil, 1930–50," *Hispanic American Historical Review* 70, no. 3 (1990): 379–404.

28 CNCD, *Boletín de Sesiones Ordinarias,* 14 June 1907, 141.

29 E. Frias Collao, "Informe de la Oficina del Trabajo," *BOT* 4 (1912): 135. Between 1911 and 1924, the Labor Office bulletin published regular news stories and announcements about foreign labor relations, citing developments in Great Britain, France, Australia, the United States, Peru, Mexico, and Argentina.

30 This project closely resembled one proposed the same year by Malaquías Concha, including hour and age limits for child workers; the eight-hour day and abolition of night work for women; Sunday rest; restrictions on piecework; fine limits; health insurance for women workers; stipulations on working conditions; safe machinery; protection of health and virtue in the workplace, such as female supervision of women; and day care or home visits for nursing mothers ("Protección obrera: El trabajo del niño y de la mujer," *La Ley,* 2 May 1902).

31 CNCD, *Boletín de Sesiones Ordinarias,* 14 June 1907, 137.

32 One editorial in a Catholic daily paper argued that "big industry really doesn't exist here; children and women have very little part in the factories; no one says that the few existing workshops are unhealthy;

dangerous and noxious industries are practically nonexistent" ("Reglamentación del trabajo," *El Diario Ilustrado*, 15 June 1903).

33 "Legislación del trabajo," *El Mercurio*, 13 August 1907, 3.

34 Cited in Morris, *Elites*, 186.

35 Even Bonificio Veas, who regarded himself as a proponent of social laws, remarked that some parts of the legislation brought to the Chamber of Deputies in 1905 by Malaquías Concha ought to be seriously debated "in order to improve them, to empty them of socialist spirit, a spirit of false and hateful doctrine that puts the stamp of impracticality on everything" ("La causa del pueblo").

36 Morris, "The Elite Opposition," in *Elites*, chap. 7.

37 Luis Carcovich, *Protección legal del niño y de la mujer obreros* (Valparaíso: Imprenta Lillo, 1918), 51.

38 For a detailed discussion of the role of individual intellectuals in policy and the ideological development of the social question, see Morris, "Intellectuals," in *Elites*, 24–43.

39 B.V.S. [Bonificio Veas], "La causa del pueblo."

40 "Conservemos a los niños y cuidemos a las madres," *El Mercurio*, 2 April 1908; emphasis added.

41 "Los grandes problemas sociales: El trabajo de la mujer y condiciones en que este debe desarrollarse," *El Mercurio*, 15 October 1911.

42 DeShazo, *Urban Workers*, 73.

43 E. Croizet, *Lucha social contra la mortalidad infantil en el período de lactancia* (Santiago: Litografía i Encuadernación Barcelona, 1912), 4–5. According to Croizet, Sweden had the best rate at 73.5 per 1,000; Uruguay followed with 104; and Austro-Hungary trailed behind with 206.

44 Ibid., 9; emphasis added. (*"La mujer obrera es una afrenta de la civilización moderna, porque ésta situación le quita generalmente el derecho de ser madre en toda la aceptación de la palabra."*)

45 Ibid., 28, 26.

46 [Rafael Edwards], "Apuntes, observaciones y propuestas sobre el tema legislación del trabajo de los niños, de las madres y de las mujeres en cinta," in *Trabajos y Actas, Primer Congreso Nacional de Protección a la Infancia*, ed. Manuel Camilo Vial (Santiago: Imprenta Barcelona, 1913), 417. Edwards founded the Sociedad de Socorros Mutuos de Nuestra Señora del Carmen, a Church-sponsored mutual aid society primarily for seamstresses, in 1907, and later became bishop and head of Acción Social for Chile. For a translation of selections from this speech, see appendix B.

47 Edwards's program included a study commission for women's and children's work; "courts of good men" to regulate disputes between labor and capital; education for working minors and worker housing; special taxes on industry to fund charitable programs for women and children;

the creation of a fund for maternity leaves; financing for industrial education; separation of workers by age and by sex (to protect morality in the workplace); and employment of women schoolteachers as "labor inspectors." His program included no reference to day care, but limited mothers' work to fifty hours a week and called for provisions to allow them to nurse their infants (ibid., 432–33).

48 Fidel Muñoz Rodríguez, "La jornada máxima y el salario mínimo," *BOT* 7, no. 3 (1913). Muñoz Rodríguez observed that foreign legislation made few exceptions to this rule, "except for certain professions and persons, and almost exclusively, for homework and the work of minors."

49 CNCD, *Boletín de Sesiones Ordinarias*, 14 June 1907, 188.

50 Ibid., 139.

51 Ibid., 141.

52 In practice, it was impossible to enforce the Sunday Rest Law for male workers because employers took advantage of a variety of loopholes to keep men working on Sundays and those employees who complained were typically dismissed. Consequently, the fledgling Labor Office could only apply fines to those factories and stores that kept women and children at work, in flagrant defiance of the law ("Infracciones a la lei de descanso dominical," *BOT* 3 [1911]: 174–79). Recognition of the law's ineffectiveness led to a 1917 proposal, eventually approved, to make Sunday rest obligatory for all workers. See CNCS, *Boletín de Sesiones Ordinarias*, 12 September 1917, 1091–95. Unfortunately, the new law (3321, 5 November 1917) was accompanied by an executive regulation that exempted so many industries that "some have said that it would have been easier for the legislators to indicate precisely the kind of work that *would* require [Sunday] rest" (Carcovich, *Protección legal del niño y de la mujer obreros*, 60).

53 Once again, the commission in charge of social legislation in the Chamber of Deputies, "desiring to facilitate the study and passage of the law," chose to separate the question of women's and children's work from the other issues brought to the commission by Malaquías Concha: factory health and safety, hour limits, and accident insurance. See CNCD, *Boletín de Sesiones Extraordinarias*, 1907–1908, 28 January 1908, 1840; "En bien de los obreros," 12.

54 CNCS, *Boletín de Sesiones Extraordinarias*, 1907–1908, 1 February 1908, 1753. This clause apparently ignored a drawback earlier highlighted in an *El Chileno* editorial on preliminary drafts of the legislation, in which the author supported the legislation but objected that "it is also unacceptable that children and men of any age are employed in jobs that are contrary to good customs" ("Legislación obrera," *El Chileno*, 17 August 1907).

55 CNCD, *Boletín de Sesiones Extraordinarias*, 1907–1908, 29 January 1908, 1419.

56 Ultimately, Malaquías Concha and Juan Luís Sanfuentes got the same legislation approved for state-owned businesses in 1917: "Until a law is passed that obliges the factories to take steps to protect their workers, the State should encourage private industries to adopt these precautions by its own example" ("Decreto del Ministerio de Ferrocarriles sobre jornada de trabajo i salubridad en los talleres de los Ferrocarriles del Estado," *BOT* 8, no. 11 [1918]: 135–37).

57 CNCD, *Boletín de Sesiones Extraordinarias* 1916–1917, 14 December 1916, 297.

58 CNCD, *Boletín de Sesiones Extraordinarias*, 1916–1917, 22 December 1916, 1163.

59 Ibid., 1161. One deputy observed that the problem with the proposed law was that it obviated the need for broader legislation to address the needs of working women, not just pregnant women and mothers. In response, Interior Minister Zañartu of the working commission responded that they could not afford to make infinite amendments on the proposed law, lest they "manage to convert it into a whole project, or into a labor code for women."

60 Ibid., 1165.

61 This is also the fundamental assumption that distinguishes the French and U.S. models of welfare provision to workers. French and Chilean legislators alike accepted the fact of working motherhood, and sought primarily to ameliorate the effects of their work through maternity leave and other protective measures. Court rulings in the United States, by contrast, established the intrinsic differences between men and women in the workplace, which led to a "two-channel" approach that granted labor protections to male workers and mothers' aid to women. See Barbara J. Nelson, "The Origins of the Two-Channel Welfare State: Workmen's Compensation and Mothers' Aid," in *Women, the State and Welfare*, ed. Linda Gordon (Madison: University of Wisconsin Press, 1990), 123–51, and Jenson, "Representations of Gender."

62 CNCD, *Boletín de Sesiones Extraordinarias*, 1916–1917, 22 December 1916, 1167, 1169.

63 Another version of the proposed legislation also included dairies, bakeries, sweet shops, restaurants, flower shops, hotel restaurants, and other food service establishments (ADGT, *Estudios y Trabajos*, 1917, vol. 36, study of *descanso quincenal*).

64 This listing is drawn from an unsympathetic review of the law (because it gave Sunday rest to too many workers) appearing in "Descanso dominical: Proyecto de reglamento," *El Mercurio*, 21 February 1909.

65 "Proyecto de lei modificando la lei de salas cunas," *BOT* 14, no. 22

(1924): 246–51; "Sinopsis de las inspecciones hechas en el año 1925 en Santiago," *BOT* 16, no. 24 (1926): 142.

66 Rojas, *La dictadura de Ibañez.*

67 Morris, *Elites,* 119–43.

68 Ibid., 208–11.

69 Francisco Walker Linares, introduction to *Veinte años de legislación social* by Dirección General de Estadística (Santiago: Imprenta y Litografía Universo, S.A., 1945). Labor Office officials were closely involved in the development of this proposal, and dedicated a special issue of the Labor Office bulletin to it: "Proyecto de Código del Trabajo," *BOT* 11, no. 17 (1921).

70 Poblete Troncoso's 1913 law thesis was on the subject of illegitimate children, and he supervised Elena Caffarena's 1926 law thesis on homeworkers, for example.

71 "Proyecto de Código del Trabajo"; emphasis added.

72 The rising interest in the area of social legislation here is demonstrated by the title of the Liberal Alliance proposal, which was the same as Malaquías Concha's 1907 law thesis.

73 Lorenzo Sazie Herrera, *La maternidad obrera* (Santiago: Imprenta La Ilustración, 1924), 38.

74 CNCS, *Boletín de Sesiones Extraordinarias,* 1920–1921, 4 November 1920, 344.

75 M., "Trabajo a domicilio," *El Diario Ilustrado,* 11 January 1921. This was also Roxane's assessment in 1928: "By nature they are individualistic and ignorant of the concept of solidarity" ("Un salario igualitario para la mujer obrera," *El Mercurio,* 11 April 1926).

76 "Reglamentación del trabajo a domicilio," *El Mercurio,* 29 October 1921.

77 "La Gran Convención Local de los Obreros en Calzado," *La Federación Obrera,* 21 November 1921.

78 "The signatory senators believe that the law should broadly protect women and children, taking sex, age, the nature of the work and their weaknesses into account"; signed by Aldúnate Solar and others (ADGT, *Sección Internacional. Comunicaciones enviadas,* 1921, vol. 77, Legislative proposal for labor contracts, professional associations, etc., presented to the Congress, 4 February 1921).

79 Alberto Hurtado Cruchaga also noted that this structure was based on the Argentine model. See *El trabajo a domicilio* (Santiago: Imprenta "El Globo," 1923), 49, 55.

80 Ibid., 49.

81 Ibid., 50–51.

82 Moisés Poblete Troncoso, "Los organismos técnicos del trabajo," *BOT* 13, no. 20 (1923): 119.

83 P. Aguirre Cerda, "Proyecto sobre el trabajo de las mujeres," *BOT* 13, no. 21 (1923): 267–71.

84 Even after a thorough examination of diaries, political correspondence, and the congressional record, Morris appears to be at a loss: "Much of what happened is clear; why it happened as it did is not so clear" (*Elites*, 235).

85 According to Charles W. Bergquist, the military version of the Labor Code combined the most coercive elements of each proposal. See *Labor in Latin America: Comparative Essays on Chile, Argentina, Venezuela, and Colombia* (Stanford, CA: Stanford University Press, 1986), 67.

86 Based on author's review of the ADGT, 1925–1931.

87 Juan Sireden Gana, *La Ley No. 4054* (Santiago: Universidad de Chile, Facultad de Derecho, 1925).

88 Flora Meneses Zuñiga, *La Ley 4054 de Seguro Obligatorio de Enfermidad, Vejez e Invalidez* (Santiago: Carrera, 1936).

89 "Protective Legislation for Working Women in Chile," *Monthly Labor Review* 25 (1927): 297–98.

90 CNCD, *Boletín de Sesiones Ordinarias*, 20 June 1928, 279–81. Sepúlveda also notes in closing that homeworkers lack insurance, "and so these women are left in total abandonment."

91 CNCD, *Boletín de Sesiones Ordinarias*, 6 August 1928, 758–60.

92 CNCD, *Boletín de Sesiones Ordinarias*, 12 September 1928, 1319.

93 Ibid., 1322.

94 The Office for the Inspection of Home Work (Inspección de Trabajo a Domicilio) was not created until 1934 (Dirección General de Estadística, *Veinte Años*).

95 Arturo Rebolledo Figueroa, *La organización de los servicios de Inspección del Trabajo, especialmente en Chile* (Santiago: Imprenta "Roma," 1948), 63–77.

96 "El trabajo de las mujeres y de los niños," *El Mercurio*, 23 April 1921. Interview with Eduardo Schmidt, Labor Office inspector, and Dr. Rolando of the General Health Office.

97 ADGT, *Inspección General del Trabajo: Informes varios*, 1931, vol. 277, Labor Office Director Thomas Lawrence orders closer regulation of women's salaries, 24 February 1931.

98 ADGT, *Accidentes del Trabajo: Notas recibidas*, 1918, vol. 47, letter from Luís Carcovich to the Labor Office, 22 May 1918. In the same year, Carcovich authored *Protección legal del niño y de la mujer obrera*. Labor Office inspector Caupolicán Ponce reported the establishment of Valparaíso's first factory day care service in 1925 (ADGT, *Varios*, 1925, vol. III, report of Valparaíso inspector to Labor Office, 19 November 1925).

99 Petitions sent to the Labor Office requested information on the industrial day care law: ADGT, *Comunicaciones recibidas del interior (I)*, 1921,

vol. 70, letter from Sociedad Fábrica Nacional de Vidrios, 27 April 1921; ADGT, *Varios*, 1923, vol. 94, letter from Compañia Chilena de Tabacos, 11 May 1923; and Labor Office letters to Ministry of Interior, 29 October 1923.

At times, the industrialists showed surprising frankness with the supposed regulators of social legislation; in 1925, the owners of the Santiago Clothing Factory reported that it was reducing the number of adult female employees from twenty-three to twenty to avoid having the day care law applied to them, claiming they didn't have enough space in their factory (ADGT, *Varios*, 1925, vol. 1114, Santiago Factory letter to the Labor Office, 16 November 1925).

100 The 179 factories visited reportedly represented one-fifth of the nine hundred registered factories in Santiago and contained almost half of Santiago's factory workers (13,858 out of 29,869).

101 Eduardo Schmidt Quezada, "Informe del Jefe de la Inspección del Trabajo," *BOT* 13, no. 21 (1923): 100, 101. Out of 7,485 total workers, 3,945 women labored in 100 of the total 179 factories inspected. On this point, officials observed, "At first glance, it seems impossible that there could be more women than men working in these particular 100 factories, but it is certain that the clothing workshops, and corset, weaving, shoe, cigarette factories, which are industries of greater capital, occupy more women than men; and since these are the most developed factories in Santiago, there is a greater quantity of women workers" (97).

102 Juan Cañepa, "Informe sobre la previsión social en las fábricas," *BOT* 13, no. 21 (1923): 90–91.

103 ADGT, *Varios*, 1925, vol. 1114, silk factory workers petition Labor Office, 25 November 1925.

104 ADGT, *Dirección General del Trabajo. Varios*, 1925, vol. 111, report from Inspector to Labor Office, 19 November 1925.

105 "Que se fije salario mínimo al trabajo a domicilio," *El Mercurio*, 27 June 1928.

106 ADGT, *Archivo 401–600*, 1928, vol. 169, letter from Ministry of Social Welfare, 6 March 1928.

107 The letter expressed particular interest in the enforcement of minimum wages and working conditions: ADGT, *Inspección General del Trabajo. Archivo*, 1928, vol. 172, letter to head of Argentine office, 21 July 1928.

108 In August 1928, the Inspección Femenina requested a list of these factories from the Ministry of Social Welfare and issued a circular to them that requested "a list of maximum and minimum wages . . . for each kind of work done by the piece or by the day paid to homeworkers, treating the men separately from the women" (ADGT, *Inspección General del Trabajo. Circulares 1–86*, 1928–1929, vol. 180, letter and circular from Women's Inspection Team, 3 and 5 September 1928.

109 See "Informe de las Inspectoras del Trabajo Srtas. Santa Cruz y Caf-

farena al Ministro del Trabajo y de la Previsión Social," *BOT* 16, no. 24 (1926): 200–206.

110 Interview with Elena Caffarena, Santiago, 22 June 1993.

111 Roxane, "Carta de Roxane," *El Mercurio*, 10 June 1925.

112 ADGT, *Varios*, 1925, vol. III, judicial section report to Labor Office director, November 1925.

113 ADGT, *Varios*, 1925, vol. III, report from women inspectors, 18 November 1925.

114 Ibid., 202. They complained that conditions were bad overall, but "tailoring, lingerie, fashion and weaving workshops in the back rooms and basements of the stores downtown," where many women worked, were the worst.

115 Ibid., 204.

116 Ibid.

117 Roxane, "Un salario igualitario para la mujer obrera." Roxane recounts here how a callous theater owner, in response to an actress who complained about her low wages, suggested, "You still have the intermissions."

118 Corinne Antezana-Pernet, "Mobilizing Women in the Popular Front Era: Feminism, Class, and Politics in the Movimiento Pro-Emancipación de la Mujer Chilena (MEMCh), 1935–1950" (Ph.D. diss., University of California at Irvine, 1996).

119 Asunción Lavrin, *Women, Feminism, and Social Change in Argentina, Chile, and Uruguay, 1890–1940* (Lincoln: University of Nebraska Press, 1995), 75–84.

120 Gordon, *Women, the State and Welfare*, 11.

Conclusion: Women, Work, and Historical Change

1 The historical literature on liberal feminism in Chile is relatively vast; see introduction, nn. 19, 20.

2 Fewer than 10 percent of economically active women were employed in white-collar jobs in 1907. Female employment in white-collar jobs increased slightly by 1930, principally through the feminization of the teaching and medical professions. White-collar jobs came to represent 22 percent of female occupations by 1930, but this proportion reflected the apparently dramatic decline in women's industrial employment, particularly in the clothing industry, more than a huge expansion in white-collar work for women (*Censo* 1907, 1299–1300; 1930, xvii).

3 Bedel, "Tendencias femeninas," *La Unión*, 6 July 1911, 3.

4 On definitions of feminism, Roxane summed up what she thought were the "natural" origins of her position: "Feminism is a philosophy of life elaborated by women . . . a tendency to improve women's social

position. . . . So that feminine or feminist can mean the same thing, we must suppose that no woman is currently indifferent to the grave problems that agitate humanity. Is being a feminist perhaps incompatible with being feminine?" ("Femeninas y feministas," *El Mercurio*, 8 July 1923).

5 Roxane, "Feminismo económico y criollo," *El Mercurio*, 29 July 1924, 3.

6 Although urban, educated women who mobilized for social reform in Latin America after the turn of the century regularly called for equal pay for equal work, their comprehensive plans for social transformation typically prioritized struggles for women's civil and political rights and stressed the emancipatory effects of female employment. See Susan K. Besse, *Restructuring Patriarchy: The Modernization of Gender Inequality in Brazil, 1914–1940* (Chapel Hill: University of North Carolina Press, 1996), Asunción Lavrin, *Women, Feminism, and Social Change in Argentina, Chile, and Uruguay, 1890–1940* (Lincoln: University of Nebraska Press, 1995), chap. 1; Francesca Miller, *Latin American Women and the Search for Social Justice* (Hanover, NH: University Press of New England, 1991), chaps. 3–5. Further research on the topic of liberal feminism in Chile might explore how this was also an instance of "mixed feminism," because liberal feminists—like socialist and Catholic feminists—combined pro-woman goals with the content and structure of their own class- and politically based objectives.

7 Heidi Tinsman, "Rethinking Gender, Dictatorship, and Neoliberalism: Temporary Fruit Workers in Pinochet's Chile," *Signs* (forthcoming); Susan Tiano, *Patriarchy on the Line: Labor, Gender, and Ideology in the Mexican Maquila Industry* (Philadelphia: Temple University Press, 1994).

8 Nicolas Stargardt argues likewise that German workers' movements were built on the paradox of simultaneous support for women's individual rights and support for the patriarchal model of the working-class family. In the German case, this tension was worked out by allowing female participation under close male tutelage. See Stargardt, "Male Bonding and the Class Struggle in Imperial Germany," *Historical Journal* 38, no. 1 (1995): 187–93.

9 Deborah Levenson-Estrada, "The Loneliness of Working-Class Feminism: Women in the 'Male World' of Labor Unions, Guatemala City, 1970s," in *The Gendered Worlds of Women Workers: From Household and Factory to the Union Hall and Ballot Box*, ed. John D. French and Daniel James (Durham, NC: Duke University Press, 1997), 224.

10 Besse, *Restructuring Patriarchy*.

11 See Thomas Miller Klubock, *Contested Communities: Class, Gender, and Politics in Chile's El Teniente Copper Mine, 1904–1951* (Durham, NC: Duke University Press, 1998), chap. 4; Karin Alejandra Rosemblatt, *Gendered Compromises: Political Cultures and the State in Chile,*

1920–1950 (Chapel Hill: University of North Carolina Press, 2000), chaps. 2, 4.

12 Klubock, *Contested Communities*, chaps. 1, 2; Ann Farnsworth-Alvear, *Dulcinea in the Factory: Myths, Morals, Men, and Women in Colombia's Industrial Experiment, 1905–1960* (Durham, NC: Duke University Press, 2000), chap. 6.

13 Farnsworth-Alvear, *Dulcinea in the Factory*; Klubock, *Contested Communities*; Deborah Levenson-Estrada, "The Loneliness of Working-Class Feminism"; Heidi Elizabeth Tinsman, *Partners in Conflict: The Politics of Gender, Sexuality, and Labor in the Chilean Agrarian Reform, 1950–1973* (Durham, NC: Duke University Press, forthcoming).

14 Emilia Viotti da Costa, "Experiences versus Structures: New Tendencies in the History of Labor and the Working Class in Latin America—What Do We Gain? What Do We Lose?" *International Labor and Working-Class History* 36 (fall 1989): 3–24.

15 See the recent studies of Servicio Nacional de la Mujer (SERNAM) and family policy in the 1990s, including Lisa Baldez "La política partidista y los límites del feminismo de Estado en Chile," in *El modelo Chileno: Democracia y desarrollo en los noventa*, ed. Paul Drake and Iván Jaksic (Santiago: LOM Ediciones, 1999), 407–29; Kemy Oyarzún, "La familia: Metáfora de vacíos sistémicos. Género, modernización y cambio cultural, Chile, 1990–1999," paper delivered at the conference "Chile: A Model Country," University of California, San Diego, 10–12 December 1998.

Bibliography

Archives

Santiago. Archivo Nacional de Chile. Records of the Dirección General del Trabajo. 1906–1930.
Santiago. Archivo Nacional de Chile. Records of the Ministerio de Industria y Obras Públicas. 1887–1911.

Government Documents

República de Chile. Comisión Central del Censo. *Censo de la República de Chile levantado el 28 de noviembre de 1907.* Santiago: "Imprenta y Litografía Universo," 1908.
———. Comisión Central del Censo. *Resultados del X censo de la población efectuado el 27 de noviembre de 1930.* 2 vols. Santiago: Imprenta Universo, 1931–1935.
———. Congreso Nacional. Cámara de Diputados and Senadores. *Boletín de Sesiones Ordinarias* and *Extraordinarias.* Santiago: Imprenta Nacional, 1900–1930.
———. Dirección de Estadística. *Censo de población de la República de Chile levantado el 15 de diciembre, 1920.* Santiago: Imprenta y Litografía Universo, 1925.
———. Dirección General de Estadística. *Sinopsis estadística i jeográfica.* Santiago: Imprenta y Encuadernación Universitaria, 1902–1907.
———. Dirección General de Estadística. *Veinte años de legislación social.* Santiago: Imprenta y Litografía Universo, 1945.
———. Ministerio de Industrias i Obras Públicas and Sociedad de Fomento Fabril. *Estadística industrial de la República de Chile correspondiente al año 1909.* Santiago, 1910.
———. Oficina Central de estadística. *Anuario estadístico de la República de Chile.* Santiago: Sociedad Imprenta y Litografía Universo, 1909–1925.
———. Oficina Central de Estadística. *Sesto censo jeneral de la población de Chile levantado el 26 de noviembre de 1885.* Valparaíso: Impr. de "La Patria," 1889–1890.

———. Oficina Central de Estadística. *Sétimo censo jeneral de la población de Chile levantado el 28 de noviembre de 1895.* 2 vols. Valparaíso: Imprenta del Universo de Guillermo Helfman, 1900–1904.

———. Oficina del Trabajo. *Boletín de la Oficina de Trabajo* (after 1925 called *Boletín de la Dirección General del Trabajo*). Santiago: Imprenta Santiago, 1906–1927.

———. Oficina del Trabajo. *Estadística de la asociación obrera.* Santiago: Imprenta i Litografía Santiago, 1910.

Daily and Labor Newspapers

(All newspapers Santiago unless otherwise indicated.)
Acción Católica, 1916–1924.
Acción Directa, 1920–1927.
Acción Obrera, 1916.
El Acrata, 1900–1901.
Actualidades, 1908.
Adelanto Local, 1924.
La Aguja (Valparaíso), 1912, 1924–1925.
La Ajitación, 1902.
El Alba, 1905–1906.
La Antorcha, 1921.
La Aurora Feminista, 1904.
La Bandera Roja, 1919.
La Batalla, 1912–1915; (Valparaíso) 1919, 1922, 1924.
Boletín Oficial, Federación de Obreros de Imprenta (Valparaíso), 1922.
Boletín Oficial de Obreros y Obreras en Calzado, Reorganizado (Valparaíso), 1922.
Boletín de los Trabajadores Industriales del Mundo, 1920
La Causa Viñamarina (Viña del Mar), 1923.
El Chileno, 1883–1924.
Ciencia y Trabajo, 1915.
El Clarín, 1924.
El Comunista, 1921–1923.
El Correo, 1925.
La Defensa Gráfica, 1914.
La Democracia, 1902–1927.
El Despertar de los Tranviarios, 1922.
El Diario Ilustrado, 1902–1927.
El Diario Popular, 1902–1909.
La Doctrina Demócrata, 1924.
El Eco del Empleado, 1914.
La Epoca, 1907–1910.

La Federación Obrera, 1921–1924.
La Federación de Obreros de Imprenta, 1918–1919.
La Gran Federación Obrera, 1911–1913.
Hoja del Hogar, 1913.
Horizontes Nuevos, 1922–1925.
La Imprenta, 1902–1904.
Jerminal!, 1904.
La Justicia, 1924–1927.
La Ley, 1894–1910.
El Luchador, 1901–1907.
La Luz, 1901–1903, 1904, 1914.
La Luz (Valparaíso), 1922.
Luz y Defensa, 1914.
Luz al Obrero, 1911.
Luz y Vida, 1911.
El Martillo (Valparaíso), 1902.
El Mercurio, 1900–1930.
La Mujer, 1921.
La Nación, 1906, 1909, 1913–1914, 1917–1927.
Lo Nuevo. (Valparaíso) 1902–1903.
Los Nuevos Horizontes, 1903–1904.
Numen (Valparaíso/Santiago), 1919–1920.
La Obrera Sindicada, 1917.
El Obrero en Calzado, 1919–1923.
El Obrero en Dulce, 1926.
El Obrero Gráfico, 1908.
El Obrero Ilustrado, 1906–1907, 1921.
La Opinión, 1915–1920.
El Oprimido, 1906.
El Panificador, 1918.
El Porvenir, 1892–1906.
El Productor, 1910–1913.
La Protesta, 1908–1912, 1924.
La Reforma, 1906–1908, 1923, 1924.
La Revuelta, 1903.
El Siglo XX, 1900–1903.
La Sindicada, 1922–1926.
La Sindicada Católica, 1915–1918.
El Socialista, 1901–1902, 1908, 1909, 1913, 1915.
El Socialista (Valparaíso), 1915–1918.
El Surco, 1924.
El Trabajo, 1910–1911, 1921–1928.
El Trabajo (Valparaíso), 1905.
La Unión, 1908–1920.

La Unión Femenina, 1926–1927.
La Vanguardia Demócrata, 1924.
La Voz del Empleado, 1917, 1921.

Journals

Acción Femenina, 1922–1930.
La Alborada (Valparaíso/Santiago), 1905–1907.
Boletín del Consejo Superior de Hijiene Pública, 1906.
Boletín de Higiene y Demografía, 1898.
Boletín Municipal de Estadística, 1908.
Boletín de la Sociedad de Fomento Fabril, 1884–1927.
La Familia, 1910–1928.
Pacífico Magazine, 1913–1921.
La Palanca, 1908.
Revista de Bibliografía Chilena y Extranjera, 1913–1918.
Revista Chilena, 1917–1930.
Revista Chilena de Higiene, 1901.
Revista del Centro Industrial y Agrícola, 1900–1901.
Revista de la Habitación, 1920–1927.
Revista Industrial Femenina, 1912–1914.
La Tribuna Libre, 1910.
Zig-Zag, 1905.

Published Primary Sources

Actividades femeninas en Chile. Santiago: Imprenta y Litografía La Ilustración, 1928.
Arteaga Infante, Claudio. *Observaciones sobre la cuestión social chilena*. Santiago: Imprenta Universitaria, 1920.
Belén de Sárraga. *El clericalismo en América*. Lisbon: Tip. José Assis and Coelho Dias, 1915.
——. *Conferencias*. Santiago: Imprenta Victoria, 1913.
Bravo Cisternas, Agustín. *La mujer a través de los siglos: Historia de lo más importante que la mujer ha realizado en el mundo y reformas de que deben venir en pro de ella*. Valparaíso: Imprenta El Progreso, 1903.
Carcovich, Luís. *Protección legal del niño y de la mujer obrera*. Valparaíso: Imprenta Lillo, 1918.
Carriego, Evaristo. *La costurerita que dió aquel mal paso y otros poemas*. Buenos Aires: Torres Agüero Editor, 1977.
Chaughi, Rene. *La mujer esclava*. Santiago: Editorial La Alborada, 1921.

Congreso Mariano Femenino. Santiago: Escuela Tipografía "La Gratitud Nacional," 1918.

Croizet, Doctor E. *Lucha social contra la mortalidad infantil en el periodo de lactancia.* Santiago: Litografía i Encuadernación Barcelona, 1912.

Cruzat, Ximena, and Eduardo Devés, eds., *Recabarren: Escritos de prensa, 1898–1924.* 4 vols. Santiago: Terranova Editores, 1987.

Cursos rápidos, para Señoras y Señoritas, internado para alumnas de provincias. Santiago: Academia Industrial Tejidos a Máquina "Rasco," n.d.

Díaz, Ramón Angel. *Del trabajo de las mujeres y los niños en la industria.* Santiago: Imprenta y Litografía "Santiago," 1910.

Errázuriz Tagle, Jorge, and Guillermo Eyzaguirre Rouse. *Monografía de una familia obrera de Santiago.* Santiago: Imprenta Barcelona, 1903.

González von Marees, Jorge. *El problema obrero en Chile.* Santiago: Imprenta Universitaria, 1923.

Hermosillo Aedo, Amanda. *La mujer en la vida económica.* Santiago: Imprenta Universo, 1938.

Hurtado Cruchaga, Alberto. *El trabajo a domicilio.* Santiago: Imprenta "El Globo," 1923.

Ibañez, Carlos. "El ahorro." In *Conferencias dadas en el año 1902.* Santiago: Imprenta Universitaria, 1902.

López, Osvaldo. *Diccionario biográfico obrero*, vol. 2. Santiago: Bellavista, 1912.

Memoria de la Cruz Blanca. Santiago: Palacios, 1929.

Meneses Zuñiga, Flora. *La Ley 4054 de Seguro Obligatorio de Enfermedad, Vejez e Invalidez.* Santiago: Carrera, 1936.

Perrin, Sara, "La mujer en las industrias." In *Actividades femeninas en Chile,* 643–64.

Poblete Poblete, Olga. *Una mujer: Elena Caffarena.* Santiago: Cuarto Propio, 1993.

Poblete Troncoso, Moisés. *La organización sindical en Chile y otros estudios sociales.* Santiago: Ramón Brías, 1926.

Poblete Troncoso, Moisés, and Oscar Alvarez Andrews. *Legislación social obrera Chilena.* Santiago: Imprenta Santiago, 1924.

Prunés R., Luís. *La prostitución: Evolución de su concepto hasta nuestros días. El neo-abolicionismo ante el nuevo Código Sanitario de Chile.* Santiago: Imprenta Universo, 1926.

Recabarren, Luís Emilio. *La mujer y su educación.* Punta Arenas: Imprenta de "El Socialista," 1916.

——. *Recabarren: Escritos de prensa 1898–1924.* Ed. Ximena Cruzat and Eduardo Devés. 4 vols. Santiago: Terranova Editores, 1987.

——. "La Rusia obrera y campesina." In *Luís Emilio Recabarren: Obras escogidas,* ed. Julio César Jobet. Santiago: Editorial Recabarren, 1965.

Santiván, F. "La mujer que trabaja." *Pacífico Magazine* (March 1913): 386–96.

Sazie Herrera, Lorenzo. *La maternidad obrera*. Santiago: Imprenta La Ilustración, 1924.

Sireden Gana, Juan. *La Ley No. 4054*. Santiago: Universidad de Chile, Facultad de Derecho, 1925.

Smith, Carmen. *Mis memorias*. Santiago: Imprenta El Imparcial, 1936.

Subercaseaux, Elvira L. de *Estudios Sociales: Trabajos leídos por señoras de la Liga de Damas Chilenas, en el Curso de Estudios Sociales*. Santiago: Imprenta Chile, 1916.

Vial, Manuel Camilo, ed. *Trabajos y Actas, Primer Congreso Nacional de Protección a la Infancia*. Santiago: Imprenta Barcelona, 1913.

Zouroff, Vera. *Feminismo obrero*. Ministerio de Trabajo, Cuadernos de la Cultura Obrera, Serie D. Santiago: Imprenta El Esfuerzo, 1933.

Secondary Sources

Ackelsberg, Martha A. *Free Women of Spain: Anarchism and the Struggle for the Emancipation of Women*. Bloomington: Indiana University Press, 1991.

Alvarez Andrews, Oscar. *Historia del desarrollo industrial de Chile*. Santiago: Imprenta y Litografía la Ilustración, 1936.

Angell, Alan. *Politics and the Labour Movement in Chile*. London: Oxford University Press, 1972.

Antezana-Pernet, Corinne A. "Mobilizing Women in the Popular Front Era: Feminism, Class, and Politics in the Movimiento Pro-Emancipación de la Mujer Chilena (MEMCh), 1935–1950." Ph.D. diss, University of California at Irvine, 1996.

——. *Movilización femenina en la época del frente popular: Feminismo, clases sociales y política en el Movimiento Pro-Emancipación de las Mujeres Chilenas (MEMCH), 1935–1950*. Trans. Ana María Ortuondo Fernández. Santiago: n.p., 1997.

Arias Escobedo, Osvaldo. *La prensa obrera en Chile*. Chillán: Universidad de Chile, 1970.

Arrom, Sylvia. *The Women of Mexico City, 1790–1857*. Stanford, CA: Stanford University Press, 1985.

Barrancos, Dora. *Anarquismo, educación y costumbres en la Argentina de principios de siglo*. Buenos Aires: Editorial Contrapunto, 1990.

Barría Serón, Jorge. *Los movimientos sociales en Chile, 1910–1926*. Santiago: Ed. Universitaria, 1960.

Bauer, Arnold. *Chilean Rural Society from the Spanish Conquest to 1930*. Cambridge, England: Cambridge University Press, 1975.

Bergquist, Charles. *Labor in Latin America: Comparative Essays on Chile, Argentina, Venezuela and Colombia*. Palo Alto, CA: Stanford University Press, 1986.

Besse, Susan. *Restructuring Patriarchy: The Modernization of Gender In-*

equality in Brazil, 1914–1940. Chapel Hill: University of North Carolina Press, 1996.

Breslin, Patrick Edward. "The Development of Class Consciousness in the Chilean Working Class." Ph.D. diss., University of California at Los Angeles, 1980.

Brito, Alejandra. "Del rancho al conventillo: transformaciones en la identidad popular femenina, Santiago de Chile, 1850–1920." In *Disciplina y desacato: Construcción de identidad en Chile, siglos XIX y XX*, ed. Lorena Godoy Catalán, Elizabeth Hutchison, Karin Rosemblatt, and Soledad Zárate. Santiago: SUR-CEDEM, 1995.

Conte Corvalán, Rebeca. "La mutualidad femenina: Una visión social de la mujer Chilena, 1888–1930." Thesis, University of Chile, 1987.

Covarrubias, Paz. "El movimiento feminista chileno." In *Chile Mujer y Sociedad*, ed. Covarrubias and Rolando Franco. Santiago: UNICEF, 1978.

DeShazo, Peter. *Urban Workers and Labor Unions in Chile, 1902–1927.* Madison: University of Wisconsin Press, 1983.

Deutsch, Sandra McGee. *Las Derechas: The Extreme Right in Argentina, Brazil, and Chile, 1890–1939.* Stanford, CA: Stanford University Press, 1999.

——. "Gender and Sociopolitical Chance in Twentieth-Century Latin America." *Hispanic American Historical Review* 71, no. 2 (1991): 259–306.

Drake, Paul. *Socialism and Populism in Chile, 1932–52.* Urbana: University of Illinois Press, 1978.

Ehrick, Christine Theresa. "Obrera, Dama, Feminista: Women's Associations and the Welfare State in Uruguay, 1900–1932." Ph.D. diss., University of California at Los Angeles, 1997.

Espinoza, Vicente. *Para una historia de los pobres de la ciudad.* Santiago: SUR, 1988.

Farnsworth-Alvear, Ann. *Dulcinea in the Factory: Myths, Morals, Men and Women in Colombia's Industrial Experiment, 1905–1960.* Durham, NC: Duke University Press, 2000.

——. "The Mysterious Case of the Missing Men: Gender and Class in Early Industrial Medellín." *International Labor and Working-Class History* 49 (spring 1996): 73–92.

Faue, Elizabeth. *Community of Suffering and Struggle: Women, Men and the Labor Movement in Minneapolis, 1915–1945.* Chapel Hill: University of North Carolina Press, 1991.

——. "Paths of Unionization: Community, Bureaucracy, and Gender in the Minneapolis Labor Movement of the 1930s." In *Work Engendered: Toward a New History of American Labor*, ed. Ava Baron. 296–319. Ithaca, NY: Cornell University Press, 1991.

Fernandez-Kelly, María Patricia. *For We Are Sold, I and My People: Women and Industry in Mexico's Frontier.* Albany: State University of New York Press, 1980.

Finn, Janet L. *Tracing the Veins: Of Copper, Culture, and Community from Butte to Chuquicamata*. Berkeley: University of California Press, 1998.

French, John D., and Daniel James, eds. *The Gendered Worlds of Latin American Women Workers: From Household and Factory to the Union Hall and Ballot Box*. Durham, NC: Duke University Press, 1997.

French, William E. "Prostitutes and Guardian Angels: Women, Work, and the Family in Porfirian Mexico." *Hispanic American Historical Review* 72, no. 4 (November 1992): 529–53.

Gálvez, Thelma, and Rosa Bravo. "Siete décadas de registro del trabajo femenino, 1854–1920." *Estadística y Economía* 5 (December 1992): 1–52.

Garcés Durán, Mario. *Crisis social y motines populares en el 1900*. Santiago: Ediciones Documentas, 1991.

Gaviola, Edda, Ximena Jiles Moreno, Lorella Lopresti Martínez, and Claudia Rojas Mira. "Evolución de los derechos políticos de la mujer en Chile (1913–1952)." Thesis, University of Santiago, 1985.

———. *"Queremos votar en las próximas elecciones": Historia del movimiento femenino chileno 1913–1952*. Santiago: CEM, 1986.

Gazmuri, Christián. *Testimonios de una crisis: Chile 1900–1925*. Santiago: Editorial Universitaria, 1979.

Godoy Catalán, Lorena. " 'Armas ansiosas de triunfo: Dedal, agujas, tijeras . . .': La educación profesional femenina en Chile, 1888–1912." Thesis, Universidad Católica de Chile, 1995.

Godoy Catalán, Lorena, Elizabeth Hutchison, Karin Rosemblatt, and M. Soledad Zárate, eds. *Disciplina y desacato: Construcción de identidad en Chile, siglos XIX y XX*. Santiago: SUR-CEDEM, 1995.

Góngora Escobedo, Alvaro. *La prostitución en Santiago, 1813–1931: La visión de las elites*. Santiago: DIBAM, 1994.

González Sierra, Yamandu. *Del hogar a la fábrica: Deshonra o virtud?* Montevideo: Editorial Nordan-Comunidad, 1994.

Gordon, Linda, ed. *Women, the State and Welfare*. Madison: University of Wisconsin Press, 1990.

Grez Toso, Sergio. "La huelga general de 1890." *Perspectivas* 5 (December 1990): 127–66.

———. "La mutualité aux origines du mouvement ouvrier chilien (1853–1890)." *La Revue de L'Economie Sociale* (1992): 155–83.

———. *De la "regeneración del pueblo" a la huelga general: Génesis y evolución histórica del movimiento popular en Chile (1810–1890)*. Santiago: DIBAM, 1997.

———, ed. *La "cuestión social" en Chile: Ideas y debates precursores (1804–1902). Fuentes para la historia de la República*, vol. 7. (Santiago: DIBAM, 1995).

Gross, Patricio, Armado de Ramón, and Enrique Vial. *Imagen ambiental de Santiago, 1800–1936*. Santiago: Editorial Universidad Católica de Chile, 1984.

Guy, Donna. *Sex & Danger in Buenos Aires: Prostitution, Family, and Nation in Argentina.* Lincoln: University of Nebraska Press, 1991.

——. "Women, Peonage and Industrialization: Argentina, 1810–1914." *Latin American Research Review* 16, no. 3 (1981): 65–89.

Hagerman Johnson, Ann. "The Impact of Market Agriculture on Family and Household Structure in Nineteenth-Century Chile." *Hispanic American Historical Review* 58 (November 1978): 625–48.

Hahner, June. *Emancipating the Female Sex: The Struggle for Women's Rights in Brazil, 1850–1940.* Durham, NC: Duke University Press, 1990.

——. "Women and Work in Brazil, 1850–1920: A Preliminary Investigation." In *Essays Concerning the Socioeconomic History of Brazil and Portuguese India,* ed. Davril Audin and Warren Dean. Gainesville: University Presses of Florida, 1977.

Hartmann, Heidi. "Capitalism, Patriarchy, and the Sexual Division of Labor." *Signs* 1, no. 3 (spring 1976).

Heisse González, Julio. *El Periodo Parlamentario, 1861–1925.* 3 vols. Santiago: Editorial Universitaria, 1982.

Hewitt, Nancy A. " 'The Voice of Virile Labor': Labor Militancy, Community Solidarity, and Gender Identity among Tampa's Latin Workers, 1880–1921." In *Work Engendered: Toward a New History of American Labor,* ed. Ava Baron. 296–319. Ithaca, NY: Cornell University Press, 1991.

Higgs, Edward. "Women, Occupations and Work in the Nineteenth Century Censuses." *History Workshop Journal* 23 (spring 1987): 59–80.

Hutchison, Elizabeth. "La defensa de las 'hijas del pueblo': Género y política obrera en Santiago a principios de siglo." In *Disciplina y desacato: Construcción de identidad en Chile, siglos XIX y XX,* ed. Lorena Godoy Catalán, Elizabeth Hutchison, Karin Rosemblatt, and Soledad Zárate. Santiago: SUR-CEDEM, 1995.

——. *El feminismo en el movimiento obrero chileno: La emancipacion de la mujer en la prensa obrera feminista, 1905–1908.* Santiago: FLACSO Working Paper Number 80, 1992.

——. "From *la mujer esclava* to *la mujer limón*: Anarchism and the Politics of Sexuality in Chile, 1900–1927." *Hispanic American Historical Review,* forthcoming.

——. " 'El fruto envenenado del arbol capitalista': Women Workers and the Prostitution of Labor in Urban Chile, 1896–1925." *Journal of Women's History* 9, no. 4 (winter 1998): 131–51.

——. "La historia detrás de las cifras: La evolución del censo chileno y la representación del trabajo femenino, 1895–1930." In *Historia* (Santiago) 33 (2000): 417–34.

Illanes, María Angélica. *"En el nombre del pueblo, del estado y de la ciencia (. . .)": Historia social de la salud pública, Chile 1880–1973 (Hacia una historia social del siglo XX).* Santiago: Colectivo de Atención Primaria, 1993.

Izquierdo, Gonzalo. "Octubre de 1905: Un episodio en la historia chilena." *Historia* 13 (1976): 55–96.

Kay, Cristobal. "The Development of the Chilean *Hacienda* System." In *Land and Labour in Latin America*, ed. Kenneth Duncan and Ian Rutledge. Cambridge: Cambridge University Press, 1977.

Kirkwood, Julieta. *Feminismo y participación política en Chile*. Santiago: FLACSO Working Paper Number 159, 1982.

——. *Ser política en Chile: Los nudos de la sabiduría feminista*. Santiago: Editorial Cuarto Propio, 1990.

Kirsch, Henry W. *Industrial Development in a Traditional Society: The Conflict of Entrepreneurship and Modernization in Chile*. Gainesville: University Presses of Florida, 1977.

Klimpel A., Felícitas. *La mujer, el delito y la sociedad*. Buenos Aires: El Ateneo, 1946.

——. *La mujer Chilena: El aporte femenino al progreso de Chile, 1910–1960*. Santiago: Editorial Andrés Bello, 1962.

Klubock, Thomas Miller. *Contested Communities: Class, Gender, and Politics in Chile's El Tentiente Copper Mine, 1904–1951*. Durham, NC: Duke University Press, 1996.

——. "Working-Class Masculinity, Middle-Class Morality, and Labor Politics in the Chilean Copper Mines." *Journal of Social History* 30, no. 2 (winter 1996): 435–63.

Lavrín, Asunción. "The Ideology of Feminism in the Southern Cone, 1900–1940." *Latin American Program*. Washington, DC: Wilson Center, 1986.

——. *Women, Feminism and Social Change in Argentina, Chile and Uruguay, 1890–1940*. Lincoln: University of Nebraska Press, 1995.

——. "Women, Labor and the Left: Argentina and Chile, 1890–1925." *Journal of Women's History* 1, no. 2 (fall 1989): 88–117.

Litvak, Lily. *Musa libertaria: Arte, literatura, y vida cultural del anarquismo español, 1880–1913*. Barcelona: A. Bosch, 1981.

Loveman, Brian. "Chile." In *Latin American Labor Organizations*, ed. Gerald Michael Greenfield and Sheldon L. Maram. New York: Greenwood Press, 1987.

——. *Chile: The Legacy of Hispanic Capitalism*. New York: Oxford University Press, 1979.

——. *Struggle in the Countryside. Politics and Rural Labor in Chile, 1919–1973*. Bloomington: Indiana University Press, 1976.

Miller, Francesca. *Latin American Women and the Search for Social Justice*. Hanover, NH: University Press of New England, 1991.

Molyneux, Maxine. "No God, No Boss, No Husband: Anarchist Feminism in Nineteenth-Century Argentina." *Latin American Perspectives* 13, no. 1 (winter 1986): 119–45.

Montecino, Sonia. *Madres y huachos: Alegorías del mestizaje chileno (ensayo).* Santiago: Editorial Cuarto Propio, CEDEM, 1991.

Monteón, Michael. *Chile in the Nitrate Era: The Evolution of Economic Dependence, 1880–1930.* Madison: University of Wisconsin Press, 1982.

Morris, James O. *Elites, Intellectuals, and Consensus: A Study of the Social Question and the Industrial Relations System in Chile.* Ithaca, NY: Cornell University, 1966.

Mujeres Latinoamericanas en Cifras. Santiago: Instituto de la Mujer, 1992.

Mundo de mujer: Continuidad y cambio. Santiago: CEM, 1988.

Muñoz, Juan G., Carmen Norambuena C., Luís Ortega M., and Roberto Pérez R. *La Universidad de Santiago de Chile.* Santiago: Universidad de Santiago de Chile, 1987.

Muñoz, Oscar. *Chile y su industrialización.* Santiago: CIEPLAN, 1986.

———. *Estado e industrialización en el ciclo de expansión de salitre.* Santiago: CIEPLAN, 1977.

Navarro, Marysa. "Hidden, Silent, and Anonymous: Women Workers in the Argentine Trade Union Movement." In *The World of Women's Trade Unionism,* ed. Norbert C. Soldon. Westport, CT: Greenwood Press, 1985.

Ortiz Letelier, Fernando. *El movimiento obrero en Chile, 1891–1919.* Madrid: Michay, 1985.

Palmer Trias, Monteserrat. *La ciudad jardín como modelo de crecimiento urbano: Santiago 1935–1960.* Santiago: Facultad de Arquitectura y Bellas Artes de la Universidad Católica de Chile, 1987.

Pardo, Lucia. *La historia laboral de las mujeres y su efecto en la tasa de salario: Una interpretación de la evidencia.* Santiago: Universidad de Chile, 1986.

———. "Una revisión histórica a la participación de la población en la fuerza de trabajo: Tendencias y características de la participación de la mujer." *Estudios de Economía* 15, no. 1 (April 1988): 25–82.

Pizarro, Crisostomo. *La huelga obrera en Chile.* Santiago: SUR, 1971.

Poblete Poblete, Olga. *Una mujer: Elena Caffarena.* Santiago: Cuarto Propio, 1993.

Poblete Troncoso, Moisés. *La organización sindical en Chile y otros estudios sociales.* Santiago: Imprenta Ramón Brías, 1926.

Poblete Troncoso, Moisés, and Ben G. Burnett. *The Rise of the Latin American Labor Movement.* New York: Bookman Associates, 1960.

Rago, Maragareth. *Os prazeres da noite: Prostitucão e codigos da sexualidade femenina em São Paulo, 1890–1930.* Rio de Janeiro: Paz and Terra, 1991.

Ramón, Armando de. *Santiago de Chile (1540–1991): Historia de una sociedad urbana.* Madrid: Editorial Mapfre, 1992.

Ramón, Armando de, and Patricio Gross. "Algunos testimonios de las condiciones de vida en Santiago de Chile: 1888–1918." *EURE (Revista Latinoamericana de Estudios Urbanos Regionales)* 11, no. 31 (October 1984): 67–74.

Ramos, Julio, ed. *Amor y anarquía: Los escritos de Luisa Capetillo.* Río Piedras, Puerto Rico: Ediciones Huracán, 1992.

Rebolledo Figueroa, Arturo. *La organización de los servicios de Inspección del Trabajo, especialmente en Chile.* Santiago: Imprenta "Roma," 1948.

Rojas Flores, Jorge. *La dictadura de Ibáñez y los sindicatos (1927–1931).* Santiago: DIBAM, 1993.

———. *Los niños cristaleros: Trabajo infantil de la industria. Chile, 1880–1950.* Santiago: DIBAM, 1996.

Romero, Luís Alberto. "Condiciones de vida de los sectores populares en Santiago de Chile, 1840–1895: Vivienda y salud." *Nueva Historia* 3, no. 9 (1984): 3–86.

———. "Los sectores populares en las ciudades latinoamericanas del siglo XIX: La cuestión de la identidad." *Desarollo Económico* 27, no. 106 (July–September 1987): 201–22.

———. *La Sociedad de Igualdad: Los artesanos de Santiago de Chile y sus primeras experiencias políticas, 1820–1851.* Buenos Aires: Instituto Di Tella, 1984.

———. "Urbanización y sectores populares: Santiago de Chile, 1830–1875." *EURE (Revista Latinoamericana de Estudios Urbanos Regionales)* 7, no. 31 (October 1984): 55–66.

Salazar Vergara, Gabriel. *Labradores, peones y proletarios: Formación y crisis de la sociedad popular chilena del siglo XIX.* Santiago: SUR, 1985.

———. "La mujer de 'bajo pueblo' en Chile: Bosquejo histórico." *Proposiciones* 21 (December 1992): 89–107.

Salinas Alvarez, Cecilia. "Antecedentes del movimiento femenino en Chile: Tres precursoras (1900–1907)." *Cuadernos del Instituto de Ciencias Alejandro Lipschutz* 4 (March 1986): 8–11.

———. *La mujer proletaria: Una historia para contar.* Santiago: Literatura América Reunida, 1987.

Santa Cruz, Lucia, Teresa Pereira, Isabel Zegers, and Valeria Maino. *Tres ensayos sobre la mujer chilena, siglos XVIII–XIX–XX.* Santiago: Editorial Universitaria, 1978.

Schell, Patience Alexander. "Educating the Children of the Revolution." D. Phil. diss., Oxford University, 1998.

———. "An Honourable Avocation for Ladies: The Work of the Mexico City Unión de Damas Católicas Mexicanas, 1912–1926." *Journal of Women's History* 10, no. 4 (winter 1999): 78–103.

Scott, Joan Wallach. *Gender and the Politics of History.* New York: Columbia University Press, 1988.

Silva Donoso, María de la Luz. *La participación política de la mujer en Chile: Las organizaciones de mujeres.* Buenos Aires: Fundación Friedrich Naumann, 1987.

Sousa Lobo, Elisabeth. "El trabajo como lenguaje: El género en el trabajo."

In *Mujeres y trabajo en América Latina*, ed. Nea Filgueira. 13–26. Madrid: GRECMU, 1993.

Solberg, Carl. *Immigration and Nationalism: Argentina and Chile, 1890–1914*. Austin: University of Texas Press, 1970.

Stansell, Christine. *City of Women: Sex and Class in New York, 1789–1860*. Urbana: University of Illinois Press, 1987.

Stargardt, Nicolas. "Male Bonding and the Class Struggle in Imperial Germany." *Historical Journal* 38, no. 1 (1995): 175–93.

Stoner, K. Lynn. *From the House to the Streets: The Cuban Woman's Movement for Legal Reform, 1898–1940*. Durham, NC: Duke University Press, 1991.

Tinsman, Heidi. "Los patrones del hogar: Esposas golpeadas y control sexual en Chile rural, 1958–1988." In *Disciplina y desacato: Construccion de identidad en Chile, siglos XIX y XX*, ed. Lorena Godoy Catalán, Elizabeth Hutchison, Karin Rosemblatt, and M. Soledad Zárate. 111–146. Santiago: SUR-CEDEM, 1995.

Tinsman, Heidi Elizabeth. *Partners in Conflict: The Politics of Gender, Sexuality, and Labor in the Chilean Agrarian Reform, 1950–1973*. Durham, NC: Duke University Press, forthcoming.

Torres Dujisin, Isabel. "Los conventillos de Santiago (1900–1930)." *Cuadernos de Historia* 6 (July 1986): 67–85.

Torres Dujisin, Isabel, and Tomás Moulián. *Concepción de la política e ideal moral en la prensa obrera: 1919–1922*. Santiago: FLACSO Working Paper Number 336, 1987.

Valdés, Teresa. *El movimiento social de mujeres y la producción de conocimientos sobre la condición de la mujer*. Social Studies Series. Santiago: FLACSO Working Paper Number 43, 1993.

Valenzuela, Erika Maza. "Catolicismo, anticlericalismo, y la extensión del sufragio a la mujer en Chile." *Estudios Públicos* 58 (autumn 1995): 137–195.

Vargas, J. E. "La Sociedad de Fomento Fabril, 1883–1928." *Revista Historia* 13 (1976): 5–53.

Veneros Ruíz-Tagle, Diana, ed. *Perfiles revelados: Historia de mujeres en Chile siglos XVIII–XX*. Santiago: Editorial Universidad de Santiago, 1997.

Verba, Ericka Kim. "Catholic Feminism and *Acción Social Femenina* [Women's Social Action]: The Early Years of the Liga de Damas Chilenas, 1912–1924." Ph.D. diss., University of California at Los Angeles, 1999.

——. "The *Círculo de Lectura* [Ladies' Reading Circle] and the *Club de Señoras* [Ladies' Club] of Santiago, Chile: Middle- and Upper-Class Feminist Conversations (1915–1920)." *Journal of Women's History* 7, no. 3 (fall 1995): 6–33.

Viñas, David. *Anarquistas en América Latina*. México City: Editorial Katún, 1983.

Viotti da Costa, Emilia. "Experiences versus Structures: New Tendencies in the History of Labor and the Working Class in Latin America—What Do We Gain? What Do We Lose?" *International Labor and Working-Class History* 36 (fall 1989): 3–24.

Wolfe, Joel. *Working Women, Working Men: São Paulo and the Rise of Brazil's Industrial Working Class, 1900–1955.* Durham, NC: Duke University Press, 1993.

Zarate Campos, María Soledad. "Proteger a las Madres: Orígen de un debate público, 1870–1920." *Nomadías* 1, Monographic Series. Santiago: Editorial Universidad de Chile, 1999.

——. "Vicious Women, Virtuous Women: The Female Delinquent and the Santiago de Chile Correctional House, 1860–1900." In *The Birth of the Penitentiary in Latin America: Essays on Criminology, Prison Reform, and Social Control, 1830–1940,* ed. Ricardo D. Salvatore and Carlos Aguirre. 78–100. Austin: University of Texas Press, 1996.

Index

Alborada, La, 100, 103–19, 136

Anarchism, 36, 63, 65–66; and the woman question, 66, 88–89, 100, 133, 136

Anticlericalism, 86–87, 100, 123, 125–27

Artisans, 4, 23, 26–27

Asociación de Costureras (Seamstresses Association), 69, 114, 118–24

Breastfeeding. *See* Mothers: and child health

Caffarena, Elena, 52, 226–29, 230

Catholic Church, 173; and elite women's activities, 2, 7, 12, 140, 171–77, 188–96; and girls' vocational training, 155, 173–77; and social action, 8, 171, 173, 189–90, 198, 204, 216. *See also* Anticlericalism; Unionization, female: Catholic

Census, industrial, 10, 27–28, 36, 47–54, 145

Census, population, 10, 234–35; methodology of, 11, 38–42; and women's labor, 37–38, 42–47

Children. *See* Mothers: and child health

Concha, Malaquías, 202, 205, 207, 212–14, 217–18

Concha Subercaseaux, Juan Enrique, 36, 201, 204–5, 207, 213, 216

Conventillos (tenements), 28–31, 83, 177, 218

Díaz, Isabel, 93, 133

Domestic service. *See* Women's employment: in domestic service

Domesticity, working-class, 2, 7, 58, 95, 109, 124, 129–30, 136, 144, 149, 158–63, 217, 235, 236, 238

Education, female. *See* Escuelas Profesionales de Niñas; Socialism: and education of women

Escuelas Profesionales de Niñas (Girls' Vocational Schools), 12, 201, 238; administration, 149–50, 163; curriculum, 147–52, 154–58; foreign models for, 163–67; graduates, 150, 154, 156–58, 162, 168, 170, 182; and organized labor, 168; reform of, 158–60; students' class origins, 150–52, 165

Factories, 16, 21, 36–37; growth of, 26–28; and sexual danger, 77–78, 81–84, 92–93; women-owned, 181–82. *See also* Census, industrial; Industrialization; *Mujer obrera, La*; Women's employment: in factories

Federación Obrera de Chile (Chilean Workers' Federation), 2, 73, 74, 98, 132–35, 237; and women, 74–76, 91–94

Femininity, 9, 57, 172. *See also* Domesticity, working-class

Feminism: Christian, 172, 190–91; liberal, 5, 8, 99, 102, 132, 134, 171, 196, 197, 229–30, 233; men and, 111–12, 126; working-class, 8, 11–12, 62, 67, 97. *See also* Feminismo obrero; Suffrage, female

Feminismo obrero (worker feminism), 12, 69, 84, 197, 236–239; critique of male domination, 57, 98, 102, 106,

Feminismo obrero (cont.)
108, 110–12, 116, 121, 124, 129, 134; definition of, 97–98; rise and fall of, 100–123; solidarity with men, 17, 103–5, 111, 112, 122, 130–33; and women's exploitation, 107–8. *See also* Feminism: working-class; Unionization, female: Democratic

Flores, Teresa, 73–76

Gender: as category of analysis, 3–14; and nature, 6, 79, 85, 94, 123, 136, 181, 183, 223, 231, 237

Homework, industrial, 5, 38, 42, 45, 51, 72, 83, 136, 180, 196, 205, 206, 221–22, 226; men employed in, 51, 221–22; regulation of, 52, 218–27; wages and working conditions, 52–54. *See also* Caffarena, Elena; Prostitution: and women's work; Women workers: in factories

Honor, of working-class women, 1–2, 52, 59, 60, 81, 92, 98, 106–7, 110, 117, 128, 147, 161–62, 164–66, 169, 172, 176, 178–80, 184, 187, 188, 195, 197, 204, 233, 239. *See also* Domesticity, working-class; Prostitution; Sexuality, female

Iconography, female, 88–89, 119–20
Immigration, 22, 65, 145
Industrialists. *See* Sociedad de Fomento Fabril
Industrialization, 2, 4, 19, 21, 127; women and, 36–37, 43, 49, 55
International Workers of the World (IWW), 73, 133

Jeria, Carmela, 72, 97, 102–3, 105, 109, 112, 117, 123, 129

Labor legislation, 8, 12–13, 72, 114, 116, 129, 132, 197, 238; 1924 labor laws, 13, 55, 76, 141, 221; compliance and enforcement, 214–16, 220, 225–26, 228; factory day care, 51, 198, 211–16, 221; and foreign models, 199,

205–8, 212, 217–18, 231; Ley de silla, 211; maternity leave, 198, 202, 205, 208–11, 213, 217–18, 220, 221, 227; and organized labor, 202; Sunday rest, 211–13, 215; women's exclusion from, 215–16; for women and children, 213, 217, 239–40; women's night work, 202, 208, 213. *See also* Homework, industrial; Mothers: and child health; Working conditions, women's

Labor Office: enforcement of labor legislation by, 224–25; female inspectors in, 226–30; and industrial statistics, 54. *See also* Caffarena, Elena; Labor legislation: compliance and enforcement; Poblete Troncoso, Moisés

Labor press, 10, 36, 65, 99–100; female contributors to, 105, 132. *See also* Jeria, Carmela; Valdés de Díaz, Esther

Living conditions, working-class, 28–32. *See also Conventillos*; Reform, urban

Masculinity. *See* Virility
Migration, 4, 16; women and, 23–24
Mothers, 128, 161; and child health, 79, 174, 199–200, 208–10, 212–14, 217; working-class, 68, 141, 199, 208
Mujer obrera, La, 9–10, 40, 60, 106, 123, 198; as cultural paradox, 9–10, 99, 109, 242. *See also* Women's employment: in factories
Mutual aid societies, 60–63, 102; female, 62–64

Palanca, La, 100, 118, 124, 238
Parliamentary Republic, 3–7, 19–20, 34, 36, 64, 68, 140–141, 198–200, 220
Partido Demócrata, 68–69, 97–98, 99, 106–7, 112–13; and social legislation, 202. See also *Feminismo obrero*
Paternalism: industrial, 191–92, 201–2, 204–5, 230, 241; in the labor

movement, 87–88, 95–96, 122, 124; state, 216

Patriarchy, 240–41; working-class, 9, 59, 68, 77, 81, 92–93, 95, 99, 111, 131, 235

Partido Obrero Socialista, 73, 125, 129, 132

Poblete Troncoso, Moisés, 217, 220, 224

Poverty: female, 2, 25, 32, 79, 147, 176, 122; urban, 23, 29

Pronatalism. *See* Mothers: and child health; Labor legislation

Prostitution, 39, 40, 45, 53–54, 81–85, 95, 110, 117, 128, 136, 147, 173, 174, 177, 187, 189, 232, 236; wages, 55; and women's work, 82–85, 194–95. *See also* Honor, of working-class women

Recabarren, Luís Emilio, 68–69, 73, 76, 79, 97, 106, 123, 125, 132; writings on the woman question, 86–87, 100–102, 126–29

Reform: moral, 146, 159, 167, 169, 171, 189; social, 36, 141, 153–54, 224

Resistance societies, 85, 191–92; female, 63, 66–67, 113–19

Roldán de Alarcón, Juana, 63, 102, 106, 243

Sales clerks, 40, 183–88, 193–96

Sales cooperatives, 178–79, 180, 196

Santa Cruz Ossa, Elvira (Roxane), 227, 234

Sárraga, Belén de, 86, 101, 125–26

Seamstresses, 39, 40, 45, 77, 81–82, 95, 100, 147. *See also* Asociación de Costureras; Valdés de Diaz, Esther

Sexual division of labor, 5, 13, 37, 59, 98, 109, 143–44, 170, 236, 240

Sexuality, female, 81, 119, 242. *See also* Honor, of working-class women; Prostitution

Social Catholicism. *See* Catholic Church: and social action

Social question, 3, 12, 16, 22, 28, 34, 55,
140–41, 171, 189, 198: contemporary studies of, 207; historiography, 6–7, 199–200

Socialism: and education of women, 65, 105, 109–10, 124, 127–28, 129, 133; and the woman question, 91–95, 123–32, 127, 129, 194. *See also* *Feminismo obrero*

Sociedad de Fomento Fabril (Society for Industrial Development), 2, 21, 140, 168, 170, 201, 205, 213; and protective legislation, 205; and vocational training, 144–50

Sociedad Protección de la Mujer, 62, 72

Soviet Union: women in, 94, 101

Strikes: women in, 67–68, 75

Suffrage, female, 134, 186, 197

Unemployment, 41–42; female, 121, 195–96

Unionization, female, 9–12, 16–17, 59–60, 69–72, 74, 121–22, 132–35, 236–38; Catholic, 12, 188–96; Democratic, 113–19; female leadership, 72, 102, 108, 137, 191–92; in mixed-sex unions, 69–72, 74, 87–88; and sexual discrimination, 87, 89–90, 131–32, 135. *See also* Anarchism; Mutual aid societies; Resistance societies; Socialism

Unionization, male: and female obstructionism, 86–87, 117, 124, 126, 130–31; and female passivity, 69, 94, 107, 114, 116, 180, 210, 219; socialist, 68–69, 73

Urbanization, 2, 16, 19, 57; rates of, 22–23

Valdés de Díaz, Esther, 69, 109, 112–23, 124, 129–30, 131, 202, 237, 243

Virility: attributed to women, 91–92, 93, 136, 237–38; of organized labor, 95; in working-class men, 9, 59–60, 94, 110, 187–88

Wages, 51, 54–57; family, 26–28, 167, 220; female, 2, 31–32, 34, 37, 55–57,

79, 83, 101, 114, 121, 144, 147, 169, 177, 184, 197, 199, 218–19, 224–25, 228–29, 230; male, 6, 17, 57, 59, 85, 87, 99, 117, 130, 211, 228–29. *See also* Homework, industrial; Prostitution

Woman question, 7, 8, 10, 65, 72, 76, 98, 110, 123, 125, 128, 132, 135, 241

Women's employment: in commerce, 44; in *conventillos*, 32–34; in domestic service, 25–26, 40–41, 44, 62, 85, 136, 147, 161, 166, 169, 175–76, 189, 215, 221, 231–32, 236; in factories, 4, 26, 40, 47–55, 58–59, 78–79, 95–96, 113, 128, 136, 173, 199, 236; in professional occupations, 8, 41, 190–91, 233–34. *See also* Prostitution; Sales clerks; Seamstresses

Women's history, 7–8, 101, 196–97

Work: definitions of, 11, 41; family, 146–47; seasonal, 52–54, 83; and skill, 41, 42, 85, 107, 154, 165, 169; suitable for men, 45, 187–88; virtue of women's, 56, 181–83, 191, 193, 197, 201, 233–34; women's domestic, 32–34, 38, 39, 44, 45, 80, 84, 148–49, 166–67, 179; women's suitability for, 77–80

Workforce: female participation in, 3–5, 34–35, 37–47, 107, 154, 164, 171–72; industrial, 20; secondary, 4–5, 37; segmentation of, 144, 170

Working conditions, women's, 2, 37, 188; hours, 37, 51, 117,121

Zelada, Laura Rosa, 1, 13–14, 56, 59, 202, 233, 237, 243

Elizabeth Quay Hutchison is Assistant Professor in the Department of History at the University of New Mexico.

Library of Congress Cataloging-in-Publication Data

Hutchison, Elizabeth Q. (Elizabeth Quay)

Labors appropriate to their sex : gender, labor, and politics in urban Chile, 1900–1930 / Elizabeth Quay hutchison.

p. cm. — (Latin America otherwise)

ISBN 0–8223–2732–5 (cloth : alk. paper)

ISBN 0–8223–2742–2 (pbk. : alk. paper)

1. Women—Employment—Chile—History—20th century. 2. Industrialization—Chile. 3. Labor movement—Chile—History. I. Title. II. Series.

HD6126.H88 2001

331.4'0983'09041—dc21   2001033109